THE INDUSTRIAL RE

MW00834152

THE INDUSTRIAL REVOLUTION

THE STATE, KNOWLEDGE AND GLOBAL TRADE

William J. Ashworth

Bloomsbury Academic
An imprint of Bloomsbury Publishing Plc

B L O O M S B U R Y
LONDON · OXFORD · NEW YORK · NEW DELHI · SYDNEY

Bloomsbury Academic

An imprint of Bloomsbury Publishing Plc

50 Bedford Square
London
WC1B 3DP
UK

1385 Broadway
New York
NY 10018
USA

www.bloomsbury.com

BLOOMSBURY and the Diana logo are trademarks of Bloomsbury Publishing Plc

First published 2017

© William J. Ashworth, 2017

William J. Ashworth has asserted his right under the Copyright, Designs and Patents Act, 1988, to be identified as Author of this work.

All rights reserved. No part of this publication may be reproduced or transmitted in any form or by any means, electronic or mechanical, including photocopying, recording, or any information storage or retrieval system, without prior permission in writing from the publishers.

No responsibility for loss caused to any individual or organization acting on or refraining from action as a result of the material in this publication can be accepted by Bloomsbury or the author.

British Library Cataloguing-in-Publication Data
A catalogue record for this book is available from the British Library.

ISBN: HB: 978-1-4742-8616-9
PB: 978-1-4742-8646-6
ePDF: 978-1-4742-8618-3
ePub: 978-1-4742-8617-6

Library of Congress Cataloging-in-Publication Data
A catalog record for this book is available from the Library of Congress.

Cover design: Sandra Friesen Design
Cover image: The first cotton-gin, illustrated by William L. Sheppard
(Harper's Weekly, 1869 Dec. 18, p. 813) / Library of Congress

Typeset by Deanta Global Publishing Services, Chennai, India
Printed and bound in India

To
Oliver, Harvey and Kerrie

CONTENTS

LIST OF FIGURES

LIST OF GRAPHS AND TABLES

ACKNOWLEDGEMENTS

I have accumulated a large intellectual debt in the research and production of this book. My interest in the role of the state and British industry was nurtured during the writing of my last work on the history of customs and excise. It became obvious to me that fiscal necessity in Britain had an extremely important connection to the country's course of industrialization. However, the centrality of the state to understanding this process took a much longer time to unravel; the interconnections between tax, borrowing, debt, industry, labour exploitation, global trade, colonization, war and knowledge are complicated but vital to a proper understanding of the Industrial Revolution.

Over a number of years I have been extremely fortunate to have encountered numerous other persons interested in this historical nexus; although we have not always agreed, the debate has been rich and informative. I would like to begin by first and foremost thanking Leonard N. Rosenband and Andre Wakefield for always providing sharp and insightful comments throughout this period; the spirit of our chat and exchanges can clearly be found throughout this book. A special mention must also go to Erica Charters, Pat Hudson and Kate Marsh, who have stepped in at vital moments to offer valuable feedback and ensure I stuck to the project. I have also profited hugely from the anonymous readers for Bloomsbury, who provided such constructive suggestions. I may not have carried them all out, but their imprint will be clear.

Elsewhere my understanding of eighteenth-century France greatly benefited from Philippe Minard and a month in Paris as a Faculty Guest at the Centre de Recherches Historiques (EHESS) in the spring of 2012. My debt, in general, to international visits is enormous. I presented arguments of this book in seminars, workshops and conferences at Amsterdam University, The Royal Netherlands Academy of Arts and Sciences, Uppsala University, The University of California, Berkeley, the Annual Meeting of the Society for the History of Technology at Las Vegas in 2007 and, also that year, the Annual Meeting of the History of Science Society in Washington, the Annual Datini Economic History Meeting in Prato in 2007, workshops at both CNRS and EHESS in Paris, the 2012 Annual Meeting of the Wolfenbüttel Working Circle for Baroque Research Congress, Ludwig Maximilian University of Munich, Leipzig University, Pitzer College in California and Chicago University. There are too many people to personally thank here but I hope they all realize how appreciative I am of all their useful feedback.

Equally fertile has been the constructive comments closer to home at talks given at an array of institutions, including Imperial College, London, The London School of Economics, Oxford University, University of Manchester, University of Aberystwyth, University of Nottingham, University of Swansea, Cambridge University, University of Warwick, University of Kent and the National Maritime Museum.

In general, I am grateful to Eric Ash, Sven Beckert, Maxine Berg, Ha-Joon Chang, Martin Daunton, Celia Donert, Charles Esdaile, Boyd Hilton, Michael Hughes, Jane Humphries, Stephen Kenny, Roger Knight, Robert Lee, Iwan Morus, Patrick K. O'Brien, Prasannan Parthasarathi, Philip Rossener, Crosbie Smith, Keith Spendiff, Larry Stewart, Ben Tate, Daniel C. S. Wilson and, especially, Simon Schaffer, for all their interest and suggestions over the course of researching and writing this book. Simon, as ever, has been a constant source of support and stimulation. At Bloomsbury my editors, Claire Lipscomb and Emma Goode, have been very supportive from the start. Their enthusiasm and commitment to the book has made the process exceptionally smooth.

The staffs at the National Archives in Kew, the Sidney Jones Library at the University of Liverpool and The Boarder and Customs Museum in Liverpool were all extremely helpful and efficient. I would especially like to thank Steve Butler for his ongoing passion for all things to do with tax. One of my greatest thanks goes out to all the students I have taught over the years. They consistently forced me to think through my arguments and clarity points I took for granted. I am also grateful for the friendly collegiality of my colleagues in the History Department at the University of Liverpool.

Lastly, but certainly not least, my family has been vital. These have not always been the easiest of years but my two sons, Oliver and Harvey, have always tolerated me. Their eyes may glaze over when I mention tax or industry, but they have continually accepted my need to disappear and write for long periods of time. Throughout my sister, Kerrie Spendiff, has been there for me and I cannot thank her enough for all her unconditional love and care.

INTRODUCTION

The British Industrial Revolution has long been seen as the spark for modern, global industrialization and sustained economic growth. Indeed the origins of economic history, as a discipline, lie in nineteenth-century European and North American attempts to understand the foundation of this process. During the following century, particularly throughout the Cold War, Britain's Industrial Revolution was briefly adopted as a blueprint for economic development. Today, however, there is no consensus over what triggered the leap into the 'modern' industrial world and therefore what lessons it may hold. Nonetheless, the ghost of Britain's manufacturing history still informs recommendations for economic development, from the type of institutions, knowledge and culture needed to an evangelical promotion of free trade and technology.

These relationships, as we shall see, were invented after the rise and dominance of Western industrialization. It was not so much an indigenous Western culture that triggered the British Industrial Revolution, but a distinct Western culture that invented such a history. As such interpretations of this process have an import of much greater significance than historical accounts of other themes; it reflects and reinforces contemporary Western politics and economics. This book will show that economics and history make awkward bedfellows when it comes to prescribing such development.

The primary subject of this book is the British state and its fundamental role in the development of domestic manufactures, importantly, those at the heart of the country's Industrial Revolution. First, state protectionist policies born of war and fiscal pressure framed the evolution of British industry such as linen, cotton, iron, steel, potteries, malt, beer, spirits, leather, soap, candles, paper and glass. The protective barriers allowed manufacturers to develop, which enabled inland taxation (excise) to expand as revenue gaugers farmed them for vital income. Excise collection became more efficient and, crucially, relatively predictable (in contrast to other sources of revenue), something essential for sustaining Public Credit and fighting costly wars. All of which – along with the specification of ingredients, process of production and system devised to measure commodities – was important in defining the shape of both taxed and eventually untaxed manufactures.

Traditionally, arguments explaining the British Industrial Revolution have tended to focus upon a narrow set of factors as the key impulse, rather than a distinctive mix of many characteristics and circumstances. This book critically weaves these univalent approaches into a broader consideration framed by the state. It will demonstrate that any understanding of the British Industrial Revolution has to take a long view from, at least, the mid-seventeenth to the mid-nineteenth centuries and be situated within a global context.

The most widely held view, currently, is that a unique rational culture and a set of favourable institutions shaped Britain's precocious industrial trajectory. Since the 1990s, scholars, including Larry Stewart, Margaret C. Jacob and Joel Mokyr, have claimed that eighteenth-century Britain fostered a fresh unmatched experimental natural philosophy that generated knowledge vital to industrial innovation.[1] This transformation took place inside a particular framework defined by a set of 'credible' components that, according to economists like Douglass C. North, included an ideal political constitution, a paradigmatic set of commercial and legal institutions and the natural cultivation of liberty and protection of private property.[2] Within this environment Britain provided the perfect setting for the entrepreneurial class to apply their intelligence free from suffocating state interference, confident that the fruits of their endeavour would be protected and rewarded.[3] This encouraged the men of the Lunar Society – such as Matthew Boulton, Josiah Wedgwood, Erasmus Darwin and James Watt – to freely meet every month and talk practical knowledge. It was men like these, who pushed the 'whole of society and culture over the threshold of the modern, tilting it irrevocably away from old patterns of life towards the world we know today'.[4] It was this distinct culture that sowed the seeds for the alliance of free markets and free minds as the formula for long-term economic growth and, eventually, the creation of the modern world. This was what triggered Britain and then the West's 'Great Divergence' from the rest.

Another popular argument, spearheaded by E. A. Wrigley, emphasizes Britain's lack of timber and easy access to the right sort of coal compared to its industrial rivals. As a result, the country was the first to cultivate a mineral economy that allowed it to escape from the restraints of an organic base, and therefore avoid Malthusian population restraints.[5] Coal, in turn, gave Britain a unique skills base in technology built around steam and furnaces; these engineers were also subsequently important in the Midland metal industries and the building of Northwest textile machines.[6] The efficient flow of raw materials and goods were, in turn, greatly aided by the creation of an elaborate inland waterway system linking coalfields to industrial centres to coastal ports.[7] On this reading, geological luck and transport, above all, made the Industrial Revolution.

Yet another prominent viewpoint has emphasized the role of relatively high male wages. This pressure, claims Robert C. Allen, triggered new divisions of labour and ultimately mechanical solutions to substitute for expensive skills. All of which, it is argued, was carried out within a relatively benign and liberal framework.[8] By contrast other historians, most notably Prasannan Parthasarathi, have claimed that it was not distinctly high wages, at least in cotton textile manufacturing, that induced technological innovation, but the inability to match the quality of Indian calicoes by Britain's indigenous labour. In particular, textile workers could not produce the warp out of cotton yarn or match Indian supremacy in the use of dyes. Quality catch-up first demanded developments in textile printing, followed by technological changes in actual textile production.[9]

This last argument is complimented by the work of Maxine Berg who underlines the vital impact, in general, of increased trade with Asia upon Britain's industrialization. In a desperate attempt to substitute domestic manufactured items for superior global goods, most notably Indian cotton textiles and Chinese porcelain, Britain devised new technological innovations to imitate such items. This was industrial invention born through frantic attempts to match superior foreign competition.[10]

Still other historians, following the earlier work of Eric Williams, stress the importance of Britain's colonies and the country's leading role in slavery. First, they claim, slaves played a fundamental role in producing staple products such as sugar and tobacco, and eventually the raw cotton needed for Lancashire cotton textiles. For some the profit generated in the American plantations also provided the capital necessary for Britain's industrialization.[11] This emphasis upon slave labour is one that periodically slips in and out of favour and, finally, depends upon the interpretation of missing and incomplete data.[12] What cannot be disputed is the first argument, namely, the fundamental role slavery played in establishing the plantation system in the Americas, and ultimately the raw cotton so vital to the British cotton industry. In addition, British American colonies became hugely important markets for the country's new export-oriented industries.[13] The Southern American slave plantations, in general, went on to become central to the economic growth of the new United States of America during the nineteenth century.[14]

In general, especially since the 1980s, there has been a shift in emphasis towards demand as the key variable in understanding the British Industrial Revolution and Western industrialization. The central focus is now upon the changing nature of the Western nuclear family household and its members' transforming consumer aspirations. The question here is whether such a change was voluntarily or forced? Of course, a ferociously hungry country for revenues, such as eighteenth-century Britain, was not going to oppose the increasing consumption of ready-made taxed goods. The new demand for an array of expanding manufactured and staple items provided, argues Jan De Vries, the vital impetus for economic growth. To enable the quenching of this desire meant families had to become more market-oriented, specialized and work harder both more efficiently and for longer. In short, there occurred an 'Industrious Revolution' long before the British Industrial Revolution. Here the key focus is household earnings rather than those of the individual male wage earner.[15]

To a certain extent, this argument compliments those suggesting that without the availability of a huge domestic pool of cheap female and child labour to exploit, there would have been no revolutionary take-off in textiles. Consequently, as Berg, Pat Hudson and Jane Humphries have shown, high – or more importantly, regular – wages were not the trigger to the Industrial Revolution but, rather, the novelty of a poorly paid section of the population for whose labour much of the new technology was specifically designed. Unlike De Vries's argument, then, this was the result of economic structural change within a highly regulated state; it was therefore not the seduction of the market that triggered this industriousness.[16] Moreover, as Leonard N. Rosenband's recent research upon a single trade – predominantly occupied by a skilled male labour force – reveals, there is no evidence of a newfound industriousness.[17] One also has to add the crucial addition of a huge coerced pool of slave labour in the colonies producing the raw materials and taxed staple goods, which Europeans so ravenously consumed.

All these arguments now take place within an eighteenth- and early-nineteenth-century national context characterized by much slower economic growth. The macroeconomic numbers produced by historians, most notably Nicholas Crafts, since the 1980s have significantly reduced the level of economic growth during the Industrial Revolution. In other words, pre-industrial Britain was actually much wealthier than hitherto thought, while the impact of the Revolution occurred much later in the nineteenth century. Crafts's best guess for growth between 1780 and 1801 is 1.32 per cent per annum and 1.97 per cent for the period 1801 to 1831. Sustained economic growth of 2 per cent per year did not occur till the 1820s. For Crafts, the primary characteristic of the Industrial Revolution was not radical economic growth, but a profound shift of employment from agriculture to industry accompanied by growing efficiency in farming.[18]

The factors outlined above, in varying degrees of importance, undoubtedly played a role in Britain's Industrial Revolution. This book, however, will emphasize the central place of an aggressive and interventionist state, and the fundamental need to situate all these explanations within such a framework. Unravelling the history of Britain's rise to industrial power requires an uncomfortable focus upon what would now be termed illiberal, rather than liberal, policies. This all took place within a context that Sven Beckert has recently coined 'War Capitalism'.[19]

Britain's large and powerful state only started to retreat and adopt a new, liberal approach and ideology when most of the country's manufacturers had become superior in world markets, and the government was faced with growing opposition to indirect taxation. This was compounded by a ballooning population, food shortages, and powerful lobbying for tax and labour reform by the new export-oriented industries (cotton, iron and potteries). In addition, the urgency of near-bankruptcy prior to and following the Napoleonic Wars created a period of desperation that propelled a new industrial and trading policy. In short, British industrial divergence was not the product of a new science of the enlightenment or any peculiarly British proclivities, skills or knowledge that provoked innovation and productive superiority. British pre-eminence was not caused by the high costs of labour or by a triumph of liberal culture. Instead, it developed out of a long era of what would now be classified as illiberal measures (state protectionism and regulation, war, colonization and labour exploitation). There is no doubt that the state was crucial to the Industrial Revolution and, as Peer Vries has recently shown, fundamental to the 'Great Divergence' with China.[20]

By the early nineteenth century the central role of the British state's economic policies in its industrial transformation was obvious to foreign observers. The political economist Jean-Baptiste Say argued that Britain's ability to borrow and service debt was the secret to its military success. This capacity rested on the large incidence of indirect taxation upon domestic manufactures that forced people to work all hours. This pattern compelled people to be industrious to ensure they could pay for basic goods and the taxes on them; it was not the market but the state that was making people more industrious. Consequently, Say diagnosed pressures on manufacturers to innovate as the room for flexibility among social labour became less and less.[21] The need to save 'on all charges of production', wrote Say, has 'brought to perfection the art of producing, and has caused the discovery of means more expeditious, more simple, and consequently more economical, of arriving at any desired end'.[22]

Say made a valid point in emphasizing the particularly high weight of taxation in total British manufacturing costs.[23] Jérôme-Adolphe Blanqui, his disciple and successor as Professor of Political Economy at the Conservatoire des Arts et Métiers, agreed: 'The all-powerful aristocracy in England finds it simple to impose upon labour all the burdens of taxation.' Like Say, he believed this was the key to understanding Britain's industrial trajectory: 'The continual increase of taxes, mainly on articles of consumption, has condemned the inhabitants of this country to a continual fever of improvement. England has become an immense factory, a universal emporium.'[24] It was certainly the case, for example, that by 1785 22 per cent of total production cost in manufacturing paper was via tax.[25] In terms of net revenue yield paper generated £133,000 per annum in 1795 and a staggering £570,000 in 1825.[26] As Parthasarathi concludes, Britain, more than any other European nation, was able and required 'to expand productive capacity in order to broaden the economic base for taxation'.[27]

Clearly, by the 1820s the ratio of tax to total production costs had significantly increased. Where figures are available the same could be seen in other excised products: for example, the annual net revenue from leather in 1800 was £250,000 and a monstrous £605,000 in 1825. The figures from net glass revenue are also telling with the excise generating £171,000 per annum in 1800 and a staggering £620,000 by 1825.[28] The duty paid for soap in 1816 was approximately the same as the cost of actually making the finished article. However, once the taxes on its materials such as tallow, barilla and turpentine were also included the actual levy of the tax was between 120 and 130 per cent of the end product. The gross yield from soap by 1815 was £747,759.[29]

Central to Britain's industrial impetus, according to these contemporary French commentators, was the country's remarkable ability – compared to its global rivals – to fund Public Credit through its relatively efficient tax system (particularly the excise on domestic industry). The increasing fiscal burden on consumers forced manufacturers to cut costs and innovate via 'the introduction of machinery in the arts which has rendered the production of wealth more economical'. The epitome of this new technology, steam engines, was only made possible too, argued Say, due to Britain's abundant 'supply of coal' compared to the rest of Europe. The French savant Sadi Carnot claimed in his *Reflections on the Motive Power of Fire* (1824): 'To take away today from England her steam-engines would be to take away today from her coal and iron. It would be to dry up all her sources of wealth, to ruin all on which her prosperity depends, in short, to annihilate that colossal power.' Thus, for these French political economists and savants, it was a combination of fiscal pressure quenched by state regulation and ecological good luck that underpinned the Industrial Revolution. However, Say did gloomily conclude that at some point 'the terrible taxes' would 'overtake, and even outstrip, the economy of the industrious producers'.[30] This was certainly a widespread fear in early-nineteenth-century Britain. Whatever its potential trajectory we can concur with Ronald Max Hartwell back in 1981: 'Of all aspects of the history of the Industrial Revolution, taxation is the most neglected by the modern economic historian.'[31]

Fixed boundaries were never, and never have been, rigid in the way academics so love; financialization, exploitation, the way things are made, and industrialization, in general, cannot be separated.[32] In the case of Britain the ability to sustain a huge National Debt relied upon a credible system of taxation; without this the country could not have successfully fought wars, controlled trade routes and guarded colonies. This, in turn, concentrated on extracting revenues from people's consumption of predominantly domestic produced (excised) and slave-manufactured goods (sugar, tobacco and other staple items). The employment of women and children in industry meant the increasing purchase of taxed goods from the marketplace, and taxed employers turning to new labour techniques.

A central theme of this book is the role of state regulation and protectionism in nurturing England's/Britain's negligible early manufacturing base. This dominated the detailed and extensive pamphlets and treatises published throughout this period. The start of this process can be traced to the Elizabethan period, but truly accelerated in the second half of the seventeenth century within a context of increasingly frequent war in Europe, the Atlantic and the Americas. Another key component within this setting was the European exploitation of the Spanish and Portuguese American Empire. Without the stolen silver, there would have been very little trade with Asia's superior manufactures – items that went on to inspire British and European industrial innovation. War demanded that the government spend ever more on military activities, especially on the creation of an unrivalled Royal Navy, and on servicing a quickly expanding debt.

The first four chapters of this book present the history of establishing fiscal stability, expanding trade, fighting European wars, extending empire and developing industry between the outbreak of the English Civil War and the end of the War of Spanish Succession in 1713. The foundation of Britain's subsequent Industrial Revolution was forged during this vital period. Central to fiscal development and imperial expansion was the institutionalization of commercial innovations forged or promoted during the republican era and frequently informed by Dutch methods; this country was then at the apex of the re-export trade and vanguard of financial instruments. The legacy of this period and the subsequent work of many of England's leading figures played a highly significant role in defining fiscal and trade policy from the Restoration era onwards.

If the Dutch offered the inspiration for England's trade and fiscal policy, it was the French Colbertian protectionist model of the late seventeenth century that informed the county's approach to industry. England/Britain's subsequent oeconomic trajectory was unique at this time in integrating both approaches bounded by a strong dynamic state. This was characterized by distinctive regulatory institutions, such as the Treasury and Excise, which helped make possible the finance for the country's aggressive commercial and territorial expansion. Over the course of the eighteenth century, fiscal credibility in Britain came to be predominantly based upon excised domestic manufactures while trade in the Atlantic and Asia grew to be significantly greater than the country's main European rivals.

The focus of Chapters 5, 6 and 7 is the role of the British state in nurturing the country's domestic manufactures. Britain industrialized thanks to strong state intervention at both the actual site of production, and via the legislative introduction of protective custom tariffs and export bounties. Protectionism allowed its relatively negligible seventeenth-century manufacturing base to develop and innovate, sheltered from adverse international competition and guarded by a powerful navy. The country, aided by a wall of sea and wood, may not have been alone in implementing such measures but it was by far the most successful. The subsequent expansion of domestic industry provided valuable employment, consumers and a vital source of revenue. Further afield the colonies, commercially controlled by the Navigation Acts (1651, 1660 and 1663), were an ever important supplier of addictive and highly taxed staple goods, certain untaxed raw materials and, of course, creating an important colonial market for British manufactures – far larger than its European competitors. All this added up to a major transformation of the domestic oeconomic infrastructure.

State institutions were also at the vanguard of recording commercial and industrial information. The English and, from 1707, the British Treasury worked scrupulously to develop an elaborate set of procedures, especially systematic accounts that tracked revenues in and out of the Exchequer. An emphasis, in general, upon political arithmetic was also employed by the Excise from its creation in 1643, the Board of Trade and Plantations founded in 1696, and an Inspector-General of Imports and Exports also established in that year to record registers of incoming and outgoing trade. No comparable set of quantitative objectives were so fruitfully pursued within other countries on the European continent, Asia or elsewhere in the world during this period. Moreover, such numerical accounts were regularly available to Parliament to interrogate and make informed decisions.[33] From this perspective the eighteenth-century British state played a major role promoting a quantifying spirit.

This book draws upon contemporary pamphlets, manufacturing petitions, Parliamentary reports, legislation and popular oeconomic treatises now, often, long for-gotten. In particular, the research covered in this book examines over one hundred years of neglected correspondence between manufacturers, the Excise and the Treasury held at the National Archives. The depth of detail exchanged between domestic industry and these two state bodies provides a crucial and, hitherto, poorly known understanding of the evolution of industry in England/Britain. The correspondence demonstrates how the Excise became the chief source of government authority over industrial knowledge and adjudicating manufacturing petitions. Here, via the Treasury, the Excise suggested levels at which to pitch tax, provided extensive details on the nature of production, interacted with manufacturers and engaged with issues of quality regarding certain items.

This last aspect was extremely important, since allowing the production of second-rate goods simply stoked the illicit importation of superior commodities and, in the long run, could destroy the survival of an industry. Taxing a good frequently required it to be rendered visible both with regard to its ingredients and the way it was produced. This, ultimately, called for attempts to regulate its qualities and for its site of production to be reconfigured to meet the Excise's process of measuring tax. In this sense, the Excise, via administrative needs, encouraged geographical industrial clusters of a particular product, dependence upon quantification, instrumentation and a standardized product. Approaches associated with enlightened thinking such as induction, counting, measurement and instrumentation were clearly being driven as much by a regulatory state than any other factor.

The state successfully pursued protection of domestic industry, especially infant sectors, through high tariffs, which represented a recognized, actively pursued and successful strategy. The protective barriers allowed manufacturers to develop and the excise revenues to expand greatly. Gradually excise collection became more efficient and, crucially, relatively predictable (in contrast to other sources of revenue). This was essential for sustaining Public Credit, thus funding expensive warfare and thence fuelling Britain's rise to power. Protectionist policies made possible the nurturing of domestic manufactures and the subsequent extensive excise of its fruits, which – along with the specification of ingredients, production and system of gauging devised to measure commodities – was important in defining the shape of both taxed and eventually untaxed manufactures. It was within this state-framed, carefully regulated context that the Industrial Revolution took place.

Chapters 8 and 9 examine the role of knowledge and foreign skills to Britain's industrialization. When the English Lord Chancellor and philosopher Sir Francis Bacon published his *Novum Organum Scientiarum* in 1620, he would have been aware that the origins of gunpowder, paper, the compass, printing press and an array of textiles and ceramics came from Asia. Importing the know-how via skilled Asians, however, was simply not a viable option. The deficiency of English domestic manufactures had been increasingly raised as a serious problem as the country sought ways to enhance its power. For example, 'letters of protection' for primarily foreign craftsmen such as weavers, saltmakers and glassmakers can be found as early as Edward III's reign (1327–77). These were designed to encourage skilled Europeans to settle in England and stimulate new domestic manufactures. These letters did not, however, offer the person a monopoly.

The incentive was rigorously revived during the sixteenth century, but this time drawing upon Italian practices, in which exclusivity was now awarded to the skilled foreigner. Managing the Elizabethan regime's quest for wooing such valuable talent over was William Cecil, later Lord Burghley, who between 1558 and 1571 was Secretary of State before becoming Treasurer in 1572. The policy was simple: namely, to encourage the manufacture of those products England currently had to import; Burghley with his close advisors, granted some thirty-one patents to foreign projectors who brought new manufacturing processes over to England. Another massive injection to England's industrialization came with a flood of French Huguenots into the country after the revocation of the Edict of Nantes in 1685. Many of these 'refugees', a word coined during this event, were highly skilled.

There is no doubt that ecological good luck also played an important role in Britain's eventual Industrial Revolution. However, royal and government intervention played a part here too. The country was clearly concerned with the level of its domestic timber supplies and, as an island, only had a limited area of cultivable forests. Consequently, James I felt compelled to ban the use of timber as energy in glassmaking in 1615. One way out of this was to extend the country's acreage via colonization to produce such scarce items as timber, although, in this particular example, the result was generally disappointing. Another solution, much closer to home, soon beckoned. The island could tap into its own uniquely accessible rich domestic deposits of the right type of coal (bituminous) as a substitute to timber.

By 1820 it would have taken a forest the size of England to have supplied as much energy as it was now using each year from coal. The switch to coal was adopted by a number of Britain's state-regulated infant industries that, in turn, fuelled the evolution of technologies connected to coal-burning. All this was developed over a long period of time sheltered behind a protective wall of tariffs. Its use in soap, malt, salt, sugar, glass, iron, dyeing and bleaching textiles commenced long before the institutional establishment of applying formal knowledge to industry; nothing comparable, on such a scale, was happening elsewhere in the world. This was not through a lack of foreign understanding but, primarily, due to ecological reasons. For example, most of Northern Europe had much superior forests and an associated timber economy. Moreover, the ease of accessibility to the right quality coal was unique at this time to Britain.

The development of the Newcomen atmospheric engine only made sense in Britain, since it was incredibly inefficient and demanded huge supplies of local coal, primarily to drain the mines in which the mineral was extracted. Much of the knowledge used to make this engine drew upon work developed in seventeenth-century continental Europe. Britain's unique access to the right sort of coal became less and less expensive throughout the eighteenth century thanks to improvements in extraction and transportation. There is no doubt that the initial surge in canal construction was driven as much by the need to reduce costs in moving coal as anything else.[34] The output of coal increased sixty-six-fold between 1560 and 1800, by which date Britain was mining most of the world's supply. Such an expansion of steam technology in Britain had an important knock-on effect in other industrial processes, most importantly, machine tool making and engineering in general.

These chapters also look at innovation within the industries that traditionally define the Industrial Revolution, namely, cotton, iron and steel. It will be shown how state protectionism played a significant role in the emergence of these manufactures. After intense lobbying from the woollen and silk textile manufacturers, printed or painted calico from India were banned from English consumption in 1701, but plain calico could still be imported and domestically printed for both home and export markets. This was followed by a total prohibition of wearing pure cotton cloth in 1721, which was the case till such legislation was removed in 1774. However, between these dates the production and consumption of mixed cotton fabrics, most notably new lighter 'fustians', were permitted, while plain pure cotton textiles were also still allowed to be imported if they were subsequently, after being domestically printed, re-exported. Thus, those textile manufacturers working with some aspect of cotton were protected from Indian competition in the domestic and colonial market – although not, of course, in other places such as Africa.

Meanwhile, France, significantly earlier in 1686, banned the importation, production and wearing of any cotton textiles – to do so became a capital offence. Many of those involved in the manufacture and printing of these items subsequently emigrated to England and elsewhere. From this period a significant and important English/British textile printing industry emerged that was too large and important to remove after the domestic ban upon wearing pure cotton textiles was introduced in 1721. Instead, the industry started focusing upon printing substitutes such as light fustians, along with other mixed cotton checks and linens. By contrast Holland kept its market unprotected for dyed and printed Asian textiles, and its hitherto European lead in bleaching, dyeing and printing subsequently declined at the expense of Britain's. The Dutch increasingly emphasized a trading, rather than industrial, future as the voice of its merchants continued to consolidate oeconomic power. By the time pure cotton textiles were once again legal in the British domestic market, the world's favourite textile was close to matching the quality of Indian cottons via mechanization and printing developments. Britain's archetypical manufacture of the Industrial Revolution had developed behind high protectionist walls. Even after 1774 the industry continued to enjoy state protection via export bounties and the continued prohibition of Indian cotton textiles.

From the start England and, subsequently, Britain, sought alternatives and strenuous attempts to find a substitute in the Atlantic colonies for vital items such as Baltic iron, pitch and tar. Much has been written upon the rise and flow of exotic goods from the Atlantic and Asia, but far less on the mesh of production networks that frequently united the entire nexus. For example, fundamental to the development of British steel was its monopoly of Swedish 'Orground' iron (the best iron in the world), which allowed the subsequent development of British tool making, cutting and shaping metals, creating exact joints, valves, cylinders and pistons. French producers and state officials also focused upon creating a domestic steel sector but, hoping to be self-reliant, prohibited the use of Swedish 'Orground' iron. This greatly undermined France's Atlantic ambitions while greatly strengthening Britain's.[35]

Britain's more patient solution to a dangerous dependence upon Baltic iron imports eventually came from the country's own iron industry and its technological transformation. British iron masters had been unable to compete with Baltic iron because they lacked the then appropriate energy and skills. Initially, the solution seemed to be to farm out the preliminary stages to the charcoal-rich American colonies; however, this never really took root. The alternative was a technological answer through the adoption of coal-fired refinery methods drawing upon innovations in other British industries, most notably, malt. After decades of work, the breakthrough eventually came with the Royal Navy agent, Henry Cort, and his puddling technique. This was anything but an overnight solution, and it was only really during the 1790s that the iron industry turned fully to mineral fuel. Even here this was not without the aid of state protection and honing the skilled workforce. Baltic iron imports were at their peak in 1793 but thereafter quickly dropped when high tariff barriers were erected, which priced both Swedish and Russian iron out of Britain.

Chapters 10 and 11 examine the swiftly changing socio-economic conditions and structural reforms of the late eighteenth century. During this period the state was straining under the weight of debt and the accompanying social agitation this was generating. This fast transforming environment had a profound impact upon the lived experience of the lower orders and growth of the middling ranks. The momentum behind subsequent state dismantling, often pitilessly carried out, had been growing since the hugely expensive Seven Years War (1756–63), accelerating in the aftermath of the American War of Independence (1775–83), and secured after the costly wars with France (1789–1815).

The result, commencing first under William Pitt the Younger, was a pragmatic switch in trade and industrial policy that favoured the newer, export-oriented, and less regulated industries (cotton, potteries and iron). Accompanying this was, crucially, a redefining of the state's role in controlling the oeconomy and thus the food and labour markets. This had a revolutionary impact upon the lived experience of the working ranks. In general, the regulated system that characterized Britain's oeconomic evolution had reached its peak by the close of the Seven Years War and had seemingly become unsustainable in its prevailing form. Consequently, the government's only way out was just that – to shrink from playing a part in adjudicating the interests of the landowner, everyday people, labour and industrialists. The disintegration of a protectionist policy and a paternalist model of food marketing was mirrored by the retreat of the state, in general, from its close intervening activities in an array of spheres. Attacks upon 'old corruption' and the size of the state were eroding social authority and something urgently needed to be done.

The regulated oeconomy had reached its zenith in 1766, three years after the Seven Years War, when a series of national protests against the exportation of English grain took place, which resulted in a rigorous implementation of the old regulatory paternal management of the market. However, it also marked a moment when a radical reform of the regulated domestic food market commenced. In particular, growing population and rapid urbanization were raising increasingly urgent questions concerning the distribution of grain. Within this context the role of middlemen and the flow of domestic grain from agricultural regions seemed to be the only practical solution rather than any ideologically driven notion of the market. The food market, this argument went, should be left to regulate itself free from all legislative and local interference. In such a model the farmers and middlemen played a necessary role in helping the flow of corn from areas of surplus to scarcity. This played well into the hands of the government's recent emphasis upon promoting the new industries, and desperate need to shrink the activities of a hugely expensive state. Indeed, it crystallized into a transition from oeconomy to a potent new political economy.

The traditional role of guilds and the state in maintaining a standard of living, including the level of wages among the working ranks, was fast dissolving towards the end of the eighteenth century before finally being severed in the nineteenth century. The bulk of this regulatory legislation stemmed from the Statute of Artificers in 1563. This confirmed an old Act of 1390 that ordered justices of the peace to regulate workers' wages and codified all the prevailing measures. Legislation such as this was viewed as the final guard against the unimpeded march of a new economic system predominantly defined by the notion of a free market. In this sense the statutes operated in much the same way as legislation controlling the marketplace for food did. The last effort to set wages came in the Spitalfields Act of 1773; this Act was passed in an attempt to rectify the increasing problem revolving around an agreed list of piece-work rates within the silk industry.

One potent symbol associated with the emerging deregulated world was the machine. The machinery pioneers were frequently viewed in the same way the old regulated oeconomy treated the middlemen in the food market. Attacks by workers against such innovators were first made by appealing to old legal regulations encoded in law and practice. Not surprisingly, then, the new mill and factory owners sought aggressively to repeal the old legislation. This protection was finally severed with the repeal of most of the industrial regulatory laws in 1809. The creation of a Leviathan state, so far described in this book, was gradually being dismantled.

Regulatory legislation was regarded as the final safeguard against the new form of centralized production which was, many workers felt, fast breathing down their necks. The machine and factory were thus seen as a reflection of the destruction of a traditional relationship between masters and workers in both the putting-out and domestic systems. The repeal of the common law and customary practices in the food market were thus joined by the application of the same form of reasoning to the workplace – therefore making it more amenable to mechanization and systematic organization. This was a battle between the old regulated world of eighteenth-century food and manufactures, and the fresh world of deregulation driven by the need to reduce the costs of the state and promote the newer export-oriented industries. The transformation in reasoning was stark and fuelled by a hostile environment driven by debt and attacks upon state corruption.

Under intense fiscal–political pressure the British regulatory state needed to shrink and thus withdraw from fields like food, industry and trade. To do this an alternative source of authority was needed and the notion of a 'free market' as a neutral umpire of disputes seemed a seductive solution. However, by severing manufacturing regulations, all legal protection of employees within the workplace disappeared; there is no doubt this served the interests of owners more than workers. The repeal of the Statute of Artificers in 1814 had a significant impact upon the shape trade unionism later took. All this delegislation was interpreted as an assault upon the labourer's property of skill and a strengthening of employer's power at the expense of the employee. The state had withdrawn its protective legislation within the food and labour markets, but still relied heavily upon the working classes for its revenues. This was a volatile situation that would have to be, sooner or later, confronted and resolved.

A delegislative attack, unlike its success in the food market, was never going to be as successful in reforming the workplace. What was needed was something else and the solution, for some, came in the shape of the machine. Within this context the latest technology took on a new meaning. For many of those with a recent liberal and deregulating cast of mind, it was perceived as an emancipating tool exposing the jealously guarded property of elite artisan skills, which was the ultimate source of their power. Unless this could be challenged, manufacturers were always going to be dependent on good relations with their skilled workforce.

In many ways the repeal of the Combination Acts in 1824 and its less liberal reinterpretation the following year, was a reluctant acceptance that labour could not be prevented from coming together to protect their interests. It also, of course, legalized what employers had long been doing, namely, also combining to promote the interests of capital. The state, however, was now let loose from its former role of regulating industry, with capital and labour now free in theory to discuss the basis of their contract; although with the Master and Servant Act legislation and the persistence of anti-conspiracy laws, the weight was very much in favour of the employer. Historically, more wage workers under the former were prosecuted and imprisoned than through anti-combination laws.[36] The eventual defence of skilled workers property would fall to Trade Societies or what would later come to be termed Trade Unions.

The final chapter will trace the rise of the new discipline of political economy legislated to justify Britain's industrial transformation. In 1640 England was a relatively weak, second-rate European power with a small and backward industrial base. Just over two hundred years later it was the world's foremost industrial and imperial power. So successful was this transition, a dramatic restructuring of tax policy during the first half of the nineteenth century was only made possible by a general confidence in the ability of Britain's entire industry, old and new, finally to thrive in the world without a protective barrier. The former combination of protection and the nurturing of domestic industries had been so successful that leading politicians ignored the fact many of these manufactures would not have existed without high tariffs. Indeed, while Britain was knocking down its industrial enclosure, other nations, most notably Germany and the United States, intensified or erected theirs.

This chapter will argue that a creed of liberalism characterized by free trade in the late-eighteenth- and early-nineteenth-century Britain originally arose out of fiscal, social and political imperatives rather than any enlightened doctrine. Pitt faced an enormous national debt along with a public outcry condemning a parasitic state. His administration decided that only by shrinking the state could these issues be diluted, aided by focusing upon the new export-oriented industries and, ultimately, securing a new form of taxation.

This argument tends to compliment recent intellectual histories tracing the changing interpretation and sense of Adam Smith's work during this period. Having initially been associated with the atheism of David Hume and the political radicalism of Thomas Paine, this part of Smith's thinking became unacceptable during the regime of Pitt. It was, especially, in the mid-1790s that his political and religious views were severed from his oeconomic ideas; the Jacobin idea of liberty was transformed into the conservative notion of free trade.[37] Likewise, many of the illiberal aspects that forged the British Industrial Revolution have been erased from modern historiography. The chapter finishes by tracing the way free trade subsequently penetrated the sinews of British political and social life; in short, how free trade, in conjunction with the creation of a small state, had become almost a spiritual creed and integral part of what it was to be British among the nation's social authority.

The Industrial Revolution

The epilogue concludes that the British Industrial Revolution was merely a short moment within a much larger and longer global trajectory. The 'Great Divergence' with other parts of the world was ecologically and imperially rooted and made possible by a distinct and strong regulatory state. The first two factors enjoy a rich historiography but the critical role of Britain's state in the Industrial Revolution remains much neglected.[38] Protectionist policies had an extremely important impact upon the development of British industries such as silk, linen, cotton, iron, potteries, malt, beer, spirits, leather, soap, candles, paper and glass. The alliance between free trade, democracy and economic success is an association superimposed after the establishment of Western industrialization.[39] Britain's single-minded pursuit of free trade during the second half of the nineteenth century was not an inevitable development of some enlightened, objective knowledge and teleological logic thrust forward by its Industrial Revolution. As this book will show, the story is far more contingent and Statist than hitherto presented.

CHAPTER 1
DEBT: TRADE, FINANCE AND EUROPEAN WAR

Everybody do nowadays reflect upon Oliver [Cromwell] and commend him, what brave things he did and made all the neighbour princes fear him.[1]

Samuel Pepys, 1667

This is a book on the history of Britain's Industrial Revolution in a world context. To understand this event, we have to examine a broad time period, commencing our explorations in the mid-seventeenth century and concluding them in the mid-nineteenth century. The path to power was wealth and this, it was generally agreed in the seventeenth century, came through trade. This led to intense European jealousy and rivalry that invariably resulted in expensive wars.[2] Revenues alone were never going to be enough to fund this fighting and borrowing was vital to military and commercial success. The question was how to create a basis to service this debt in a trustworthy and reliable fashion. It was within this environment that protectionary and regulatory state policies were introduced in England, which provided the subsequent framework to Britain's eventual Industrial Revolution. The evolution of Britain's national debt and taxation of domestic manufactures, therefore, requires a clear understanding of this symbiosis. We have to recognize that one of the greatest gifts Britain gave to the world during this period was debt and how to credibly service it. Our starting point is the 1640s and the turbulent period of the English Civil War followed by the restoration of Charles II.

The Restoration and the institutionalization of republicanism

A young and weather-beaten man exhausted from a long voyage east, across the Atlantic, stepped upon revolutionary English soil in 1646. The new arrival was George Downing, the son of Emanuel Downing (one-time attorney and clerk of the English Inner Temple) and Lucy Downing (sister of the puritan John Winthrop, the first governor of the colony of Massachusetts Bay). George was born in Ireland in 1623 but brought up from the age of three in London and, from 1638 in Salem, Massachusetts. It seems likely Emanuel's fur trading business with the governor's son, John Winthrop Jr., and the London merchant, Francis Kirby, persuaded them to relocate to this American colony. Emanuel became a leading member of the Massachusetts Company and enthusiastic advocate for developing English-America with African slaves. George went on to be educated at Harvard University, where he subsequently became the second-ranking member of the newly established institution's first-ever graduating class.[3]

Extremely ambitious, supported by a privileged background, George gravitated to the source of Massachusetts's authority, which was not the colony's Assembly, but the country he had spent his early childhood. In 1645 he left Salem for England via Barbados and other Caribbean destinations as a ship's chaplain. Soon after, he made his way to London loaded with letters of introduction. Here, he quickly assimilated into and climbed the ranks of the new republican regime by first becoming the chaplain of Colonel John Okey's dragoon regiment in the New Model Army, and then becoming chaplain of Sir Arthur Hezilridges's regiment in Newcastle. He was then appointed by Oliver Cromwell as Scoutmaster-General of the English army in Scotland – a position in which he proved to be ruthlessly efficient. Ten years later, as a result of his rigorous effort here, he was rewarded with the position of Teller of the Receipt in the Exchequer on a very lucrative salary of £500 per annum; this posting was quickly followed by his appointment as Cromwell's diplomatic envoy to The Hague (a position he resumed under Charles II).[4] This was an unprecedented and incredibly impressive trajectory for a colonial graduate.

Downing's experience of virgin English republicanism, more mature Dutch oeconomic praxis and, no doubt, experiences from his former colonial life, would become important to English Restoration reforms. In particular, like many of his contemporaries, he knew that the heart of power was fiscal credibility and commercial plenty. Philosophical thought and religious devotion do not seem to have been at the vanguard of Downing's ambition. The Dutch, especially, were demonstrating the centrality of trade and finance, and it was increasingly deemed vital that England emulated their commercial practices. This was an objective Downing worked extremely hard to achieve. Here he joined a growing groundswell leaning towards a commercial, but by no means unified, vision of England's future.[5] Far from an end to the republican regime, the Restoration would see many of its key policies thrive, especially around the issue of credit.[6]

In 1659 the relatively brief period of English republicanism was coming to an end and resort to earlier royalist methods of rule beckoned. This was not without danger, but such a reversal seemingly had greater potential for social and political stability than sticking with the prevailing prospects. Nonetheless, the restoration of the Crown in 1660 by no means ended English radical activities. The subsequent Exclusion Crisis (1679–81), the Rye House Plot (1683), Monmouth's Rebellion (1685) and, finally, the Glorious Revolution (1688–9) are all a series of related events stemming from the revolutionary period. Melinda S. Zook writes: 'If we take the entire decade of the 1680s into account, the Glorious Revolution begins to look less glorious, less smooth and bloodless, and more like other modern revolutions.'[7] Likewise, recent research demonstrates how much of the Commonwealth's commercial and fiscal policy remained central in the decades following the Restoration.[8] It was, in short, republican approaches to financial borrowing that would ultimately provide the resources to establish long-term reliable credit for the Crown.

One major problem to the success or fall of the newly restored Crown in 1660, as it would equally be for the post-Glorious Revolution period of the 1690s and beyond, was the issue of credit – both financially and politically. This rather vague but fundamental term, 'credit', is defined by faith and trust. Critical to the survival and strength of any emerging – or mature – nation state revolved, as it still does, upon this issue. Power required political and social stability along with a mechanism to allow debt; it also invariably needed credible information that, in turn, required trust in a process of fact-gathering, the people collecting such knowledge and the method used to reduce such intelligence into trustworthy information.[9] Historically, credit also demanded national security (a strong military), probity (regular and predictable revenues), the generation of wealth (typically seen as via trade, labour, services and industry) and stability (food and employment).

Despite a concerted, but futile, attempt by royalists to blank out the republican era and restore things to how they had been prior to the Revolution, the subsequent fiscal basis of the Crown retained fundamental key innovations made during the last two decades with, perhaps, the excise being the most controversial. The king was granted a permanent annual revenue of £1,200,000 that he was expected to live entirely upon. The sources of the fund, however, were no longer his own and no attempt was made to restore the former royal demesne that included feudal fiscal revenues.[10] In terms of raising additional revenue, the options open to Charles II were certainly limited and, unlike his father, he could no longer hope to force loans and trigger a deeply embedded hostility to direct taxation. In particular, despite the retention of certain traditional types of direct taxation and the locally collected land tax (that went on to provide an important income between 1694 and 1798), the memory of Charles I's ship money and Commonwealth assessments were simply too strong to allow any new form of direct tax.[11]

Borrowing became an essential part of Restoration finance, with over 12 per cent of government receipts paid into the Exchequer stemming from loans, the figure reaching a third in some years. The ultimate guarantee that the money would be paid back was the king's word. Remember, as far as Parliament was concerned, unless it was an urgent matter such as war, the king had been granted enough annual revenue to live from. Consequently, any other loans were a result of the Crown's personal endeavours. For extra revenue, the king, left to his own devices without Parliament, relied upon four main sources to draw upon: the East India Company, the City of London, tax farmers and goldsmith bankers. Relations between the Crown and all these sources were frequently strained and demanded a great deal of wheeling and dealing, and not a little careful coercion on the part of the king's negotiators. In particular, great care had to be taken not to upset the city since its role in breaking the Crown in 1640 was still fresh in the memory of the restored regime.[12]

With the king's word central to borrowing, the first thing Charles II had to do was build up his credibility as a safe pair of fiscal hands. This is neatly summed up by one of the few historians of the hugely important English Treasury, Henry Roseveare: 'The time had come, at last, for the Crown to offer purely business-like inducements to its lenders, to build up its credit as a marketable commodity founded upon the probity and punctuality, as well as profitability, of its dealings. Here was a special incentive to administrative efficiency which did much to stimulate the Treasury's evolution after 1660.'[13]

English eyes gazed enviously across the Channel at the Dutch and desperately sought to replicate the key factors underpinning that nation's fiscal credibility, namely, regularity built upon a prosperous oeconomy, trustworthy revenues and a centre for commercial information. The Dutch, at this point, were also Europe's primary audit society.[14] At the vanguard of emulating them in England was Cromwell's former Scoutmaster-General Downing.[15] In general, the impact of the Dutch upon England went way beyond finance, accounting and trade with important aspects also informing manufacturing, printing, agriculture and natural philosophy. As both Gils Rommelse and Jonathan Scott claim, it was the Anglo-Dutch connection that created the modern British state and, at the heart of this, was commercial competition[16] although, as we shall see, France and South Asia, in particular, had more of a say in this development than implied here.

This evolution was, of course, by no means instantly easy or manageable. Credibility requires stability, consistency and therefore, above all, proof of time. When the Treasury was initially put into commission in June 1660, the commissioners were all privy councillors and recorded as a committee of the Privy Council. It was soon apparent, however, that Treasury business was not being efficiently attended to. In an attempt to improve the situation, the white staff was handed to the staunch royalist, Thomas Wriothesley, the fourth Earl of Southampton. This is important in the sense that the Lord Treasurer was now no longer one of the Exchequer officials, and was deliberately removed geographically to his own set of offices at Whitehall. Instructions to Exchequer officials concerning the reserve and pay of the king's money now flowed from the Lord Treasurer seated in his own dwellings. None of this, however, meant that the Earl of Southampton was independent of the Privy Council, with all fiscal issues still debated and resolved at the council. The principal duty of the Lord Treasurer was to apply the council's revenue orders and ensure they were performed. In terms of the day-to-day running of Treasury matters, much of Southampton's work was most likely carried out by his secretary, the royalist Sir Philip Warwick, who subsequently sat on 258 committees. He was also a key player in persuading Parliament to vote a new tax of £70,000 a month for the duration of the Second Anglo-Dutch War (1665–7).[17] It appears that Southampton, along with Warwick, ensured many of the key developments forged during the Interregnum were retained.[18]

Southampton's position was later bolstered with the appointment of his nephew, the former royalist turned parliamentarian, turned ambiguous royalist, Baron Anthony Ashley Cooper of Wimborne St Giles, as Chancellor of the Exchequer and under-treasurer. A staunch Protestant, Cooper had earlier turned against Charles I in 1644 because he did not think the king was committed to the preservation of the Protestant religion, to English liberty and to hastening the commercial future of the country. Regarding the latter, Cooper was committed to England's increasing Atlantic ambition, most notably making a significant investment in the part-ownership of a plantation in Barbados along with a quarter shares in a small slave ship. Cooper's notion of liberty did not extend beyond Albion's shores. He sold his percentage of the plantation in 1655 for the lucrative figure of £1,020. During this period, Cooper had also become an important figure in the Interregnum administration and, at one time, had been quite close to Cromwell. He continued to pursue his commercial and colonial policy during the Restoration, with the North American colony of Carolina becoming the central focus of his interests.[19]

In the first year of the Restoration, Cooper was appointed as a member of the Privy Council's Standing Committee of Trade for Foreign Plantations. This body subsequently became redundant, then mutated into two committees, and from 1670 simply became the Council of Trade to which Cooper, now first Earl of Shaftesbury, became president. In the same year, he invested in the Hudson's Bay Company and became its deputy governor four years later. Despite his former republican sympathies, Shaftesbury was at one point an important confidant to Charles II, the king clearly valuing his alliance and, moreover, feeling it important to keep his potential enemies on his side. However, Shaftesbury's anti-Catholic and ambivalent royalism would forcefully rear their head once again during the Exclusion Crisis of the late-1670s.[20]

After only five years Charles II faced his first military engagement with the Dutch. Parliament granted an additional aid of £1,250,000 as an emergency wartime measure. It came with a clause, an appropriation, that all the money had to be used for the purpose intended, that is, only for matters concerned with the war. The money for this loan would be received and disbursed by the Exchequer, with all relevant records made available to Parliament. Those creditors subscribing to this loan would receive something called Treasury Orders, which was a fiscal device instigated and enthusiastically driven by Downing. These were chronologically numbered with half-yearly payments at 6 per cent interest, which would mature at the close of the specified eighteen to twenty-four months. The time span was decided upon by the estimated length it would take to collect the necessary revenue used to service the loan. This was a device that Downing learnt during his time spent during the republican era. As well as the ordered and paper-based element to this legislation, it meant, crucially, that the untrustworthy credit – the 'word' of the king – was replaced by Parliament. It also actively encouraged public investment by expanding the then limited number of negotiable financial instruments.[21]

Parliament was putting *its* reputation and weight behind the sustenance of credit. Credible commitment was something being dealt with long before the post-Glorious Revolution period. This was not born of enlightened thinking but commercial aggression, emulation and a realization that fiscal credibility was vulnerable. This was in all but name a republican usurpation of royal authority, namely, if you do not trust the king you can trust the Parliament. This wartime measure was subsequently systematized and applied to the ordinary revenue from 1667. The Treasury (be it in the form of a Treasurer or Treasury Commission) and the Exchequer would now have to be far more precise and punctual in its duties to maintain public confidence.

This significant shift in power from the king to Parliament did not, of course, go down well everywhere. A bank was a republican institution and thus attempting to make the Exchequer function like one was, for many, a sinister move. In a world of slippery loyalties, Downing's former republican sympathies and association with Cromwell was not lost on the staunch and fallen royal loyalist, Edward Hyde, first Earl of Clarendon. As far as he was concerned: 'Bankers were a tribe that had risen and grown up in Cromwell's time.'[22] In addition, he fumed:

> Downing … told them … by making the Payment with interest so certain and fixed, that … it should be out of any Man's Power to cause any money that should be lent To-morrow to be paid before that which was lent Yesterday … he would make [the] Exchequer … the best and the greatest Bank in Europe … and all Nations would sooner send their money into [it] … than into *Amsterdam* or *Genoa* or *Venice*. And it cannot be enough wondered at, that this intoxication prevailed so far that no Argument would be heard against it … without weighing that the Security for Monies so deposited in Banks is the republick itself, which must expire before that security can fail; which can never be depended on in a Monarchy, where the Monarch's sole word can cancel all those formal Provisions.[23]

Downing was simply pursuing a policy that was increasingly viewed as another piece in the puzzle for establishing universal commercial power, which was a relationship linked with Protestant religious domination. As the merchant and republican Slingsby Bethel wrote in 1671: 'Banks such as are in use in Venice, Amsterdam and Hamburg, where the states are security, keeping particular accounts of cash, for all men desiring it, are of great advantages to merchants and traders.'[24] However, it was not to be the Exchequer, and the realization of such a bank would have to wait until 1694 and the creation of the Bank of England.

Central to Downing and the Treasury Commission's concerns was the precise gauging and accurate recording of fiscal records. Roseveare emphasizes the purpose of this aim, namely, it was hoped this would 'mobilize the king's credit on a basis of efficient bookkeeping. This campaign is the key to almost everything the Treasury Commission did and was the source of its control.' Having more credible and separate records enabled it to act on its own information rather than relying on the unreliable Exchequer accounts. All of this enabled the Treasury to plan ahead by allocating current expenditure through the prediction of future revenue yields and establishing credible authority. Again, this was a theme that had been pursued during the Interregnum.[25]

The emphasis upon trading expenditure and revenues became a repetitive theme. For example, early in the eighteenth century, the one-time Excise Commissioner and prominent commercial commentator Charles Davenant made such probity central to public credit; all the accounts connected with revenue should, he stressed, be 'methodiz'd, so as to be kept very clear and intelligible without altering the Course of the Exchequer, or interrupting any of the present Methods of keeping the public Accounts'. Again similar sentiments were underlined by the Tory leader, Robert Harley: 'It [credit] is produced, and grows insensibly, from fair and upright Dealing, punctual Compliance, honourable Performance of Contracts and Covenants; in short, 'tis the Off-spring of universal Probity.'[26] This view now transcended ideological and political boundaries.

The work had already been done and institutionalized. In 1668 the confusing system of various revenue farmers harvesting the excise around the country was centralized.

The collection of duty became the responsibility of the London excise farmers who were now accountable to the Treasury. Although they could still sub-farm the various counties, this move gave the Treasury greater control of the excise revenue. Six years later, in 1674, the collection was brought wholly under one authority with the abolition of sub-farming. In 1683 farming was finally abolished and excise collection became a state institution, giving full control of this revenue to the Treasury. Both the Excise and Customs departments became the key advisors to the Treasury in drafting any fiscal, commercial or industrial legislation.[27] The nationalization of the country's revenue would go on to prove to be a vital step to ensuring the nation's credit and rise to power.[28] By contrast, France and the United Provinces had far more diffuse fiscal systems. As Rommelse writes regarding the latter: 'The States General found it almost impossible to reach unanimous decisions because the provinces often had conflicting political and economic interests. The tax system was decentralized and the percentage contributed by each province became fixed. The institutional structure of the United Provinces and the political deadlock between the provinces made changes to this system impossible.'[29] The advantage and ability to nationalize the revenue was far easier in England than its European and Asian rivals.

Clarendon, rightly suspicious of these republican-inspired English reforms was, prior to his fall, always alert to anything he perceived as a threat to royalty, and was the prime force behind the preservation of Privy Council power. A committed believer in the 'ancient constitution' and power of kings, he had been a key architect in the early years of the Restoration.[30] He was keen to ensure that Parliament's power remained restricted, which made him unpopular, and he was subsequently unfairly blamed for the disastrous second Anglo-Dutch War (1665–7), resulting in his impeachment in 1667 and his subsequent banishment. This was the same year, perhaps not coincidentally, that Downing passed, as we have seen, one of his most important fiscal reforms (Treasury Orders). In his departing reflections, the hurt and bewildered Clarendon claimed: 'In my humble opinion, the great misfortunes of the kingdom have proceeded from the war, to which it was notoriously known, that I was always most adverse; and many without vanity say, I did not only foresee, but I did declare the mischiefs we should run into, by entering into War before any Alliance with the Neighbour Princes.'[31] War would, however, be a principal architect of England/Britain's industrial trajectory.

With the fall of Clarendon the Privy Council's power became diluted. The Lord Treasurer, Southampton, also died in May that year resulting in the acceleration of the growth of Treasury influence and authority. The expanding state departments subsequently became more independent and the Lord Treasurer's duties were put into a Cromwellian-style commission. Southampton's expected successor to the position of Lord Treasurer was his nephew, Shaftesbury; however, his support of the opposition's Irish Cattle bill in 1663 and his subsequent involvement in the impeachment of Lord Clarendon put him out of favour with the king. Despite this, Shaftesbury's political capital was too high for Charles to simply erase and, consequently, the king grit his teeth, and agreed to make him one of the new Treasury commissioners. Along with Shaftesbury, the first commissioners were the Duke of Albemarle, Sir William Coventry and Sir John Duncomb. The most important, perhaps imperative, position of Secretary to the Treasury was given to that other pragmatic republican and colonial-educated advisor Downing. The Treasury was now well on course to becoming an independent and powerful state department.[32]

Unlike a Treasurer, a Treasury Commission had to make collective decisions. The board quickly established a fixed timetable for business and regularized meetings. The nature and content of Treasury work was primarily classified into distinct books created by Downing, while a minute book commenced recording the daily proceedings of the Treasury Lords. Their aim was to find out as near exactly as possible the financial state of the kingdom.[33]

Downing was an exceptional and scrupulous administrator. His overriding objective was simple; namely, to nurture national power and therefore generate the wealth this required. This was an aim he was happy to pursue drawing upon Dutch but also, where appropriate, French practice. Towards the end of the Interregnum, Downing had warned that England was dangerously languishing in both trade and industry with its main European competitors: 'They are far too politic for us in point of trade, and do eat us out in our manufactures.' It was here that Downing made such a difference; he articulated, perhaps even more than his contemporaries in political power, that there was an intrinsic relationship between military success and a coordinated commercial and industrial policy with nurturing wealth and raising tax revenues. In this sense the origin of modern capitalism, as Sven Beckert has recently argued, was war.[34] The furtherance of national power depended upon a robust fiscal system hinging upon the regular and visible flow of revenues – with all such information carefully charted.[35]

Downing and others learnt from the French the indispensable need for industrial protection, and from the Dutch a strong navy and a fiscal machine that, in an altered shape, would eventually bring stunning success to the eighteenth-century British state. First, they found that the Dutch relied primarily on the excise for revenue at the expense of customs duties, and emphasized the close alliance between Dutch naval military might and trade. Downing wrote to the suspicious Clarendon in 1661, 'The Trade of England cannot have its necessary protection and incouragement unless his Majesty have a much greater Revenue.'[36] To aid this objective Downing came up with eleven proposals that emphasized the excise and practical ways to improve revenue collection. His commitment to domestically generated revenues had already been crucial in preserving the retention of the Commonwealth's excise.

The primary aim of Downing and numerous others of his ilk, now long forgotten, was to make England a leading force in Europe and the Atlantic. The means justified the end whatever the regime. This objective, too, was recognized by Charles II when he appointed Downing to the post of Secretary to the new Treasury Commission in 1667, much to the horror of the impeached and now powerless Clarendon, who later grumbled at the king's patronage, regarding it as having 'so little reverence or esteem for antiquity, and did in truth so much condemn old orders, forms and institutions, that the objection of novelty rather advanced than obstructed any proposition'. This was the voice of an understandably bitter and fallen star, whose feet remained firmly planted in the pre-Revolution past. The notion of the divine right of the monarch had clearly not been resurrected with the passion and decisiveness many in the Restoration hoped for. Nonetheless, in the short term, Downing's energetic attempt to introduce a general excise never made much headway, much, no doubt, to Clarendon's relief.[37]

In the long term, however, the views of Downing and other like-minded folk would become central to English and British finance, trade and industrialization. This was part of the comparatively weak English state's continuing transformation since 1642, from a relatively unreformed body to joining a central and Western European period of state building. Much of this, as Jonathan Scott, Michael Braddick, James Scott Wheeler and D'Maria Coffman have so well argued, was a legacy from the failure to deal with the fiscal problems of the second half of the sixteenth century. Obviously, without money the Crown was unable to fund a successful foreign policy.[38] Reflecting upon the republican military success of the Interregnum, Downing wrote from the Netherlands in March 1662: 'I would to God … something [was] done … for the augmentation of his Majesties Revenue … nothing being more certaine, then that … his Majesty cannot keepe … neither honor nor interest with his neighbours … unless his Majesty have a much greater Revenue.'[39]

Very early on in the new Restoration regime, Downing had penned a number of policies that pointed the way to attempt a rectification of the situation. In August 1661 he produced a blueprint, capturing prevalent commercial sentiment, for viable revenue that would enable the new king to gain the credentials and fiscal backing to challenge the Dutch for commercial supremacy. The ability to defend trade through a strong navy required lucrative and reliable revenues, which he wrote, 'is the mystery of this [the Dutch] state'. It was also something clearly demonstrated during the Interregnum – a point impregnating most of what Downing set out to achieve. A priority would be to snatch as much of the Dutch carrying (re-export) trade as possible, and Downing was ruthlessly precise in his prescription. To begin with, the English had a massive advantage when it came to time: 'There is three or four months' time commonly in the year in which the Hollanders are frozen up whereas all that time the English are at liberty both to fit their ships and make their voyages.' However, he further cautioned, this 'must be gone about very calmly and by degrees that soe it gives not too great an alarm at once, but yet it is a most plausible way of encouraging his Majesties shipping and discouraging foreign shipping'. This was something the French had introduced with an additional five shillings being added to the lading and unlading of ships, 'that if observed must in time make France wonderfully considerable in shipping'. As well as recognizing Dutch commercial might, Downing was, like many of his contemporaries, now also dwelling upon an increasing awareness of French commercial ambition and industrial superiority.[40]

Downing calculated that the king needed at least £150,000–160,000 per annum to fight a war with the Dutch. To try and achieve this, he proposed a number of possible new sources of revenue and fiscal reforms. The latter included two new acts for improving the collection of customs and excise, while the former advertised a controversial new excise upon salt (except that used in fishing) and one on the fledgling paper industry. He warned, if 'the king should have an Excise, he must have sufficient power for the collecting of it; and as to the Customs, there is nothing more destructive to the merchants and to trade if … Duty's should be imposed and not well collected'. As to a new duty on sealed paper, he predicted, 'It may be made a very handsome revenue, as it is in Spaine and this country [the United Provinces].'[41] Here Downing was a little premature since there was a need to first nurture a robust English paper industry to be taxed. Before excise revenues drawn from manufacturers could lie at the heart of fiscal credibility there needed to be an established industrial base.

Nonetheless, Downing had done his homework; he had scrutinized Europe for best fiscal and tax-raising practices and attempted to apply them to England. Again, for example, with his suggestion for an excise on salt, Downing was drawing upon the experience of another nation: 'It is known that a vast sum of France's ways is by this commodity,' although he further cautioned, 'it must not be layd in England as in France upon the persons spending it, but upon the commodity itself as it was done by the last'. In this sense, Downing situated success within a more carefully defined commercial, fiscal and industrial policy. To ensure the salt manufacturer in England was encouraged, a duty had to be passed in Parliament that 'foreign salt may pay more than they do'. Consequently, the tax would be on the producer who, in turn, would accept the burden because he was protected from foreign rivals. The emphasis upon protectionism and inland taxation upon manufacturers would become integral to English and later British policy. Indeed, this would directly and indirectly frame the Industrial Revolution. Downing also recommended, for equitable reasons, that home-brewed beer as well as commercially sold beer should be taxed, since 'the poorest pay who are not able to brew, and the rich who are able to brew pay not'.[42] Downing and the emphasis of numerous others on the republican tainted excise, however, was not as yet publicly supported and evoked widespread hostility. Arguments that crystallized around the introduction of this tax drew upon and fed an increasingly prominent political concern over the notion of an Englishman's liberty.

The great fear was the introduction of a general excise, with the political and oeconomic arguments from both sides forged during the English Civil War and Interregnum period. The brewers of London early on expressed views that would become extremely common throughout the later seventeenth and eighteenth centuries as the excise expanded. In *Free-men Inslaved*, published in 1642, they claimed the excise was 'contrary to the Fundamental laws of this Land' and 'targeted a necessary which like bread was vital to the poor'. The law was decided by excise commissioners and sub-commissioners and thus 'denying us Tryals either by the Judges of the Land, or Jurors, which is our birthright'. The power given to these excise officers was far too much and 'contrary to *Magna Carta*, which faith, Everyman's *House is his castle*', while the levying of fines or imprisonment was in violation of '*Habeas Corpus*, and consequently the benefit of the Common Law due to free-born *Englishmen*'. These sentiments were something that subsequent governments had to take seriously right up until most excises were dismantled in the nineteenth century. The usual response to such accusations was stated in *An Act of the Commons of England. … For the speedy raising and levying of Monies by way of New Impost or Excise* in 1649, which claimed that the excise was 'the most equall and indifferent levye that can be laid upon the People'.[43] Downing, of course, was of this view.

Downing's enthusiasm for the republican tax had numerous less well-known advocates. An anonymous author tried to sell the equitable nature of the excise in his pamphlet of 1647 entitled *The Standard of Equality in Subsidiary Taxes and Payments, or a Just and Strong Preserver of Publique Liberty.* The writer pressed an argument that would become the standard fodder of subsequent eighteenth-century governments defending the tax, namely, that people via an excise would only have to purchase that which they could afford. Thence the tax would fall heaviest upon the wealthiest since they consumed the most. The anonymous author concluded, 'The Excise, rightly ordered, is the ready way to raise a Masse of Money, with the least sensible pressure of the People, appears by the practice of our Neighbours in the Low-countries.' Here the Netherlands had shown that the excise was the 'surest, speediest, easiest provision for the publique, as in which what hath dropt out of private purses, by un-perceived degrees, flowes in a full and faire streame into the common Banke'.[44] He then tried to refute the array of excise critics and reasoned, 'Wee shall soone observe that the new and strange in sound, is old and familiar in the practice thereof. For all Impositions, Taxes and Customes, formerly imposed upon wares and commodities, were in effect the same with the Excise, though under another name and notion.'[45]

However, these views were balanced by a number of tracts issued against the excise. The pamphleteer and lawyer, William Prynne, launched a torrent of biblical evidence to prove the injustice and irreligious nature of the excise. It 'was altogether a *stranger, and thing utterly unknown to our Fore-fathers*, the *Name* and *thing* being never found in any *Histories*, or *Records* of former Ages in this *Island*'.[46] Nonetheless, an excise upon domestic manufacturers would go on to be the most important tax in eighteenth-century Britain and a vital key to its fiscal, commercial, industrial and military success.

'Barbarous Tyranny of the Hollanders': The Dutch wars and fiscal reform

The targeting of the Dutch as England's primary trading rival had been a prominent issue, particularly since the Interregnum, and lurking behind the work of Downing and others was a renewed quest to usurp Dutch commercial superiority. This, along with strategic fiscal reforms needed for aggressive oeconomic expansion, became ever more urgent.

The success of the first Anglo-Dutch War of 1652–4 under the Cromwellian republic was obviously not a distant memory in the 1660s. Sentiment, earlier, had been stoked by the alleged barbarism of the Dutch towards the English. One of many well-read pamphlets on the subject included a shocking account by the merchant James Ramsay in 1651, in which he claimed to have been an eyewitness to the torture and brutal death of a number of English merchants and factors at Amboyna (Maluka in Indonesia) in 1623. This had become an infamous incident involving the persecution and murder of twenty men working for the English East India Company by agents of the Dutch East India

The Industrial Revolution

Company. The men were hung, tortured and then beheaded in a 'macabre fashion', such was the 'barbarous Tyranny of the Hollanders' concluded Ramsay. Whether the incident took place to the level of brutality then painted, of course, can never be known but it became a significant event in later legitimating the first Dutch War.[47]

The question now was whether the newly restored monarchy had the stomach for war with the Dutch. Clearly, Clarendon and Southampton were suspicious of such warmongering; however, the tide of aggression was rising in tandem with English commercial expansion. In particular, English trade for bullion from the Spanish Americas, slaves from West Africa, fishing in Atlantic waters, cloth and spices from Asia and trade with Portugal were increasingly clashing, especially with Dutch commercial interests. There were new English companies such as the Company of Royal Adventurers Trading with Africa, which in this case had powerful backing from the controversial Catholic Duke of York.[48] Charles II's brother and heir to the throne was a keen advocate of war with the Dutch but not just for commercial reasons.

With the French increasingly displaying expansionist ambition in the Low Countries, many English figures were confident that the Dutch would back down and offer generous trading concessions to England. For Downing, in particular, it was important to be uncompromising and forceful in negotiations. Since 1663 he had been employed to carry out such discussions on behalf of the Crown, the Royal Adventurers and the East India Company. Downing and many others, still nostalgic for the respect England achieved during the republican era, hoped that the glorious memory of victory in the last war with the Dutch would be enough to persuade the United Provinces of the folly of another military encounter with England.

Clarendon, especially, was understandably keen to prevent or delay hostility for as long as possible due to scarce Crown finances and a House of Commons reluctant to grant additional taxes. Nonetheless, the Downing lobby was increasingly impatient, considering any indecisive posturing as simply a dangerous display of weakness, which would convince the Dutch that England would never go to war. Over two days in April 1664, the Committee of Trade outlined all the trading complaints against the Dutch. Two days later, on the 21 April, Thomas Clifford presented the committee's findings to the House of Commons, which duly approved its contents. Crucially, the House pledged that it would support action, namely, grant additional taxes if war commenced. This was then presented to the House of Lords, which also passed the resolution. Instead of persuading the Dutch to back down, however, it inflamed the situation and accelerated the path to war. Events were put beyond doubt when the gung-ho naval captain, Robert Holmes, with a naval force sent by the Duke of York, apparently exceeded his orders off the African Gold Coast and attacked any Dutch shipping he encountered (Figure 1). This resulted in him capturing several Dutch forts and trading posts, but triggering a decisive and successful Dutch counter-attack upon the Royal Adventurers Company. War was inevitable.[49]

It was not just commercial incentive that triggered the second Anglo-Dutch War (1665–7). It was also greatly aided by a prevalent fear that the republican United Provinces sought universal domination. By now, it was almost taken for granted that

A Profpect from Cape-Coaft Road of Elmina, S.ʳ Jago, Phipps's Tower, Cape-Coaft-Caftle, and Fort-Royal, 172

ELMINA Caftle was firft built by the Portugueze, but afterwards taken from them by the Dutch, anno 1638. It certainly the Strongeft, Largeft, and beft Garrison on the Coaft of Africa, the not so airy, or pleasant as Cape Coa from whence it is distant about three Leagues. In Short the Dutch Forts in General fony'Coaft of Guinea) are far better Arm'd and mann'd than the Englifh, who have not such goo d Encouragement to Support a Trade of so great importance to their Nation

Figure 1 'English settlement and slave trading centre at Cape Coast Castle on the Gold Coast.'

the key to such a quest, for either a republic or a monarchy, was trade and this required command of the seas. The Dutch control of trade in the East Indies, the West Coast of Africa, the Caribbean and the Mediterranean was a clear indication for many that the Dutch were set upon such a universal quest.[50] It was during this period that the increasing importance of traders as a fiscal resource was met with the merchants need for state naval protection. This was frequently a tense relationship but, ultimately, the duality of common aims overcame conflicting differences.[51]

Downing, writing in December 1664 as the king's envoy to the United Provinces, was in no doubt of the Dutch republic's ambition. In typically bullish manner, he claimed they were set upon nothing less than universal domination of trade. He further snarled that 'new injuries' were 'daily heaped, and the same designs of the *East* and *West-Indie-Companies* carried on for the utter overthrow of all the *Trade* of His Majesties Subjects in those parts of the world'. While all the time the king was trying to seek a peaceful settlement, the Dutch, he claimed, had begun arming 'in an extraordinary manner, ordering the fitting out with all speed a great *Fleet*, and *hundreds of carpenters* forthwith dispatched to work upon it night and day, (holy days as well as working days)'. They would stop at nothing, even godly respect, in the quest for global commercial might and universal domination. The Dutch may have been Protestants but they were a mad, bad and dangerous people.[52]

Commercial anxieties were, in one way or another, the prevalent theme, but the sense of these fears differed among merchants. The leading historian of this theme, Steve Pincus, has argued that they were far from united over the wisdom of war with the Dutch. Religion, of course, penetrated the sense of these concerns. It was those 'most committed to the Anglican and Royalist cause', who 'were convinced that the religiously pluralist and politically republican Dutch policy was the source of England's political and economic woes' that spearheaded the attack upon the Dutch.[53] In short, despite Downing's macho posturing, it was the Anglican royalists that were the most aggressive in their stance towards the Dutch partly to crush domestic religious dissent and the possible return of political republicanism.[54]

Meanwhile, although Protestant Nonconformists and some Church of England members were not yet united in fingering Catholic France as the true enemy, they were nonetheless starting to view them with unease and as a potentially more dangerous trading rival than the Dutch. Such sentiments, however, made little headway in Charles II's pro-French court and the Dutch republic remained the primary enemy. It was increasingly claimed that to stop them achieving their aims would mean preventing them monopolizing trade. As the Anglican royalist John Evelyn summed up, for 'whoever commands the trade of the world, command the riches of the world, and whoever is master of that, commands the world itself'.[55] Feeding on such fears, Downing fiercely argued that the Dutch had gained much of their trade via 'fraud and treachery'.[56] In the event the second Anglo-Dutch War was a humiliation for England, culminating in the Dutch sailing up the Medway and sinking fourteen of the Royal Navy's largest vessels docked at Chatham.[57] This disaster both triggered a renewed speculation of another civil war and underlined the need to dominate the seas. Losses like this undermined social stability, oeconomic ambition and the fact that England would always be vulnerable to a superior navy.[58]

Accusations of Dutch commercial success being built upon unfair trading practices and part of a policy for universal domination again reared its head in the events leading up to the third Anglo-Dutch War (1672–4). One commentator sneered in 1672: 'The Netherlanders from the beginning of their trade in the Indies, not contented with the ordinary course of a fair and free commerce, invaded diverse islands, took some forts, built others; and laboured nothing more than the conquests of countries, and the acquiring of new dominion.' Another irate Englishman, also writing that year, slammed the Dutch as set upon suppressing the whole of England's foreign trade through 'bloody and inhumane butcheries'. Such rhetoric was fed by Restoration fears that the Dutch republic, rightly seen as a haven for former English republicans, was set upon destroying the English monarchy. This time, however, the war was more political than commercial and fuelled by the hope it would bolster the English Crown at home. It was underlined that the immoral Dutch quest for universal power had particularly taken root after it switched rule from the House of Orange to republicanism in 1650.[59]

During this period of political suspicion and commercial ambition the anti-French voice was, once again, beginning to get louder. Although the Dutch threat loomed large, a significant minority of predominantly English radicals were increasingly insisting that the real threat was the growth of Catholic French power via commercial expansion and the increasing intensification of King Louis XIV's absolutism. The only thing stopping French universal dreams, they claimed, was the Dutch. Thus, war against the latter would be a great mistake. The only benefactor in such a clash would be the French, with Louis gleefully rubbing his hands as the Protestant English and Dutch cancelled each other out. The result would be French usurpation in trade and the eclipse of Protestantism by Catholicism. The weary English republican, Algernon Sidney, sighed, 'The king of France will gain all the traffic, and increase his power at sea, as fast as either of ours can diminish.' England was simply being manipulated, it was alleged, to aid French interests.[60]

Widespread support for military conflict against the Dutch soon dwindled after fighting commenced and the anti-French voice increasingly seemed verified. English seamen accused the French Navy of deliberately doing nothing and letting the Royal Navy take the full brunt of encounters with the Dutch. The fears of English radicals were seemingly confirmed, and further bolstered by the dilution of any anxiety towards Dutch republicanism after the restoration of the House of Orange. In addition, it was also a period of growing domestic alarm of Catholic plots and suspicious French sympathies within the English court. This was triggered by the ill-conceived Declaration of Indulgence in 1672 and its cancellation the following year. Such ever-present trepidations were given real substance in 1673 by the official news that the Duke of York and the Lord Treasurer were Catholic. If the English and Dutch ended up destroying each other and their respective trade, the path would be totally clear for French Catholic universal monarchy. Within such a climate, Charles II was forced to sever his alliance with the French king and sign a peace treaty with the Dutch.[61]

If England was increasingly suspicious of French activities, such fears were mutual. Certainly, by 1670 France was becoming concerned with the strength and increasing emergence of English maritime power in Europe and the West Indies. In particular, Spain had become dangerously reliant upon the Royal Navy, which provided England with a prominent position in Spanish commercial policy. France now worked to challenge Dutch and English trade in the region, which meant trying to bring Spain and its American empire under French influence.[62]

The long-term result of these events was the significant erosion in the original trajectory of the restored monarchy. The right of the king to make war or peace was absolute and needed to be severed by Parliament. For Pincus, the significance of all this 'lay not in the revival of fears of Roman Catholicism, but rather in the conviction that only an English Parliament could protect the nation from French universal dominion and a French style of government'. The fear of a Catholic successor to Charles II, his brother the Duke of York, was seemingly eroded by the marriage of York's eldest daughter, Mary, to Prince William of Orange in 1677. Tim Harris also places the emphasis of England during this period on a tension between religious issues and political fears over royalism and a potential return to republicanism. Likewise, as Richard Greaves has shown, suspicion regarding a possible return to republicanism had actually never gone away since the republican era. Under the leadership of Cooper, the first Earl of Shaftesbury, a strong faction had emerged that stoked up fear over the threat of a Catholic succession. This culminated in the explosive Popish Plot crisis of 1678–81, with attempts at bringing a bill to exclude the Duke of York from the future Crown.[63]

The exclusionists may have gone on to lose the battle, but they eventually gained a prominent voice in the post-1688 Glorious Revolution regime. Thereafter, Dutch and French policies were welded, with the former's commercial and fiscal experience combined with French industrial protectionist policies to create a unique English, and subsequently British, oeconomic trajectory. This would be a significant factor in the country's subsequent Industrial Revolution.

Not long after the arrival of Prince William of Orange, England was plunged into a hugely expensive military conflict with France that lasted nine years. To fund such an expensive war required a revolutionary extension of prevailing fiscal measures and creation of new financial innovations. In February 1689 Parliament introduced a monthly assessment for six months, regarded by MPs as a land tax, which was the first time such a levy had been introduced in ten years. One problem with the assessment was its unequal distribution, with the east half of England contributing more than the west. By 1694 the landed gentry was getting fed up, in general, of shouldering the burden of increased tax to pay for war with France. The government increasingly turned to an inland tax on its, as yet rather negligible, domestic manufactures as an alternative source of revenue. However, it had to be careful not to appear to be attempting to introduce a general excise, despite the idea of such a universal tax being popular with well-known commentators like Davenant. For example, he feared that if a 4s. levy in the pound remained on the landed class, they would probably become so indebted that their estates would be confiscated by the greedy moneylenders making massive profits at their expense.[64] For numerous others, however, a general excise could give William the power to rule without Parliament. Moreover, if this was a tax upon everyone then the 'common people' could turn upon traditional social authority.[65] The landed tax was thus seen as having the potential to trigger a revolt among the aristocracy, while an expansion of the excise could do the same among the great masses. A decision, however, had to be made sooner or later on which way the axe would fall. In the short term, the state's fiscal administrative system could be tackled through efficiency savings.

William brought with him Dutch advisors with experience of their more developed fiscal system, and an acceleration of Dutch capital into London. In short, the 1690s drew heavily upon English republican and Dutch experience in the initial building of what John Brewer terms a 'fiscal-military State'. Accompanying the dramatic increase in costs through war was a greater urgency, fuelled by Tory and Whig divides (although far from black and white), for even greater accountability. Trust between the executive and Parliament was strained and characterized by mutual suspicion. The account commissions that sat between 1691 and 1713 were relatively effective at trying to establish greater visibility. However, since they were composed of MPs (unlike its precursor of 1667) it often degenerated, especially during its final years, into a vehicle simply for political attacks. The primary source of darkness was, as ever, the Exchequer, in which positions of power were held for life and, frequently, hereditary. As such the occupants were not accountable to any person or institution; as their positions were private property, they could not be sacked for incompetence or inefficiency. The real work was done by their deputies who they paid with part of their stipend. Consequently, the Exchequer was able to ignore the Treasury's pleas for the improved performance of their duties. This meant serious delays in the Exchequer's auditing and release of public accounts. The result was an important act in 1696, building on the Order of Council of 1668, for improving the tracking of such accounts in and out of the Exchequer. Roseveare describes this act, drafted by William Lowndes, as 'brilliantly original in establishing Treasury control over the men who actually performed those duties – the deputies to the patent officers'.

The latter would now be appointed by the Treasury with the patentees still safe in their sinecures.[66]

The 1690s witnessed a high level of scrutiny of public accounts by various commissions characterized by a traditional country and anti-executive stance. The emphasis upon greater information and visibility of income and expenditure continued to grow in the eighteenth century. The reams of reports concerning fiscal matters 'were part', argues Julian Hoppit, 'of a continual use of political arithmetic which had been' developing during this period.[67] In other words, the increasing emphasis upon tracking revenue and solidifying borrowing payments provided an impetus towards a technology for achieving such objectives. Induction was, arguably, being spearheaded within the state's fiscal apparatus more than natural philosophy and the interrogation of nature. The huge expense of war, quest for money and the sheer urgency of the situation was a much greater fuel for such innovation. National oeconomic necessity was, in this sense, a leading impetus to a method of state empiricism and a quantifying spirit.

The outward embodiment of these attributes was correctly kept account books without deliberate alterations or suspicious erasures; this was also a key feature of the Excise's instructions in making and recording all tax-gauging charges and keeping a diary.[68] Such was the importance of good accounts that Daniel Defoe devoted a significant chunk of his *The Complete English Tradesman* (1725) to this imperative. 'Next to taking care of his soul', he advised, 'a tradesman should take care of his book' – a measure, as just underlined, drummed into him via his former occupation as an excise officer. Consequently, they 'should always be kept clean and neat; and he that is not careful of both, will give but a sad account of himself either to God or man'.[69]

The values of probity and prudence, allied to good bookkeeping, came to be offered equally as ideal business and state administrative habits. Elsewhere, such moral attributes and accounting practices were becoming key features of good natural philosophy. Bookkeeping and mercantile practices became a vital resource for late-seventeenth-century natural philosophers seeking a method for recording knowledge production. For example, it became an important resource for the early members of the Royal Society of London.[70] To read a description of an experiment was to literally believe you had witnessed it,[71] while correctly kept accounts gave a seeming objective knowledge of revenue flows. Arguably, more than other institutions it was the Treasury and the Excise that really put such an approach into practice during this period.[72] These two fiscal bodies were soon joined by the establishment of the Bank of England to complete what would become a crucial alliance during the eighteenth century; trust in the fiscal future was certified via this credible trinity.

A key part, then, in the development of England's fast-expanding fiscal, trading and industrial system was the establishment of the Bank of England in 1694. This was rightly seen at the time as a republican institution that drew inspiration from the cities of Genoa, Venice and Amsterdam. There had been advocates for such a creation since at least 1641, when Henry Robinson proposed a national bank, followed ten years later by a similar scheme put forward by the Dutch art agent, painter and architect Balthasar Gerbier.

Robinson was, according to Robert Brenner, an 'ideological republican', who became a prominent figure within the Commonwealth government and was valued for his theory and proposals regarding trade. His two most important and widely read tracts were *England's Safety in Trades Encrease* (1641) and *Brief Considerations, Concerning the Advancement of Trade and Navigation* (1649). Robinson's suggestions had the support of some powerful figures such as Cooper, who had also supported his earlier doomed fight to become postmaster general. Robinson's proposals for a national bank were considered by the Protectorate Council in 1654 and during the Restoration. However, despite Charles II authorizing a patent for the scheme the plan made no further headway.[73] Nonetheless, his views, in general, were representative of prominent fiscal arguments then emerging in England.

The bank, however, would have to wait till the Glorious Revolution before it would be established. William Cunningham caught the significance of its subsequent founding: 'Hitherto the continuity of the government had depended chiefly on the succession to the throne; and there were possibilities of violent reaction with each new accession; but the existence of the Bank gave an important guarantee for the maintenance of the same general principles of rule under any monarch.' The bank was partly made possible because, under William and Mary, the monarchy was now weaker and constitutionally limited, while the powerful influence of wealthy Protestant immigrants, who formed a significant part of London's moneyed interest, also added a great deal of impetus to its establishment.[74] However, these two factors were only half the story; the other part of the problem was the limitation of private bankers. From the start, William had struggled to raise the loans needed from creditors and, especially, the prevailing system of private banking. Since the Protectorate an array of elaborate financial services were on offer to both city merchants and the gentry from, especially, goldsmith bankers. With the arrival to the throne of William, the credibility of the Crown in fulfilling its pledge to repay loans was far from high.

The constitutional reforms made after the Glorious Revolution went some way to improving the Crown's credit potential. Certainly powerful goldsmith bankers, who had not been hit by the earlier Stop of the Exchequer in 1672, like Sir Francis Child, started purchasing government tallies in 1689 for the first time.[75] To do this Child moved funds from his usual concentration in the private sector and lowered his reserves to asset ratio. He could have made significantly larger loans to the Treasury but decided not to. Instead, as Stephen Quinn has shown, he chose to maintain 'reserves sufficient to handle severe runs rather than further extend his exposure to government debt'.[76]

It was entirely because of this prudent approach by the private financial sector, in general, that forced the Treasury to examine other ways of funding its increasing need for money. 'The reluctance', concludes Quinn, 'of private bankers to decrease their reserve ratios created a gap between what William III wanted to borrow and what private bankers like Child were willing to fund. This gap spurred famous innovations in public finance at the heart of the Financial Revolution.' William and his now predominantly Whig advisors were keen to exploit the sudden growth in new joint-stock companies and people willing to invest in them. War was forcing merchants to look inwards to invest domestically and fuelling this drive for greater financial opportunities. It was within this context, of course, that the Bank of England was established in 1694 to improve both William's situation and to offer better returns (and credibility) for investors in public stock. The bank raised £1.2 million and loaned this to the government; in return the subscribers were incorporated as the Governor and Company of the Bank of England.[77]

Despite the three wars with the Dutch, England did not yet have the overwhelming burden of a huge debt that its main European competitors had, while its central state bureaucracy – especially the Treasury, revenue bodies, Navy Board and Admiralty – were firmly under parliamentary control. In general, the tax system was much more unified than its European rivals and more effectively controlled by the staff at Whitehall.[78] The impressive centralization of the country's fiscal system, via the filtering of all the state's receipt and disbursement through the Treasury, has led Brewer to rightly declare that Britain had 'become the first major European state to keep full accounts of total government revenue and expenditure'.[79]

Prior to the Glorious Revolution, certain important offices could still be purchased but, with the exception of the Royal Household, a purchasable office by 1700 was almost invariably a sinecure or quasi-sinecure.[80] Influence, rather than purchase, was by far the most important criteria. After 1689 the pressure exerted by a more confident and powerful standing House of Commons created an element of accountability. This is not to say there was no corruption, far from it, but it was generally not on the scale that characterized European fiscal administration. In addition, tax collection in most countries in Europe was still predominantly (although not totally) in the hands of a consortium of private financiers and tax farmers. By contrast, in England by the late seventeenth century, Customs and Excise had been nationalized.[81]

The credit of a nation was, ultimately, only as good as the source and gathering of its taxes. Over the course of the eighteenth century, these would become heavily reliant upon domestic industry in Britain. Fiscal and state administrative reforms were accompanied by a strategic approach to nurturing trade, naval power, colonization and, especially, domestic manufactures behind protective tariffs. Any understanding of Britain's subsequent Industrial Revolution has to comprehend this interlinked nexus. From the start, the manufacture and trade of cloth was central to a nation's success. In the following chapter, we trace the early emergence of various textiles in England and Britain's history.

CHAPTER 2
'THE GREATEST DOMINION OF THE WORLD': TRADE AND TEXTILES

In 1649 the staunch commercial reformer and republican Henry Robinson underlined the aim of establishing England as the centre of the world's trade and navigation.[1] Just over thirty years later in 1680, a leading barrister, oeconomic commentator and one-time active exclusionist, William Petyt, added to this objective the need to also nurture domestic manufactures:

> Whereas Manufactures and a great Foreign Trade, will admit of and oblige an increase of people even to infinity: And the more the Manufacturers increase, they will the more enrich one another, and the rest of the people; it may then be proper to inquire how the *Manufactures* of a Nation may be *increased and improved*. This may be done either by enlarging former Manufactures, or by introducing new ones.[2]

This chapter charts the gradual shift from an emphasis upon trade to a growing concern with the quest to nurture domestic industry.

For many, like Robinson and Petyt, there was an expanding, although at some point static, commercial pie and England's share fell far short of what it should be. During the seventeenth century, the world seemed a fertile possibility of great plenty dented by the fear, uncertainty and risk of investing in foreign lands, a negligible domestic industrial base and vast seas populated by powerful trading rivals and unknown peoples, as well as ruthless privateers and pirates. New trading networks stemming, partly, from a growing demand for exotics from the Americas and, especially, Asian manufactured imports, were stoking a political fear over the balance of payments and need for ever-greater supplies of bullion from the Iberian American empire. It was also eroding traditional trading relationships as the rise in long-distance commerce to the Americas and Asia continued to increase.

It should be remembered that as late as the mid-sixteenth century, England's main trade was concentrated in the Low Countries. To expand the geography of this commerce required obtaining valuable mercantile information and the navigational skills to enable long-distance trade. In terms of the former, this meant knowledge of market dates, the nature of local commodities, currencies and conversion rates, duties, and local weights and measures. Moreover, on a simple matter of practicality it required emulating the navigation skills of the Dutch, Portuguese, Spanish and Italians. To achieve this required the wooing and importation of such skilled persons from these countries, which was a project that actively commenced during the Elizabethan period.[3]

The commercial transformation stemming from the Elizabethan period dramatically accelerated during the early Stuart period and, especially, from the 1640s and into the Restoration. The catalyst for this surge was the lucrative import and re-export trade, and not the traditional northern European export of English textiles. By 1663 the total value of trade to Italy, the Levant and East India was £1,031,000. In contrast, the export of the Merchant Adventurers of English textiles to Germany and the Low Countries was just £406,000.[4]

Success would be heavily dependent upon aggression – one asset England was not short of. However, in terms of technology, navigation skills and maritime superiority, England was still no more impressive than any of its European and Asian rivals. Indeed, in many ways the country was subservient in comparison. Stanley J. Stein and Barbara H. Stein wryly comment: 'Under-developed nations should not overlook the fact that the English amassed a mercantile fleet from the seventeen hundred-odd merchant vessels seized as prizes from the Dutch in two years (1652–4). They were not the only nation to act in this way, but they were the most successful.'[5] England like its European rivals concentrated its attention upon mastering the world's seas. It was this concerted global maritime policy that separated Portugal, Spain, the Low Countries, England and France from much of the rest of the world.

John Thornton concludes his important study of the African continent and the Atlantic thus: 'By discovering this key [navigation], Europeans were able to unlock the commerce of the Atlantic, and because they had single-handedly developed the routes, their domination of the high seas in the Atlantic was ensured in a way that was not possible in any other extra-European area of navigation.' This is not entirely true as the Chinese and other Asian countries had skilled navigators but tended to concentrate on local maritime trade. In addition, as Chris Bayly rightly adds: 'Crudely, Europeans became better at killing people than its Asian and African counterparts; they quickly learnt that the best path to power was to exploit, eliminate, connect and control "other peoples' industrious revolutions".'[6] These illiberal skills and aggressive policies were particularly harnessed by Britain and played an important part in its industrial trajectory. In short, they were key features of what Sven Beckert has usefully termed 'war capitalism'.[7]

Recent work has persuasively shown that a combination of Atlantic and Asian overseas trade and a policy of import and re-export substitution lay at the heart of British industrialization during the eighteenth century.[8] This is dramatically supported by the fact that England imported 34.7 per cent of raw materials and 31.7 per cent manufactures between 1699 and 1702, and 62.3 per cent raw materials and a mere 4.3 per cent of manufactures by the mid-1840s.[9] However, the story is not quite so simple and a number of competing factors also informed this transition.

The European cloth trade had become saturated by the seventeenth century – a situation made far worse by the arrival of cheap Indian textile imports. This, Robert Brenner argues, led to an emphasis upon cost-cutting, especially in trying to reduce the price of labour and in the production of inferior textiles such as the new draperies. He concludes that this was not driven by fashion but, rather, the urgent need to compete. Likewise, Robert C. Allen places the emphasis upon expensive domestic labour and the need to innovate to save on such costs.[10] By contrast, Maxine Berg's argument places the focus upon changing tastes: 'Europeans responded to Asian luxuries by learning from their imports, developing knowledge of markets and adapting processes.' Moreover, the importance of these 'Asian luxuries demanded the making of consumer markets both at home and abroad for things never before needed or even desired'. Consequently, the reaction to these imported Asian goods played a significant role in informing both consumption and new production techniques.[11] This has recently been demonstrated, too, in the case of cotton textiles, in which innovation was all about attempting to match Asian quality.[12] The above perspectives, of course, do not necessarily undermine each other. As Leonard N. Rosenband has argued, a vital factor fuelling British innovation was simply desperation, triggered by the array of superior manufactures arriving at the country's shores. In this instance, it activated an array of domestic manufactures imitating, as Berg puts it, the new consumer goods from Asia that, in turn, mutated into distinct innovative British products.[13] This argument also applied to Britain's attempt at matching superior European items such as glass, soap, spirits and paper.

Aspects of these strategies can be seen in Robinson's suggestions for commercial catch-up during the seventeenth century. His arguments were a succinct synthesis of what were fast becoming a set of standard axioms among the views of numerous contemporaries. His publications made enough of a splash for the Council of State to appoint a committee to discuss with Robinson a way of applying his proposals.[14] His views, which the Commonwealth took so seriously, were characteristic of what would define the oeconomic policy for well over a century. In 1641 he emphasized the importance of encouraging the exportation of domestic goods and doing everything to hinder the imports of foreign competition. Fundamental to success, he underlined, was the nurturing of a strong Royal Navy and merchant fleet. Robinson's seventh proposal was the need to create new domestic manufactures: 'These manufactures are one maine cause hath made the Hollanders so numerous and brought them to their greatnesse.' England thus needed foreign skilled labour, which should be encouraged to set up industry in the country.[15]

These arguments were reiterated again and again by later writers. One of the most forceful and most read of these arguments came from the pen of Petyt. He argued: 'New Manufactures must be first taught, and then encouraged, and if made of Foreign Materials, the Materials must be Imported.' This would require, he concluded, the greater encouragement of skilled foreign labour: 'Without these primary Encouragements and Superintendence of the Government, it will be hard to nourish up any new Manufacture, or to enlarge any old ones, at least, suddenly, to any degree.'[16]

The key to reducing imports of foreign rival goods was to cut or sever duties on the export of English equivalents and increase the duty on imports. If this was not done, Robinson warned, all other nations 'who have already begun to make Cloth, will be able to undersell and beate us quite out, so that a Master-piece it would bee, if possible, to give them so good cheape abroad, as others might not make to live by it'. Likewise, a great deal of money was to be had by making England the emporium and centre of re-exporting East India spices, calicoes and other goods from that region. The best way of doing this would be to establish a corporation 'able to plant Colonies by degrees and make head in the Indies if need be against the Hollanders'. Such a body, he advised, should be formed by joint and well-governed stock.[17]

Robinson earlier also revealed how taxation could act as a tool of social engineering and presented an argument that would become very popular for justifying the excise, the bedrock of public credit, in the eighteenth century: 'I have knowne a policie practiced elsewhere amongst people over-slothfull, that would not worke above halfe the weeke, if they could get money enough to feed them for the whole, and that was by clapping excises and taxes upon what they eat and drank.' In this way they would have to be more industrious by working longer and harder for their necessary items.[18] It was not the market that first made people industrious but the state.[19]

Despite Robinson's inequitable promotion of a monopoly corporation to run the East India trade in 1641, his views by 1649 had significantly changed upon this issue. He now attacked the monopolistic nature of trading companies and advocated the need for opening trade 'to all men'. Like an increasing number of other writers on the subjects of trade and industry during this period, Robinson advocated the need for a specialized body to direct commercial policy. He first proposed this in 1641 and underlined its urgency again in 1649: a 'Court of Merchants, and others well versed in Merchandizing, erected, for speedy determining all differences about Trade and Navigation'. No other body would be so well equipped 'for deciphering the intricate and various differences (which seeme to many as darke obscure Hieroglyphics) arising from this profession'.[20]

This increasing embrace of the pursuit of commercial wealth was also accompanied by a changing intellectual legitimacy. Perhaps more than any other historian, Steve Pincus has traced and unravelled a new political positioning during this period, in which a hybrid of older and new themes combined to produce a justification for the push towards making commercial wealth. 'The political economy they defended', he writes, 'assumed that wealth, not civic virtue, was the basis of political power.' At the heart of this, he claims, was labour rather than land coupled with a dynamic notion of the market as opposed to a static one.[21]

By the 1690s the whole commercial and industrial context had changed due to the urgency of financing the expensive war with France. In this sense 'the balance of military power' had become 'a balance of economic power'.[22] The City broker and oeconomic writer, James Whiston, cogently articulated this sentiment: 'War is become rather an Expense of Money than Men, and Success attends those that can most and longest spend Money.' Petyt had stated the same in 1680, adding that it had been the wealth generated from the West Indies that made this military success possible. And, as was typical of writing in this period, the point was once again reproduced by the Bristol merchant John Cary and former Excise Commissioner Charles Davenant, in 1695.[23]

A significant transformation had been recognized by contemporaries that, more than ever, money, rather than courage and valour, was the key factor to military success. Debates over virtue had become usurped by the pursuit of wealth. By this stage, too,

Dutch William had reluctantly accepted that Whig support was the only way to make this possible. This would also mean the creation, as Pincus shows, of an accompanying oeconomy based around industry at the expense of the leading emphasis upon agriculture and the role of the colonies.[24] Much of the scaffolding for this had already been made during the Interregnum and Restoration. The war with the Dutch and then the French would ensure that the edifice would be strengthened and enlarged.

It was particularly during the Interregnum period that the navy was underlined as a crucial instrument within English commercial policy. The significant legislation was the Navigation Act of 1651 along with naval competition and war with the Dutch. The prequel behind the 1651 act played upon the fear of Spain seeking, as Benjamin Worsley put it that year, 'Universal Monarchie of Christendom'. Equally sinister was the Dutch quest for 'Universal Trade, not only of Christendom, but indeed of the greater part of the known world'. People like Worsley and Robinson became important architects of the oeconomy being constructed during this period. From what historical records we have, Worlsey was probably raised in London, educated in Dublin at Trinity College and then served in the English army in Ireland during the 1640s. He was a staunch advocate of colonization and the aggressive pursuit of trade, and became a leading figure in Samuel Hartlib's intellectual circle.[25]

Worsley spent two years in the Netherlands scrutinizing their oeconomic policies and intellectual resources. He was wooed back to England with the prospect of going to the American colonies and setting up a sugar business in Barbados along with various other projects in Virginia. The latter venture was primarily to do with securing the political and commercial fortunes of this colony. When Virginia, led by the planters, declared its royalist declaration in May 1650, the Commonwealth was outraged. A fleet was quickly dispatched and the Virginia planters were squashed. Thereafter, Worsley was put in charge of coordinating the Commonwealth's response to royalist rebellions throughout the American colonies. To secure the loyalty of such places the Commonwealth allowed them a degree of self-government. By now, Worsley was considered too valuable as a commercial advisor to lose to the colonies, and ended up contributing to the new Council of Trade and spearheading the drafting of the first Navigation Act. He was now at the heart of Commonwealth power and rooted in the metropolis.[26] Like Downing and Robinson, Worsley emphasized the need to imitate Dutch commercial practices including the way they built and sailed ships.[27]

Quality, trade and regulation

Whether the subject was the navy, tax or trade, domestic industry was never far away from the debate. For example, John Bland's tract, *Trade Revived,* written in the last days of the republic in 1659, was subsequently plagiarized by numerous writers. Like Downing, Bland had spent a formative period in the mainland American colonies although, in his case, further south in Virginia, where he became a significant investor in the region from the mid-1630s. His son, Giles Bland, later became Collector of Royal Customs in 1673 before being executed three years later for his role in Bacon's rebellion (a civil war that raged in the colony in 1676).[28]

John Bland had made a fortune through trade, particularly in the Mediterranean, and as a London landlord (including property rented to the Admiralty Committee of the Privy Council). He was extremely well connected with his family related to the powerful colonial entrepreneur, slave trader and administrator, Thomas Povey, who he collaborated with on a number of commercial projects. Povey held positions on the Council of Trade and for a time, was Secretary of the Committee for Foreign Plantations; he also had business dealings with influential merchants and financiers, such as the powerful Cromwellian slave trader and revenue farmer Martin Noell. It was through the marriage of Povey's daughter, Francis, to Giles Bland that the two families were united.[29]

Initially, Bland was keen that corporations and companies were restored to enable adequate resources for large-scale trade. Corporations would also discipline domestic-produced manufactures by keeping them 'true according to their Standard and Rule, for weight, Measure, and Breadth and all falsifying of them prevented'. He was a keen advocate of promoting the quality of domestically produced goods and the standardization of weights and measures. He wrote 'that all sorts of Commodities fabricated in *England* and its Dominions, be made by an exact Rule and Standard, be it cloth, stuff, silks, or any other things whatever, both for length, breadth, weight, and measure'. Bland claimed that establishing one measure and one weight throughout England and the colonies would aid commerce and help prevent fraud.[30] Commerce was teaching an ambitious country the need for standardized goods and metrology to ensure quality.

Having stringent manufacturing regulations would help prevent the forging of domestic goods by inferior copies. Forgeries were costing the nation a great deal of money, damaging the reputation of its one true competitive manufacture, woollen textiles and adding to the decay of trade. As such, enforced regulations would raise their quality and restore their reputation abroad by making them instantly recognizable. Consequently, via 'the true and exact makings of our own Manufactures', Bland concluded, buyers could be sure that they were not 'deceived in the Commodity'. However, such a national process of regulation would have to wait for the reorganization of the Excise later in the century and its expansion during the eighteenth century. Here the Excise created, as William Cunningham once observed, 'a system of industrial supervision on national lines', which was important in maintaining 'a high standard of quality for goods of every kind, manufactured for sale either at home or abroad'.[31]

The emphasis upon quality and the detrimental repercussions of second-rate products was frequently emphasized. For example, the anonymous author of *England's Interest Asserted in the Government of its Native Commodities* (1669) was scathing of the deterioration of domestically produced woollen cloth. In particular, the

want of some new Laws for the new Drapers, hath occasioned the woollen Manufacture to be rendered contemptible both at home and abroad, and so much more, or rather, because the *Dutch, Fleming,* (and it is feared in time the *French* also) do by care and industry endeavour to excel our *English*; the consequence is to lose our *English* trade.

In contrast, the care and regulation of the Dutch revealed how production should be managed. The author continued,

> the Advantage the *Dutch* have of us in all their Native Commodities is their exactness, by which means their credit is so, that it is taken by its contents, (and ours not) which is very advantageous, which is done by the qualifications of those persons that have the oversight, and are intrusted in that affair, which is not done in *England*, but generally the contrary.

The credibility of the system of administration and personnel involved was crucial, with the value of 'exactness' a central requirement.[32] England urgently needed, according to this anonymous writer, a similar process of quality regulation. Any defective Dutch cloth would result in a fine for the manufacturer. Reputation was everything and unless England regained its credibility in its only successful manufactured export, woollen textiles, it would suffer in trade.[33]

Another policy that Bland emphasized was the need to aid domestic manufactured goods by removing any export duties while keeping only minimal customs on imported raw materials. Any loss in customs revenue on manufactured imports could easily be made up by an increase in excise duty and by a rise in customs duty on goods such as fruit, wine, sugar, spice, and luxury items that could not be made or grown in England.[34] All these policies would soon be implemented. This last view of Bland's was repeated by Samuel Fortrey in his hugely successful tract entitled *England's Interest and Improvement, consisting in the Increase of the Store and Trade of this Kingdom* (1663). Fortrey's emphasis upon protectionist policies, an aggressive anti-French stance and the need to encourage the immigration of skilled foreign Protestants to help nurture England's industry, made it a firm favourite at a number of key historical moments – leading to its republishing in 1673, 1713 and 1744.[35]

Fortrey was the son of a successful London merchant, also called Samuel Fortrey, whose Protestant family had fled Flanders to escape religious prosecution during the Elizabethan era. Fortrey the elder married Katherine de Latfeur, daughter of James de Latfeur of Hainault, and made their home in an impressive Flemish mansion at Kew, known as the Dutch House. In 1642 Katherine died, followed five years later by Fortrey the elder leaving his son with a significant fortune. Some of this he invested in the Bedford Company, a Norfolk land drainage corporation we will examine later, and subsequently became one of the company's conservators with an annual salary of £150.[36]

Like Bland, whose tract he was clearly aware of, Fortrey underlined the need to encourage the export of successful domestic manufactures, free from unreasonable taxes so 'that the merchant may afford his commoditie abroad, as cheap as others, or else he could not be able to vent it'. Secondly, those foreign items that 'cannot be raised here, should be brought to us under easie customs, the better to enable us at an easie exchange, to vent our commodities abroad'. Lastly, all those luxury goods imported into England that could not be domestically produced 'should pay extraordinary customs'. In this way, 'the State will raise a good revenue, and the country save their wealth, that would be wastefully spent abroad, and so increase our own manufactures at home'. He famously calculated that England was swamped by French goods by a trade deficit of £160,000.[37] In language very similar to Downing and subsequent commentators, Bland emphasized the equity of the excise as the ideal source of revenue:

> There being not any way or duty easier born by all people, than an excise upon the consumption of goods with the Land, be they Foreign or Native commodities, it is the most equitable imposition to a people that can be for hereby everyone poor and rich bears his part and proportion according to his expenses, for he that spends much, payes a great deal of Excise.[38]

By this point, sea power had become intrinsic to state defence, trade and ambition. The relationship was also reciprocal; in the sense revenue from commerce funded the navy. The Commonwealth Navigation Act of 1651 stipulated that only goods coming in from the country of origin, or that which had first exported them, would be allowed entry to the English or Irish market. Further, the merchandise had to be carried in English ships or vessels belonging to the country from which the items originated. It was a policy explicitly aimed at taking some of the lucrative Dutch carrying trade and putting an end to the reliance of English merchants upon the Hollanders. Although the Dutch ships were technically superior they were, as Worsley and others underlined, at this stage largely unarmed and inadequately protected by the Dutch navy. It was primarily because of this that the first Anglo-Dutch War of 1652 brought them such terrible losses much to the delight of English merchants, who subsequently found it hard to forgive Cromwell when he decided to stop the hostilities for political and religious reasons.[39]

The first and subsequent Navigation Acts were a key part of the scaffolding framing English and later British illiberal protectionist policy. This became a vital factor in fuelling the export aspect of the Industrial Revolution. As well as theoretically confining trade between the colonies and England to English ships and seamen, it greatly stimulated the recruitment – often forced (both domestically and from the colonies) – of a valuable seafaring labour force. In addition, much employment was nurtured around English ports that, in turn, became linked to the industrial activities of the hinterland. The acts were designed to maximize revenue through the extension of commerce and, ultimately, via the nurturing of domestic industry.[40] At the centre of aggressive European trade were textiles.

Woollen textiles

A London merchant, signed I. B., earlier emphasized in 1644 a growing belief that 'the chiefest way of enriching a Kingdome, is the expanse of its native or home commodities (that can well be spurred) in forraigne parts'. This was difficult since England was not, as yet, an established industrial nation. Its only really significant manufacture during this period was woollen textiles. Since the early seventeenth century a series of new, lighter, woollen-based fabrics had started to make headway that were offsetting the decline of the old, heavy, woollen-based broadcloth textiles. The latter was a thick fabric made of short carded yarn providing both warp and weft that was also a very expensive cloth. The developing fabrics, by contrast – were lighter, coarser and cheaper – and made of long-combed wool that made both warp and weft (worsteds). Another textile was composed of carded yarn (linen, cotton or silk) that was the weft, while the warp was of wool or also combined yarn. These newer, lower quality mixtures – the so-called new draperies – were increasing while the higher quality pure woollens stagnated and declined.[41] This new trade in mixed fabrics and worsteds had first been introduced into England by so-called 'strangers', Walloons and Flemish, during the 1560s. In particular, something like 4,600 immigrants settled in Norwich and a further 1,300 came to Colchester in 1586.[42]

There are a number of factors that induced the rise of the woollen-based new draperies. F. J. Fisher argued that it was connected with a shift of trading emphasis from Northern to Southern Europe. This was aided by the end of the war with Spain in 1604 and subsequently the penetration into Spanish trade in the Mediterranean, where the climate suited the new lighter fabrics. By the eve of the English Civil War 'the trade in the newer fabrics', wrote Fisher, 'almost equalled in value the trade in the old, and the ports of Spain and the Mediterranean were taking a large share of London's exports as were those of the Low Countries'.[43]

By contrast, P. J. Bowden put the emphasis upon the transition of the available wool. The regions in England that produced high-quality wools were also the areas that experienced the most agricultural enclosures during the sixteenth and seventeenth centuries. This introduced a heavier fleece and a longer staple from the sheep, resulting in coarser wool that was much more suited to the new draperies. The quality of wool was less than it had been and certainly inferior to that imported from Spain. Bowden concluded: 'Enclosure made light fleeces heavier, fine wool coarser, and short wool longer. … It made wool unsuitable for the manufacture of worsted fabrics and, to a lesser extent, the coarser varieties of cloth.' This is an argument more recently emphasized by Robert C. Allen in his account of the British Industrial Revolution.[44]

However, the story is far more complicated. The original development of the woollen mixtures that became the defining ingredients of the new draperies stemmed from Italy; the Italian technical methods then came to England via Flanders. In addition, the homespun and woven cloth products of the peasant communities, items that hardly entered traditional and international commerce, generated different practical knowledge and technical processes that were also subsequently utilized and commercialized.[45]

The combination of these shop-floor Italian and peasant methods in Flanders to produce the new draperies was triggered by competition from England's old draperies and the demands stemming from Antwerp's pool of Italian merchants. Already there was a shift in product variation towards lighter and cheaper textiles in England through its development of kerseys in and around Halifax. These were still part of the old draperies but were made of short-stapled English wool and fulled less heavily than traditional broadcloth. The cloth was lighter, cheaper and narrower than the traditional old draperies. Not surprisingly, attempts were made in the rural areas of the Netherlands to imitate this cloth.[46]

Another important development was the introduction of the Houdschoote say, which was made not from the quality wools from Spain and England, but from local inferior wools from Holland and other nearby regions. It was produced through a mixture of traditional old drapery and worsted techniques, and originated from peasant practical knowledge and innovations. This textile was another example of the array of fabrics falling under the umbrella of new draperies. Donald Coleman observed that these new cloths 'embodied no single recognizable major act of invention. All sorts of familiar inputs were simply being combined in ways different from those apparent in the major export products of the English industry'. It was simply innovation out of fierce competition and spearheaded by peasant know-how. These were not always in the direction of future developments. For example, it became even more labour-intensive and retained the traditional use of the spindle and distaff (wool in the old draperies had always used the wheel). Nonetheless, the final result was the creation of new products albeit via a new combination of traditional techniques.[47]

By the seventeenth century, a demand for less robust but lighter and brighter fabrics had become embedded in European demand. The new draperies had restructured the traditional English and Northwestern European wool-based textile industry. Old divisions were smashed as new combinations of fabrics between different types of wool, silk, linen and cotton were devised. Coleman concluded his history of the new draperies claiming, 'It seems likely that the lighter and more colourful nature of these fabrics helped to encourage in consumers a taste for a wider range of choice, thus easing the acceptance of the still lighter and still more colourful Indian cottons when they appeared later.' Importantly, it was the North European Protestant migrants that introduced the finishing and dyeing shops that enabled England to produce the more colourful fabrics. This, in turn, enabled the English, ultimately, to export its textiles to the European continent, parts of Africa and the Americas in a finished, as opposed to hitherto unfinished, state.[48]

The period also witnessed the decline and almost disappearance of Italy as a major woollen fabric producer. Italian woollen textile regions were deeply affected by the collapse in Spanish, German and Turkish markets due to war from 1618 in central Europe and the Turko-Prussian War between 1623 and 1638. Italian products were generally of superior quality but the costs of production were much greater due to a combination of strong guild control, high taxation and greater labour costs. Moreover, the Italians were unable to tackle the changing nature of fashion that increasingly wanted brighter colours and lighter textiles.[49] A report to the Italian Senate in 1668 claimed that the Turks wanted light and cheap cloths, and not the expensive and heavy textiles offered by the Venetians.[50] As a result, England and the Netherlands captured a great deal of the former Italian trade in the Levant.

By the mid-seventeenth century, the largest single centre of woollen-based cloth production was Leiden. Its main competition now came from England and the region of East Anglia where skilled Flemish and Walloon textile workers had settled in and around the towns of Norwich and Colchester. By the late seventeenth century, the old Leiden woollen industry had shrunk and was rapidly being outstripped by the English new draperies. Nonetheless, the production of pure heavy woollens (*lakens*) remained a vital product at Leiden and continued to be more competitive than the English equivalent.[51] As a result, the English won the market for the cheaper and lighter new draperies, while the Dutch secured the market for high-quality textiles. All this was at the expense of the Italian and Flemish cloth producers.[52]

England had an advantage over its competitors in terms of access to lower material and labour prices compared to its main competitors. The result, as we have seen, was the collapse of Leiden's cheaper worsteds. By contrast, English producers of upmarket quality pure woollens struggled to be competitive. Lurking in the background were French manufactures from Languedoc who were producing medium quality ranges of woollen-based cloth, but these would not become powerful competitors until well into the eighteenth century. The immediate threat came, rather, from the illicit export of raw English wool to Holland, Sweden and France, and the perceived danger from ever-increasing imports of popular textiles from Asia. This accelerated a new phase of innovative woollen fabrics that became even cheaper, lighter and brighter.[53]

Despite the increasing success of England's woollen industry and certain re-exports – such as Indian calico cloth, tobacco and sugar – the country's commercial and industrial base was still vulnerable in comparison to its main European rivals. The need to nurture domestic manufactures to improve the balance of trade and, increasingly, as a source to tax to underpin public credit, was increasingly coming to the forefront of oeconomic policy. Within this nexus, the French were fingered as the main manufacturing threat but, also, inspiration as a model to nurture domestic industry via protectionism.

Nurturing industry: France and the 1674 scheme of trade

To survive in the increasingly competitive international textile market, required English cloth industries to become ever more flexible and innovative to meet existing and new changes in demand. This was achieved via a very successful state protectionist and regulating policy; here the country's manufacturers were sheltered more robustly than its rivals, which enabled the country to innovate, safe from superior imported equivalents. In addition, trade was carefully regulated via the Navigation Acts; enumerated colonial goods heading for Europe had to first enter via an English or Irish port before being re-exported, while enumerated commodities from Europe heading to a colony also had to initially enter through an English or Irish port. Lastly, some colonial goods were given a subsidy, such as naval stores and indigo, while certain other items like manufactured fur hats were prohibited. The general impact of these acts amounted to a common market between England and its colonies, with the huge advantage lying with the former. Although the acts protected the American merchants from Dutch and French competition, they forced them to compete with English merchants. The encumbrance of the acts on the colonial merchants was considerable and it is not surprising to find them prominent among those seeking American independence over a century later.[54]

Also commencing in the 1660s was a concerted targeting of Irish trade to England. In 1664 Parliament erected a duty of £2 per head on all Irish cattle and 10s. on sheep to protect English and Welsh stock (and therefore the rent and value of land). Three years later a total ban on all foreign cattle, sheep and pigs was enacted. The English owner of Irish land and propagator of political arithmetic, William Petty, claimed that before this legislation was passed something like three-quarters of all Irish foreign trade went to England, sinking to less than one-quarter after these laws were passed. In addition, after years of enjoying trade parity to the English colonies, Ireland was brutally shut from all participation in the 1671 Navigation Act.[55]

For the historian Margaret Priestley and, more recently, David Ormrod, the 1670s represents a major moment when Parliament's view towards the balance of trade changed. Prior to this decade, it was much more the case that fiscal and commercial interests tended to follow parallel paths. However, from this period the House of Commons became much more involved with the balance of trade and nurturing of domestic manufactures. In particular, it was the need to remedy the adverse trading relations with the French that came to the fore. To cure this negative balance a commercial treaty was strongly advocated by the City merchants between 1663 and 1672.[56] An example of this growing pressure came in June 1673 when the king experienced mounting pressure to only wear home-produced cloth. The lobbying worked and the king agreed not to wear foreign manufactures.[57]

The gathering force to forge a new commercial treaty with France gained further momentum in November 1674, when a petition by 'Merchants trading to France to the Lords Commissions appointed for the Treaty of Commerce with France' was published. The merchants wanted the Treaty of 1606, in which the English were denied 'free liberty' in France and its provinces, to be overturned. In other words, English merchants were currently not entitled to guaranteed 'safe-conduct' to live or trade in such areas. The petition also wanted 'the Customs and Impositions' on English woollen and silk textile manufactures to be reduced to their pre-1606 treaty levels, and for shipping restrictions to be deregulated. In general, the treaty was held up as being detrimental to English interests – in particular, the new draperies. The French dominance over England in manufactures was such, the merchants claimed, that 'without a Reduction, not only the manufacturers of *England* will decline, but the stock of the Nation will be consumed and exhausted by the Continuance of such a destructive and unequal Trade'.[58]

England's increasing vocal realization that it was industrially backward was being expressed at a hitherto unprecedented level. The royalist Carew Reynel, desperate to gain a public office, penned his *The True English Interest* in 1674. Drawing strongly upon Jean-Baptiste Colbert's policies, particularly via the work of Jacques Savary (a key figure in revising French trade laws between 1670 and 1673), Reynel underlined England's lack of productive self-sufficiency. He wrote, 'We make not our own silks we wear, our own house-hold furniture, I mean Tapestry, nor our own shirts to our backs, which these manufactures, if we had them full stockt, would make us infinitely rich and populous to Eternity.' As with others he stressed the need to encourage the domestic populace to consume home-produced goods and thus greatly increase the customs on foreign equivalents. Reynel was also emphatic that a negligible amount of duty, or even better, no levy should be placed on English goods exported.[59]

Reynel targeted the need to nurture, among other items, a linen industry and to greatly stimulate the fledgling silk manufacturers. The former, he emphasized, was potentially more profitable than woollen textiles. The knock-on effects of cultivating such an industry would be immense: 'The Linen Trade will save an infinite deal of money we send to *France* and *Holland*, and employ half a million people; keep in Tillage much Land, set many Husbandmen on work by the great quantity of Hemp and Flax, that will be sown for the carrying of it on.' The cultivation of the latter would save money currently going, again, to France and Italy, while the setting up of a linen industry would make possible the long-term establishment of a paper industry. Without linen rags, Carew rightly explained, it simply would not be possible to produce paper since such rags were the main raw material in its manufacture: 'No Nation uses more Paper than we, and yet make none ourselves.' While many lobbied for the expansion of an English linen and silk industry, others emphasized more loudly the need to protect the key woollen textile sector. One of the main issues was the rise in illicit exports of raw wool. Joseph Trevers, a one-time clothier and customs officer, spoke for many when he feared such trade would lead to the terminal decline of English woollen textiles.[60]

The eventual result of this clamour was the implementation of French-inspired industrial policies; drawing upon Colbert's protectionary policies, rather than the Dutch, England set upon an intensified nurturing of domestic manufactures. As the Dutch continued on their path as primarily a trade-based oeconomy, the English complimented their adoption of the policies of their old foe with those of their primary new industrial enemy. A number of copies of the French Arête of 1686 can be found in the papers belonging to the Commissioners of Trade and Plantations, while numerous contemporary pamphlets liberally quoted from it.[61]

An example of the success of Colbert's policies was the establishment and protection of the French Royal Glass Company. This was initially greatly aided by the wooing over of skilled Venetian glass artisans in 1665, and by the mid-eighteenth century was very likely the second-largest manufacturing concern in France. Its products were verified by a company seal to protect trade from illicit Venetian and, especially, domestic rivals. Within this fierce state-regulated context, the company made a number of important innovations. Most importantly, it replaced traditional blowing glass techniques with a process of casting or rolling plate glass.[62]

In addition to protectionary tariffs, new English policies included the introduction of bonded warehouses for the re-export of prohibited printed Indian textile imports; this was a system that was greatly expanded under Walpole and William Pitt the Younger. However, unlike the English Calico Act of 1701, the French had also earlier suppressed its domestic printing calico industry in 1686. This resulted in the emigration of numerous skilled French artisans and craftsmen travelling across the channel to England and elsewhere. In hindsight, France was also significantly hindered by their established and confusing fiscal infrastructure, and by an emphasis upon dominating the European continent rather than channelling their energy, at least initially, westward to the Americas and eastwards to Asia.[63]

The most important English commodity and primary source of contention was the export of woollen-based items to France. A number of significant City merchants drew up a commercial treaty during 1668–9, in which Article 7 argued that all woollen and silk tariffs in both England and France should be abolished. Sentiments were further stoked when Charles II controversially dragged England into war with the French against the Dutch in 1672. In 1673 London weavers attacked French weavers living in the capital, resulting in the destruction of their materials and houses. By 1674 reforming the tariffs with France was considered the only solution by the Lords of Trade and Plantations in tackling the balance of trade. Spearheading the debate was a City merchant and commissioner of the newly nationalized Board of Customs, Sir Patience Ward. The inequality of the textile tariffs between the two countries was alleged to be the reason France was flooding England with its silks and linens. The former paid only 5 per cent import duty as opposed to the 50 per cent demanded in France for English woollen textiles.[64]

Downing presented Parliament with a document entitled 'A Scheme of the Trade', which revealed a table of Anglo-French trade purporting to demonstrate that French exports to England exceeded England's to France by £965,128 per year. The table was signed by fourteen leading and extremely powerful merchants trading with France: Patience Ward, Thomas Papillon, James Houblon, William Bellamy, Michael Godfrey, George Torriano, John Houblon, John Houghe, John Mervin, Peter Paravicine, John Dubois, Benjamin Godfrey, Edmund Harrison and Benjamin Delaune. In Parliament, it was forcefully supported by Colonel John Birch who mocked the Commons by sarcastically remarking: 'You may make war with France, with the money he overbalances you in your trade, which you get back, like bees, by industry.'[65]

Birch was a one-time wine merchant, a successful soldier in the parliamentarian army and a member of the Long Parliament. In 1661 he was made an auditor of the Board of Excise for life with a salary of £500 per annum. During the second half of the 1670s he became very concerned about the threat of Catholic France and fought hard to try and prevent the Crown's unpopular decision to enter war with the Dutch. Although an exclusionist, he was careful in his support and moderate in his demands. He also remained very active in trying to increase the Crown's revenues via the excise. Nonetheless, he became marginalized during the reign of James II and, not surprisingly, became an enthusiastic supporter of William of Orange.[66]

The Scheme of the Trade was submitted to Parliament at a time of growing suspicion of popery among the English court, and at a time when there was a fear of French industrial and commercial expansion. The signatures to the scheme are extremely illuminating. Ward was an active politician, fierce Protestant Dissenter and important trader of English woollen cloth to France. He was elected alderman for the Farringdon Within ward in

1670 and sheriff of London and Middlesex from 1670 to 1671. He was a key member of urban dissenters attempting to block the 1670 Conventicle Act and leader, in general, of London dissenters and those concerned with the commercial and military threat from France. These views were reinforced by his close connections with French Huguenots. Like many of the other signatories he was at the forefront of the exclusion movement. He was elected Lord Mayor of London in September 1680 and shortly after became a fellow of the Royal Society. Ward was often in the company of the first Earl of Shaftesbury and the Duke of Monmouth. However, after the backlash to the exclusion movement he, like numerous other exclusionists, was forced to flee to the Netherlands after being sentenced to the pillory and fined £5,000. It should also be remembered that Ward was just one of a large number of English and Scottish exiles who utilized available resources to aid William's invasion in 1688. In fact, the English merchant community, in general, gave some £200,000 towards the cost of the Dutch offensive. Ward returned to England after the Glorious Revolution and resumed his trading and political commitments. In 1694 he bought £4,000 worth of the original stock of the Bank of England.[67]

Thomas Papillon was a forceful exponent of commercial, industrial and political reform. He was the son of a hard-nosed Huguenot refugee who became a prominent military engineer and leader of the French Protestant congregation in Threadneedle Street. His great-grandfather had been killed in the St Bartholomew's Day massacre of 1572, and Thomas, who had been brought to London as a boy, retained his family's deep dislike and distrust of Catholicism. He was apprenticed, along with his cousin Michael Godfrey, to Sir Thomas Chambrelan, a top London merchant and one-time governor of the East India Company, and went on to take the mastership of the Mercer's Company in 1673–4, 1682–3 and 1698–9; he also served on the East India Company Committee in 1663–71, 1675–6 and 1677–83. In politics, he became a constant thorn in the side of Charles II's court and, like Ward, was a staunch exclusionist. He was eventually also forced to flee to the Netherlands after being massively fined, before returning to England in the aftermath of the Glorious Revolution.[68]

Papillon expressed his views in a forthright oeconomic tract that claimed trade with France was simply adverse and unfair:

A Trade, that takes off little from us in Commodities, and furnisheth us with little or no Goods for our Foreign vent in other places, but with abundance of either unnecessary and superfluous things to feed our vain humours and fancies, or with such, though useful, as hinder the consumption of our own Manufactures, can never be profitable but destructive; and such a Trade is that to France, as it lies under those exorbitant Impositions on our Manufactures, of 50 to 60 *percent* amounting almost to a prohibition.

Thus, the trade of English draperies to France had sunk, he claimed, from £600,000 to £50,000, while the French continued to freely export wines, linens, paper, silks, ready-made garments, beds, toys and numerous trinkets. This, the tract concluded, was a 'ruinous and destructive' trade. Colbert's oeconomic policy, particularly tariffs upon

English cloth, was deemed to be having a damaging impact upon England's exports. Although this well-known treatise is identified with Papillon, it was actually written by the Scottish nonconformist and political plotter, Robert Ferguson, who also penned the Duke of Monmouth's *Declaration* in 1685.[69]

Another signatory was Sir John Houblon, a descendant of a predominantly Protestant French-speaking (Walloon) family from Lille. His father was born in England but retained very close links with the French Reformed Church in Threadneedle Street of which, like Papillon's father, he became an elder. Houblon became a prominent merchant trading with Portugal, Spain, Italy and the Mediterranean. During the Franco-Dutch conflict of 1674–8 he made a great deal of money in trade with Spain, with most of the silver being profitably sold to the East India Company. Like Papillon and Ward he was a fervent exclusionist and was elected as sheriff of the City of London just after the Glorious Revolution. He served on the directorate of the Levant Company between 1691 and 1695 and became the first governor of the new Bank of England in 1694 (of which he subscribed £10,000 to the original floatation). In 1698 he became a director of the New East India Company and in 1702 he was appointed a commissioner for navy victualing. Houblon lived in a mansion off Threadneedle Street and helped organize funds to set up a trust to assist French refugees in linen manufacturing at Ipswich. His brother, Sir James Houblon, also sat on the first directorate of the Bank of England and was a key advisor in funding the Nine Years War. In addition, he was also appointed as commissioner of accounts in April 1694 and was given the new and important task by Parliament of scrutinizing government expenditure. Like his brother, he was a forceful advocate of industrial protectionism.[70]

Michael Godfrey was the son of a wealthy London merchant, also called Michael, whose brother was Edmund Berry Godfrey (the magistrate murdered in mysterious circumstances in 1678, an incident that went on to further feed the fear of a Catholic conspiracy); he was both cousin and one-time fellow apprentice of Papillon. Not surprisingly, Michael Godfrey the elder was a fierce exclusionist and deeply immersed in City politics. Michael the younger, on the other hand, was involved in the wine trade and was a key figure in trying to set up a new East India Company. However, it is the younger Godfrey's central role in supporting and lobbying for the establishment of the Bank of England where he made his biggest impact. He was rewarded by becoming the first deputy governor to the bank in 1694 (the governor being, as we have just seen, Sir John Houblon).[71]

John Dubois was a son of a French Protestant refugee, Jean Dubois, physician of Canterbury, and his wife Catherine de L'Espine. He was brought up in the French Reformed Church community of Canterbury in Kent and later became active in the congregation at Threadneedle Street in London – where he became a deacon and an elder. In terms of commerce, he worked mainly in trade with France, while politically he became involved with the cause of civic nonconformists. Here he joined Papillon, Ward and various other well-known dissenting and French Reform Church merchants – all of whom energetically pedalled the views accompanying the Scheme of the Trade. Dubois was elected to the London common council for Cripplegate Within ward in 1674. In 1679 he was returned as an MP for Liverpool, and also became an important advocate of excluding the Duke of York from the throne. Like Papillon, Dubois was prevented from taking shrieval oaths after the 1682 election due to the anti-exclusionist backlash.[72]

The Scheme of the Trade became the central piece of reformist oeconomic opinion in the late seventeenth and eighteenth centuries. The statistics of this document were frequently cited in Parliament and at meetings of the Committee of Trade. The data was also incorporated in various treatises such as John Pollexfen's *Discourse of Trade, Coyn, and Paper Credit* in 1696. While the key advocates for a protective trade treaty with France in 1713 wheeled out the scheme's numbers to demonstrate an adverse balance of trade with France, the numbers were clearly misleading as the scheme, while published in 1674, took its numbers from 1668, which as the pro-French trade organ, *The Mercator*, pointed out later in 1713 was a 'low year' for English exports. It is true that the total market for different types of woollen-based cloths had declined; however, after 1668 they had started to once again increase. The type of cloth to suffer the most was kerseys from Yorkshire, but serges enjoyed a rapid expansion – especially between 1676 and 1685.[73]

The Scheme of the Trade, however, continued to carry a punch even by the end of the eighteenth century. William Pitt the Younger, in promoting the 1786 Anglo-French Trade Treaty, felt obliged to confront the statistics, and he is worth quoting at length:

It has been asserted that no beneficial Treaty of Commerce can ever be formed between this country and France; that there is no line of reciprocity that can ever be adopted by this country, so as to make it prudent to form any Treaty that would lead to a mutual interchange of commodities. In order to ground this doctrine, it has been asserted, that the trade with France has always been detrimental to this country. They allege, that in those periods in which the commerce has been open between this country and France, the balance has been uniformly unfavourable to us. The only periods from which this conclusion is drawn, are those of a few years in the reign of Charles the II [1674] and the accounts of that period, depending upon such facts as were collected at a Treaty of Utrecht [1713].

These accounts, of course, were the Scheme of the Trade, and Pitt dismissed them more successfully than earlier commentators as strategically deduced from the Custom House records that were 'kept very inaccurately'.[74] The scheme was obviously, as with all such arithmetic, politically motivated. They were geared towards depicting as negative a picture of trade with France as possible. In addition, the table completely excluded the lucrative role of re-exports from English colonies to France. Between 1674 and 1678, this particular sphere grew significantly partly due to England's neutrality during the war between the Dutch and the French, although they were nowhere near the size the pro-French trade treaty organ, *The Mercator*, later claimed.[75]

Pressure for the prohibition of French trade finally bore fruit in 1678 when an act was passed implementing such a policy. This was seen by older, and now relatively un-cited, historians as a major moment in commercial policy. Cunningham and William Ashley, for example, argued that this marked a key juncture in the distinct shaping of English commerce and industry. Despite James II briefly lifting the prohibition and introducing high tariffs, the total prohibiting policy was reintroduced after the Glorious Revolution. 'From the Revolution till the revolt of the colonies,' wrote Cunningham, 'the regulation of commerce was considered, not so much with reference to other elements of national power, or even in its bearing on revenue, but chiefly with a view to the promotion of industry.'[76] This claim, however, is only half-right, since it was actually the linking of revenue with home manufactured goods that came to the fore. Both the reigns of James II and William III recognized the need for a strong state, but while the former looked to revenues primarily via trade, the latter put the emphasis increasingly upon taxing domestic manufactures; the two approaches would join and pay dividends over the course of the next century.

In his latest book, Steve Pincus, like Cunningham earlier, has placed even more emphasis upon a major shift towards the importance of manufacturing, rather than trade and land, as the key to England's future. This departure really became established, he argues, after the Glorious Revolution and the demise of James II's emphasis upon landed property and trade as the key vectors of oeconomic policy. As such, Sir Josiah Child, Director of the East India Company, had been an important advisor to James, and had peddled a commercial approach that saw proficiency as based in land and snatching as much as possible of a finite international trade. By contrast, an emerging Whig view placed the emphasis upon labour and manufactures as the basis of wealth. In the case of the former view, property was ultimately the king's and thus he had the right to grant monopoly charters to companies like the East India Company and the Royal African Company. Consequently, the emphasis was upon land (colonies) and trade in which the enemy was the Dutch. However, where the focus was upon labour and manufacturing the target was the French. Whig merchants, Pincus claims, were furious with James's exclusive trading policies that quickly turned them against his regime. He concludes: 'Arguments about political economy played a pivotal role in generating the ideological energy that gave rise to the Revolution of 1688–9; interest in political economy was not an unintended consequence of those events.'[77] Although, as we shall see, the policy divide was not quite as black and white as this.

It was not, of course, just the French that were seen as the primary industrial rivals but other European and Asian countries. In January 1696, a House of Commons Committee was hurriedly appointed to examine the reasons for the recent 'Great Tumults of the Multitude' who had gathered about the House of Commons. The objective of the 'multitude', it was found, was to ensure a bill was passed to restrain the wearing of all imported wrought silks and Bengals from Asia and Persia. The unrest was triggered by apprehension among weavers that members of Parliament had received bribes to hinder the passing of the act. In particular, a prominent linen draper dealing in East India goods, Gabriel Glover, had given £1,000 to parliamentary members to prevent the passing of the act. He was overheard saying: 'That they would take care to give the weavers such a Fall, that they should never be able to rise again.'[78]

Whatever the basis of these allegations, a massive impetus to the establishment of industrial protection and nurturing domestic industries was coming as much from the phenomenal growth in imported Indian calicoes during the 1680s and 1690s as it was from French and European goods in general. A certain William James, probably a merchant in woollen textiles, complained in 1689:

> The great Obstruction to the Consumption of Wool hath been our wearing great quantities of silks and other Commodities from Foreign ports; especially from *France* and *India*; as silks called *Persians*; and *Callicoes* imported by the *East-India* Company: Besides the silks, the *calicoes* last mentioned, contribute more to the lessening the Consumption of Wool, than most people are aware of, and is little regarded.

He concluded that it was vital to erect a 'fence' around England's woollen and relatively new silk industries, 'that it may be as sacred as *Magna Carta* itself'.[79]

The 1690s, especially, was a period in which numerous Acts of Parliament and regulations affecting an array of trades were implemented or revised. The English woollen interest also joined the weavers in East Anglia and the silk weavers of London and Canterbury in condemning the threat of imported silks and calicoes by the East India Company. This time they had a battle on their hands; although the wool industry had strong interests in the House of Commons, the East India Company was equally powerful in the House of Lords. The result was a compromise with the introduction of a special duty of 20 per cent on imports of cheap Indian and Chinese textiles, followed in 1701 by an actual prohibition of all Asian cloth that was painted, dyed, printed or stained. The company could, however, still re-export such items and, crucially, plain calicoes could still be finished and sold in England. This, as we shall see in a later chapter, in turn stimulated the growth of English calico printing and, eventually, the cotton industry – the archetypical representation of the Industrial Revolution.

In terms of quality, the cottons from India were the best and most successful textile in the world and could not be beaten in terms of scale, quality and cost.[80] All of this was a product of labour intensity and experience characterized by superior skills built upon centuries of know-how and market penetration.[81] The question of whether or not Indian labour was less expensive than European, especially British, has become a hotly contested debate. Prasannan Parthasarathi claims that when factoring in the cheaper cost of food, Indian labour was just as well off as its British counterparts. However, Stephen Broadberry and Bishnupriya Gupta claim that much higher silver wages were paid in Britain compared to labour in India. Thus, they claim, British producers could not adopt the labour-intensive approach of the Indians and were thus forced to turn to labour-saving technology – a point also recently made by Allen and earlier by Ralph Davis. Parthasarathi has recently countered this argument, claiming the reason Britain turned to technology was primarily due to the fact that its labour could not match the skills necessary to meet the quality of Indian textiles. The key divergence was superior

Indian skilled labour and not cheaper wages. We shall return to innovation and cotton in a later chapter.[82]

As a substitute to European, especially French, textiles, the East India trade was initially seen as generally a good thing. However, possible negative implications were soon recognized and aired in various broadsides, debates and pamphlets. First, the balance of trade with India was adverse with far more goods being imported into England than exported to India. Second, such was the growing demand for Indian textiles that it was predicted that it would decimate the English woollen and young silk textile industries. Third, the unfavourable balance of trade meant that the imports had to be paid with silver that, along with gold, was the basis of national wealth. Lastly, the trade was a monopoly carried out by the East India Company via a royal charter.

The East India Company was established in 1599 and initially dominated by the Levant Company; the trade had grown from an Elizabethan thrust towards new import-based commerce with the East. The company and numerous other merchants were not seeking new markets for English-manufactured exports but, rather, new locations for lucrative imports. During the first twenty years of the East India Company's trade, some £840,376 of exports were made, of which only £292,286 were goods (predominantly foreign), and the rest was bullion. The company tried to fight the growing hostility to its trade by first wheeling out the early-seventeenth-century defensive thesis of Thomas Mun that was written about 1630 but not published until 1664. He argued that such trade did not drain the treasure of the country and that the balance of trade should be judged generally and not per country. Without the export of bullion, he argued, there could not be any trade with the East, and thus there could be no lucrative re-export trade of such items (something that returned bullion with interest) – a key point in the company's defence. There were also numerous other important aspects this trade produced, such as the promotion of shipping and the cultivation of sailors that were fundamental to the Royal Navy in times of war. Despite these claims, the argument against the trade was gaining an almost unstoppable momentum, and by the close of the century, defending the company became a much harder task.[83]

Pressure to ban East Indian cotton textile imports was joined by a number of other developments. For instance, raw wool was also haemorrhaging illicitly out of the country and feeding the French woollen textile industry. The French were also accused of hindering the English silk industry by the illegal export of their superior silk textiles into England.[84] Two years later in 1698, the Board of Trade and Plantations similarly warned of the levels of unwrought wool being illicitly exported to France, Holland, Sweden and other foreign countries. They were also concerned by the increase in woollen textile production in Ireland and the North American colonies. The board concluded that imported woollens textiles from Ireland and North America should be prohibited, while skilled English woollen workers should be banned from going to Ireland with those already there strongly encouraged to come back. The issue of the transnational flow of skilled labour was recognized as crucial to industrial development.[85]

Meanwhile, a House of Commons Committee set up to consider the several petitions from dyers, setters, callenders, tillet-pressers and packers from London, Norwich and

Coventry, reported their conclusions in May 1698. The petitioners dramatically alleged that much of the printing of perpetuanas (woollen serge fabric) and the rest of the new drapery had been transferred abroad, where foreigners obtained cheap dyes from England due to the generous drawback they received when re-exported. Thus, most of the English textiles were being exported unprinted, they claimed, to be finished in Holland or Hamburg. The result over the last twelve years had been, the petitioners complained, the demise by a factor of ten of the English dyeing industry. The situation was made even worse by the fact that the Dutch prohibited the importation of such English finished cloth. The committee, under the chair of the staunch Whig, Sir Rowland Gwyn, concluded that some way had to be found for taking the duties from the necessary dyes: 'Resolved, That it is the Opinion of this Committee, That a Drawback be allowed upon the Exportation of all sorts of our Woollen Manufacture, in proportion to the Duties laid upon the Materials and in the dyeing the same; or a Bounty be given upon the Exportation of all Woollen dyed Goods, fully manufactured.'[86] Ultimately, the decision would be made to import most vital raw materials duty-free, thereby greatly aiding domestic industry by eliminating drawbacks.

Pressure was also being exerted by the powerful west of England woollen manufacturers on the dangers to its industry from Irish woollen rivals. This, once again, pushed Parliament into action. The result was the suppression of a part of the Irish woollen industry in an act of 1699. The lobbying for the ban also came from East Anglia and London, and was motivated by the fact that they were experiencing a drain of skilled workers to Ireland. The Irish industry traditionally produced a basic, coarse woollen cloth called 'frieze', which went entirely into domestic consumption. However, certain Protestant rural areas were now successfully branching out into the area of 'new draperies'.[87]

It was the production of woollen cloth from this more recent and lucrative realm that was subsequently banned and not the traditional production of frieze. As a commentator wrote in 1698, the Irish exported 'great Quantities of new Draperies ... which although they endeavoured to shroud under the Name of Friezes, yet are known to be Bays, Perpetuanas and Serges'. It was predicted that they would soon perfect the production of lustrings (a silk fabric with a gloss) and alamodes (a silk textile made of a plain weave). Other commentators were also signalling the potential threat stemming from the North American colonies. For example, T. Tryon, a merchant, claimed in 1699 that the 'considerable settlements' in America were being frustrated with the supplies of clothing and utensils from England. Consequently, 'it hath put them upon breeding all Sorts of Cattles, and making their own Clothing, which is certainly very detrimental to us'. There was a frenzy of such fears and threats periodically published throughout the eighteenth century.[88]

The impetus to do something with Ireland's industrial and commercial base had been building for a number of years. An anonymous writer in 1691 was not out of place when he argued that Ireland should be cultivated as a plantation colony; a place to grow or produce products England needed and for it to become a market for English manufactures:

Ireland I take to stand in its Relation to *England* much in the *same* Nature with our Foreign Plantations, and might be made more beneficial than them all. ... The next thing *Ireland* may be considered in, is how it stands as a Foreign Plantation to *England* in part of its trade, and Consumption of our woollen, iron, and other Manufactories; and in that, by an Account I have seen, it exceeds all the *West-India* Plantations, as also in that of our Natural Product, Corn, Hops, Salt &c.

The author, who would subsequently become a legislator, also wanted a ban on the Irish production of the new draperies and for all raw Irish wool to be only sent to England. As an alternative, he suggested that Ireland should concentrate on another textile, namely, linen. William III wrote to the Earl of Galway in July 1698: 'The chief Thing that must be tried to be prevented, is, that the *Irish* Parliament takes no Notice of what has passed in this here, and that you make effectual Laws, for the Linen Manufacture, and discourage, as far as possible, the Woollen.' An anonymous commentator was also convinced that such a policy would bring 'the Multitude of *Irish*' into 'a more civilised Way of living, which would tame them faster than any Severities we can use'.[89]

It was hoped that the introduction of French Huguenots to cultivate and concentrate on building a linen industry would go a long way to appease (and assimilate) those Protestant Irish woollen workers affected by the new act of 1699. In general, linen was pencilled in as a low-cost alternative to expensive European linen, and shortly later as a clear import substitute for banned Asian printed calicoes and subsequently plain calicoes too. This has to be put within a context in which linen imports were very lucrative for the exporter and clear savings could be made by creating a new supply – especially from the Irish colony.

By the 1730s the policy was working with European imports of linen into Britain greatly diminished, while British linen also benefited in 1743 and 1745 with the introduction of bounties on exports. The latter allowed producers to successfully challenge European, predominantly German and Austrian, exports to colonial markets, although drawbacks on foreign linen imported and then re-exported remained. This was primarily to prevent North American colonial consumers encouraging domestic manufactures of their own, since the colonial market needed more linen than Ireland and Britain could supply. Nonetheless, the bounties gave a mighty boost to the growth of domestic British linen production. This was all made possible by a clever deal made with Austria, in which the bounty on linen would be paid for by an additional duty on imported foreign cambrics (originally a fine white plain-weave linen cloth made in and around Cambrai in Northern France). This type of textile mainly came from Austrian Netherlands and thus did not really interest high-ranking Austrian officials. The export of British linen grew from a value of £87,000 in 1740 to over £200,000 in 1750. Here is a very good example of import substitution policy aided not insignificantly by Parliament.[90]

It seems fairly obvious that the promotion of the British linen industry was part of a three-pronged plan. Imports of Indian calico cloth had challenged the European production of linen and silk (a good thing), however woollen textiles – despite the new draperies – were unable to act as a satisfactory domestic substitute for calico, silk and linen cloth; to make things worse, the Irish woollen industry seemed, or at least had the potential in its new drapery trade, to erode the competitiveness of the English equivalents (a bad thing). Within this context, it made good domestic sense in terms of employment to replace the Irish new drapery industry with a linen one. It was believed this could, possibly, eventually become a substitute for European linens and the clear demand for Indian calicoes. This position was certainly the implication of Papillon's (Ferguson's) work of 1680. Papillon, however, said that before this approach was established, it would certainly be

> much better for the Kingdom to expend 150 thousand pounds in Calico, than 4 or 500 thousand pounds in French, Dutch, and Flanders Linnen: And if the linen Manufacture were settled in *Ireland*, so as to supply this Kingdom, the Callico now consumed here, might be transported to other Markets abroad, and so bring a farther Addition of Stock to the Nation.[91]

After briefly lifting the ban upon French silks, linen, brandy and wine under James II, a complete prohibition was, once again, introduced on such French goods after the arrival of Dutch William and Mary to the throne. In one long sentence the act made its objectives crystal clear:

> Forasmuch as your Majestyes upon just and honourable grounds have been pleased to declare an actuall warr with France and to enter into severall Confederacies for carrying on the same and that it hath beene found by long experience that the Importing of French Wines Vinegar Brandy Linnen Silks Salt Paper and other commodities of the Growth Product or Manufacture of France or of the Territories or Dominions of the French King hath much exhausted the Treasure of this Nation lessened the value of the native Commodities and Manufactures thereof and greatly impoverished the English Artificers and handycrafts and caused great detriment to this kingdome in generall.[92]

Prohibitive duties also appeared on other French goods between 1693 and 1696 that were kept in force for nearly the whole of the eighteenth century. In addition, whenever possible privateers were encouraged to intercept and suppress French trade. All these measures were designed to protect domestic industrial interests by stimulating the substitution of French silks, spirits, linens, glass and white paper with English supplies. Nonetheless, French traders still found it possible to penetrate England through a vast illicit market, or simply shipping such goods under the cloak of another European country, most notably the Dutch. Ideally, to fight this huge alternative oeconomy required the production of goods of an equivalent quality, which was where excise stipulations, surveys and duties came in. In taxing infant industries – such as certain textiles, alcohol, and later, paper, candles, leather, glass and soap – it was also important that they worked to try and reach the quality of foreign equivalents.[93]

In this sense, the Excise, to begin with at least, helped nurture the quality of many goods. Additionally, as a memorial on contraband trade commented in 1719: 'The true remedy against these evils [smuggled manufactured goods], is to encourage the Manufactures already established, and establish those that are wanting in this kingdom of which now come from France at no considerable rates.' In sum, when it came to policy, the objectives were to first usurp the Dutch carrying trade followed by European and Asian industry. Central to the latter was the substitution of foreign imported goods with domestically produced ones that could be protected and, where possible, excised.[94]

In 1697, for example, an act was passed to encourage the domestic production of lustrings and alamodes to replace foreign imported equivalents. This act was explicit in its objectives: 'Whereas it hath been always found of greate Advantage to encourage the setting up and making of new Manufactures within this Realme whereby the Exportation of Money to procure forreigne commodities is prevented the Wealth of the Kingdome increased and the Poor are imployed.'[95] A year later the import duties upon foreign lustrings and alamodes were increased and additional legislation introduced to further encourage their domestic production.[96]

Developing domestic industries also required the necessary skills. For certain manufactures, this was solved by the huge influx of skilled Huguenot refugees during the 1680s and 1690s. Their role in papermaking, glassmaking, textile printing and silk is well known, but they also spearheaded linen production in Ireland and elsewhere in Britain. Many also came with impressive trading, banking and contracting credentials. Their capital and financial skills, in turn, helped support the costly Protestant war against Louis XIV. According to Ormrod, approximately 10 per cent of the national debt was underwritten by French Huguenot investors during the 1690s. Many of them combined their financial and mercantile activities, while a staggering twenty-five directors of the new Bank of England between 1719 and 1785 – along with a number of directors of the East India Company – came from this group.[97]

The 1690s, as well as instigating many of the features associated with P. G. M. Dickinson's 'Financial Revolution', was thus obviously also dominated by connected questions of tax, industry, employment, bullion, foreign immigration and trade. Not surprisingly, perhaps, it was during this important decade that criticism of export duties began to intensify. First to be abolished were the export duties upon woollen cloth in 1700, roughly at the same time that imported printed Indian cottons was banned, and this abolition represented a clear attempt to place policy on an export footing. However, it was not until Robert Walpole's extensive customs reform of 1722, which abolished export duties on most British goods, that this objective really took root. This, again, was roughly the same time that all pure cotton textiles were banned for domestic consumption. By this time, most export duties were eradicated and a series of bounties had been enacted to stimulate home industry. Protective duties on competing manufactured imports were simultaneously increased, while raw materials imported or produced at home were prioritized for the benefit of domestic industry. This all helped to strengthen the young and vulnerable British manufacturing base and expand the excise upon domestic production – crucial for public credit. Within this complicated nexus, the role of labour and the colonies became ever more important, and a way of integrating them properly within British interests gained a much greater urgency.

So far, we have traced the vital interrelationship between trade and industrial expansion to increase wealth and revenues needed to fight expensive wars. What was also becoming apparent to many merchants and commercial commentators by the end of the seventeenth century was the need for a more coordinated, visible and structured oeconomic policy. A growing popular suggestion was for the creation of a new Board of Trade consisting of experienced merchants to guide and monitor trade, nurture industry and define colonial policy. In the following chapter we shall see how this culminated in the establishment of the Board of Trade and Plantations in 1696 and the intensification of appropriating American silver, expanding the African slave trade, and the continual task of nurturing domestic industry and dealing with superior European and Asian manufactures.

CHAPTER 3
SILVER AND SLAVES: BRITAIN AND THE ATLANTIC WORLD

Revenue, trade and industry were just three interlinked areas that needed to be joined to aid England's ambitions for wealth and power. Earlier, most of the leading lights of Charles II's court were also involved in the country's expanding empire, which was considered yet another factor vital to the country's prosperity. This was a deeply held view by the successor to the throne, the Duke of York, who headed the Royal African Company's monopoly trade in slaves.

During the sixteenth century, it had been predominantly Spanish notions of empire that had informed much of England's imperial thinking but, by this stage, out of necessity, a much more home-grown approach had been forged. Indeed major differences between Spanish and English colonies had now become stark. No doubt if England's North American colonies had been rich in silver, a Spanish-type extractive empire would have been pursued leading to a wealthy elite. By contrast, however, there was very little silver or native labour there to exploit. This led, as John H. Elliott has argued, to a 'developmental' as opposed to 'exploitative rationale'.[1]

In this sense, the North American colonies were of less obvious value to England and there was, thus, less incentive to adopt a type of Spanish high-profile approach to empire. Likewise, with a lower and more diffused population the English Crown and Church had less reason to get involved, unlike the Spanish Catholic Church, whose missions attempted to convert and 'civilize' the peoples of South America. As a result, North America provided a popular destination for a transatlantic English and later British mix of ambitious merchants, religious dissenters seeking freedom of worship, a few risk-taking aristocrats, hopeful settlers and indentured servants wanting a better life.[2] This, perhaps, made colonies such as Massachusetts appear a 'reflection of the growing pluralism of English society'. However, as Elliott concludes, 'It was also a reflection of the relative lack of concern felt by the British Crown in these critical early stages of colonization over the character of the communities that its subjects were establishing on the farther shores of the Atlantic.'[3] One should also add that the colonies were also becoming in parts, to a certain extent, the dustbin of England's dispossessed, criminal and unwanted population.[4]

However, it would be wrong to conclude that there was a consensus of views towards the colonies. For example, by underlining the increasing emphasis upon the importance of labour to a nation's wealth during this period, Steve Pincus demonstrates that the role of the colonies and trade took on a new direction. The Spanish and

Portuguese empires and their predominant emphasis upon bullion were perceived as making these countries lazy and unproductive. This was a chance for the growing ambitious commercial classes of England to take more of the world's trade. For Tories the future wealth of England was via imperial expansion and the erosion of commercial competition from the Dutch. By contrast, Pincus concludes, Whigs underlined the need to nurture domestic industry through state support, and fighting the French to ensure European markets remained open to English goods.[5] The political party terms may have been more blurred than this implies but the historical divide over oeconomic matters was very apparent, although all would have understood the intrinsic value of plugging into the Iberian empire for bullion.

From the outset, England and, from 1707, Britain's colonial oeconomy in the Americas was an agricultural-based commercial form of imperialism. As such the appropriated land concentrated upon staple goods like sugar, tobacco, rice, grain, fish and manufacturing raw materials, including dyes, cotton and shipping supplies. Plantation imports to England grew by 100 per cent between 1663 and 1701. This, to repeat, was in contrast to Spain's silver-based and elite-driven extractive empire.[6] Moreover, the Americas had also become a vital market for English manufactures with, as Nuala Zahedieh has shown, manufactured exports to the colonies growing as fast as the re-export sector in colonial staple goods. In general, New World imports and exports to the colonies stimulated both commercial and industrial innovation in England; during the Restoration period colonial trade accounted for some 20 per cent of all overseas commerce. By 1700 English colonies had hugely risen in population to some 400,000 people compared to the country's domestic market of 5 million consumers. In comparison, the French colonies of only had a population 70,000 and the Dutch some 20,000. The hub of English colonial trade was London which, on the back of this colonial surge, had become Europe's largest city by the close of the century.[7]

Colonial Atlantic trade clearly had a crucial impact upon England's subsequent industrial trajectory, as it resulted in not only innovation to meet diverse colonial demands, but also in the stimulation of domestic consumption. Indeed, because of the distance to colonial markets an emphasis emerged upon product standardization, predictable quality due to the large batches of goods dispatched, and thus the need for manufactures to have a credible reputation. In this way, Zahedieh concludes, England started to concentrate upon 'an industrial revolution based on cheap export goods' rather than top-of-the-range craft-produced items.[8]

Early colonial policy and the establishment of the Board of Trade and Plantations in 1696

In 1672 about two-thirds of all the English Western plantations were governed by private companies or by proprietors. Only Barbados, the Leeward Islands, Jamaica and Virginia were under royal control. The new Lords of Trade, led by the first Earl of Shaftesbury (Anthony Ashley Cooper), quickly directed their attention on trying to remedy this situation. Their primary focus, to begin with, was the unruly and fiercely independent province of New England; the key area here was Boston and the surrounding Bay region. However, the first colony to be taken under royal rule was the far less powerful proprietary government of Bermuda in June 1684. From here the speed and commitment to removing proprietary governments intensified; in just over two months even the charter of Massachusetts would be revoked.[9]

The Lords of Trade were heavily dependent upon the newly nationalized Board of Customs (established in 1671) over policy matters. It was the task of the board to write the trade instructions for the colonial governors and, importantly, to monitor and review colonial laws. All of this meant consulting merchants, planters, colonial agents and numerous other interested bodies.[10] The key personality at the board was Sir George Downing, who was in frequent contact with the Lords of Trade. Other prominent board members included Sir Dudley North, Sir John Buckworth, Sir Patience Ward, Sir Robert Clayton and Sir Robert Southwell. In fact, Southwell was also appointed permanent secretary to the Lords of Trade by Charles II with the initial task, aided by four clerks, of trying to knock the new committee into some organized shape. The subsequent work of the permanent secretary was half-yearly rotated among the clerks. The post of assistant to the secretary went to William Blathwayt, who was the nephew of the wealthy London merchant and colonial administrator, Thomas Povey. Blathwayt would soon rise to become 'the chief man of all work' in colonial matters.[11]

By the reign of James II, Blathwayt's accumulated colonial knowledge and experience had massively risen in importance. Those colonies, without London agents, relied upon Blathwayt to lobby the king and Parliament over their concerns. Under James II, the committee of the Lords of Trade and Plantations became a standing committee.[12] Clearly, if a single figure had exerted and made the largest impact upon colonial policy it was, by the 1680s, Blathwayt, known as 'the Elephant' to his clerical staff, presumably because he never forgot anything. By the summer of 1687 he was, among other positions, Secretary to the Committee of Foreign Plantations and Secretary at War. His various state positions combined to make him, as one of his historians put it, 'the chief technician of an adolescent empire, an imperial "fixer"'.[13] Blathwayt's guiding principle was military defence and preservation of the colonies. In a commercial world still predominantly perceived as finite, a colony lost was a gift to England's enemies. This meant packing them with dependable and skilled military men.

Blathwayt's regime set out to 'royalize' each colony, and erode proprietary and charter colonies wherever possible; Blathwayt now, theoretically, had the power to call each colony to account. However, by this point it was probably too late to succeed with such a programme. The American colonies were now swamped with diverse political views and interests fed by the wave of sectarian Protestants that had entered North America after the collapse of the English Republic. In addition, there were far too few immigrants from the upper ranks of English society to recreate the social hierarchy and structure of the mother country.[14]

By now, the colonial viceroys had become reliant upon Blathwayt for advice, since neither the secretaries of state nor the Lords of Trade replied regularly to their correspondence, in contrast to Blathwayt who always did. This, claims Stephen Saunders Webb, made him 'the bureaucratic pivot on which imperial administration turned'. Blathwayt wanted a consolidated empire run by London, as he put it, to 'bring about the Necessary Union of all the Plantations in America which will make the King great and extend his royal Empire in those parts'. This meant a revocation of charters and the rights of government within the colonies, which became an aim that Blathwayt and those of his ilk would only have limited success in achieving.[15] He had loyally supported James II during the Glorious Revolution, and so was briefly replaced by Sir William Temple as Secretary of War on the accession of William and Mary in 1689. However, Temple quickly found the post too daunting and ended up, no doubt for other reasons, committing suicide. As a result, Blathwayt was quickly reappointed. His approach and objectives remained the same, namely, to restore royal government to America; although this time, he had much greater opposition to contend with. The governor of Maryland, Lionel Copley, who opposed the implementation of royal rule, accused Blathwayt of being a Jacobite.[16]

Despite such suspicions, Blathwayt continued to make headway and was appointed Secretary of State on the instigation of the Earl of Nottingham. He was now Secretary for War, for Plantations and the State, which put him in a position to construct a far more coordinated policy. He soon became a key advisor to the new Dutch king and, while William was away, frequently acted on his behalf. Blathwayt was at the peak of his power and in a very strong position to pursue his aim for English dominance of all North America and attempt to obtain all the richest West Indian Islands. To begin with, he wanted a much greater commercial connection with Spain's American empire, and to totally exclude the French from it. However, with the downfall of his primary patron, the Earl of Nottingham, Blathwayt increasingly found that he had to defend his royal absolutist view of empire from the opponents of arbitrary government and defenders of individual property rights.[17] Soon after Blathwayt's responsibilities were replaced by the creation of a Board of Trade and Plantations. Although Blathwayt was appointed to the new body, established in 1696, he was increasingly isolated from the other predominantly Whig members.[18]

A new dominant interest was emerging. The momentum and resources that informed this drew upon an array of views, which included those put forward by Charles Davenant and the broker, James Whiston. The former's 'Memoriall concerning a Council of Trade' along with the latter's plan was presented to the House of Commons. Their combined suggestions advocated a specialist group of those best suited to improve English trade, namely, men with extensive experience of trade. Whiston, who operated from a building close to the London Custom House, was no stranger to the Treasury or politicians and, since 1680, he had published the *Merchants Remembrancer*. This publication provided an up-to-date array of financial and commercial information such as insurance rates, exchange rates, stock prices and the prices of commodities, including bullion.[19]

If R. M. Lees is right to emphasize the views of Davenant and, especially, Whiston, as the architects of the new board, their inspiration was very likely that of John Bland and his tract, *Trade Revived*, published in 1659. Here Bland advocated the creation of a committee of some fifteen to seventeen merchants, who were 'the ablest, understandingest, and experiencedst men trading into foreign parts', and meeting at least every two weeks. Their task, he wrote, should be to outline policies to advise trade policy and deal with trading abuses. This idea was recycled by Carew Reynel in his *Trade Revived* in 1674 and pointed at in Sir Josiah Child's treatise on the *East India Trade* of 1681. Child pleaded for greater merchant counselling in government: 'I am of Opinion, the Dutch, *Nationally speaking*, are the wisest People now extant, for the contriving and carrying on their Trades for the publick advantage of their Country … for the Dutch have most Merchants in their Councils.' Child was certainly consulted over the establishment of the Board of Trade and Plantations in 1696. The West Indies merchant Sir Dolby Thomas and the Bristol merchant John Cary also strongly advocated the creation of a commercially experienced Board of Trade in the early 1690s. The latter suggested it should be modelled on the new Bank of England.[20] It was the work and writings of people like these, as Sophus A. Reinert underlines, that mattered in England's and, subsequently, Britain's trade and industrial rise and not those subsequently eulogized in a more recent anachronistic historiography. For example, Cary became an important advisor to the new board and important resource in defining Ireland's future oeconomic trajectory.[21]

The new Board of Trade and Plantations was introduced in 1696 with the remit of promoting English trade coupled with the task of inspecting and improving colonial plantations. In particular, producing a close study of the state of general trade such as the nature of imports and exports, the origin and destination of goods, those trades that 'are or may prove hurtful and what beneficial to this Kingdom; and by what means the Advantageous Trades may be improved, and those that are prejudicial discouraged'. Fundamental to this was the need to nurture domestic substitutes for adverse imports and promote any lucrative manufactures in general. As the Board of Trade and Plantation Commissioners reported in 1700: 'To consider by what means profitable Manufactures already settled may be further improved, and how other new and profitable Manufactures may be introduced.'[22]

Despite the pleas of men like Whiston, Davenant and Cary, and earlier Bland and Carew, the membership of the board was not completely endowed with men of commercial experience. For example, the former state colonial authority, Blathwayt, was appointed to the new board and it was headed by John Ederton, third Earl of Bridgewater. The earl had been a fervent supporter of the Glorious Revolution and the succession to the throne of William. The new king clearly held Ederton in high esteem and had already appointed him on the 7th of May 1689 to the Privy Council and to the position of Lord Justice during the king's frequent absences. Thus, he was an important figure in linking the Lords of Trade with the Privy Council and protecting royal prerogative from parliamentary attacks.[23] The early officials of the board were an unusually committed and active group with, arguably, the new body making its greatest impact during the first fifteen years of its existence. It was also during this period that much of the subsequent commercial and industrial policy implemented during the first half of the eighteenth century was defined.

Another member of the board was Sir Philip Meadows (sometimes Meadhouse) who was a late replacement for the initial appointment of Samuel Clarke of the Customs Commission. Meadows had been a leading diplomat under Oliver Cromwell's regime, where he had been active as an envoy to Portugal to ratify an important Anglo-Portuguese treaty in 1654. His success here led to him spearheading another diplomatic mission in 1657, with the intention of diluting Charles X of Sweden's ambitious policies in the Baltic and attempting to prevent war between Sweden and Denmark. Having successfully served Cromwell he was subsequently evicted from his Whitehall lodgings at the Restoration but otherwise left unpunished for his loyal service to the republic. He must have smelt a comeback just after the Glorious Revolution and published a rambling treatise entitled *Observations Concerning the Dominion and Sovereignty of the Seas*, first drafted in 1672, and aimed to underline his diplomatic knowledge of maritime affairs. He was right to be optimistic and subsequently became a commissioner of accounts in January 1692, and then appointed to the new Board of Trade. A few months later, he was also made an excise commissioner.[24]

The Earl of Bridgwater, Blathwayt and Meadows were joined by Abraham Hill, the son of a wealthy London cordwainer and alderman, who was someone who had also thrived under the Cromwellian regime. He spent a great deal of his time within philosophical circles meeting in and around London's coffee houses, living off his inheritance; he became an important member of the administrative side of the relatively new Royal Society of London. His republican leanings kept him away from state officialdom until the accession of William and Mary. Hill was a member of the new Board of Trade until 1702, during which time he spent most of his time being responsible for the colonies of New England, Newfoundland and New York.[25]

John Methuen was also an original member of the board and was the eldest son of Paul Methuen, one of England's leading and most wealthy clothiers from Wiltshire; his success was built on a successfully wooing skilled Dutch workers.[26] In May 1691 he was appointed minister to Portugal and over the next three years developed good relations with Pedro II. He returned to England in December 1694 to attend to matters at the House of Commons needing his input, leaving his son in Portugal to act as his deputy. Two years later, he was appointed to the new Board of Trade and, soon after, made speaker of the Irish House of Lords. His task here was to try and settle the deeply divided Irish administration, which was still squabbling over the spoils of war in the aftermath of the Jacobite defeat. Methuen had a tough time. Tempers were fraught when the English suppressed the Irish woollen industry in 1699, compounded by William's decision to keep a standing army in Ireland after his attempt to have one on English soil was blocked.[27]

Probably to his relief, Methuen was once again dispatched to Portugal in April 1702 as special envoy. His objective was to consolidate Portuguese neutrality as the implications of the War of the Spanish Succession became increasingly worrying. He helped persuade the Portuguese to break their alliance with the French, which culminated in a very significant commercial treaty signed in December 1703. In return for importing English cloth, the Portuguese were given preferential customs duties on exported wines (at the expense of the French). The deal served both countries ensuring a regular market for Portugal's important wine and port producers, and equally for English textile makers who gained access to Portugal's South American empire and silver; this would remain a key and symbolic treaty until 1786.[28]

Another member and first secretary to the board (1696–1707) was the merchant and commercial commentator John Pollexfen, brother of the radical Whig legal authority and promoter of William and Mary's Declaration of Rights, Henry Pollexfen. His early business seems to have been in the Iberian trade, particularly in Portuguese wines; and whose experience here no doubt also fed into Methuen's successful work. He was elected to the House of Commons in 1679 for Plymton Erle, which he held as a Whig in 1681, 1689 and 1690. He was an advisor on various trade committees, including one on the commerce of tobacco and another on the balance of trade with France. In addition, he was a commissioner for assessment between 1689 and 1690 and a Devonshire justice of the peace from 1689.[29]

Pollexfen, like Blathwayt, took a strict stance towards the American colonies and greatly disliked the proprietary governors. Earlier in 1677, he had been appointed to a special committee examining the East India Company and had defended the rights of 'interlopers', claiming monopolistic joint-stock companies had 'no souls'. He argued that the East India trade was a massive drain on English bullion and accused the company directors of jobbery. In 1689 he took the opportunity of pressing the fresh Williamite regime to create a new East India Company. He proposed the establishment of a regulated company for twenty-one years with each member contributing 20 per cent to the overheads. A few years later in 1698 Parliament eventually agreed to open up the Indian trade. Pollexfen also held strong views on the huge expansion of paper money and emphasized the importance of retaining metallic coin and having a fixed monetary standard. He joined Hill and Meadows in supporting John Locke's views concerning England's imminent recoinage and the importance of labour in the generation of wealth. The latter included the imperative of importing skilled foreign workers and the advantages of populating colonies.[30]

A one-time wine merchant based in Bordeaux, before fleeing back to England after the Edict of Nantes in 1685, William Popple was another original appointment to the board. His uncle was the Cromwellian Andrew Marvell, author of a key exclusion text, *Account of the Growth of Popery and Arbitrary Government* (1677), who used both William and his father, Edward Popple, as bankers. William married Mary Alund, daughter of Matthew Alund, a fervent republican and parliamentarian colonel, who served both Oliver and his son Richard Cromwell. Popple's circle of friends included the Quaker, William Penn, the natural philosopher, Robert Boyle, the first Earl of Shaftesbury and his fellow board member, Locke, who was very probably instrumental in getting him appointed. This may have been a strategic move on the part of Locke to prevent his rival, Blathwayt, getting his brother-in-law, John Povey, appointed.[31]

The staunch royalist, Blathwayt, now found his dominance in colonial matters challenged by that of Locke. The political philosopher and oeconomic commentator was yet another member of the board with deep connections to the republican and exclusion era. Under the patronage of the first Earl of Shaftesbury, he had formulated a distinct view towards the colonies between 1668 and 1675. During this period Locke had become closely involved in Shaftesbury's attempt to develop the colony of Carolina, and was also the second secretary to the then Council of Trade from 1673 until its disbandment in 1675.[32]

Locke was convinced that America was the solution to England's future prosperity. An important argument here was the need to go beyond Dutch commercial practices, and invest capital and people in the American colonies and cultivate the Americas to generate new wealth and resources. This could be achieved by promoting such lands as a depository for England's unwanted people and, ultimately, cultivating staple products via African slaves. Here they could help to nurture the land as a source of agricultural goods and as a supplier of raw materials that England currently purchased from its European competitors.[33]

To begin with, it was hoped English labour would be enough. The key to understanding Locke, and similar-minded folk, is the centrality of industrious labour rather than quantity and quality of land. For example, Locke claimed English plantations were twice as productive as the Swedish due to the superior ability of English labour. In particular, he claimed that land in America would be hundred times more valuable if it was cultivated by Devonshire farmers than any comparable ethnic labour. Moreover, the increase in colonial agricultural production would create manufacturing jobs in England due to the need for necessary tools and clothes to supply the colonists. Moreover, the need to transport such items and, in turn, colonial staples would generate further maritime employment, something already embodied in the 1660 Navigation Act. Like Mun earlier, Locke also emphasized the potential of the colonies to supply England with all its shipping needs such as timber, pitch, hemp and tar. Lastly, to ensure that property was recognized and defended in the colonies, Locke argued that land should only be increased in proportion to the availability of labour and only near towns where the law could be safeguarded. Locke's notion of natural rights was confined to hard-working white male English Protestants, with Devonshire farmers at the apex of an 'industrious and rational' being. Through such superior and intelligent people, others, such as indigenous Americans, could be transformed from a 'natural to civil man.'[34] There was nothing strange or original about Locke's views. During the eighteenth century, various experiments were devised to measure the amount of work that could be squeezed out of a human. The conclusions were frequently nationalistic and ethnic. For example, the French Huguenot refugee John (Jean) Desagulier claimed five Englishmen were the equivalent to a horse whereas in France and Holland it was seven men.[35]

Another early member of the board was George Stepney, a close friend of Blathwayt. Hitherto, Stepney had spent most of his career as a diplomat, becoming the most well-known foreign envoy during William and Mary's reign. In 1698 he was dispatched to Saxony, Prussia, and three years later to the Palatinate. Stepney's knowledge of German issues was invaluable and was regularly drawn upon by the board. From the Palatinate he was appointed envoy-extraordinary in 1701 and then envoy-extraordinary and plenipotentiary (a diplomat with full authority) in 1705, where he played an important part in the early period of the War of the Spanish Succession.[36] In his tract *Essay upon the Present Interest of England*, first published in 1701, Stepney fiercely argued that the power of France was too great and had to be reduced.[37]

The board, as we have already seen, was dominated by former republicans from the English Civil War and Interregnum era, and/or fervent exclusionists with religious dissenting sympathies. Ford Grey, Earl of Tankerville, had been at the forefront of trying to exclude the Duke of York from succeeding to the throne during the exclusion crisis. With the failure of this movement, he had plotted with the first Earl of Shaftesbury and the Duke of Monmouth to use force to ensure a Protestant succession. Although, ultimately, there is no proof that Locke was involved in the Rye House Plot, he was certainly very close to several of the key schemers. He was removed from Oxford University under a Royal Order in 1684 and was in exile in the Netherlands by the end of the year. Shaftesbury, likewise, had already had to flee England two years earlier (along with numerous other exclusionists) which put a temporary halt to the plan. However, the quest to replace the new Catholic king quickly resumed with Grey and Lord William Russell, culminating in the ill-planned Scottish insurrection led by Archibald Campbell, the ninth Earl of Argyll. Grey's house was searched and a hoard of nearly ninety muskets and armour was found, which Grey feebly claimed were weapons meant for his estates in Essex, Sussex and Northumberland. Grey also fled to the Netherlands and was indicted for high treason in July 1683. Russell was not so lucky and was beheaded at Lincoln's Inn Fields later that year.[38]

Propaganda against the fleeing conspirators was quick to rear its head in broadsides and short pamphlets.[39] It was in the Netherlands that Grey joined Monmouth and sailed with him on the disastrous attempt to invade England in June 1685. Grey was subsequently caught but spared after the intervention of Lord Lumley and Grey's willingness to provide a full confession. Perhaps even more important was the fact that Grey owed the Earl of Rochester £16,000, which was funded from Grey's estates that would cease upon his death. He was pardoned in November 1685 and had his title restored in June 1686. Not surprisingly, he declined to fight for James II when William invaded in November 1688. William asked Grey to join the Privy Council in May 1695 and created him Earl of Tankerville the following month. A year later, he was appointed to the Board of Trade, a position he held until 1699 when he was replaced by the second Earl of Stamford (originally proposed as a member back in 1696).[40]

Thomas Grey, the second Earl of Stamford, had also been a staunch exclusionist. He was accused of stirring popular unrest, along with Grey and Sir Thomas Armstrong, in the London shrieval election of 1682. The shrievalty had played a key part in the pro-parliamentary impetus to London politics in 1641–2. In 1680 the republican Slingsby Bethel had been elected sheriff of London with help from Algernon Sidney.[41] Both these prominent republicans shared a long history, especially while in exile in the Netherlands and drew a great deal of inspiration from the Dutch.[42]

The Corporation of London was a hotbed of radicalism, with numerous members having deep roots in the republican era and the not unconnected events of the recent exclusion crisis. Some of the leading Whig leaders in the corporation were directors of the new Bank of England and East India Company, and important voices in helping to inform colonial, fiscal, trade and industrial policy for example, the one-time Lord Mayor of London Sir Patience Ward and Sir Robert Clayton who, as we saw earlier, had sat on the Board of Customs, while other members included the Huguenot merchants, Papillon, and Godfrey. All these men, it will be recalled, were signatories of the 'Scheme of the Trade' (1674). Again, like the Board of Trade and Plantations, the Corporation of London was predominantly composed of religious dissenters. Indeed, of the twenty-five Whig radicals responsible for trying to remould the City around popular government during the 1690s, Gary Stuart De Krey found some twenty were nonconformists with many having former connections to the exclusion crisis. Not surprisingly, then, the Tories worried that the City Corporation was going to become a 'commonwealth' and, certainly, the new Dutch king, William, also feared such a possibility. De Krey writes, he (William) became 'suspicious that many Whigs were crypto-republicans' and thus viewed 'the City as a potential trouble spot'.[43] This, of course, was right, but they were also very important to his successful transition to the English Crown and subsequent work in bodies such as the new Bank of England (1694) and Board of Trade and Plantations (1696); the pursuit of wealth and power required risk, changing allegiances and compromise.

In the aftermath of the Rye House Plot, Stamford's house was also searched. He was eventually prosecuted and imprisoned in the Tower in July 1685, but then pardoned in April 1686. Undeterred, Stamford joined William's invasion in November 1688 with several hundred men. He was subsequently rewarded with the high stewardship of the honour of Leicester in April 1689. It is sometimes forgotten that over half of the Dutch invading force were composed of nationals from the British Isles.[44]

Like Pollexfen, Stepney and Blathwayt, Stamford was hostile to proprietary colonies, claiming that they were contrary to the interests of the Crown. He subsequently played a major role within the board in drawing up the ruthless Piracy Bill of 1700, with the provocative clause that any proprietary and charter colonies that failed to enforce the new law should lose their charters. He was dismissed from his office in 1702 by Queen Anne but, once again, reappointed as first lord of the Board of Trade in April 1707 and made a fellow of the Royal Society the following year.[45]

The last of the early members of the board was Robert Sutton, second Baron Lexington. Like many of the others on the body, he had diplomatic experience and was an ardent supporter of the new Dutch king. Very early on in June 1689, William sent him to Prussia to promote and improve the alliance with the Prussian elector and secure closer cooperation among the Northern Protestant allies. The following year he was made a commissioner of the Admiralty and, from March, he was a member of the Privy Council before finally being sent to Vienna as envoy-extraordinary in April 1694. He was appointed to the Board of Trade in June 1699, which he served upon until dismissed, along with Stanford, by Queen Anne in 1702. Released from official duties he spent the rest of his life sinking various coalmines in his Nottinghamshire estate.[46]

The board synthesized their views within two early reports written for the House of Commons. These policy announcements clearly drew upon the whole gamut of diplomatic, political and hard-nosed commercial experience of the board. The first document appeared in December 1697, and the meeting was chaired by the first lord of the board, the Earl of Bridgewater. The other signatories comprised the Earl of Tankerville, Meadows, Blathwayt, Pollexfen, Hill and Stepney. An early objective of the trade team was a consideration of 'what means the severall usefull and profitable Manufactures already settled [in England] may be further improved, and how, and in what manner new and profitable manufactures may be introduced'.[47]

South American silver and African sweat: The work of the Board of Trade and Plantations

The Board of Trade and Plantations underlined that the nurturing and promotion of domestic manufactures was inseparable from commercial policy in general. It was the balance of trade that moulded such a policy and the tool used to carve this was numerical information; the emphasis upon quantification allowed calculation, which led to direct decision-making and, perhaps, diluted conflicting views among its members. In this sense, the board was formed to practically utilize such knowledge, with the almost simultaneous introduction of an Inspector General of Exports and Imports specifically created to help collect the necessary trade data.

David Landes's suggestion that 'the effort to find a surrogate for the replicated experiment by the use of explicit international comparisons' is apposite if it is inverted: namely, that principles associated with natural philosophy actually drew on commercial and state administrative developments. The 'careful accumulation of data' and 'the use of inductive reasoning' was unfolding within merchant practices – most notably in mercantile and slave plantation labour bookkeeping – and certain state bodies – most notably in the Excise and the Treasury departments.[48] In this way the state, commercial practices and plantation business, as much as any other interest, can be seen as spearheading practical empirical observation and placing faith in a quantifying spirit.[49]

The board began their first report with a wide survey of trade. The first region they turned to was Sweden and the South Baltic, which had significantly increased its exports since 1670 (the date the board commenced their calculations). This was a crucial region for English supplies as the bulk of shipping materials came from here, namely, iron, hemp, rope, pitch, tar, copper, masts, furs and certain other goods. The board was concerned by the recent activities of the Swedish king, who had placed a duty of 50 per cent upon English woollen textile imports in order to nurture and protect Sweden's infant woollen industry. What was even more worrying was the fact they were also using raw wool smuggled from England via Scotland. Nor was it just English woollen textiles being blocked, but a number of other items leading to a negative balance of trade. The board concluded, 'We are over balanced about Two hundred thousand pounds per annum in Goods and Freight.' The reliance, particularly upon Baltic iron, would dominate concerns throughout the eighteenth century.[50] Elsewhere, imports of timber from Denmark and Norway had also greatly increased, especially since the rebuilding of London after the Great Fire of 1666, leading, once again, to an overbalance of trade.[51]

Not surprisingly, the country that occupied the board's attention the most was France. The trade team anxiously emphasized the repercussions of the prevailing balance of trade with France:

> The importations from France have gradually increased from anno 1670 to the beginning of the late War, in wines, Brandies, silks, Linnen, and many sorts of other Goods, For tho there was a prohibition of French Wine during some of those years, yet it was brought in under other Names: and in the same years Our Exportations thither have decreased.

The first computation the board found concerning the balance of trade with France was taken from the document we earlier examined, constructed by London City merchants in 1674, entitled 'A Scheme of the Trade'. The board reproduced the report's findings concluding that trade from France that year was £1,136,150. By contrast, they claimed, English exports to France for the same year amounted to just over £171,021.[52]

The board were particularly concerned by the degree of French protectionism. In 1654, 1660, 1664 and 1667, the French king had increased the import duties upon English woollen textiles as well as on lead, tin, coal, tobacco, sugar, fish and various other goods. In addition, a hefty tax was placed on English ships with the stipulation they could only land goods at Calais and Dieppe. This further eroded the export of woollen textiles and other items. Then, after their ban of re-exported Indian cotton textile imports in 1686, large duties on all East India goods were implemented with, once again, the order that such goods could only be deposited at certain ports. The board underlined that the rationale behind this was to encourage the consumption of French 'Cloths, Stuffs, Silks and other Goods made by his [the French king's] own people, all which amounted to a Prohibition in many cases, of receiving Goods from England'. They concluded, 'we have been overbalanced in that Trade, in most of the said years' by about £1 million per annum.[53]

A sense of what the board was planning had already been proposed by the radical Whig and staunch Protestant Dissenter, John Cary. This Bristol-based merchant was the son of Shershaw Cary, a successful trader in the Iberian Peninsula and the West Indies and a sugar refiner; he was also the master of Bristol's Society of Merchant Venturers in 1671. John Cary trained as an apprentice to a linen draper and followed this living until 1679, before concentrating solely upon trading where he became a Warden of the Merchant Venturers in 1683. In a career that rapidly took off, he was soon appointed to the Common Council of Bristol in 1688 and became their representative in London. Cary's published occonomic views were clearly well thought of and reached a wide audience. For example, his *Essay on the State of England* (1695) was reprinted in various editions throughout the first two-thirds of the eighteenth century, including translations into French in 1755 and from French into Italian in 1764.[54] For Cary international dominance was based upon 'hegemony rather than harmony', guns and protectionism rather than free trade and peace; the foundation of civil society was commerce and the growth of civilization a product of an ever 'intensifying division of labor'.[55]

Cary speculated that 'if Linnen Manufacturers can be settled in *Scotland* and *Ireland*, Distilling, Paper, and Silk Manufactures, encouraged here [England], the Balance will soon be altered, especially if the *Portuguese* make Improvements in their wines, for which they now receive great Encouragement, the People of *England* being not so fond of the *French* as they were'. This emphasis upon an alternative supply of linen, silk, paper and wine was widely recognized as crucial. France was draining England's wealth with its promiscuous exports of both luxuries and certain necessaries. By contrast, 'they prohibit our Manufactures, in order to set up the like amongst themselves, which we encourage by supplying them with Materials; and not only so, but they lay Tax on our Ships for fetching away their Product, which must else perish on their Hands'. Because most French imports were luxuries, Cary, like the members of the board, condemned them as unnecessary and simply based upon whim or fashion and, therefore, a dangerous waste of domestic wealth.[56] If people were going to intoxicate themselves with such luxuries, it was far better that they were domestically produced and, ideally, excised.

Equally alarming were the goods now being imported from Asia. A particular source of contention for the board was the East India Company trade. According to the board's calculations, the country had imported something like £1,000,000 per annum of Asian goods between 1670 and 1688. Of this figure, they claimed, approximately half was re-exported but only about £70,000 of English-manufactured goods were exported to Asia; most of the wealth used to purchase Asian goods was exported bullion. A far more rabid and public attack upon the company came from Pollexfen in two consecutive tracts. By contrast, the balance of trade was all positive with Spain, Portugal, Italy, Turkey, Barbary and Guinea.[57]

By the close of the seventeenth century, the trading and industrial bases of England, the Iberian Peninsula, Iberia America and Asia had become interlinked. The rise of the English new draperies found a fertile market in Portugal and Spain (as well as the Mediterranean) that provided an impetus to the English carrying on trade to those regions. Stanley J. Stein and Barbara H. Stein write: 'Textiles, first woollen, later cotton, whether carried to Africa to exchange for slaves, to Cadiz for silver to exchange at Calcutta for calico, or contraband or Caribbean shores for dyewood and silver, were to be England's key to economic development and its challenge to the European continent.'[58] Likewise, it was England's increasing dominance of the global cotton trade that ultimately, Sven Beckert argues, was a crucial precondition for the Industrial Revolution.[59]

If silver was the main source of wealth extracted from Spanish and Portuguese colonies in South America, what was the equivalent for the English colonies further north? A major focus of the new board, as its full title specified, was the various colonial plantations. The trade team cogently explained the precise role the North American mainland and Caribbean colonies played in the English oeconomy: 'From your Majesty's Plantations in America, great quantity's of Sugar, Tobacco, and other goods are annually imported, exceeding much in value the goods exported thither. But the better half of such goods being sent from hence to Markets abroad, after having paid considerable Duties here'. The board acknowledged a North–South divide in the productivity of the North American colonies but pointed out that, although the northern areas lacked a staple product, they were important purchasers of English woollen textiles, handicraft goods, farming implements and other items. In addition, 'to maintain and increase our Navigation … we humbly conceive the Trade to and from those Colonies deserve the greatest incouragement, and will be very advantageous, as long as the Acts of Navigation and Trade be duely observed'. Importantly, the board wanted an added injection into the slave trade – the planting and harvesting of goods like tobacco, sugar, cotton, rice, indigo and ginger was 'best carried on by the Labour of Negroes'. It was therefore vital to supply the colonies with as many African slaves as achievable and as cheap as possible.[60]

These latter sentiments were also expressed in a very similar manner by Cary who, also, strongly emphasized the lucrative nature of the African slave trade. It was, he claimed, 'a Trade of the most Advantage to this kingdom of any we drive, and as it were all Profit, the first cost being little more than small Matters of our own Manufactures, for which we have in Return, *Gold, Teeth, Wax*, and *Negroes*, the last whereof is much better than the first'. It was only through slaves, he continued, that 'great Quantities of *Sugar, Tobacco, Cotton, Ginger*, and *Indigo*, are raised'. This trade, he claimed, was 'our Silver Mines, for by the Overplus of *Negroes* above what will serve our Plantations we draw great Quantities thereof from the Spaniard'. The African continent and English-American colonies were England's equivalent to Spanish mines and, to continue with the metaphor, the Caribbean colony of Jamaica was initially a major warehouse. This West Indian colony was 'a Magazine of Trade to *New-Spain* and the *Tera Firma*, from where we have yearly vast Quantities of Bullion imported to this kingdom both for the Negroes and manufactures we send them'. Cary concluded by condemning the monopoly of the African Company as stifling England's potential enlargement of the slave trade.[61]

Similarly, the board emphasized what everyone knew, namely, that the slave trade with Spain was a key avenue to gain vital silver and dispose of English goods. England started quite late, in comparison to other European countries, in its scramble for a slice of this lucrative trade. From the time the Portuguese and Spanish had shared the same monarch in 1580, the former had enjoyed a monopoly of the slave trade with the latter – supplying as many as 300,000 Africans to Spanish America by 1640.[62]

However, from the mid-seventeenth century other European countries started to increase their participation. After a period of launching attacks on Spanish convoys and sponsoring piracy in the Atlantic, the English, along with the Dutch and the French, turned to planting colonies in the region. These provided a foothold in a region hitherto dominated by the Spanish. It was during the Interregnum that England invaded Jamaica and started a lucrative trade that quickly flourished, particularly after the Treaty of Peace with Spain in May 1667. From Jamaica a number of provisions, manufactured goods and slaves were sold to the Spaniards. In short, the island soon became the entrepôt for English goods (be them material or flesh) in the Caribbean. In exchange, an important supply of silver and gold was given that both enriched England and its colonies with a hard currency. Spain had no slave-trading status and imported Africans via contractors known as 'assientists', and Jamaica soon became one of the contractor's main sources of slaves. Not surprisingly, then, the assientists wanted protection in and around the island from the increasingly hostile opposition of the local English colonial planters, and attacks from the privateers and pirates also operating from the island.[63]

Elsewhere Portuguese Brazil, especially, was demonstrating the great wealth to be made from extensive sugar plantations worked by slaves. Likewise, the English planters in Jamaica emphasized through the Island Assembly in 1688, 'the only means to Enrich and Support this Island' was via the 'plentifull supply' of 'Negroes'. Armed with this argument, the assembly condemned the well-endowed assientists, claiming they both inflated the price of slaves and picked all the fittest bodies, while draining much of the island's crucial provisions.[64]

In the battle against the assientists, the planters subsequently joined the pirates and privateers. These latter 'outlaws' and semi-legal operators depended upon the plundering of both Spanish coastal towns and vessels to line their purses.[65] By contrast, in order to maintain the valuable slave trade with the assientists (and thus the Spanish), it was vital for the English government to suppress such attacks. It was also the case that the country that supplied the Spanish Indies with slaves typically gained a massive advantage selling European and global produce here. Moreover, through this channel much silver was obtained that was fundamental in funding the East Indian trade. This was certainly the policy of the East India Company between 1657 and 1666, before the Duke of York and Company of Royal Adventurers imposed their presence and took over the slave trade. Such was the importance of this commerce that the English government turned a blind eye to violations of the Navigation Acts when it came to Jamaican trade with Spain. Stein and Stein have argued: 'American silver galvanised Europe and set in motion the development of the market economy and nation-state.' In short, the Spanish extractive bullion-based empire became far more important to Western Europe than Spain itself. This expansion of trade also led, as Phyllis M. Martin has shown, to the demise of African cloth production as European and Indian textiles increasingly penetrated Africa.[66]

Silver from the Americas became vital in enabling the growth of trade to Asia. Between 1600 and 1800, a significant amount of the world's silver ended in China and India where it was partly used as currency. For Europeans the silver thus acted as a commodity to exchange for Asian silks, ceramics, cotton textiles and spices.[67] Spanish American bullion entered Europe and its re-export significantly stimulated trade. It provided a credible source of exchange, promoted exports to Spain and the vast Spanish American empire, and enabled the purchase of manufactures from Asia – all of which fuelled the growth of production and consumerism in Europe. In addition, this Atlantic slave-based commerce fed the growth of British shipping, including their building and services such as insurance.[68]

The promotion of trade with Spain was thus an extremely high priority for England and the members of the Board of Trade. The Jamaican planters and their various actions to prevent the exportation of slaves, along with the activities of pirates and privateers off the Spanish coast, were eventually defeated. There was also a concerted attempt in 1694 to gain the assiento itself; however, the contract was awarded to a Portuguese company. The large, experienced Iberian trading element within the Board of Trade, no doubt, was utilized to ease this transfer and keep the slave trade thriving with the new contract holders. The board, in addition to strongly recommending the further encouragement of this trade, also lobbied hard for the monopoly of the Royal African Company to be terminated and the business to be legally opened up to private traders. 'This step', wrote Curtis Nettels, 'was taken because the opportunities of the Spanish trade and the growing labour needs of the English colonies required the resources of the interlopers and the African Company combined'. By the end of the seventeenth century, the trade between the English West Indies and Spanish America was worth about £1,500,000 of bullion per annum into Jamaica and Barbados.[69]

However, the situation was more complicated than this. The historian William A. Pettigrew has shown that the extensive debate between supporters of the Royal African Company and the independent traders took on overt political dimensions. The demise of the former and the victory of the latter was by no means a straightforward event. Pettigrew shows that the development was defined by three main stages. First, the company lost a great deal of power when its governor, James II, took flight. Secondly, the independent traders took advantage of the post-1688 context to successfully lobby Parliament and lastly, they harnessed the power of bodies like the Board of Trade and the anti-company campaigning of the colonials to successfully petition Parliament. This resulted in the slave trade being opened up to private traders in 1698, initially only for thirteen years. However, when the act expired, the independent traders continued to convince politicians that the trade was best pursued by them. Thus, the private traders benefited not only from the opportunities presented by the Spanish trade and growing labour needs of the English colonies, but also from the new political and institutional changes forged in the post-Glorious Revolution period. During those thirteen years, there was a great expansion of slave-based goods, with the state's coffers greatly benefiting from the growing tax on goods like tobacco and sugar.[70]

However, the English situation in the West Indies had also gained an added menace. Just as England was enjoying a strong position in trade with the Spanish, the French revealed their commercial ambition in the area. They first targeted England's jewel, Jamaica, and seized English vessels trading to the Spanish coast. Blathwayt nervously told the former exclusionist and, from 1692, Secretary of State Sir John Trenchard: 'The situation of the Island is such that, if it be lost to the French, all that profitable trade we now enjoy (though underhand) with the Spanish colonies, as well as the negro traffic, will be cut off.' By the close of the century, France had greatly expanded its commercial interests to a point where it was challenging for hegemony over Spain and its American empire.[71] The Spanish market had become a key lucrative source for French goods.

Between 1668 and 1672, France, under Jean-Baptiste Colbert's guidance, also made a concerted attempt to challenge the Dutch, English and Portuguese Asian trade. This was a venture that ultimately failed, primarily due to the French inability to reconcile the country's emphasis upon its traditional dynastic ambition in Europe and commercial overseas objectives. Colbert had managed to gain a substantial amount of money (15 million livres) to establish a company with a monopoly of trade to Asia for fifty years. The first fleet left for Madagascar in March 1665, followed by another fourteen ships and 1,700 men to the Isle Dauphine. In contrast to the Dutch and English, Colbert's company, argues Glenn Joseph Ames, did not obtain the 'solid support' from the growing commercial class. Instead, it relied primarily upon 'the controller-general's power and his ability to arrange investment and support from a Crown and aristocracy that, despite his best efforts, continued to view the campaign as merely an extension of dynastic struggles in Europe'.[72]

Ultimately, the French military expedition was undermined by the advance knowledge obtained by the Dutch of its impending launch and overt mission to erode Dutch interests. Not surprisingly, the Dutch reinforced their already impressive naval presence in the region. Moreover, European dynastic issues were beginning to once again dominate and preoccupy Louis's concerns, which left the French Asian fleet in a much more vulnerable position. The French king, ultimately, neglected Colbert's initiative as he focused wholly on campaigning in Flanders and on a reversion back to traditional foreign policy.[73] The French Asian experiment, however, had alerted many English that France, rather than the Dutch, were now emerging as England's true commercial rivals. Pollexfen wrote a few years later in 1697: 'We formerly looked on the *Dutch* as our only Rivals; now the *French* by their indefatigable industry to promote Trade, and by additions made to their strength at sea appear more dangerous.'[74]

France was far more successful in the Atlantic than Asia. From the commencement of their expansion west, a strategic commercial objective first by the Dutch, then the English and later by the French was to take a slice of the huge, fertile and rich Americas held by Spain and Portugal. The slave trade provided both a lucrative commerce and an umbrella for an illicit one. The Portuguese, followed by the Dutch, English and French, found that the slave trade provided the best means to evade Spanish colonial prohibitions and swamp the markets of South America. This required a foothold in the Americas resulting in the Dutch, for example, gaining Curacao, the English taking Jamaica and the French establishing colonies in the Antilles, all aiming to obtain as much of the African supply of slaves.[75]

France may have become the largest exporter to Spain but it was not until 1697 that it penetrated the Spanish American empire. This was achieved with the acceptance by Spain of French rule of Eastern Hispaniola (or Saint Dominique). No doubt, this event helped to speed up the release of the Board of Trade's report in the same year, with matters further heating up after French privateers seized English vessels carrying slaves from Jamaica to Spain. England's response to the French activity was to station two regiments in Jamaica and order the English naval commanders in the West Indies to provide full protection for all English vessels travelling to Spanish ports. France, however, gained a real prize when they obtained the contract for the assiento in 1701, with the French Guinea Company appointed to provide Spain with 4,800 slaves per year. This development clearly weighed heavily in England's decision to enter the War of the Spanish Succession in 1702, and within ten days of the assiento deal being signed, a joint military force between the English and Dutch against the French was being discussed. The English Secretary of State Sir Charles Hedges later commented in January 1706 that it was 'the chief aim of the French in possessing themselves of Spain, to make themselves masters of the West India trade'. The crowning of a Bourbon on the Spanish throne in

1700 had led the French to hope for a reform of Spain and that its empire would suppress trade with its competitors. However, by the close of the war, the French (and the Dutch) were crowded out of the Spanish colonial trade, and England (now Great Britain) via its colonies and naval might, had gained the pre-eminent access to the money trade of the New World and increasingly a monopoly of the lucrative clandestine trade of the region.[76] This was a momentous moment in Britain's commercial and industrial fortunes.

Portugal's geographic position next to Spain gave it great strategic importance and it was no wonder that the English Board of Trade and Plantations contained so many members with Portuguese commercial and diplomatic experience. The country was clearly a major component in England's pursuit of power and plenty. The country was not just a gateway to wealth but, equally, valuable skills and practices. Over a century earlier, Portugal, like Spain, had been at the vanguard of navigation and colonization of South America. These navigational skills were greatly informed by Iberian Jewish astronomers and mathematicians who, in turn, were drawing upon the work of Muslim philosophers. As well as dominating the Indian Ocean and the trade in spices, silk and porcelains in exchange for South American silver, Portugal was also the first to introduce slaves from West Africa to farm its sugar estates. Here it plugged into the west coast of Africa and purchased slaves from the existing African Saharan slave trade.[77] Within this trading nexus a form of plantation organization was developed that would subsequently be used by English and British plantations. Techniques developed here also went on to inform aspects of industrial development in Britain.[78]

Despite the Spanish occupation of Portugal between 1580 and 1640, any chance of a monopoly of Brazil's sugar was eventually broken by English and Dutch sugar planters in the Caribbean. As a result of the 1703 Anglo-Portuguese Trade Treaty, Portugal and its colonial American empire were commercially linked and now dependent upon England.[79] Portugal, primarily out of a credible fear of a Franco-Spanish invasion, had allied itself to England during the War of the Spanish Succession. Under the treaty, the Portuguese lowered duties on English woollen textile imports in exchange for England importing Portuguese wine instead of French or Spanish. Even prior to the treaty in 1700, approximately 11 per cent of all English exports went to Portugal and Brazil. The treaty confirmed Spanish fears over England's ambition for an even greater slice of the Iberian American empire.[80]

This was fully realized in the 1713 Treaty of Utrecht that was a crucial moment in Britain's commercial trajectory. Spain lost all its European dependencies along with the gateway to the Mediterranean, Gibraltar, but was allowed to keep its American empire in exchange for trading privileges to Britain. France retained access to Spain's American colonies through an unspoken toleration of its merchants in the country for their assistance in administrative and structural reforms. The assientists subsequently passed into English hands under a thirty-year contract with the South Sea Company, along with permission to send a vessel of 600 tons carrying merchandise to the Spanish Indies every year. This became known as the 'vessel of license' or 'permission ship' and became an extremely profitable warehouse for London merchants to flood the great fairs at Cartagena and Porto Velo, from where the goods would then often go on to

Peru, Chile and the South Sea via Panama. Invariably, the vessel was much bigger than the designated 600 tons and was almost constantly being restocked in the colonies of Jamaica and Barbados. In 1716 the official tonnage was increased to 650 tons and the assientists were now permitted to dispatch the vessel before the fairs commenced.[81]

Opportunities for fraud were rampant and greedily exploited by British merchants. The South Sea Company spent more time developing the huge profits to be made through contraband trade with Spanish South America as it did in the slave trade.[82] Nonetheless, the increasing demand for slave-based goods increased the demand for coerced Africans to work European colonies, which also lowered the cost for such slaves. Britain quickly became one of the largest markets for tobacco, sugar, cotton, dyestuffs and spices for both domestic consumption and, crucially, re-exports. This, in turn, fuelled the establishment of its plantation colonies in the Americas as it sought to replace foreign suppliers; Virginia became important for tobacco and Barbados followed by Jamaica for sugar.[83]

Scarce resources in the British Caribbean required innovative thinking from planters. To establish a successful plantation required new intensive processes of labour organization and nurturing of agricultural resources. A combination of slaves, water and wind power working twenty hours a day was required to keep the sugar mills going. A great deal of this drew upon Portuguese and Dutch experience but, speculates Robin Blackburn, also probably upon labour discipline within the Royal Navy. Sidney W. Mintz describes plantations as 'a synthesis of field and factory' and 'unlike anything known in mainland Europe at the time'.[84] A great deal of innovation took place within this illiberal space. By the 1700s, English exports to the American colonies was also becoming important with something like one-fifth being shipped here.[85] This figure greatly increased over the course of the eighteenth century and has been, rightly, seen as an important factor in Britain's industrialization.[86]

The role of capital derived from the slave trade and its importance to Britain's Industrial Revolution has, however, been questioned by a number of historians. Like so much of the economic debate concerning the eighteenth century, the data is frequently questionable and easily manipulated to support a particular argument. It is also the case, as Javier Cuenca Esteban astutely points out: 'It is too frequently stated that those who insist on linking British economic growth with colonialism and slavery are motivated by ethics or ideology; it would be equally conjectural to ascribe similar motives to the initial and continuing opposition to Eric Williams's thesis.' David Eltis and Stanley L. Engerman conclude that although 'it [slavery] did not by itself cause the British Industrial Revolution. It certainly "helped" that Revolution along.' However, they also speculate that in the absence of slavery the revolution probably would have happened anyway. This also builds upon earlier arguments made by Engerman with Patrick K. O'Brien.[87] As we shall see, this book, however, follows Robin Blackburn, Joseph Inikori, Sven Beckert and others in underlining the important impact African slaves played in expanding Atlantic commerce and domestic manufactures that became integral to the Industrial Revolution.

A solution to the adverse balance of trade with Sweden and the South Baltic, argued the board, could be answered by Ireland. This problematic colony, they claimed, could be successfully cultivated to grow hemp and flax to be shipped in English ships. It would not be long, they claimed, before its production would be so 'improved, and increased to be as good, and as cheap as what comes from those places'.[88] This was part of a wider scheme the board had for making the navy totally independent of supplies from potential hostile or competitive nations. The other region the commissioners were looking closely at for naval stores (timber, pitch, tar and copper) was New England (although the board, keeping all avenues open, also argued that pressure should be kept up upon the king of Sweden to revoke his order of 1680, which had introduced large duties on English goods).[89]

As for prohibitory tariffs on French goods, the board were quite clear what the policy should be. As long as they retained prohibiting tariffs upon English goods, the 'impositions now charged on French goods cannot be taken off without laying this nation open to a great disadvantage by that Trade'. This would have to remain till a commercial treaty could be organized that prevented such a trade overbalance. This view, of course, was tame to that subsequently unleashed in the early 1710s during the debates leading up to the trade treaty with France in 1713. The board was also concerned with the rapid rise in popularity of French brandy among the English masses and the subsequent harm to their health. In other words, it was a preamble to the forthcoming introduction of an extremely important excise upon malt (fundamental to beer production), which would become the most lucrative source of revenue throughout the eighteenth century; this was also a major period for the nurturing of the domestic spirit industry, most notably gin.[90] The English state quickly learnt the fiscal advantage of taxing addiction – so much for the health of the masses.

The board concentrated its attention on the prevailing condition of England's manufactures in general, and how they could be improved. Understandably, they first examined England's most important, if not only mature industry, woollen textiles. Although the woollen industry had greatly increased since 1670, it was being seriously challenged by other countries using English raw wool. 'We are informed', the board anxiously reported, 'that great quantities are frequently landed in Holland from Scotland which we suppose is most carried thither out of England or Ireland.' Further supplies were illicitly exported from the coast of Kent and Sussex – especially from Romney Marsh. In addition, 'according to the best computations we can get', something like 2000 sacks of unwrought wool had been exported to France per annum since 1698 and the commencement of the Nine Years War. This, they complained, 'is so great a help to the working up the wool of forreigne growth that other Nations doe now make great quantities of Woollen Manufactures, to the great hindrance of those made in England, and detrimental of this Nation'. The result of all this would be the establishment of the rather ineffectual Riding Officers patrolling the south coast.[91]

It was also this report that provided the impetus to force Ireland to switch from manufacturing woollen textiles to manufacturing linen textiles. Pollexfen underlined the board's argument in his own treatise of 1697: 'The increase of the woollen manufactory in that kingdom may prove fatal to those of *England*, if speed can be not taken.' Instead, he advised, the colony should concentrate on the manufacture of linen. This, as we saw earlier, was actively pursued, with prohibiting duties passed in 1699, specifically targeting the Irish production of the new draperies.[92]

Likewise, the busy Bristol merchant, Cary, had spilt a great deal of ink over the importance of sorting out Ireland. He claimed, 'Of all the Plantations settled by the *English* [Ireland] hath proved most injurious to the Trade of this Kingdom, and so far from assuming the ends of a Colony, that it doth wholly violate them.' Cary feared that if left alone, the Irish woollen industry would outdo England. This colony, he wrote, 'produces as good or rather better wool' than England, while provisions for its woollen workers were cheaper. Instead, he argued, Ireland should concentrate on agricultural items where its true interest to England lay. Working in husbandry made a 'hardy People' committed to the land, whereas trade and industry was much more temporary with merchants frequently leaving the place. Ireland, he warned, should be reduced 'to the state of our other Plantations' and if it was to have an industry it should be linen. This would potentially 'draw over Multitudes of French Refugees, and put them upon an Imployment wherewith they were formerly acquainted'.[93] The result would, indeed, be the cultivation of a linen industry – spearheaded by Huguenots – that would come to act as a substitute to supplies from the Continent.[94]

The board next turned to silk. They reported that although the growth of the English silk industry had greatly increased since 1670, it was still significantly hindered by illicit superior silk imports from France. In particular, consumers wanted the fashionable designs and quality coming from France far more than anything 'invented by our Weavers here'. In other words, urgent intervention needed to be taken to improve the quality, design and fashion of English silk production. Action here meant improved access to raw silk and, especially, French designs.[95]

The young silk industry had been given a massive impetus after some 13,000 French Huguenots from Lyons and Tours settled in Spitalfields in East London after Louis XIVs edict in 1685. A huge fund was subsequently granted by Parliament to finance the French silk workers in 1687, and in 1692 a charter for the Royal Lustring Company was passed giving a monopoly in the manufacture of lustring and alamode silks. Soon after the company convinced Parliament to introduce large duties on equivalent imports, although French silks still found their way illicitly into the country.[96]

Similarly, the domestic paper industry had barely improved, let alone established itself, since early attempts commencing in the 1670s. Like linen textiles, the stock subscribed to nurturing this manufacture had not been well used, with 'the Corporation now in being having but eight Mills of their own, they make, as we are informed of all sorts, about one hundred-thousand reams per annum of white paper'. The board strongly advocated 'all incouragement' of this industry, 'that we may improve to make as good as what comes from abroad'. One problem, and clearly the nurturing of the linen industry would help this, was the want of linen rags, which was the primary raw material used to make paper. To help matters the board underlined its central policy, namely, protectionism, 'that all paper imported ought to pay a higher duty than paper made at home'.[97]

Pursuing this principle further the board strongly argued the need for a new Book of Rates, since the prevailing tolls had been made in 1660 and were now hopelessly out of date. In particular, they wanted a revised set of rates and duties that would ensure no advantage would be given to 'Neighbouring nations'. Thence no unfinished goods should be exported to countries where such items were finished for re-export. In short, the export and re-export trade should be protected. By 1700 the board had some of its way and export duties on woollen manufactures, corn, grain, biscuit and meat were repealed, while a new Book of Rates was passed that included goods not originally specified in the original rates. However, it was not till Robert Walpole's administration that all commodities and merchandise manufactured in Great Britain could be exported duty free.[98]

Many of these themes were further emphasized and pursued three years later when another report outlining the board's proposals was released. This time it was headed by the new first lord of the board, the Earl of Stamford. The other signatories were Hill, Pollexfen, Stepney, Blathwayt, Meadows and second Baron Lexington. The first objective of the report was to further safeguard the English woollen industry by, once again, underlining the need to crush the Irish new drapery producers. Despite the legislative ban on such Irish textiles they continued to manufacture them. The Board of Trade concluded, as before, that the best way of eradicating their production 'was by giving them [the Irish] such Encouragement in the Manufacture of Linnen as might engage them heartily in it'.[99]

This time the board's recommendation was put into action and the plan for extending linen production in Ireland was entrusted to a skilled French Huguenot refugee, Louis Crommelin. His family had been one of the leading French linen manufacturers and flax growers in the region of Picardy. However, following the Edict of Nantes in 1685 the family's estates had been forfeited to the Crown and their buildings subsequently destroyed. The family initially fled to Amsterdam where Louis's father became a partner in a bank. William III personally asked Crommelin to come to Ireland and draw up proposals for improving Irish linen production. Many exiled Huguenot linen workers had already been attracted over to the Northern Irish town of Lisburn, following the English Parliament's act inviting foreign Protestants to settle in Ireland in 1696. There was also a significant linen industry in Antrim and Down established earlier by weavers from the North of England following the English Civil War.[100]

Crommelin's proposals were sent to the Treasury and the new Board of Trade, whereupon both bodies recommended their implementation. His plans were given a royal patent and he was made overseer of the royal linen manufacture of Ireland. For this he was provided with an unprecedented advance of £10,000 to carry out necessary investments with an additional 8 per cent paid on this sum by the Treasury over the next ten years. He was rewarded with £200 per year as director and a further £120 to each of his three assistants. One of the first things he did was to employ a number of skilled foreigners and order 300 looms, which he soon increased to 1,000, imported from Flanders and Holland. All of this was a massive English investment in Ireland of foreign skills and technology. In addition, Crommelin managed to employ one of Europe's best reed makers, the Frenchman Henry Mark du Pre, to improve the combs used to separate threads and ensure the weft was in its proper position. As for flax production, Crommelin attracted over a number of Dutch to teach methods of flax growing to Irish farmers. This also involved the drainage of land and the importation of flax seeds from Holland, the German states and Russia. The board was confident Crommelin would make a large impact; they certainly had gambled as much, writing 'we have reason to believe he will be able to make a considerable advance therein'. All this took place under a highly protective policy and by 1727 the plan had succeeded with a third of all Ireland's exports now linen cloth. Such was the quality of Irish linen that by the 1740s both Scottish and German linen makers were counterfeiting Irish textiles.[101]

The linen scheme in Ireland was part of a broader English and, subsequently, British policy of destroying woollen textile competition wherever possible. The board cast their roving eyes across the Atlantic and similarly disliked what they saw. They thus advised Parliament to crush the activities of those colonies in America trying to manufacture woollen textiles. The result was the introduction of restrictive legislation that had the desired result.[102]

Instead the more Northern American colonies that lacked a staple product were persuaded to concentrate on trying to provide naval stores. As such the Navy Board had been instructed to send officials to New England where, in collaboration with commissioners of that colony, they were advised to view and inspect the forests lying upon the east coast. They wanted to ascertain the potential of the timber for masts and other necessary materials required for building ships that included pitch, tar and rosin. Specimens of each were sent back by the said officials for examination by the Navy Board. There was great optimism that this would both provide a utility for the northern colonies, which lacked a staple product like the southern colonies, and sever the potentially dangerous reliance upon Northern Europe for naval stores.[103]

The 1700 report, no doubt, was also deliberately presented the same year the first Calico Bill was being discussed by Parliament to ban imported Indian printed calicoes. As a clear preamble the board wrote:

> We did also (upon another occasion) humbly propose that the wearing or Consumption of the Manufactured Goods of India, Persia or China, made of Silk or Herb or mix'd with either of those Materials, as also of painted or stained Calicoes, and of all Handy craft Wares imported from those parts, should be discouraged and lessened in these Kingdomes, and in his Majesty's Plantations.

By contrast, the board underlined its determination to further nurture the domestic silk industry and encourage the Royal Lustring Company – both objectives subsequently became official policy.[104]

In general, the emphasis was the continuation and intensification of nurturing domestic industry and to promote exports to balance trade. The origins of this policy date back to at least the Elizabethan period, but the necessary momentum did not really commence until the mid-seventeenth century. This is the subject of the following chapter.

CHAPTER 4
SOUTH ASIAN 'WEEDS': THE BALANCE OF TRADE AND TEXTILES

The 'Golden-fleece': Foreign skills and industrial development

A primary emphasis of the new Board of Trade and Plantations was on the critical need to attract foreign know-how to develop domestic industry. This emphasis had been intensifying since the sixteenth century. As John Blanch wrote in 1707:

> She [Queen Elizabeth] wrapt herself up in her Golden-fleece, and resolv'd to be *Semper Eadem*; She built upon the good Foundation laid by her Brother King *Edward VI* and studied the Imployment of her own People. The Lord *Clarendon* tells us, *That she endeavour'd by all means to draw over Numbers of foreign Manufactures, by enlarging the Priviledges in all Places, while for the Convenency of the Trades they chose to reside*, (true policy) *and granted them churches in* Norwich, Canterbury *and other Places of the Kingdom*, as well as London.[1]

The year 1561 was an active year with skilled workers from the German states brought in to run and manage a new company operating the mines in Northumberland and to search for copper in Keswick. French and Dutchmen were brought over to aid in the tin mining happening in Cornwall, while others were wooed across to assist in the development of iron, lead and other metal mines. A German captain, Gerard Horrick, was hired to cultivate domestic supplies of gunpowder, and another German, Gaspar Seelar, was employed to manufacture salt in 1563. The aim of Elizabethan policy – managed by Sir William Cecil, Lord Burghley and his numerous advisors – far exceeded just industrial catch-up, and was equally dedicated to the quest of expanding England's maritime power. The problem was England's rapidly diminishing supply of timber and other necessary naval materials such as hemp, flax and canvas, the last of which was used for making sails. How could England challenge, let alone usurp, European competition without the necessary raw materials and skilled labour?

The year 1561 was a busy year, in general, for immigration to England, with some 406 people expelled from Flanders and Brabant being permitted to settle at Sandwich in Kent and carry on their weaving trade, with a community also established not far away in Canterbury. Another colony was created at Maidstone, also in Kent, in an attempt to improve its flagging prosperity, while a settlement was formed at Southampton on the Hampshire coast in 1567. Immigrants tended to come to the south and east of England, to places such as London, Kent, East Anglia, Sussex and Hampshire. Many of the early

Dutch who came to England fled from Spanish Catholic oppression, while the French came over in droves following the St Bartholomew's Day massacre in 1572. England's success in developing the new draperies was, concludes Carlo M. Cipolla, 'above all the result of "Walloon" immigration'. Another period of religious wars commencing in 1621 led to more French coming from Normandy.[2]

In *England's Interest* (1663), Samuel Fortrey underlined the need to attract the right sort of immigrants by selling the notion of English liberty. In this way, he claimed, 'we should quickly attain to the perfection of those manufactures, which now we so highly value and purchase so dear abroad'. Legislation was subsequently introduced that year to encourage the manufacture of linen and tapestry that would be reliant upon imported European skills.[3] Fortrey and these seventeenth-century commentators need not have worried too much, since talented French Huguenots would soon be crossing the channel in vast numbers.

The obvious benefits of skilled foreign labour soon crushed indigenous prejudice, and their impact played an important role in developing eighteenth-century British industrialization and trade. Skilled Huguenot workers and merchants provided a major impetus to the development of the British Atlantic by remoulding the shape of Northern European commerce in general and linking such trade to North American markets (especially New York and South Carolina). Perhaps, more than any group, French Huguenot immigrants during the 1690s helped fashion the 'cosmopolitan character', as David Ormrod puts it, of London as a trading centre, and to fuel product specialization, primarily in the silk, linen and paper industries. Although the Huguenots fled to all Protestant strongholds in Europe and the New World, the wealthiest went to England, Holland and to a lesser extent the German countries. The Dutch emphasis upon the re-export trade and the German lack of Atlantic penetration helped the immigrants in England find a more fertile environment to, especially, ply their manufacturing skills; in other words, aside from religion, it was industrial encouragement and the potential Atlantic markets that was the carrot.[4]

Louis XIV's revocation of the Edict of Nantes in 1685 was clearly an important moment in England's nurturing of domestic manufacturers; such immigration was also important to English global finance. The term 'refugee' was coined to describe this flood of French immigrants and, such was their global diffusion, that they became a vital component in an international Protestant network. There were already a large number of Huguenot refugees prior to the revocation of the Edict of Nantes, but this dramatically boosted their number to a further 150,000 to 200,000 people; somewhere between 50,000 and 100,000 ended up in England. Huguenot's proved exceptionally adept in the world of commerce, where they were bound by religion, a sense of persecution and strong family ties, which were all crucial to establishing and sustaining early transnational financial credit and trading networks. J. F. Bosher writes: 'For the average Huguenot merchant of that time, religion was stronger than nationality, and he was usually ready to link his fate with American, Dutch, English, or any other Protestant merchant.' In addition, merchants in Catholic Europe tended to obtain lesser social status compared to their equivalents in England and the Netherlands.[5]

Huguenots, along with other ethnic groups and indigenous peoples, found in England an industrially backward but hugely ambitious place to defend their religion. Moreover, it was a relatively accommodating and exciting environment to ply their commercial and industrial skills and, not to mention, line their purses. As such, they formed a fundamental resource for nurturing crucial industries and a hitherto relatively unimportant fiscal and commercial centre. The English context undoubtedly added a drive and determination to the refugees that made them more successful in establishing manufacturers than other examples. For instance, the attempt by Spain to introduce certain industries by attracting over skilled and foreign labour, on the whole, failed.[6]

Already, in the aftermath of French dragoons being set loose in the province of Poitou to convert Huguenots, Charles II announced in August 1681 that all Protestant immigrants would be welcomed to England. They would, he pronounced, be allowed to pursue their commerce, arts and trades with complete freedom. During this period, and particularly in the earlier French purge of Protestants in 1665, there was a general fear that England was seriously underpopulated. Within this context there was an additional growing groundswell to encourage immigration, which, in turn, led to a controversy over the issue of naturalization. Between 1660 and 1709 there were a dozen attempts to pass an act for a general naturalization of Protestant immigrants. The fear, however, for many was that admitting so many clear nonconformists would disrupt the power of the Church of England and the Restoration religious settlement. By contrast, others argued toleration and naturalization were vital to increasing England's dwindling population and manufacturing power.[7]

Generally, those advocating naturalization had a Whig bent and those opposing it were predominantly, although not always, of a Tory inclination. An anonymous commentator in 1689 summed up the urgency of attracting foreign skilled labour: 'We are now supplied from *foreign parts* with divers Commodities, which, if the kingdom were replenished with Artisans, they would furnish us with here at home.'[8] Opponents of naturalization were eventually defeated in 1709 with the passing of the Naturalization Act, which subsequently triggered a flood of German immigrants from the Palatines. This stirred the wrath of Tories who were all too ready to find an excuse to end the increasingly unpopular Whig regime; the exodus from the Palatinate region along the River Rhine was far more than expected. The majority were farmers and many were encouraged to go to Ireland and, eventually, the British Americas. In Ireland they were pushed into the production of flax and hemp to aid the new linen industry, while in North Carolina they were encouraged to concentrate upon the cultivation of naval stores. The majority, however, ended up being sent back. This helped speed up the collapse of the Whig government and the election of a Tory administration in 1710.

Another key interest that disliked naturalization were those who benefited, especially within the City of London, from the revenue generated from alien duties placed upon foreign merchants operating out of London.[9] Despite such opposition, the influx of international immigrants to London had a profound impact upon the trajectory of City trade, particularly from the 1670s onwards. The most important were French Huguenots, Jewish merchants mainly of Iberian-Sephardic origin and Dutch merchants. Perry

Gauci concludes: 'It is clear that the traders of foreign extraction constituted the most dynamic element within the mercantile world of post-Restoration London.' Almost a third of merchants of known origins were born abroad, and nearly 8 per cent more were the descendants of foreign immigrants. In general, too, the City of London contained a phenomenal number of religious nonconformists.[10]

A demonstration of the importance of foreign immigrants came later in the eighteenth century when a declaration of loyalty to King George II in 1744 by City merchants, consisted of numerous persons of foreign origin or descent. Wilson found about hundred were Huguenots, another forty were Jewish (Samson Gideon and Joseph Salvadore being the most well known) and a further thirty-seven were Dutch (perhaps most famously Matthew Decker and Joshua and Gerard van Neck). This last group may have been the smallest but they were the most powerful and influential. In addition, there was also a great deal of intermarriage between these groups. These powerful merchants and financiers were clustered around their churches, synagogues and charitable centres, primarily in and around the financial centre of the City of London.[11]

Of even more importance was the role of foreign immigration in nurturing British manufactures. Consider the example of silk. Although England had attempted to produce silk cloth since the early seventeenth century, the country still imported large quantities of French silk textiles. For example, between 1686 and 1688 England bought more than £700,000 worth of silk cloth from across the channel. Consequently, there was a great deal of desire to cultivate a more competitive domestic silk industry, which triggered an aggressive pursuit of attracting appropriate foreign know-how. As a result all French Huguenot immigrants skilled in silk were encouraged to establish such manufactures, with most settling at Blackfriars in Canterbury in Kent, Spitalfields in London's East End, and Ipswich in East Anglia. In 1692 a group of French, Dutch and English entrepreneurs bought the patent to manufacture alamodes (a soft and light silk) and lustrings (a fine and shiny broad silk), which culminated in the Royal Lustring Company that established some 768 looms at work in Ipswich and London by 1695. Most of the skill and management in these new establishments were provided by French refugees. This growing domestic silk textile industry was also given an annual subsidy, and an Act of Parliament in 1697 prohibited all silk textile imports.[12] All this was not without a fight.

In 1693 some thirty-eight mercers and manufacturers of the industry, once again including numerous Huguenots, combined to take on the company. In the subsequent battle, the predatory group were aided by the French Lyon silk interest who tried to supply large quantities of their silk into England.[13] The Royal Lustring Company soon caught on and petitioned the House of Commons concerning 'a very destructive trade carried on with France during the war for illegally importing such silks whereby the king has been defrauded of customs and our own manufacture has been greatly discouraged, that the same vessels which imported such silks exported great quantities of wool'.[14] The operation was actually being managed by Huguenots out of London and Canterbury; large fleets of illicit French silk textiles and raw English wool cargoes were operating between Kent and Picardy. Clearly, making money could still transcend Protestant loyalties and fervent anti-Catholicism. The move was successfully defeated by surveillance at the ports and the perpetrators were brought to trial in 1698.[15]

The French Huguenots, despite some of their illicit activities, came with far more valuable industrial skills and practical knowledge, which helped introduce the prized secrets of the Lyon silk industry. Not surprisingly, Frenchmen from this region were deeply worried that they would lose most of the English market, and consumers would come to prefer the English silk textiles that were developing at such a fast rate. Numerous French commentators expressed their concern that the backward English silk manufactures would soon catch up and produce items as good as the mature French industry.[16]

The Frenchman Nicholas Dupin, the first Deputy Governor of the Linen and White Paper Corporation in England, Scotland and Ireland, worked hard to bring over European skilled labour and provide adequate training establishments. He also advocated the need for parish workhouses to be created where the poor could be taught by 'a competent number of English, French, and Dutch Protestant Artists, both Men and Women'. Here, he recommended, they should be paid 18 pence per week over and above the common wage for such work as spinning and weaving linen cloth along with a number of other textile jobs. The aim was to aid the nurturing of domestic industry, especially those manufactures that could potentially be a substitute for French and Asian goods.[17]

Huguenots also established other rival industries to the French, including the production of sail cloth in Ipswich and elsewhere. In addition they educated Englishmen in the production of the 'finest grades of woollens and velvets and how to weave such linens as batiste'; this was fine plain-weave cotton developed by Baptiste of Cambrai in the thirteenth century. In general, Huguenots were important in aiding the establishment of the hugely important domestic production of printed calicoes and aiding the acceleration of the production of substitute Indian cotton textiles in general.[18]

Elsewhere, the Huguenots were important in greatly improving and expanding the English paper industry; despite already providing some coarser grades of paper, England imported most of its white paper from Holland, France and Germany. In the words of Scoville, Huguenots 'fortified what had been a rather sick industry by bringing improved paper moulds and forms, by disclosing to the English some of their most important and secret processes of manufacturing and bleaching, capital, managerial ability, and skilled manpower'. Despite the attempt by the French ambassador to bribe the manager and workers of one mill back to France, the English paper industry was in a much healthier position than hitherto. Gerald de Vaux established a paper mill at South Stoneham in Hampshire, Henri Portal built one at Laverstoke also in Hampshire and another was constructed on the Darent in Kent. The Portal undertaking went on to gain the contract to make the paper for Bank of England notes until 1924. Nicolas de Chaps set a mill up near Glasgow, while French workers manufactured good quality blue and grey paper at Dalry Mills near Edinburgh (taken over by Nicolas Dupin in 1693). Dupin also obtained a patent in 1691 to make white paper in Ireland, and established a mill that briefly supplied Dublin with paper for books and pamphlets during the 1690s. Although French and Dutch writing paper remained far superior throughout most of the eighteenth century, the English did start rivalling them in some of the lesser grades of paper which became a useful source of revenue.[19]

In addition, the French played an important role in the improvement of other English sectors such as glass, felt hat making, laces, gloves, buttons, gold and silver items. In the case of glass, French Protestants from Normandy and Picardy were fundamental in the manufacture of crown glass used for windows, cast plate glass and mirrors. The experiments with coal-fuelled furnaces were primarily an English development; although an early furnace patent dated 1610 had liberally drawn upon experiments conducted in France. T. S. Barker writes,

> Although the English appear to have possessed a distinct advantage in furnace design, they still relied for the greater part on skilled, foreign craftsmen to work the molten glass – or metal, as it was called – which their furnaces heated. In the early seventeenth century when coal-fired furnaces were introduced, foreign names loomed very large among the makers of window glass.

This seems to have commenced in the second half of the sixteenth century with, for example, an Antwerp merchant along with his partner gaining a patent to produce window glass in England in 1567, followed by the arrival of Norman and Lorraine glassmakers further improving this small industry. These manufacturers initially relied upon timber as their source of fuel; however, with the increasing depletion and competition for wood demanded by the Royal Navy, James I banned its use in May 1615. Such was the value of timber anyone found defying the law was subject to the death penalty. Instead, they were instructed to use coal that, unlike elsewhere in Europe, was plentiful, really accessible and of a good quality.[20]

Foreign labour was also important in a variety of other areas such as leather trades, brewing, potteries, soapmaking and furniture-making.[21] England's leading botanist and Leiden-trained physician, Nehemiah Grew, underlined the absolute importance of such labour in 1707. He boiled England's emerging success as a manufacturing country down to the successful wooing of Dutch, Walloon, French, Venetian and Spanish skilled labour.[22] He should, of course, have added the Germans and Portuguese to this list.

Clearly, then, foreign skills played a vital role in helping to nurture England and Britain's early infant industrial base. This was not lost on two French officials dispatched to Britain to help negotiate the crucial trade treaty after the Peace of Utrecht in 1713. They warned:

> The privileges and favours which he [king Charles II] accorded to our Protestants who withdrew to England in great number and who carried there our manufactories of silk, hats, hardware, paper, linen, and several other commodities have broken the usage in England of all similar imported goods which they formerly obtained from us. And the refugees have carried the manufactories to such a degree of perfection that even we begin now to import some of their output.

In addition, the flood of French immigrants was impacting upon the price of English labour: 'Labour which was formerly very expensive in England when employers hired only Englishmen has become as cheap as in France since our religious refugees have gone there in such great number.' It was not just European refugees who were fuelling the development of English and British industry; a key set of political policies within the realm of trade related manufacturing was also contributing to this development: 'The raw materials used in these manufactures', the French officials continued, 'pay no import duties and neither do the drugs used in dyeing. And all manufactured products which pass outside the realm are also exempted from export levies.' The two French officials were right to be apprehensive and to recognize the outline of a successful industrial strategy.[23]

However, Grew pointed out that English industry still had a long way to go. After giving an array of items that England should be making rather than importing, he made a number of recommendations to rectify the situation. Instead of just encouraging foreigners to come and settle, he suggested, England should send its countrymen to its industrial rivals to master their techniques. It was inexcusable, he said, to continue to export 'undrest and undyed' textiles since the profit was in the finished item. Hence, for example, it was vital that England worked harder at gaining and perfecting dyes. He underscored the need for protectionism and finished with a swipe at guilds without referring to them by name. By keeping the trade skills 'secret in a few hands', they had limited the extent of production and had kept the wages high. Not coincidentally Grew, like Henry Martyn, sang the praises of mechanical invention and the need to reward ingenuity 'as in France'. He concluded that a repository for all industrial instruments and developments should be created in every county, which would inspire and fuel invention.[24]

However, it was the menace of Asian, rather than just European, textiles that was for many the immediate concern. This was soon addressed on 19 October 1721 – the same year the consumption of pure cotton textiles was banned – when Robert Walpole, the new First Lord of the Treasury, made the following remarks in an address to both Houses of Parliament via the king's speech:

> It is very obvious that nothing would more conduce to the obtaining of so public a good, than to make the exportation of our own manufactures and the importation of the commodities used in the manufacturing of them, as practicable and as easy as may be; by this means, the balance of trade may be preserved in our favour, our navigation greatly increased and great numbers of our poor employed.

By the late 1730s such a view was taken for granted.[25] The British and Irish manufacturers of linens, threads and tapes wrote: 'From hence we must be convinced, that when any Nation has a Mind to set up a Manufacture, which a neighbouring Nation is in Possession of, they must particularly encourage it, 1. by Bounties; 2. By loading its Rival, The foreign Manufacture, with Duties; and 3. by making it the Fashion to wear it.'[26]

It was China and India as much as the French that were the manufacturing rivals of England's industrial aspirations. The most energetic advisor at the Board of Trade and Plantations, John Pollexfen, was in no doubt about the adverse trade with South Asia:

> As ill Weeds grow apace, to these Manufactured Goods from *India* met with such a kind reception, that from the greatest Gallants to the meanest Cook-Maids, nothing was thought so fit, to adorn their persons, as the Fabricks of *India*; nor for the ornament of Chambers like *India-Skreens, Cabinets, Beds* and *Hangings*; not for Closets, like *China* and *Lacquered* ware; and the Melting down of our Milled Money, that might by the name of Bullion be Exported to purchase them, not at all considered.[27]

The importation of such sophisticated foreign goods, especially those deemed luxuries, was not only a drain on the country's bullion but also destructive of domestic employment. England, at this time, had no industrial answer.

William Petyt had earlier warned in 1680, 'as home trade grows worse and worse, Industry itself must be tired and foiled, to the great amazement, as well as affliction of the People'. This would also, if left unaddressed, lead to an exodus of England's indigenous as well as foreign skilled workers to its commercial rivals – accompanied by the growth in the number of unemployed poor – something that, according to Petyt, had already risen tenfold in the last two decades. In addition to traditional occupations declining, land values had sunk and rents had massively fallen: all of which, he claimed, was undermining traditional social authority. The only people to benefit, he sneered, were parasites such as merchants dealing in foreign goods, and an explosion of useless 'Lawyers, Attorneys, Solicitors, Scriveners, and Pen-men of all sorts'. The nation was being 'dis-peopled, as well as impoverished by a consumptive Trade'. Crucially, he concluded, the draining of wealth meant less tax revenue leading to the country being unable to fight future wars.[28] War clearly looms large in trying to understand Britain's industrial trajectory over the course of the long eighteenth century.

In his tract entitled *An Essay on the State of England, in Relation to Its Trade, Its Poor, and Its Taxes* (1695) the Bristol merchant John Cary, like Pollexfen, spent a significant amount of time condemning the East Indian trade in silk and cotton textiles. These two items, he claimed, 'do us more prejudice in our Manufactures than all the Advantage they bring either to private purses or to the Nation In general'. Not only did they erode the domestic woollen textile industry, but they also nurtured competitors abroad. For example, because English people were buying Indian calicoes instead of German linen, the latter were now producing woollens that they would previously have purchased from England.[29]

A long pamphlet published in 1696 by the successful Gloucester woollen clothier John Blanch, similarly condemned the East India Company for the same reasons as Cary and Pollexfen. The fashion craze for Indian calicoes was damaging traditional English woollens in general. He pleaded: 'I cannot see what reason may be given against a total Prohibition of their being worn in England, which will be the quickest way to have them disused.' And if that was not an option, he prophetically predicted, then nurture an English cotton industry instead. The Southern plantations in North America, he suggested, could be used to cultivate raw cotton by slave labour to supply such a potential industry. On this subject Cary was also confident and in 'no doubt we might in time make Calicoes equal in their sorts with those Imported from *India*'. He also expanded these arguments the same year in a separately published pamphlet entitled *A Discourse Concerning the East-Indian Trade* (reprinted the following year).[30]

Pollexfen was less flexible and described the Indian trade as the 'worse foundation of any trade' and wheeled out all the usual arguments concerning the negative export of bullion from Albion's shores. The East India Company responded firmly to these allegations and explained that, on the contrary, the seeming counterbalance in trade aided England: 'There is nothing imported by us but is exported again. Two thirds in value is exported. This is to be made out by the Custom House Books. Our books will not show it. We sell them here, and the buyers export them. What we export is all profit to the nation.' The company's argument was supported by Daniel Sheldon in the House of Lords, who declared,

> If a right calculation could be made of the value of those East India goods they have exported from England to other countries, verily believe it would amount almost to as much as the value of the bullion they have sent to India, without deducting what would have been drawn from the nation by the commodities of other [rival] countries if we had not been supplied from India.[31]

The primary attack against the Indian calico trade was two-pronged: it was detrimental to the nation's woollen cloth and silk textile industries, and secondly, it was draining the country's bullion. Europeans may have wanted the Asian calicoes but they, in return, had little – apart from silver – that Asians wanted. In this way Spanish American bullion became ever more crucial and the African connection to Asia was solidified, with slavery being vital to gold and silver mining in South America.[32] As C. Knick Harley succinctly observes: 'Asian demand for bullion and coin was so great that the rise of European trade with the east should be seen primarily as a consequence not of trade routes to the east but of the discovery of America.'[33] Whether China and India really did become the world's sink for silver need not concern us; our concern can be limited to the fact that it was vital to trade with these regions.

Cotton textiles were the most obvious of the new goods coming in ever larger quantities into England; other items included silks, porcelain, raisins, spices, cocoa beans, tobacco, tea, coffee and, of course, sugar. The speed of these goods entering England mirrored the rise of the country's commercial and colonial power. This enabled prices to lower as England's purchasing power increased and, above all, it was the fact this phenomenal growth in imports was controlled increasingly by English traders and shipping.[34]

By the last two decades of the seventeenth century, attacks upon the East India Company had become engrained in London Whiggism. Ever since the Huguenot Whig Deputy Governor of the Company, Thomas Papillon, had been ousted by Sir Josiah Child, the company had been dominated by the latter and Tory shareholders (although this divide was never totally clear-cut, with a number of Whig and nonconformist investors continuing to have interests in the body). Likewise, although there remained Whig stock owners of the African and the Hudson Bay companies, these institutions remained the target of Whig criticisms. Eventually, in 1698, the Whig Junto now running William's policies in Parliament managed to secure a parliamentary charter for a new East India Company. Although it did not end the old company, it placed its future in doubt and the two bodies eventually amalgamated in 1708, while the Hudson Bay and African companies had their exclusive trading rights removed in 1697 and 1698 respectively.[35]

Within this context the sharp and pragmatic oeconomic commentator and ambiguous Tory, Charles Davenant, in his defence of the East India Company's trade just prior to the first Calico Act (1701), argued that English trade to the East and West Indies provided a surplus in the balance of trade and was not causing a drain on the nation's wealth. He agreed that it was vital the woollen textile trade was encouraged, 'but 'tis its Exportation Abroad, and not the Consumption of it at Home, that must bring Profit to the kingdom'. Davenant was also, of course, conscious from the point of view of revenue that woollen cloth was not subject to a national excise tax.[36] It was, however, the source of certain local regional taxes.

Although the importance of wool to employment was not questioned by anyone, the banning of domestically printed Asian cloth had real social implications. For example, a petition of 1696 pleaded that it would potentially be putting thousands of women and children employed at 'second manufactory' of Asian imported cloth out of work. It was only through their employment, the petition continued, that 'the Weaker Sex have been preserved from those Temptations to which Want might otherwise incline them and, by this Housewifery, many Modest Virgins have recommended themselves to Frugal and Industrious Husbands'.[37] The now large number of people employed in the domestic calico-printing industry would be an important factor in the imminent Calico Act. Woollen cloth manufacturers were already aided in 1700 by the repeal of duties on the export of finished items; this was a policy Walpole extended to all British manufactured goods exported in 1721 – along with the duty free importation of numerous raw materials.[38]

Davenant deeply opposed any attempt at prohibiting cloth from the East, a view entirely understandable when your paymaster was the East India Company, although he was also far too clever not to have a valid argument. He claimed since a market had been created for these products throughout Europe, a monopoly in their re-exportation had developed between the English and the Dutch. Consequently, since the rest of Europe did not trade in cotton textiles, they purchased them, often in violation to their national legislation, from the Dutch and English East India Companies. As such the trade was really not at the cost of English gold and silver but that of the European continent.[39] Much of Davenant's polemic had already been made by the Scottish radical and congregationalist, political militant and defender of nonconformism Robert Ferguson in his book *The East-India-Trade: A Most Profitable Trade to the Kingdom* (1667). The treatise was clearly sponsored by his patron, who republished it, as we have seen, in 1680, rather misleadingly under his name ('wrote at the Instance of Thomas Papillon') with a slightly altered title. This has subsequently been believed to be the work of Papillon.[40]

Ferguson underlined the usual emphasis upon the importance of trade to a nation's greatness and the adverse nature of commerce with France. By contrast, he continued, the East India trade supplied England with 'necessary and useful Commodities' at 'the cheapest rates'. In exchange, they took a significant quantity 'of our Native Commodities and Manufactures' (mainly drapery, tin and lead), although he was careful to add 'not altogether so much as some other Trades do'. Crucially, East India goods supplied the nation with large quantities of goods for the lucrative re-export trade. The knock-on effect was vital, he claimed, in maintaining English shipping in readiness for 'warlike service' and defending the kingdom. The trade also cultivated seamen and provided a considerable amount of revenue.[41]

At a superficial level, the East India Company balance of trade looked negative, agreed Ferguson in 1677, with about £110,000 of English and foreign goods exported to India and £200,000–240,000 of goods returned. However, of these items some such as saltpetre were vital to England's military and saved the country from having to rely on a potential European enemy. It was also better to import Indian silk than French or Italian, while calico cloth was an ideal substitute for linen cloth imported from France, Germany, the Netherlands and Flanders. Even better would be to nurture a domestic linen industry or, as would happen, one in Ireland, 'so as to supply this kingdom'. Crucially, Ferguson argued, much of the imported calico from India was re-exported to Europe and thus already provided 'a further Addition of stock to the Nation'. Consequently, through the re-export trade England was bringing in much more bullion than it was losing.[42]

The ambitious Director of the East India Company, Child, like Downing, had prospered during the republican era and was equally pragmatic in his politics. It is fair to say his main concern was his purse rather than his conscience.[43] Child, unlike Davenant and Ferguson, did not think there was any point in engaging with the bullion argument. Instead, he simply dismissed it as a red herring: 'I am of Opinion, that silver and Gold, coined or uncoined, tho they are used for a measure of all other things, are no less a Commodity than Wine, Oyl, Tobacco, Cloth or Stuffs; and may in many cases be exported as much to National advantage as any other Commodity.' He warned, 'No Nation ever was or will be considerable in Trade, that Prohibits the Exportation of *Bullion*', and if the English East India Company did not pursue the Asian trade, it would all go to Holland. In a swift dismissal of Indian calico and silk imports challenging England's young and vulnerable silk industry, he instead stressed, like Fergusson and Papillon earlier, the damage Indian re-exports of silks and calicoes were doing to England's European competitors.[44]

Perhaps the most well-known defence of the East Indian trade came from the pen of Henry Martyn (Martin) entitled *Considerations Upon the East-India Trade* published in 1701. Martyn, who succeeded Davenant as Inspector-General of Imports and Exports in 1714, claimed that the East Indian trade increased the bullion, domestic manufactures and land rents of England. For one thing, Indian textiles were more valuable than bullion and, as Davenant and Ferguson emphasized, via re-exportation they actually brought in more bullion than was originally used to purchase them (even after transportation costs). Despite European prohibitions of Indian goods, Martyn argued: 'Foreigners will find out ways to get such into their own countries, or they will come after 'em into ours'. In short, Europe had nothing to compete with Indian textiles and such goods would find their way in one way or another.[45]

Despite this robust counter defence of the East India Company, a flood of short pamphlets continued to spew from the printing press attacking the trade. For example, an anonymous publication, signed by a certain T. S. in 1701, claimed the arrival of vast quantities of Indian calicoes had destroyed the production of certain textiles, such as tammets (a type of light worsted woollen cloth) in Suffolk and Norfolk. It was also eroding the London Spitalfield and Canterbury silk manufactures along with the Gloucestershire woollen clothing trade, while the 'pernicious trade' had also 'brought stained Linnen into Fashion'. In short, claimed the angry writer, 'whatever Commodity is made in *England* of wooll may be imitated, and in many ways exceeded in Cotton Manufactured in *India*, and afforded Cheaper than our English Trades-Men can afford theirs'.[46]

Pollexfen, through the Board of Trade and via his own published works, relentlessly attacked Child and, especially, Davenant. He accepted that gold and silver could be seen as simply commodities and that keeping them hoarded would not make England richer. However, he pointed out, 'Yet it being that in which the Riches of the Nation doth so much consist, and so necessary for the Payment of Fleets and Armies, and carrying on of commerce, that we cannot be safe, nor Rich without it.' Thus, the wasteful export of bullion for Indian textiles was a disaster in waiting to happen. Instead, he advised what was fast becoming mainstream policy: 'It is more our Interest to apply ourselves to increase our Products and Manufactories, and Consumption of them.' All that the export of bullion for Indian textiles did was drain England's wealth, promote luxury and erode the country's most important industry, woollen textiles.[47]

There can be no doubt that by thus diverting more Indian calico cloth to Europe the export of English woollen textiles must have been simultaneously reduced.[48] The shift towards imported Asian textiles dislodged traditional foreign trade which had important ramifications. For example, the Turkey Company used English woollen textiles to exchange for imported raw silk and silk goods from the Levant. Thus, when the East India Company imported cheaper silk from India and Persia, the Levant silks became redundant thence also having a negative impact upon English woollen cloth. Similarly, when German linen was no longer wanted due to imported Indian calicoes, English woollen textiles normally used in exchange for German linen also suffered, leading to the Germans starting to use their linen looms to make woollen cloth. Crucially, any erosion of the English woollen industry was accompanied by a reduction in land rents, thus raising the fear and wrath of the gentry. These concerns played a major role in the cotton controversy leading up to the first Calico Act in 1701.[49]

The priority, as far as Pollexfen and the Board of Trade were concerned, was to encourage English domestic industry, the exportation of home-produced goods and the discouragement of imported equivalents: 'For the more variety we have of Goods of our own make, the less we shall need from Abroad, and have the more to *Weavers*, and instruments for the setting up of Manufactures there.' One issue was the large joint-stock companies abusing their monopolies. The problem being that once they started to make a profit, like the East India Company, they became closed affairs, 'not easily broken' and dominated by just a few people. Pollexfen concluded: 'All will agree that Trade ought not to be situated and contracted to the Advantage of some few, but diffusive for the incouragement of Industry, and free for all persons to ingage in.'[50]

Davenant claimed each country around the world should specialize in the production of what suited their environment – what 'Providence intended'. This, of course, became a popular argument later propagated by nineteenth-century free-traders. He argued that the calico trade did not harm the woollen manufactures because it was the industry most suited to England. According to this reasoning, no other nation should be able to produce woollens as cheap and good as this country. By contrast, the silk industry was not natural to these shores. This proved to be a dangerous, albeit durable, argument that could easily backfire. In this instance, the silk weavers were furious and hit back claiming their industry was as much English as was woollen cloth (albeit raw silk still had to be imported despite attempts to produce it domestically). This, in turn, helped to support the view that if the silk manufacturers were right, then the linen drapers and calico printers were also as natural to England as woollen manufacturers. Davenant also suggested that competition with cheap Indian cloth would aid the woollen industry by forcing it to make cheaper textiles. Similarly Martyn argued: 'Manufactures made in England the like of which may be imported from East-Indies by the labour of fewer hands, are not profitable; they are a loss to the kingdom; the Publick therefore loses nothing by the loss of such manufactures.'[51]

A clever and robust response, specifically to Davenant, came once again from the energetic man at the Board of Trade, Pollexfen. He disputed Davenant's figures and, instead, calculated that the Indian trade had drained England of £400,000 of bullion per year since 1690. He further claimed that such a negative drain could be traced back to 1666, which had been further fuelled by the need to purchase timber and iron from Northern Europe for rebuilding London after the Great Fire. He accused Davenant, indirectly, of fiddling the books: 'if the accompts be not true, then the Arguments grounded thereon cannot be good'. Ironically, perhaps, Davenant went on to become the second official person to be in charge of calculating England's trade figures in 1703.[52]

Pollexfen dismissed the argument that if calico imports were banned the Dutch would get all the trade: 'at last the old Bugbears the *Dutch*, are called upon to frighten us into it, who, as upon all occasions when any contest hath happened about this Trade, are usually Summoned for that purpose'. He persuasively brushed the argument aside: 'But this needs no answer here, it being not proposed that the *English* shall be prohibited from bringing these Goods into *Europe*; but only the Consumption of them in *England*.'[53] Pollexfen's and Cary's arguments were joined by a wash of popular pamphlets such as the one signed by N. C., an apparent 'Weaver of London', in 1697. He also emphasized the small number of merchants benefiting from the trade at the expense of the nation. These people were unpatriotic and a danger to the country. Their work, he concluded, should be made a capital crime as it was in France.[54]

Another self-proclaimed 'London Weaver', signed T. S., also published a tract against the East India Company in 1697. Like the previous tract he explained that the way ahead should be to further imitate French policy. The legislation he had in mind was the French decree of 1686, which banned the domestic painting and printing of Indian white calicoes. This meant the physical destruction of the utensils and other fixed capital used in the process throughout the country. Moreover, the actual wearing of cotton cloth should be prohibited and made a capital offence. This, however, would be a step too far at this stage for the English legislators and one part in the story to the eventual rise of the British cotton industry.[55]

Pollexfen and the anti-East India trade arguments won the day, and the government believed a ban on imported silk cloth and Eastern *printed and dyed* calicoes would aid the domestic silk and woollen industry, ease unemployment, dampen increasing social protest and stem the export of bullion. The title of the 1701 calico legislation was 'an act for the more effective employing the poor by encouraging the manufactures of the kingdom'. The safeguarding of employment was considered vital to national prosperity and getting the balance between this, revenue, trade and industry could be difficult. The import of chintzes (printed patterned cotton with a glazed finish from India) for domestic use may have been banned, but they could still be imported into bonded warehouses for re-export. The legislation also still allowed the importation of plain calicoes (white or unbleached cotton fabric) and cotton yarn. All of this helped fuel the already significant domestic printing and dying cloth industry, which was precisely the fear earlier expressed by the London weaver, T. S. Indeed, it was after the 1701 Act that the domestic printing of designs upon calico, mixed cottons and linen greatly accelerated. Although the printing was of a far inferior quality, they were much cheaper and diffused far further down the social scale. Probably, as a result, custom duties were also placed on plain calicoes in 1701 followed by rises in 1704 and 1708, while excise duties were subsequently put on domestically printed calicoes in 1712 and 1714.[56]

The initial region for the production of calico and fustian printing was London and, generally, the Home Counties. It seems the first patent was given to an English engraver and pioneer of the Dutch mezzotinting process, William Sherwin, in 1676. He opened a factory in the Lea valley and then another one at Well Yard near St Bartholomew's Hospital. He later told the House of Lords in 1696 that he employed four hundred people, but also admitted his printed cloth could not survive washing. In other words, his production was based on the pigments used by the French and not the technically superior water-resisting process of Indian printed cotton textiles. The first, large, calico-printing manufacturing complex was introduced by a Frenchman, Rene Grillet, in 1690. Interestingly, he was not a Huguenot but a Catholic, who came to England to continue the pursuit of his trade after the French ban on cotton textiles in 1686. Before coming to England he had first gone to Holland to perfect his techniques by working with skilled Dutch master-printers who, at the time, were the best in Europe. Grillet's manufactory employed a large number of predominantly Catholic Frenchmen described by one contemporary as 'a saucy and independent lot'.[57] The quest to further industry could transcend religious boundaries.

Another large textile printing site was opened in Essex by another Frenchman, Francis Pousett, in 1694. Soon after other establishments appeared in Lewisham, Mitcham, Wandsworth and further locations south of the River Thames. They all mainly worked on printing imported plain Indian calicoes for the domestic market. As a result of the 1701 Act, the East India Company started to import far more plain calicoes, which they hoped would also dilute hostility towards the trade by the creation of employment via the finishing of such goods. However, in terms of quality and durability it was not till well into the second half of the eighteenth century that the Indian method of printing was effectively imitated.[58] Moreover, to actually match the quality of the Indian fabric would take longer and only come with mechanization.[59]

From at least 1704, the domestic printing calico industry started to flex its growing muscle and commenced a campaign of defensive lobbying. For example, they faced attacks from the English stuff weavers who were clearly concerned about their jobs due to the rise of the calico-printing producers. In response, the printers claimed they deserved protection as much as weavers, since they had become an important source of domestic employment. The printers also emphasized that the Dutch had established manufactures to substitute their 'several sorts of Strip'd and Chequered *Indian* stuffs … in imitation of Calicoes, which are printed there, and will better serve instead of Callicoes than English Stuffs' – a fear also noted by the Board of Trade in 1707. By 1711, however, domestic printed calicoes had successfully stemmed the trade of imported chequered, stained and striped linens from Holland. Their attempt to take advantage of the English 1701 ban on printed Asian textiles had failed.[60]

The Commissioners of Trade and Plantations concluded that the Calico Act had simply encouraged the domestic printing of plain Indian calico imports:

> Though it was hoped that this prohibition would have discouraged the consumption of these goods, we found that the allowing calicoes unstained to be brought in has occasioned such an increase of the printing and staining calicoes here and the printers and painters have brought that art to such perfection that it is more prejudicial to us than it was before the Act.[61]

The act had, underlined the pro-woollen textiles Customs Commissioner John Haynes, simply fuelled a domestic calico and linen printing industry, 'that greater quantities of Calicoes and other Linnen have been Printed and worn in *England* Annually, since the importing of it was prohibited, than ever was brought from India'.[62]

By 1707 the board was even more precise in their analysis, claiming that 'the painters and printers have brought that Act to such perfection, that it is more prejudicial to us than the importations of printed calicoes was before the passing that act'. It seems that prior to this legislation the Indian calicoes had been predominantly purchased by the 'Richer sort of people while the poor continued to wear and use our woollen goods'. However, the English printed Indian calicoes were now so cheap 'that persons of all qualitys and Degrees Cloath themselves and furnish their houses in a great measure with them'.[63] From the beginning, textile printing was an industrial concern unlike the local village and household nature of Indian production. The premium paid for printed Indian textiles was eclipsed by the much cheaper plain imports and domestic printing.

Introducing sumptuary legislation in England for all types of cotton textiles was seriously discussed during this period. Such a policy had been especially used by the French since at least the late sixteenth century, when the Superintendent of Finances between 1598 and 1601, Maximilien de Bethune, suggested introducing a ban on wearing silk due to the flood of imported Italian silks along with gold and silver thread. The argument behind his reasoning was simple, namely, to stem the loss of bullion out of France paying for these items. However, the French king, Henry IV, did not ban the wearing of silks but just the importation of foreign manufactured silks. This successfully aided the French domestic industry and was a prelude to Jean-Baptiste Colbert's subsequent harsher protective legislation in the second half of the seventeenth century. The French banned, unlike England, the wearing and printing of linen and cotton textiles in 1686 to protect its silk industry.[64]

This ban, as Prasannan Parthasarathi remarks, 'hampered the development of the [French] cotton industry for decades', while many of the country's skilled textile printers came to England and elsewhere to continue to ply their trade. Giorgio Riello agrees: 'The 1686 ban might have retarded and in some case halted the development of domestic calico printing' in France. In short, 'while Britain allowed printing for export and fustian and mix cottons, France upheld a total ban that included also domestic production'. Britain's other great European commercial rival, the Netherlands, never enacted any prohibitory legislation due to the dominance of its trading interest.[65]

One merchant in 1719 claimed that since imported Indian calicoes didn't even compete with woollen or silk textiles, there was no legal reason to oppose them; 'that many of those that buy Callicoes, would not buy any Thing else instead of it, if there was no such Thing in Being as Callicoes'. For example, a far larger threat to the English silk industry were Dutch, Italian and smuggled French silk textiles, while unemployment among weavers was simply the result of Masters and Journeymen employing too many people. Finally, the excise tax from domestically printed Indian calicoes had now also become a useful source of revenue funding a part of the rising national debt.[66]

However, such arguments were aggressively challenged by a growing number of angry commentators. One anonymous critic, also writing in 1719, claimed the wearing of domestically printed Indian calicoes would soon destroy the home wool and silk textile industries. The model Britain should adopt was, once again, that of the French and their passing of the 1686 edict banning the printing, using and wearing of all (including plain) Indian wrought silks, cottons and calicoes. 'It was', wrote the author, 'without question, an unaccountable Mistake in those who solicited the first Prohibition of *Indian* Printed Callicoes, that they contented themselves with prohibiting the use of calicoes Printed Abroad, but did not insist upon prohibiting the Wearing and Use of those Printed at Home, as Things in themselves equally ruinous to our Manufactures.'[67]

The one-time financier, MP and debtor John Asgill reiterated an argument we have already met, namely, that double standards were at play. For example, silk cloth was not a staple product since raw silk had to be imported, while raw cotton was imported from the British colonies to fuel its young mixed cotton textile industry, and thus since the cotton came from British possessions it was a staple commodity. As a result, 'if the Silks, as well as that Imported Thrown as Raw, is, by reason of its being manufactured here, intitled to Protection and Encouragement; then the Callicoes made of Cotton, imported from our *American* Plantations is, by reason of its being manufactured here, intitled to the like Protection and Encouragement'. Not surprisingly, to counter such arguments, the British silk manufactures quickly published a proposal to try and domestically cultivate the growth of silkworms within Britain in 1720.[68]

Pursuing his argument further, Asgill thus claimed linens made in Britain and Ireland were also a staple commodity. As for the domestic woollen industry, he smirked, that was simply a deviation: 'That the Printed Callicoes (against which the Complaint is made) not being worn or used for the same Purposes with the Woolen Manufactures, do not therefore interfere with them, nor ought to be suppress'd in favour of them.' The real threat to woollens came, Asgill continued to emphasize, from linen and a new lighter type of domestically produced and printed mixed cotton (such as fustian) cloth, 'against which no complaint is made' and yet these were 'being worn and used for the same purposes with the Woolen Manufactures'.[69]

In turn, Asgill was condemned that year by an apparent weaver called Claudius Rey, who fumed there could only be a handful – if any – of looms in the country making cotton textiles unlike the extensive silk industry. This must have been right since the English had not yet found a way of making cotton yarn strong enough to be warp and therefore match the far superior quality of Indian cottons. In addition, the fact that flax and raw cotton were imported to aid the linen and mixed cotton industries undermined the idea that both could be considered staple manufactures. This, of course, ignored the fact that raw silk was imported. Rey returned later that year with an even more detailed attack upon the domestic printing of calico and linen cloth. His argument was simple: 'That the wearing of any Commodity whatsoever, which taketh away the Labour of the Poor, and impoverishes the people, is an *Evil*, with respect to the *Body Politick*.' Consequently any product eroding the domestic labour involved in the production of home goods was a very bad thing. At the heart of the problem, he claimed, was, once again, the fickle fashion of women. Rey was furious and accused women for 'the utter RUIN AND DESTRUCTION of our most *famous* SILK AND WOOLLEN MANUFACTORIES! Which are so beneficial, and whose welfare I so nearly linked with that of the whole *Nation*!'.[70]

The continual lobbying of the English woollen and, especially, silk manufacturers eventually resulted in the Calico Act of 1721 that further legislated a total ban on the importation of any Indian plain cotton fabric for domestic consumption. It was now illegal to wear such cloth – although muslins, neckcloths and blue calicoes were still legal. Printed calicoes could still be imported for re-export and plain calicoes could also be imported to be domestically printed and then re-exported. The English domestic calico printers had already conquered the British market since the 1701 ban and, after 1721, their position was consolidated by concentrating almost wholly on the printing of fustians along with other types of mixed cottons and linens for domestic consumption and export.

It was the Lancashire production of these light fustians and other types of mixed cotton–linen check cloths, which subsequently became an important export to Africa and the West Indies. Thus, while France, and most of Europe, banned the importation, printing and wearing of *plain calicoes* in the late seventeenth century, England had encouraged it. The end product was then protected from superior Indian competition of *printed calicoes* (1701) and, by the 1721 Act, nurtured by producing substitute textiles to print like light fustian and other mixed cotton textiles. Importantly, too, plain Indian cottons could still be domestically imported and printed for re-export. This, as Alfred P. Wadsworth and Julia De Lacy Mann concluded long ago, was eventually vital to the subsequent British pure cotton textile industry.[71]

The 1721 Calico Act also led to some confusion since, although fustians were exempt, they looked and felt very similar to pure cotton cloth. At one level the similarity of English fustian with Indian calico enabled manufacturers to exploit both the demand in the domestic and increasingly European, colonial and African markets. However, their similarity was such that the British government was forced to pass a subsequent act in 1736, stating in very clear terms that fustians were exempt from the legislation of 1721 as long as the warp was entirely of linen yarn.[72] And since British manufacturers were, as yet, unable to produce textiles with a cotton warp this was a redundant legal demand.

Interestingly, the issue was not black and white between trades. For example, the Manchester fustian manufacturers were supported by woollen textile producers from Halifax, Wakefield and surrounding areas. This seeming paradoxical support can be explained by the commerce such woollen traders were involved in. A large market for their textiles was Africa and the West Indies. On the return trip from selling their woollens large quantities of raw cotton was brought back and sold to the Manchester fustian producers.[73] The standard of textile printing continued to improve in and around London and increasingly in Lancashire. Indeed, such was the progress that the directors of the East India Company, acknowledging increased competition abroad, wrote in 1744 to their suppliers in India warning them to stick strictly to their orders: 'Printing here has come to so great perfection that unless you can keep to these instructions you must lessen the quality.' British mixed cotton textiles had also gained a good reputation on the European continent, with one French printer from Bayle, Jean Rhymer, hugely impressed with the English imitation of Indian work in prints.[74]

The eventual winner in the 1701 and 1721 legislation was not silk or woollen textiles but domestic linen, fustians and ultimately pure cotton cloth. As we have seen, the government was keen to encourage the linen and fustian industry to offset European imports. Therefore, the domestic prohibition of East Indian textile imports, far from securing the future of woollen cloth, actually stimulated the emergence of these other textiles. The archetypal representation of the Industrial Revolution, the cotton cloth industry, was a product of state protectionist policies while, after 1774, it was only lightly taxed in relation to other domestic industries. It was, as Wadsworth and Mann argued, protection that provided the necessary incentive to print imitative calico textiles and then British-made cotton cloth.[75] This was not an overnight process and took the first seventy years of the eighteenth century for manufactured British mixed and cotton textiles to begin to match the quality of Indian cottons, and establish a decent reputation in export markets. The innovation that made this possible all took place behind a protective wall.

In conclusion, a key impetus behind the development of certain industries in eighteenth-century Britain was inspired by the manufacturing world of France, China and India. Asian taste and know-how fuelled, argues Maxine Berg, 'a programme of product innovation in Europe in attempts to "imitate" and to make indigenous these products'. However, and this is a fundamental point, they did not have the experience and knowledge to also import the same production process, equivalent ingredients and identical techniques that Asian manufacturers used. From this perspective, therefore, the rise in such consumption was thus an extremely important factor in shaping British industrial innovation. Goods such as ceramics and calicoes were mature everyday items in China and India, and yet traditional historiography normally locates their development to eighteenth-century European industrialization. Empire, if anything, gained access to the products of other nations. Imitative innovation was promoted as a way of overcoming Asian supremacy and, crucially, conducted behind a wall of prohibitions and tariffs. In the following chapter, we further trace the development of England's and, subsequently, Britain's, regulatory and protectionist policy forged in the late seventeenth and early eighteenth centuries.

CHAPTER 5
STATE PROTECTION AND INDUSTRIAL DEVELOPMENT

In no country has the taxation of manufactures been carried to such an extent as in England.[1]

Stephen Dowell, 1884

The rise of the British cotton textile industry and other manufacturers took place behind closed doors and after nearly a century of nurturing. It was particularly from the 1690s that trade protection intensified through the rapid implementation of tariffs and bounties. It was not by accident that this decade was also the period in which many of the fiscal innovations, described by P. G. M. Dickson as a 'financial revolution', were established.[2] Bans and prohibitive import duties were fixed on an array of items, including certain textiles, alcohol and hardware. This also heralded a huge escalation in smuggling and competing debates over the pros and cons of more liberal trade with Europe (especially France) and Asia (especially India). Britain's future oeconomic trajectory was still far from settled, but this was all about to change as the contest leading up to the Anglo-French Trade Treaty of 1713 was decided; revenue needs, colonization, labour exploitation, trade and industry were to intensify their interrelationship.

In the aftermath of the Glorious Revolution, unprecedented warfare expenses were putting a strain on customs revenue and, especially, the land tax. The gentry were at breaking point and the only solution was an expansion of the excise. For example, in 1695 an additional prohibiting duty of 25 per cent was placed on French goods, resulting in a reduction of customs but compensated by a doubling of the excise duty on domestic beer. Inland duties were also briefly placed on salt, glass, paper, tobacco pipes, stone bottles, hackney carriages and windows. In addition, a new excise duty on low wines (spirits extracted after the first distillation) was introduced, and the hugely important duty on malt (made from barley or other grain used in beer or spirits) was passed two years later in 1697. This expansion of the excise would be significantly extended with the election of a Tory government in 1710 and consolidated under Robert Walpole's administration during the 1720s. All of this brought excise officers into contact with ever-greater sections of, in most cases, a relatively new manufacturing community. It also complicated their work due to the increased sensitivity and technical nature of gauging many of the new goods.[3]

This concerted move to taxes on the manufacture of domestically produced goods and certain addictive colonial imports like tobacco and sugar, has to be situated within a context increasingly characterized by an aggrieved landed class. The cost of war under William and Mary had pushed the land tax to a rate of four shillings in the pound. Unable to shift the burden upon their tenants due to a series of poor returns on harvests, the landowners were at the end of their tether. This resulted in the removal of Whigs from power in 1710 and the landslide election of a new Tory administration, which attempted to reduce the burden of tax upon the landed ranks and speed up peace with France.

This potent sense of frustration and flexing of landed power was never forgotten by Walpole. The only solution was to try and keep the land tax low and, working through the Treasury, develop ways of increasing revenues from indirect taxes.[4] This, as has been charted in earlier chapters, was one major factor in the impetus to increasingly target the excise. It was a move that had particularly accelerated under William and Mary during the 1690s and then, once again, under the Tories during the regime of Robert Harley, who became in 1711 the first Earl of Oxford. The Whigs, especially Walpole, were chastened by the electoral defeat in 1710 and learnt that the land tax was politically dangerous; this became clear to them not only because the Tories won, but also because some Whigs themselves – landowners, in particular – had become disillusioned with the party's policies.

According to figures calculated by Patrick K. O'Brien, direct tax constituted 47 per cent of all revenue in 1695, 40 per cent in 1710, 26 per cent in 1720 and reached a low of 17 per cent in 1735. By contrast, the excise increased from 27 per cent of all revenues in 1695, to 36 per cent in 1710, 46 per cent in 1720 and a mighty 55 per cent by 1735 (Graph 1).[5]

Interestingly, the increasing reliance upon excise revenues also roughly paralleled the reduction of interest rates presented in David Stasavage's work, which reveals a drop

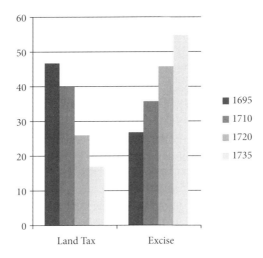

Graph 1 Percentage of direct tax and excise revenues 1695–1735.
Source: O'Brien, 'The political economy of British taxation', 9.

from 8 per cent in 1695 to 3 per cent by 1730. What is also interesting is that, as S. E. Fine has shown, the efficiency of the Excise collection in proportion to gross and net revenues shrank from 15.8 per cent in 1684 to 7.7 per cent in 1730. Walpole's rightful fear of a discontented landed gentry also, partly, informed his attempt to lower, and possibly terminate, the land tax in 1733. His aim was to compensate for the loss by improving the revenues from tobacco and wine by shifting their collection from the inefficient customs to the excise.[6]

Douglas North and Barry Weingast have emphasized the importance of British institutions in protecting private property and ensuring political rights as the key to underpinning credible commitment and thence economic development.[7] Regardless of how persuasive this argument is, there is no doubt that one state institution they miss is the body central to raising revenues, the Excise, which became absolutely fundamental by the 1720s to fiscal credit. Lenders would ultimately only judge credibility by the borrower's ability to gather revenue to pay back such loans. The Glorious Revolution had already seen a decisive emphasis upon nurturing domestic manufactures, which was increasingly driven by the need to create more income via excise taxes. This was a view that had been promoted by numerous commentators since the mid-seventeenth-century English Revolution, and was seen as the only way to dilute the landed financial burden and the political volatility of this fundamental interest. In this sense Tory landowners, on the contrary, were far from all being anti-excise. Hence, the home market had to be first taken back from foreign imports and, as protected domestic-produced goods gained in quality and competitiveness, they could supply crucial revenues that lay at the heart of public credit.

The model here was French Colbertism rather than Dutch commercial trade. French influence did not end with the reign of James II and the dilution of the monarchy's power, while the turn towards taxing manufactures was clearly not dominated by the Whigs. Even Sir Josiah Child, the embodiment – according to Steve Pincus – of James II's commercial views and Tory oeconomy, fiercely advocated replacing tax on land with excises in his 1694 tract on trade. By this date, the new land tax of 1689 was causing increasing anger among the landed ranks as they seemed to be shouldering the financial burden of war against France. Child suggested that public taxes on land 'might not much better be laid on the produce thereof, by way of Excise, and by easing those few that are the Proprietors of Land'. Here, he had in mind a tax upon 'Iron, Lead, Tin, Salt, Wool, Leather, Tallow, Corn, Hay, and on Plate, Glass, Brick, Earthen Ware, Paper; and many Manufactures in this Nation, which pay no Customs or Taxes'. He then justified the switch in the usual way, namely, such excises were sustainable and equitable. This was because so many people consumed these items that the burden was significantly reduced, and since they only needed to purchase what they could afford, it was comparatively fair. This view was also clearly supported by the new predominantly Whig Board of Trade and Plantations in 1697. The ambiguous Tory, Charles Davenant, also repeated the argument in his memorial on credit. The best foundation for credit, he claimed, was the excise: 'Hardly any other thing can yield so great an Annuall Income, and upon which the Government may so well rely'[8]; advocates of the excise transcended clear political boundaries.

The unique aspect of Britain's evolving Dutch and French hybrid oeconomy was the administrative structure, approach and success of the Excise. It was under Queen Anne's Tory government that eight important excises were reintroduced or established for the first time. These were placed upon candles (1712), leather (1711), hops (1711), soap (1712), paper (1712), printed or stained cloth (1712) and wire (gold and silver, 1712). Thus, it was under the new Tory regime that the Excise was greatly extended. By 1785 there were twenty-five excises that now generated more revenue than the land tax and customs combined.[9]

Already, by the 1720s, the Excise employed a greater number of people than all the other revenue departments combined.[10] However, with the exception of woollen textiles and one or two other items, English exports of manufactured goods were not yet performing that impressively. As we have seen there had been a significant move, for some time, to emulate the Dutch trade in re-exports. In his capacity as Inspector General of the Exports and Imports, Davenant advised the Commissioners of the Public Accounts in 1711 that Britain had to reduce duties on all those goods that were advantageous to British trade and industry, improve the system of drawbacks on re-exportation, make Britain a free port and focus on excise revenue.[11] This, of course, was exactly what Walpole attempted a few years later and it remained the central objective of eighteenth-century British oeconomic policy until the crisis of the final third of the century.

The importance of re-exports cannot be underlined enough. Fundamental naval items such as timber, hemp, bar iron, pitch and tar from the Baltic were paid for by re-exporting slave-produced colonial goods like sugar, coffee, tobacco and Asian tea, spices and textiles. The connection between Europe, the Americas, Africa and Asia was sealed through global trade.

The 1713 Anglo-French Trade Treaty and establishment of eighteenth-century oeconomic policy

The Anglo-French Trade Treaty of 1713 was a vital moment in confirming and solidifying British oeconomic policy. The debate building up to the settlement was typically cast under the political umbrella of Whig versus Tory with, for example, one anonymous commentator writing in 1713: '*Torism* can never agree with Trade which is in other Hands, and can never be in theirs, while Persecution and Discord are so much encouraged by them.' For this writer, at least, all Tories were Catholic, pro-French and a threat to Britain's wealth and liberty.[12] An English merchant, who claimed to have lived in Languedoc for twenty years, underlined the rapid expansion and danger of French white cloth. In general, he warned, if trade barriers were erased the British market would be flooded by cheaper French textiles.[13] Religion, politics and oeconomic policy frequently became conflated and fuelled heated and emotive debates.

Despite the realization that markets could be created, as demonstrated by the phenomenal success of Asian imports, the prevailing view was still that there was a fixed market and the task was to snatch as much of it as possible. Consequently, as spelt out so clearly in the Board of Trade's two earlier reports, trade with some regions – particularly Europe (especially France) and South Asia (especially India) – was classed as injurious, and with some others – American colonies and parts of Africa – as beneficial. Numerous products imported from France were deemed luxuries, while others were condemned as adverse to the sale of domestic manufactures. It was therefore legislated that trade with countries like France and India had a negative impact on the balance of trade, resulting in both a loss of bullion coupled with higher unemployment.

The above sentiments had reared their head periodically for some time, and came to the fore with the election of a Tory government in 1710 and subsequent negotiations for a peace treaty with France.[14] At this time, the main objective of the government was to try and expand British influence in South America, which was the key impetus behind the establishment of the South Sea Company and its credibility in taking over much of the national debt.[15] The Tories, unlike the Whigs, were less bothered about the nationality of the Spanish king. It was hoped that the acquisition of Spanish mines would wipe out the warmongering Whig-induced national debt and bolster the domestic landed basis of power; this all required a quick peace and potential trade treaty with France.[16]

The political temperature dramatically rose. The naturalized French Huguenot lexicographer and journalist, Abel Boyer, was hostile and deeply worried by the prospect of closer relations with Catholic France. In January 1711 he established a new periodical entitled the *Political State of Great Britain*, which ended up becoming an organ for his feud with the pro-French Tory writer and propagandist, Jonathan Swift.[17]

In September 1711 Boyer's war of words with Swift reached a climax when he published *An Account of the State and Progress of the Present Negotiation of Peace*. The tract spent most of its time refuting the arguments given for the financial need to bring peace, and stating what the criteria of a settlement should be if such a treaty was made. Not surprisingly it went to the heart of the matter; in particular, the fate of the Spanish Crown: 'The Address of the Lords, Nov. 19, 1708, professing, *They are more convinc'd, that no Peace can be safe and honourable until the Whole Monarchy of* Spain *be restor'd to the House of* Austria.' There was no good reason, he continued, 'why the Allies must now dwindle as to the Terms of Peace'. Crucially, Boyer assured his readers, Britain's financial situation was healthy, '*our Debts are fully provided for; and that our Credit is entirely restor'd*'.[18] In the meantime some forty-six anti-treaty petitions from around the country were submitted to the government.[19]

The French Commerce Bill of 1713 provides a lens that reveals the crystallization of oeconomical policy during the Augustan period, and the relationship between the state, trade, revenue and industry. Hitherto, no completely clear party position had yet materialized over the question of these oeconomic issues. Nonetheless, Perry Gauci reveals just how close the Tory administration of 1710, led by the Earl of Oxford, came to passing a liberal commercial treaty with the French. He writes: 'Tactically, trade presented a good platform for his [Earl of Oxford] administration, since it echoed previous Tory attacks on the warlike stance of his Whig rivals, which they had decried as inimical to British interests.' However, as soon as the French commercial treaty was presented to

Parliament, a torrent of pamphlets and propaganda swirled from the pens of worried Whigs, manufacturers and merchants. The Tory government reacted by launching a mouthpiece for its pro-treaty views entitled *The Mercator*. There is a slight confusion over who wrote the essays, but it was probably a combination of Daniel Defoe, Arthur Moore and Charles Davenant.[20]

The treaty proposed that both British and French subjects should be given the same commercial privileges, while the duties upon French items were not to be more than the levies on those placed on any other nation. In addition, all prohibitive laws passed in England and Britain since 1664 should be repealed, all French and British goods should be rated according to the tariff of 1664 and all the laws contrary to that tariff should be repealed.[21] A great deal of time was also spent negotiating fishing rights and claims to Canadian and New England colonies.[22]

The opponents of the treaty responded by launching a patriotic attack that condemned the pro-treaty advocates as undermining Britain's true interest. One of the most sensational events happened on 18 June when some seventy Tories voted against the bill. Spearheading this revolt was the High-Church Tory and fourth baronet Sir Thomas Hanmer, who, despite being initially in favour of the treaty, now felt it would actually be detrimental to the woollen and silk manufacturers; here he was probably concerned about the livelihoods of his constituents. Nonetheless, the pro-French Tories persisted and started to once again make headway, with publications from both sides continuing to spring forth from propagandists. The most significant was the opposition's *The British Merchant*, which was set up as a challenge to *The Mercator*, and written by Henry Martyn and a handful of experienced and powerful merchants, including the staunch protectionist, Joshua Gee, the Dutch-born financier and MP Sir Theodore Janssen and the Italian merchant Nathaniel Toriano (a possible relation to the earlier Torriano who signed the Scheme of Trade).[23]

Despite the hitherto lack of success of the Tories with the commercial treaty, they pushed it to the forefront of their agenda. Any chance, however, of successfully introducing it was severely eroded in June when the Tory politician, financier and one of the leading writers of *The Mercator*, Moore, referred to by the opposition as 'the Prime Minister of Trade', was condemned by both Houses of Parliament for corruption. He was alleged to have shipped nearly 30 tons of Dutch linen to the West Indies on his personal account, and therefore having abused his position as a Director of the South Sea Company. He was dismissed from the company in July 1714, much to the joy of the opposition who wasted no time implicating the episode to the credibility, in general, of the Tory government. In short, their leading exponent for the treaty, having drawn up or commissioned most of the articles, was none other than a corrupt, unpatriotic and untrustworthy person. Since September 1710 Moore had also been a Commissioner on the Board of Trade and Plantations.[24]

In addition to this gift to the Whigs, *The British Merchant* had launched a remarkably successful campaign in its own right. The authors' main points were, for contemporary ears, clear and convincing. In a series of robustly made arguments, the journal repeatedly gave reasons why a trade treaty with France would be devastating to Britain's manufactures and balance of trade. The case put forth from the start was one that had already been growing and applied, but it would now be greatly emphasized. Here is what the authors said: 'Wise Nations are so fond of encouraging Manufactures in their Infancy, that they not only burden foreign Manufactures of the like kind with high Impositions, but often totally condemn and prohibit the consumption of them.' Trade with France was bad because they supplied many of the lucrative goods that Britain was now trying to produce but, as yet, were far inferior in quality. For example, silk, spirits and linen (rags from the latter were also crucial to the fledgling paper industry) were produced in France on a much greater scale and of a much better quality. Consequently, to once more open up the British market to them would destroy its equivalent weaker domestic producers. *The Mercator* countered this by pointing out that Italian silk was being imported into Britain and it was not challenging domestic producers; given this, why would, *Mercator* argued, French silk textiles affect domestic producers of silk?[25]

France also had a natural advantage over Britain, it was claimed, regarding the cost of labour. According to *The British Merchant*, the French lived on a diet of roots, cabbage and in some regions entirely upon chestnuts. In other words, they cost a great deal less to feed than British labour. The speculation of cheap French labour was a huge one, although it was not just over the subject of food. *The British Merchant* also acknowledged the superior skills of the French labour force and wrote, 'There is a Slight of Hand in almost every Manufacture that is much more necessary than strength; and 'tis plain, that we are not yet arrived at that Slight, if a Fat with five Pair of Hands, is able to work off more Reams of Paper than the same Number of Hands can do in England.' The same argument, of course, was applied to the skill of Indian spinners, dyers and weavers of cotton cloth.[26]

Elsewhere, it was argued that if the prohibiting duties upon French brandy were removed, it would destroy Britain's newly developing spirits industry, which was an increasingly important source of excise revenue. The point being that the country was not yet at a level to compete with superior French brandy (or Dutch jenever) but, protected, was developing a substitute spirit, simultaneously providing employment and crucially servicing the debt via more reliable revenues. In addition, British gin also soaked up grains that were not good enough for brewing beer. The same protective argument was made regarding paper, silk and linen, 'so that we must be out of our senses if we permit the *French* to import their Manufactures to the Prejudice and Destruction of our own'. Later on, one of the authors of *The British Merchant* stipulated: 'The best way to preserve our Commerce, is to recommend the preservation of the best Markets for the Product and Manufactures of our Native Country.' Apart from woollen textiles and a couple of mined minerals, the market for most of Britain's infant manufactures was, as yet, a protected home one, although it was a market increasingly taxed and supplying vital revenue to Britain's fiscal system and rise to power. Thus, to open it up to more established European and Asian goods would have a devastating impact, leading not just to the demise of young domestic manufactures, but unemployment, a reduction in excise revenues and huge threat to public credit.[27]

The theme of retaining skilled labour was a central argument for *The British Merchant*. A particular issue, here, was religion and keeping the country relatively open to diversity since, they claimed, many of 'the lowest Rank, Mechanicks, Artisans, and Manufactures' differed from the teachings of the Church of England. Thus, if they were driven out of Britain for their beliefs, as had happened in France, they would also take with them their valuable skills. The country had relied on inward European migration in the first place to establish a great many of its domestic manufactures.[28] In this sense, the embracing of transnational diversity was born of aggressive ambition rather than liberal enlightenment.

The British Merchant revitalized the old Scheme of the Trade (1674), which we looked at in Chapter 2, to demonstrate the adverse balance of trade England had prior to the introduction of prohibiting legislation in 1678.[29] Of course, as we have already noted, at least one of the writers for *The British Merchant* was a signatory of the Scheme, namely, Toriano, who wrote: 'Our Trade never was so good before, as it has been since the Prohibition of French Goods.'[30] However, *The Mercator*, rightly, challenged the veracity of the data used by the document. They wrote:

> It is well known, the Plague had in the Year 1665 put an universal stop to all Trade, except such as Necessity forc'd the People to, for meer Provisions. The next Year the Fire of *London* happen'd; and as the Fire began near the waterside, and among the Warehouses and Cellars of the Merchants, the Quantities of *Wines* as well as other Goods which were spoil'd or destroy'd were very great.

This was compounded by the war between France and Holland, which ended only in July 1667. Not surprisingly, then, French imports greatly shot up, temporarily, that year.[31]

Another prominent issue between those who favoured greater liberal trade with France and those that did not was over commerce with Portugal. The Anglo-Portuguese trade treaty of 1703 had been negotiated by one of the original members of the Board of Trade and Plantations, John Methuen. *The British Merchant* claimed this crucial treaty would be undermined if trade commenced again with France. Portuguese commerce had become a vital outlet for British woollen textiles of all types, which would be undermined if the proposed terms of the new Anglo-French Trade Treaty were repealed. It was true France would allow in British-grown and manufactured goods but not items of a re-export nature. This restraint was a real source of contention because Britain would still allow 'all sorts of Goods, of all Countries whatsoever, to be imported upon us from France'. Moreover, France had introduced, as we have seen, an edict prohibiting the importation and use of any East Indian manufactures since 1686, which was a law that was subsequently periodically tightened up – one change even made the importation a capital crime. Trade with Portugal was better since wine was purchased by the proceeds of woollen cloth, thence according to prevailing doctrine, it was as good as having domestically made wine. In addition, French production of woollen textiles had improved so much since 1664, it was claimed, they would no longer want British woollen goods. By contrast, *The Mercator* argued that the only reason British exports to Portugal had increased was due to the recent discovery of gold mines in Portugal-Brazil. It was this, they stated, that allowed them to purchase such items that they had hitherto been unable to. Lastly, contrary to the remark of *The British Merchant*, they argued, once France removed the tariff duties on British woollen textiles they would flood into France.[32]

The debate was about the future basis of British trade, industry and taxation. On the one hand, *The Mercator* claimed that the revenues from the customs made from French goods would lower the burden of the land tax and agriculturally related excised malt. In short, the focus was upon an agrarian oeconomy, revenue from customs and a fixed global market with an emphasis upon productive agricultural labour. By contrast, *The British Merchant* placed the emphasis upon cultivating domestic manufactures, industrial labour and increasing revenues via the excise upon consumption. Here, the future was an industrial oeconomy, revenue from excises and selling increasingly diverse products to the Atlantic market. It was only at this point, at least in print, that a clear demarcation was made between Whig and Tory. The *British Merchant* warned: 'The certain and infallible Consequences of the Bill of Commerce are, that we shall import from *France* a World of Manufactures already wrought to the utmost Perfection.' The unpalatable truth was the superiority of most French manufactures over British manufactures; in their present state, British producers simply would not survive.[33] The same argument, of course, had already been made regarding porcelains from China and cotton cloth from India.

The anti-French sentiment eventually won and the final agreement ensured that the trade between the two countries remained highly regulated for most of the eighteenth century. Prohibiting duties and bans acted to try and keep nearly all French manufactures – except certain necessary items like quality paper and types of glass such as plate that could not as yet be substituted – from the British domestic market. Although an illicit trade in prohibited French goods found their way into the country, the legislation worked well enough to protect and nurture many excised and untaxed British equivalents.[34]

A contentious and prominent issue that had been underlined by the 1713 trade debate, stemmed over the continued taxation of raw materials used for British industry. This constituted something like 15 to over 25 per cent of the total cost of production for most domestic manufactures. A minor concession was given to the textile industries with the abolition of duty on cochineal and some minor dyestuffs in 1714, followed by a reduction in the duty on Turkish raw silk and mohair yarn in 1718. But it was not until Walpole's measures in 1722 that more substantial reductions were made. Implicit within these debates was the issue of drawbacks and the concern that if imported raw materials were re-exported, a foreign country with low duties could get them cheaper than British manufacturers. The argument was particularly relevant to goods for which Britain was an important entrepôt, which were mainly British colonial and Asian commodities destined for Europe, along with British, Asian and European goods going to the British colonies and Africa. Despite the concession of 1714, the greatest complaints remained over drawbacks on dyestuffs, which eventually led to their total abolition under Walpole in 1722.[35] This was a year after the total ban on wearing Indian calico cloth, and can be seen as compensation to the now powerful textile printing industry for the loss of plain

Indian calicoes to print for domestic use. Preventing the re-export of valuable dyes to Britain's competitors would make domestic manufactures more competitive in foreign markets as well as in the home market. This was a government that knew what it was pursuing in terms of trade, industry and taxation.

Walpole's decision in 1722 to remove all export duties on most domestic-produced goods in order to make them more competitive within the foreign arena was also important here. This policy was combined with the abolition or reduction of import duties on foreign materials used in the production of all domestic manufactures. The nurturing and regulation of domestic industry had become the centre of commercial and fiscal policy. The impetus to British industrialization was not new enlightened knowledge but illiberal protectionist measures that allowed technical innovation by erecting a prohibitory wall.

The Americas were simply seen as land for the cultivation of raw materials used to fuel Britain's domestic manufactures, a place to nurture naval supplies and, of course, as a land to grow lucrative slave-produced staple products to feed the addictions of its domestic and foreign markets. Nor should one forget mainland America's importance, especially since the Transportation Act of 1717, as a depository for British convicts and, crucially, as an increasingly important market for British products.

The emphasis upon the American colonies for raw materials led to, for example, one of the authors of *The British Merchant*, Joshua Gee, in partnership with others including Augustus Washington (father of the first president of the United States of America, George Washington), obtaining 12,000 acres in North America to cultivate iron ore. Gee was also a strong advocate for the transportation of domestic convicts and the unemployed poor to aid colonial labour problems. Gee's well-known tract, *The Trade and Navigation of Great Britain Consider'd* (1729), went through numerous editions and reprints during the eighteenth century and was translated into French in 1750.[36] Most British commentators agreed on the lucrative wealth to be made from colonies and controlling as much of the re-export trade as possible.

The aim to increase turnover in foreign trade, primarily colonial re-exports, by expanding London as a free port, continued with tea, coffee and cocoa beans in the early 1720s. This was the successful prequel to Walpole's subsequent doomed excise scheme on wine and tobacco in 1733.[37] Bonded warehouses enabled re-exports to be placed in excise-managed warehouses prior to re-shipment, and therefore avoid the frustration and delay of customs procedures (as well as various scams involving drawbacks). However, in the long run Walpole's policies were not enough to remove obstacles in the way of commercial expansion. Rather, that would come from Lord Chatham's aggressive policies during the 1740s when French competition in the Mediterranean, India, Africa, the West Indies and North America would be taken head-on, culminating in the commencement of the Seven Years War in 1757. Nevertheless, the Walpole era had consolidated the trading, industrial and fiscal structure that would enable successors to fight expensive wars.

Protecting Britain's infant domestic industry from more mature foreign competitors was a clearly recognized, actively pursued and ultimately successful industrial strategy.

The protective barriers allowed manufactures to develop, which enabled the excise to expand and farm industry for important revenues. This made tax collection more efficient and, crucially, relatively predictable compared to customs and the land tax. In turn, this allowed more of the population to be employed, which resulted in the alleviation of the threat of domestic social unrest and of the nation's bullion dwindling, all of which made the country more self-sufficient, compared to its European competitors, at a time when it was so often at war.

It was by first cultivating and securing the home markets from foreign competition that the organized pressure from manufactures opposed to government taxation policies lost much of their bite.[38] Protectionist policies, then, made possible the fertility necessary to nurture domestic manufactures and the subsequent extensive taxing of its fruits, all of which, along with the specification of ingredients, organization of production and system of gauging devised to measure commodities, was important in defining the shape of taxed manufactures.

Merchants originally taught the state to measure and count and, subsequently, the state during the eighteenth century taught manufacturers to measure and count like the state. In this sense, a quantitative spirit during this century was greatly aided by this development, in particular, the Excise. The pragmatism came in the setting of domestic excise rates; here it was up to the manufacturers to lobby and secure the best rate they could at the expense of another domestic industry or within an industry. Britain clearly pursued its revenue as part of a general oeconomic policy. By contrast, as J. F. Bosher points out, France by the eighteenth century 'valued the customs for their financial yield. It treated them primarily as a tax rather than an instrument of economic policy'.[39]

The role of tax in informing a more general oeconomic policy was recognized by contemporaries as early as the late seventeenth century. For example, an anonymous tract of 1689, purported to be by Daniel Defoe, wrote: 'In other kingdoms they place Taxes only to raise Money, and have no regard to the Trade of their Kingdom, that so their Taxes may not prejudice their commerce. But in England care is always had that Impositions may not impede our Trade and Manufactories.' This was done by taxing adverse imports and actively nurturing domestic industry. It 'seems plain', he wrote, 'that some Trade may impair a Kingdom, and such Taxes and Impositions may abate by imposing such Duties as they cannot bear. So far then it will be allowed, that they improve Trade, as we commonly say, saving is Gain; so, if we keep out a destructive Trade by Duties, we may allow that an Improvement of our own.' Tax was also good for increasing employment elsewhere, since by spending the revenues on the navy and army meant work for a significant number of the population in the armed forces.[40]

Unlike the characteristic growth of trade in the seventeenth and early eighteenth centuries, the rapid expansion of commerce from the mid-eighteenth century took with it much of the new produce stemming from Britain's relatively new and sheltered domestic industries. Two English regions especially benefited. First, the West Midlands in terms of the production of metalware, increasing experience in steam engineering for mining, the production of guns to Africa, exports of nails for building purposes in the American colonies and, of course, the new potteries. Secondly, the growth of northwest textile industries that was predominantly export-led and benefited greatly from the ease of waterway access between Manchester and the port of Liverpool. Canals, crucially, solved the issue of energy by making accessible cheap coal from Lancashire's collieries easily available.[41] In addition, Cheshire salt works supplied the fundamental material for the growth of Britain's chemical industry in the northwest.[42] In other words, industrialization in England and Britain was very much a regional affair.[43]

Regional success can partly be explained by a particular regions ability to snatch both growing overseas markets from not only other nations but also *regional* domestic competition. Joseph E. Inikori concludes: 'These leading regions were individually more internally integrated and tied more closely to their overseas markets than they were connected to the other regions in England in the early stages of the process.' The story of Britain's Atlantic trade also sheds light on the technological transformation in Britain. In the words of Jacob Price:

> Just as the British market demand helped create the plantation economies of the West Indies and the more southerly parts of north America, so did overseas demand make necessary or at least hasten the technological transformation of several long-established branches of British industrial life.[44]

Critical to this development was also cheap labour. As European consumers became increasingly addicted to the fruits of Atlantic trade, there was a huge demographic movement of slaves to the colonies. Equally, as production rapidly grew so too did the efficiency of the slave trade; the result was a cheap and regular supply of African slave labour that led to lower production costs and the greater consumption of Atlantic goods in Europe. The significant reduction in prices of plantation products, especially tobacco and sugar, moved them from the status of luxuries confined to the palates of the rich to a mass market. By 1780 the British Caribbean was populated by just over 90 per cent Africans. Again, on mainland British America the production of plantation crops, such as tobacco, rice, indigo, sugar and raw cotton for export, were produced mainly by imported slave labour from Africa.[45] Closer to home the growth of Britain's new manufactures, especially textiles, started to increasingly employ cheap female and child labour.[46] If there was an 'industrious revolution' it was spearheaded by a coerced and distinct part of the labour force – many excluded from the new delights of the marketplace.

In addition to this development was the rapidly expanding thirst for British produced manufactures in New England and among the middle mainland American colonies. These areas lacked the natural resources, compared to the southern colonies, for large-scale plantations; instead they tended to specialize in mercantile activities such as maritime services – most importantly shipbuilding. This nurtured an important consuming market in northern mainland British America; between 1768 and 1772, New England and the middle colonies took between 66 and 72 per cent of its imports exclusively from Britain. By the 1770s over half of Sheffield's cutlery along with other metalwares and West Midland chinaware went to the Americas. This was unique to Britain and had no equivalent in any other European country.[47]

Almost all English-manufactured Atlantic re-exports in the late seventeenth century were of foreign origin. However, by the latter half of the eighteenth century this had dropped to 25 per cent, and by the mid-nineteenth century it constituted just 14 per cent. Spearheading this transition were exports of woollen cloth, mixed cotton textiles followed by metals, potteries and finally the dramatic rise in pure cotton cloth.[48] So, again, the impact upon protecting British industry from foreign competition in the Atlantic trade is clear to see. Even when tobacco and sugar are excluded, nearly 41 per cent of all raw materials imported into Britain between 1814 and 1816 came from the Americas and Africa, including dyestuffs, timber, hides and skins, ingredients for soapmaking and, of course, nearly all the slave-produced raw cotton. If slave-produced sugar and tobacco are also included, between 1784 and 1856 the annual average alternates between 92.2 and 96.6 per cent.[49]

There is no doubt international demand played a crucial role in fuelling the domestic manufactures spearheading the British Industrial Revolution. Despite this, J. V. Beckett and Michael Turner claim certain excises played a regressive role and may have actually slowed down industrialization. They conclude, following Nicholas Crafts, this would explain why the Industrial Revolution, as measured by national economic growth, was more significant after 1830. In other words, the impact of a regressive tax regime may have reduced domestic demand, but the gaining of overseas markets and acquisition of raw materials created a surge in overall national economic growth later in the nineteenth century. This, however, is to ignore the fact many of Britain's industries would not have existed in the first place if they had not been protected and nurtured. Equally, the foreign markets Beckett and Turner emphasize would not have been available without the excise revenue from domestic industry to fund crucial loans needed for imperial expansion and military aggression.[50]

The point here also depends upon what industries you decide to focus upon. Do you concentrate on the more mundane and predominantly domestically consumed and heavily excised, such as malt, beer, soap, leather, glass, leather, paper, spirits and candle-making? Conversely, do you look at the predominantly newer, more dynamic and export-oriented industries like iron, potteries, mixed cottons and later pure cotton textiles (all also protected by prohibitory or high import tariffs and export bounties but either not or lightly excised)? Whatever way you look there is no doubt that protectionism, taxation and the expansion of empire were fundamental factors in Britain's Industrial Revolution.

The combination of repealing duties on imported raw materials, monopolizing colonial trade via the Navigation Acts and Royal Navy, disciplining certain domestic manufactures through excise regulations and surveillance and implementing bounties and drawbacks on home-produced manufactures, all combined to provide a crucial input in the initial shaping of English and British production, and commercial practices. Nor did the Excise necessarily act as an agency of stifling innovation on the more taxed industries. For example, at the start it helped ensure certain goods came up to a particular standard of quality and thereafter regulated via a national system of gauging. The industrial techniques that characterized British industry after 1830 would not have been possible if the prior shape of manufactures sculptured, directly and indirectly, by the government's dominant preoccupation with funding war and sustaining public credit had not evolved. It is also the case that some of the traditional excised-produced goods were eventually undermined, at the expense of those industries traditionally associated with the Industrial Revolution; this became a calculated industrial policy under William Pitt the Younger during the 1780s. It was hoped the wealth and employment from these new, booming export-oriented industries would increase the home consumption of the more established domestic-produced excised goods. These traditional taxed manufactures may not have been as well protected as they once were but, hopefully, were now mature enough to survive. This, to emphasize, would be aided by the growing taxed consumption of the expanding workforce of the new industries.

It is certainly the case that many more people were buying taxed goods at the end of the century than at the start, and this was not simply a result of population growth. To generate revenue from, say, malt, candles, leather, tea, coffee, textiles, spirits, paper, glass, sugar, beer, salt, soap and starch, required people to ideally consume them after they had been manufactured. The taxing of these goods also lends some weight to those historians who have emphasized the importance of the household and the impact of women moving into the manufacturing sector, and therefore no longer being able to produce many of these goods at home. Instead, they bought them from manufacturers, making them potentially much larger sources of revenue. The point here, whether one agrees with it or not, is that income was increasing, people out of necessity were certainly buying more taxed goods and the country's revenues were benefiting. As the one-time excise officer and political radical Thomas Paine wrote in 1792, 'Whatever the [British] constitution may be in other respects, it has undoubtedly been *the most productive machine for taxation that was ever invented*.'[51] So how did Britain's taxation and regulation of manufactures compare to its primary eighteenth-century European competitor, namely, France? This will be the subject of the next chapter.

CHAPTER 6
THE STATE AS ARBITER OF PRODUCTION

The British government's manufacturing knowledge came primarily from the Board of Excise, whose members had a combination of technical training and simple practical knowledge gained from years of experience. This is clearly demonstrated by the correspondence – neglected by historians – between the Treasury and the Excise that the following chapter draws upon. Whenever the former was lobbied by disgruntled producers or whenever the Parliament requested precise information over a manufacturing issue, the Treasury would invariably turn to the Excise for advice. Moreover, their guidance was nearly always acted upon. Clashes between taxed manufacturers and the state over the process of gauging tax, production techniques, procedures and ingredients were typically decided by the knowledge of this body and by the strength of the trade lobbying Parliament. The situation in France also revolved around state regulation, but was much more complicated, opaque and harder to administer. Another advantage Britain had over its main European industrial adversary was an integrated domestic market that could be very easily taxed nationally and prompted to change in a standardized manner; excise taxes were the same throughout the country.

By the last third of the eighteenth century, the role of the British and French states in regulating manufacturing was beginning to come apart, and with it the place of the Excise and the French Bureau of Commerce. In the case of the latter, the Bureau worked with inspectors of manufacturers and guilds as the experienced arbiters of production. Now manufacturers and certain spokesmen in both countries started to stress the need for deregulation and for leaving the producers (via the market) to decide upon the specification of goods; price and variety rather than quality and state certification were coming to the fore. As Philippe Minard explains regarding the French context, 'The regulating regime that functioned in France took only one commercial situation into account: a situation in which competition mainly concerned not price, but quality. Colbert only envisioned a competition over guaranteed quality for top-of-the-line products.'[1] In this sense the consumer's demand was, in theory, fixed at a stationary moment. However, this was only the case had the French state been able to regulate according to its edicts, which in many trades it could not.[2]

The British Excise was experienced in the methods, skills and tools used by the manufacturers they taxed. The Treasury and relevant figures in government trusted the Excise's authority in such matters and therefore looked to them as specialists in such things. After all, they really had no other alternative and, with all decision-making requiring some form of closure, they needed an authority to provide this. The experience of the Excise certified an agreed level of credibility to offer the necessary legitimation to enable this.

In the case of France, the approach to production, spearheaded by the Council of Commerce created in 1700 (changed to the Bureau of Commerce in 1722), was significantly less effectual. In particular, France did not have the institutional framework to intervene in manufacturing quite as successfully as Britain. Trades in the latter could lobby Parliament as a whole and know, if they got parliamentary approval, their concerns would be acted upon nationally. Any change in regulations would be applied across the whole country since the Excise was a national institution, which was not hindered by fragmented regional interests in the way the *commissaires* at the Bureau of Commerce were. Added to this was the simple fact that not only was Britain a nationally integrated market, its geography was also significantly smaller and therefore easier to govern than France.

Many of the problems facing the eighteenth-century French oeconomy were down to the fact that the king was the ultimate source of authority. Moreover, in contrast to Britain's much newer, geographically contained and more unified oeconomy, the French nation was a diffused 'mosaic of conflicting and overlapping jurisdictions, added piecemeal during several hundred years of conquest, marriage, and inheritance'. This made the task of pursuing a coordinated trading, fiscal and industrial policy extremely difficult for the king and his advisors. It meant the Crown frequently had to allow local concessions that prevented applying uniform policies. 'In effect', concludes Hilton L. Root, 'the Crown had to buy off the localities of key local groups [such as local guilds and merchants] by supplying local institutions and acknowledging local privilege'. The Crown in Britain, working through a semi-elected national Parliament, did not face such regional and independent governments. Moreover, there certainly were no internal tariffs disrupting the free flow of domestic trade in Britain; the most notorious example in France being the toll wall of the Farmers-General built around Paris between 1785 and 1788. Members of Parliament could bring local issues to the House of Commons and abide by the decisions made there. Consequently, it was much easier to implement a national tax, trading and manufacturing policy than in France.[3] This is not to say, however, that this was all-enveloping. On the contrary, it could work the other way and the British system could reinforce traditional techniques and procedures. By contrast, the French system of privileges could, sometimes, offset administrative restrictions leading to the prompter diffusion of technological innovations. Nonetheless, the balance was much more favourable to Britain during this period.

The process of industrial decision-making was simply more involved, dispersed and complicated in France than in Britain. When manufacturing queries were raised, they were first sent to the Controller General or Secretary of State for the Navy, who would, in turn, forward them to the *commissaires* at the Bureau of Commerce. This body would then pass them on to merchant-deputies, who were basically representatives of the French mercantile elite. The merchant-deputies would prepare an answer, the *avis*, which would then be discussed by the *commissaires* at a weekly meeting. They would then post the report and their reflections to the relevant provincial intendant and inspector of manufacturer. They, in turn, would meet the local producers and/or guild to discuss it. Their conclusions would subsequently be returned to the *commissaires*, who would vote on the issue and draft an official response. This would then, finally, end up on the desk of the Controller General or Secretary of State for the Navy (or both). If it was a particularly difficult technical issue, advice would be sought from either the French Academy of Sciences or the Parisian craft guilds. By contrast, such an awkward and lengthy process was not so characteristic of the British approach. France's extensive procedure – which was made even more complicated by the hiring of legal lobbyists in Paris to present the point of view of the local guilds if it had manufacturing implications – could take months or even years to complete. However, this is not to generalize across all trades and this issue was taken on by the French Director-General of the Finances, Jacques Necker, in 1779 and, at least, in the case of textiles the process was speeded up.[4]

Further, the urgency of creating and sustaining domestic manufacturers was simply not such an issue in France as it was in Britain. For one thing the country already had a robust industrial base. Thus, when Jean-Baptiste Colbert, Controller-General of French Finances, introduced his edict in the second half of the seventeenth century, it was with the assumption that domestic industry in top-of-the-line goods had already reached the desired level of quality and therefore needed preserving. His concern at this time was particularly with Dutch and Italian competition and thus the need to further protect existing French industry. Driven by the aggressive ambitions of Louis XIV, the demand for gold and silver bullion kept increasing. Thence, under Colbert's direction, a series of policies were introduced to further stimulate French industry, especially the promotion of export-oriented luxury goods, the reinforcement of guilds to police quality, huge hikes in protective tariffs and the introduction of a national body of inspectors of manufactures.[5]

The inspectors were created to ensure that the right raw materials, number and length of yarns, along with dyeing and finishing were all done correctly. If the standard was met, it would gain a mark in the form of a lead seal, which became the symbol of market trust. All that Colbert introduced was a codification, via a legal statute, of what already existed within manufacturing customs.[6] He was underlining the strength of French industry and the need to preserve its leadership in certain trades. Likewise, Britain followed the example set by France and implemented a similar protectionist and regulatory policy to industrialization – although in an attempt to nurture and, at least to begin with, promote the quality of an item. Lead seals were also applied to British woollen textiles but, in the case of excised manufactures, verification of products was simply via a national excise stamp.

Unlike woollen cloth, textiles such as linen, fustians and cotton were *nationally* regulated by the Excise. For most home-produced goods, the nationwide Excise was the key institution of regulation; this normally entailed close control of manufactures at the site of production by this institution. By contrast, much of the regulation and measurement of goods in France took place at the local guild office or internal toll stands. In Britain this was not altogether a one-way process but involved, certainly to begin with, attempting to create or elevate the products of infant industries. The brutal truth was that no end of regulation was good enough if the product did not reach a certain intrinsic quality. The Excise knew this and so did the legal trader and smuggler. This is not to generalize across all taxed items, but it was certainly the case regarding woollen textiles just referred to and excised goods such as other textiles, paper, leather, soap, beer, glass, spirits and candles. It was not until after the Seven Years War (1757–63) that regulation took on a much more mechanical approach and became far less concerned with a nurturing component.

The eventual method and form of gauging established a correlation between the product and the revenue demands of the state. In this way the Excise, to begin with, worked as a kind of mediator between producer and Parliament's revenue concerns that roused disputation but also permitted compromise, production change and sometimes inertia; this was acceptable as long as the protective tariff exceeded the excise. It also made the Excise, the Treasury's and government's foremost source of experience concerning knowledge of manufacturing.[7]

There were many features of the Excise administration that were novel for the period and revolved upon effective surveillance and execution. For example, prospective excise officers had to go through a period of technical training in the art of measuring goods followed by a written and practical test; a degree of merit rather than mere connection was required. The excise officer was also deliberately plucked from areas suitably distant from his tax round to ensure his face was unknown in his place of business. In other words, his relationship with the local community, at least to begin with, was not based on familiarity but anonymity. To ensure this process was sustained, the officer, after a specified period, was duly removed to serve another district. This was in contrast, for instance, to the collection of the land tax, which was maintained by locally respected landed figures.[8]

In recasting trust and objectivity in this way, the Excise pursued a rigorous method of reflexive endeavour and practice. The whole process involved in the production of a taxed good had to be detectable, in theory, to the excise officer. They, thus, had to have a complete knowledge of the manufacturing process of all taxed goods. In turn, the excise officer's own activities and method had to be visible to his watchful superior's and, indeed, to the manufacturer. Clear rules enabled regularization across the country and therefore a seeming equity in the Excise approach. This also demanded the creation and maintenance of a similar quality of product. For this reason, and equally for administrative efficiency, the Excise far preferred industrial monopolies in the sense manufacturers tended to concentrate within certain regions. Therefore, standardized products were as much state-driven as they were by producers and/or consumers. Manufacturers turned to quantification because they had to learn to calculate like the state. Consequently, the quantitative spirit was as much instigated by the state as by simply enlightened individuals applying it to further their manufacturing endeavours.[9]

Disputes centring upon the trade and manufacture of such addictive goods as tea, sugar, tobacco, spirits and beer, along with increasingly necessary items like soap, candles, leather, certain textiles, paper, starch, glass and malt, saw contests between the standards and stipulations of the state and those defined by local customs, public preferences and deliberate acts of evasion. It was a place where the law sought to make the practices and spaces of manufacturers and merchants observable through regularized laws, inspection, product qualities, procedures, weights, measures and product packaging. It was within this nexus that the visible hand of the state – via its revenue departments – implemented and gained an empirical knowledge and understanding of manufactures. Consequently, it increasingly bred experienced revenue officers who could illuminate this process.

This was an interfering strategy to force manufacturers to improve the quality, or simply to regularize production to ease national gauging, of the product. Thus, initially, the Excise not only had to gather revenue from these young and highly protected industries but also, in some cases, help to ensure their survival and improve their products to meet continental and illicit rivals; superior choice and the black market obviously cost the government considerable revenues. As such, was the manufacturer really capable of producing what he or she purported to produce? Were the right mordants and dyes being used in the production of textiles (poor ones would rinse away after one wash)? Was the leather correctly tanned and really from the stated animal? Was the paper of the designated quality? Were the candles made from the fat or oil stated and thus from the class they purported to be from? Were the hops being used of the required quality? And was the soap really made of the specified ingredients and the certified size? As a memorial written in 1719 on the state of contraband trade between France and England concluded: 'The true remedy against these evils, is to encourage the Manufactures already established, and establish those that are wanting in this kingdom of which now come from France at no considerable rates.'[10] In other words, the true remedy was to work harder at imitating French imports behind a protective trade barrier.

From its establishment in the mid-seventeenth century, the Excise gradually evolved into an ever more systematic institution that helped shape production and markets. This, in turn, informed state policy as it responded to the particularities of manufacturing (including the nature of the commodity itself). This reveals how the state, through the Excise, created an effective framework for the rise of industrial capitalism, while supplying itself with revenues necessary to protect and guide this development. This was an essential reciprocity that was crucial to Britain's fiscal base and thence military power. The relatively young institutional oeconomic framework born of the mid-seventeenth-century English Revolution, Restoration period and later Glorious Revolution was integral to this evolution. Unlike France, British excise regulations had to ultimately pass through Parliament. This not only allowed some manufacturing trades to lobby MPs, but also offered a level of credibility to the legislation.[11] No such opportunity existed for French manufacturers.

In France, the king's authority may have been absolute but this did not, of course, equate to his ability to exercise absolute power. As Harold T. Parker writes: 'In the interests of assuring obedience the French kings had negotiated bargains, contracts, and understanding with the towns, the provinces, and the leading privileged classes of clergy, nobles, merchants, and manufactures.' The result was a maze of diverse 'local laws, local tolls and tariffs, local weights and measures, privileged exemptions from taxation and quartering troops, and privileged monopolies of manufacture and trade'. This also made it much harder for the king to build up fiscal credibility; since power was concentrated in the king, he could renounce his debts whenever he liked, which was something impossible to do in both Britain and the Netherlands.[12] Moreover, the Minister of Finance and his department were dependent upon venal accountants, who owned their offices, to ensure the collection and spending of revenue. They were extremely hard to control and operated as private individuals rather than public officials.[13] All this gave much greater control to British governments when it came to making budgets, policy and planning ahead. The situation in France made it impossible to pursue such a 'rational' system of indirect taxation or have anywhere near such a clear knowledge of revenue income and expenditure.[14]

Although there was no equivalent to the Excise in France, they did have the Inspectorate of Manufactures that was created by Colbert in the seventeenth century. This body became the focus of intense criticism by the new liberal critics of manufacturing policy during the eighteenth century. Colbert began reorganizing the rules regulating textile production in 1669, commencing with a general code for woollen textiles that set standards for its products that included the 'size of the pieces, quality of the raw materials, number and section of yarns, dyeing, and finishing' right across France. This attempt at a unified approach was then applied to all top-end French textiles, with the Corps of Inspectors established soon after to try and enforce the stipulations. If the item was approved it was given an inspection mark in the form of a lead seal fixed to the edge of the product. In contrast to British excised goods, this was both harder to institutionally enforce nationally and, for the less unified French trades, especially difficult to lobby for changes.[15]

It was not till 1704 that the inspectors of manufacturers came under the control of the fairly new Council of Commerce and, from 1722, rebranded Bureau of Commerce. Until this point the Crown did not even know who the inspectors were or the source of their salaries. From this point on the *commissaires* made sure the inspectors conducted their surveys and submitted their biannual reports. The inspectors, along with the local intendants, subsequently became the council's key source of commercial information and tool of regulation. The provincial intendants were, claims David Smith, extremely important in communicating 'with the local royal and municipal officials who investigated or clarified the local contexts that might affect a decision'. As such the intendants were the primary liaison 'between the Parisian administration and administrative officials throughout France with regard to commercial and manufacturing policy'. The relationship between the intendants, inspectors and Bureau of Commerce, and manufacturers became an increasingly close and important one throughout the century.[16]

Prior to, and in addition to, the role of inspectors and intendants, the French approach also demanded a great deal of self-regulation, which was done by the *Gardes-Jurés* (guildsmen elected by their colleagues). They had the duty of preventing the sale of cloth that did not meet the specified standards. Once a month they were also expected to inspect the shops of journeymen and master manufacturers to ensure, for example, their looms fitted the particular sizes ordained by regulations. The policing did not stop here and another check was made by merchants in the Bureaux de Contrôle, which was situated where the cloth was retailed. These two seals, one by the guild and the other by the merchants, confirmed the cloth met the official standards and place of origin. The item was then allowed to be freely sold.[17]

Any cloth that failed to meet these standards was seized by the *Gardes-Jurés*, while local mayors or aldermen then decided whether the seizure was permanent and or the level of fine to be imposed upon the manufacturer. The regulating system also provided internal checks on the officers and judges to ensure they were doing their jobs. The process of marking within the guild system had been around for centuries, but Colbert's innovation was to try and standardize the process and create a body of inspectors to police each region. This was the first time a national institution, stemming from central administration, had been created to manage the system. The new establishment expanded and became a dense group of men that were concentrated within designated jurisdictions.[18]

The similarity between the structure of the Bureau of Commerce and the Excise is clear in a number of key areas. Like the Excise, the bureau, under Daniel Trudaine between 1749 and 1769, had an inspection system structured by a hierarchy of inspectors and sub-inspectors. They were also, like the Excise, more disciplined than other French bodies since they did not own their posts. However, pay, unlike the Excise, was predominantly from income produced via fees charged, in this case, for marking goods. Nonetheless, claims Minard, compared to other French state officials, the bureau embodied characteristics that 'gave it the status of civil service decades before such a service was formerly established during the Revolution'. The French inspectors defended their role by describing their work as safeguarding the public interest concerning the standard of items. In addition, the goods had to meet a recognized quality because without this they could not export and meet rival foreign equivalents.[19] The consumer needed to trust that the item was what it purported or else trade would collapse. This was the rationale behind the mark.

From this perspective, the Bureau of Commerce and inspectors of manufactures were there to protect consumers and prevent manufacturers cutting corners to produce an inferior product. This was clearly a role the Excise shared in Britain; some form of regulation ensured product credibility and therefore consumer trust. Consequently, it was the role of the state, as a perceived neutral arbiter, to prevent the corruption of goods by enforcing a set of standards confirmed by a mark of guarantee and also to teach producers best practices. There was thus a twofold policy: on the one hand, to regulate the production process and, on the other, to encourage industrious manufacturers to produce goods that met an expected standard. French manufacturers had evolved under a different set of circumstances to Britain; on the one hand, many of their top-of-the-line items were simply older and predominantly superior and, on the other, they were not so intrinsic to the country's fiscal system.

In most trades Britain was a great deal more nationally integrated and, to begin with, flexible, because it had to be; unlike France, Britain was more industrially backward and European survival demanded revenues generated by trade and, especially, industrial development. To ease the volatile relationship between producers and the Excise required the creation of a new means of collection. The general unpopularity of the excise tax among the population since its introduction by Parliament during the English Civil War made it vulnerable, which was perhaps one factor behind its particular bureaucratic structure and practices. In the words of Theodore Porter, 'The drive to supplant personal judgement by quantitative rules reflects weakness and vulnerability.'[20] However, in the case of the Excise three features were more important: first, the fact that such rules enabled *regularization* across the country, thus making it appear equitable; secondly, an attempt to create and sustain a certain *national quality of product*; and, thirdly, to ease *administrative efficiency and policing*.

Consider the impact of the Excise on the early-eighteenth-century fledgling spirit industry. The distillery claimed the well-known excise authority, public lecturer and astronomer Charles Leadbetter 'is the very *Apex*, or highest Pitch that can be aimed at by man in Gauging'. As well as being the author of numerous editions of *The Royal Gauger* (1739), he taught manufacturers to count and measure like the state in public lectures at the Head and Pen in Cock Lane, close to the Thames in Shoreditch.[21]

The tax on spirits was made on the 'wash' just before the first distillation; the wash contained all the legally specified materials used in the production of a spirit – the type and mix of grain, malt and water that on fermentation was termed the 'wort'. The officer first noted the quantity of wash and then made a charge on the amount of spirits that would be distilled from it. In other words, a certain number of gallons of wash produced a specific quantity of spirit, which meant the tax would be paid both upon this amount and, crucially, its strength. The latter was ascertained by various techniques till an arbitrary standard calibrated into a hydrometer was adopted in the mid-eighteenth century. The original legislation of 1698 ruled that a distiller had one month to demolish any concealed vessels, pipes, stop-cocks, or holes in the wash-back (where the wort is fermented), and any secret warehouses. If he did not, and was caught, the producer would be fined £100.[22]

As with all Excise products, the officer had to map the distillery by drawing and describing all the relevant details of production – from the places of the various utensils to the positions, lengths and directions of the vast array of pipes. This was vital for ensuring that much of the production process was visible to the officer and thus open to inspection; obviously illicit activities were a constant threat to the revenue.[23] To aid the Excise in this task, the pipe carrying wort or wash had to be red, the pipe carrying low wines or feints had to be blue, while spirits had to be pumped along white pipes and water through black ones. This strict set of procedures again reveals the extent to which the Excise went in organizing the space of the distillery. If the officer suspected any distiller of evading these regulations, he was allowed, day or night (with a constable), to break up the ground and walls of the distillery and search for illicit pipes. An extensive level of quality control was also involved: brewers were strictly told not to use 'unlawful and unwholesome Ingredients' in their beer. For example, an act of 1698 legislated that no brewer or retailer of beer or ale could use 'any molasses, course sugar, honey or composition of sugar'; if found using such ingredients he could be fined £100. In addition, he could not use other 'unwholesome ingredients' such as foreign grains, *Guinea* pepper, essentia brine, coculus indiae, broom, wormwood or any other bitter substance.[24]

The Excise's technique of gathering revenue became gradually more fearsome over the course of the eighteenth century. The officer surveying textile printers was told to measure the distance between his home and the site of production, in order to gauge the time it would take him to get there. At the printers he had to 'keep a Dimension or White Book' for taking an immediate account of all the goods the printer received from the drapers or other sources. More specifically, he had to enter the name of each proprietor and record 'the Lengths and Breadths of all the Silks, Silk-Handkerchiefs, Calicoes, and Linens, under their respective Titles, as fast as they are measured'. On surveying a printer's workhouse or warehouse he then had to take a note of the number of tables being used, the kind of goods being printed, followed by a precise measurement of 'the exact Length and Breadth of every Piece of every Kind, and in a frame prepared for that Purpose, fairly to imprint the Length upon each Piece of Calico, and also the Breadth, if over or under the Statute, on the End thereof'. To ensure quality, it was important the officer made 'quick Returns, on your Traders, at Times unexpected' in order to check, for instance, that the printer was not using inferior and illegal dyes. To do this, he could normally tell by the preparation of the cloth, by the intensity of the colour or by tasting the cloth. It was obviously fundamental that an officer had the ability to distinguish different types of cloth, which was something born from experience.[25]

Taxed manufactured textiles such as the above were marked at each end by an Excise stamp. If they were found without such a mark then the cloth was 'forfeited', and taken to the local Custom House or Excise Office where it would be sold to the highest bidder. For such a crime the manufacturer would be fined £200, while if the owner tried to bribe an officer to mark the textiles without payment of tax, a fine of £100 would be levied coupled with two hours in the pillory. However, the worst crime a manufacturer could commit would be to counterfeit the Excise seal, which was 'deemed felony, without benefit of clergy'. A similar set of regulations surrounded printed silks and linens and, again, if any used a counterfeit stamp they would 'suffer death as felons'.[26]

The Excise ruled that a good quality tallow candle must legally 'be half sheep's tallow, and half bullock's', while the production of common candles had to be either moulded or dipped. A manufacturer had to pay an annual licence and varying duties depending upon the quality of the candle. As well as making a detailed map of all the candle maker's utensils and the layout of the workhouse and storehouse, the Excise officer had the power 'to have entrance on demand, between five in the morning and eleven at night, with or without a constable' (during the night a constable was required). Before production could commence, the chandler had to inform the excise officer and provide precise details of the mould, size and number of times he intended to fill it. If he did not he would have to pay £50, and if he manufactured candles in a secret location he would be fined £100. The maker also had to supply robust fastenings to furnaces, coppers, pans and other utensils that he was not allowed to use without informing the excise officer. If he failed to comply and was caught, he would be fined £100.[27]

The pattern was similar for all excised manufactures. For example, the officer was allowed at all times (at night in the presence of a constable) to enter a papermaker's premises, and make a note of all the rags and other materials found there. A ream of paper was to consist of twenty quires, and each quire to be of twenty-four sheets, while a bundle of paper was to have forty quires. If a ream or bundle did not match this requirement, the producer would be fined £50, and to confirm the legality of the paper the officer would stamp it.[28] If the producer used a counterfeit stamp he would be fined a crippling £550 as, for example, befell the papermaker George Blackman in 1801. The instructions did not stop here: all the paper had to be tied and wrapped in an elaborate and defined way, and the excise officer could at any time open a ream or bundle of paper to check that it was the quality specified.[29]

Soap manufacturers were strictly forbidden to 'set up, alter, or make use of any boiling-house, work-house, warehouse, &c. for making, or keeping sope, nor use any copper, kettle, fat, &c. without first giving notice thereof in writing at the next office'. If caught breaking any of these rules, the manufacturer would be fined £50. Again, producers had to supply locks and covers for all their utensils, while soap frames had to be 2 inches thick and not above 45 inches in length or 15 inches or more in breadth. If the manufacturer was found illegally manufacturing soap, he would be fined £100 and have all the produce seized. Waste from the manufacturing process, including the question of what constituted waste, was an ongoing problem in soapmaking and glass production. Soapmakers were allowed one pound in ten as compensation for waste. If the manufacturer was suspected of using illicit pipes to siphon soap, the excise officer, as in the case of spirits and beer, was allowed to smash up the manufacturer's floor (all pipes had to be above ground). Moreover, if the producer was found guilty of illicitly siphoning lees or soap, the person would be fined £50. The tax was charged by weight; additionally, hard soap had to be made into specified shaped cakes or bars.[30]

Though the production of British spirits remained fairly static between 1723 and 1820, the excise rate and efficiency in gathering such revenue greatly increased during this same period. This led to the percentage of total excise revenue generated by spirits increasing from 3 per cent in 1723 to nearly 10 per cent in 1820. Spirits and, especially, beer and malt were the most important excises; although this significantly decreased as the other excised manufactures, developing behind protective tariffs, greatly expanded. Thus, between 1746 and 1825 the production of printed textiles increased by 4,300 per cent, leather by 122 per cent, candles by 265 per cent and soap by 310 per cent. All this, of course, generated a significant amount of extra excise revenue.[31]

The success of the Excise was particularly due to its eventual achievement in taxing goods at the point of production, and encouraging larger and fewer producers preferably combining in a particular region. This made revenue collection cheaper through a more efficient use and allocation of employees, it created greater consensus among manufacturers about the equitable nature of gauging techniques and increased specialization among excise officers. Through its technical emphasis, crucial support from the legislature, protectionist policies and, ultimately, backing from the army, the Excise overcame rival calculative agencies. This enabled the boundaries of excise extraction to be stable enough to sustain its revenue-generating capability. The following chapter will continue with this last theme and further concentrate upon the imperative, but rather overlooked, intersection between the revenue demands of the state and the evolution of domestic manufacturers.

CHAPTER 7
BALANCING TAX AND INDUSTRY: THE REGULATION OF DOMESTIC MANUFACTURES

By the second half of the eighteenth century, many of Britain's formerly backward industries had reached a more robust state. This, in summary, was primarily the result of state protectionism and regulation, the arrival of a significant number of skilled foreign immigrants, combined with a huge increase in global trade and colonial expansion guarded by state-funded maritime might. Added to this was labour exploitation (slaves, women and children), an element of encouragement via patents, premiums and bounties, a unique ecological environment and, in some cases, via the actual process of excise gauging.

The Excise was the most important revenue-generating body that lay at the heart of public credit and therefore Britain's power. The hardest balance was weighting the incidence of inland tax and customs tariffs, with the aim of nurturing and aiding the health of domestic industry and employment. By the close of the Seven Years War (1756–63), the unprecedented level and expansion of the excise became a leading financial concern for certain domestic manufactures.[1] By this point the level of tax had become a highly significant factor in total production costs.

It was certainly the case that by 1785 22 per cent of the total cost in manufacturing paper was via the excise.[2] In terms of the net yield made in revenues, paper generated £133,000 per annum in 1795 and a staggering £570,000 in 1825. Clearly, by this stage the ratio of tax to total production costs had also significantly increased.[3] Where figures are available the same could be seen in other excised products: For example, the annual net revenue from leather in 1800 was £250,000 and a monstrous £605,000 in 1825. The figures from net glass revenue are also telling with the excise generating £171,000 per annum in 1800 and £620,000 by 1825.[4] The duty paid for soap in 1816 was 6d. per pound making the levy on the article 100 per cent of its price. However, once the taxes on its materials such as tallow, barilla and turpentine are also included the cost of the tax was between 120 and 130 per cent of the product. The gross yield from soap in 1815 was £747,759.[5] Not surprisingly, the principles behind the method used to gauge tax at the site of production became increasingly contested. Within this context experiments to test arguments over levels of precision and accuracy of measurement became ever more utilized.

Consider the case of glass. During the eighteenth century the prime factor influencing the location of glass manufactures was the availability of coal. The cost of transporting fuel was hugely expensive prior to the extensive building of canals and later railways. Instead, it made sense to invest in locating manufacturing as close to the key material of production, in this case coal, and the lesser ingredients such as sand, alkali and clay. This was the case for most domestic industry. The perceived shortage of timber, which had become an increasing concern during the Elizabethan period, had triggered pre-Newtonian experiments by iron producers to try and smelt iron using coal. The attempt during the seventeenth century to remove impurities from iron by devising the reverberating furnace (keeping iron ore and fuel separate), developed by Thomas Percival, proved largely unsuccessful in iron production. However, it was found acceptable in meeting the requirements of glassmakers. This was probably out of desperation after James I banned the use of timber as a source of energy for glass production. As early as 1612 a coal-fired furnace in Southwark was producing green glass for windows.[6]

During the early seventeenth century the story of glass was dominated, until the English Civil War, by the naval admiral, administrator and courtier Sir Robert Mansfield (sometimes also referred to as Mansell). Through his fraudulent activities as Treasurer of the Navy, Mansfield amassed a fortune that he invested in various trading ventures, including the purchase of a monopoly for glass production. Here he pumped at least £30,000 into improving his London Southwark works by eliminating impurities in the glass such as unevenness and spots. He initially used Scottish coal due to its having lower content of sulphur and, thus, less adverse impact in discolouring the glass. However, this superior quality coal was extremely expensive and awkward to transport. As a result, Mansfield shifted his glass furnaces to Newcastle-upon-Tyne, where there was still reasonably good quality coal that was extremely accessible. The move was successful and provided the foundations to the Northeast glass industry.[7] In spite of the initial limitations in transporting coal, other early glass centres included London, Gloucester and, eventually, southwest Lancashire. This last region had local access to Cheshire salt and the right type of sand; crucially it was in easy reach of the required type of coal after the opening of the Sankey canal in the late 1750s.[8]

The history of glass production in Britain is a disjointed story prone to stops and starts. An attempt to excise the domestic manufacture of glass to aid the war with France was tried in 1695, halved in 1698 and totally removed the following year. The 1695 Act had triggered a number of petitions and generated a great deal of noisy parliamentary discussion. A committee on glass duties reported in 1695 that the tax would fail to generate much revenue due to the levy on coal being too much, and thus, the owners of mines finding it uneconomical to dig out. Consequently, since coal had become the primary fuel for making glass many manufactures were therefore already being hit hard. The report claimed: 'Glass-houses at Gloucester have been obliged to extinguish their fires' since they could no longer afford to purchase the taxed coal. Similarly, another report, the following year, concluded that duties on glass did much more damage than the revenues they generated.[9]

The industry simply was not yet capable, skilled or large enough to be taxed safely. John Cary complained in his *Essay on Trade* in 1695:

> I fear the glass-makers will now groan under the excise, especially those in and about London, who have another load by the duty on coals, besides the swarms

of officers to which we lay open the houses of those men, who deserve all the encouragement we can give them and ought to have things made as easy to them as may be.[10]

One petition warned that the bill would lead to the emigration of the limited number of English skilled glass workmen and artificers abroad. Another commentator claimed that since the duty had started, a number of established glass-houses had closed and, eventually, all would be forced to shut down. The petition reiterated the warning that glass-houses were uprooting and setting to work abroad, in this case in Holland. They proposed that alternative items be considered for tax such as soap, lead, hemp, flax or an additional levy upon the post.[11]

However, a pamphlet purporting to answer the glassmakers petitions accused them of inventing the whole situation. The author(s) claimed, 'For at the same time that they affirm want of Demand for Goods occasion'd them to put out their Fires, the want of Goods is so great among them, that the prices of all Glass are considerably risen.' It was true, the author(s) wrote, that the demand for bottles, particularly in Gloucester and Sturbridge, had diminished, but this was due to the fact that cider had suffered a two-year problem in supply. In addition, contrary to the glassmakers complaints, far from there being that many workmen involved in glassmaking, the number amounted to no more than 800. In short, the pamphlet concluded, 'the Glass-Makers to make good their Petition are forced to fly to Fictions and Falsities'.[12] Nonetheless, legislation was passed in 1697 to reduce the duties upon glass – along with tobacco pipes and stone and earthen wares.[13]

This, however, was not enough for the glassmakers who continued to lobby Parliament to do more. As a result, a House of Commons Committee was set up in 1698 to examine the flurry of these petitions, and interviewed a number of glass producers. They concluded that the remaining duty was indeed having a dire impact upon the industry. Not only would the tax destroy the infant industry but also lessen the revenues from coal, since the glassmakers would no longer be there to purchase the fuel. Equally worrying was the wooing of the 'best Workmen … into foreign Parts, where there is great Encouragement given: Many are already gone; and many more will soon go, if the Duty be not taken off'. The House read the report twice and agreed that the remaining duties upon glass should be, and subsequently were, removed.[14]

Despite the repeal of all the glass duties it was still not enough for the manufacturers. A petition from the glassmakers in and around the City of London in 1699 persisted in emphasizing the detrimental impact the duties upon coal were having upon the competitiveness of English glassmaking in general. To import a chaldron of coal into London from the Northeast was not cheap and provided another reason for Newcastle being such a great location for glassmaking. The petitioners, and this was the real point, also wanted much higher duties placed upon all imported glass. This was the key to developing domestic glass with the same true for all domestic infant industries. For example, thanks to protectionist duties as early as the 1720s two-thirds of all home-consumed paper was now British.[15]

The excise tax on glass was not revived until 1746 when the Prime Minister, Henry Pelham, desperate for new revenues to help pay for the costs of crushing the 1745 Scottish rebellion, reintroduced the duty. In addition, taxes were also placed upon the imported materials used in the production of glass, although to ease the pain, further protective tariff duties were put on all imported glass. Thus, despite these new inland levies, British glass was now well protected from foreign competition and continued to make headway.

As with all products that were excised the process of gauging was intricate and extensive. First, since the manufacturing process and the materials used for the various types of glass differed, the system of measurement also varied. For example, crown glass used kelp, barilla, pot ash, Lynn sand and cullet. It was then heated, blown into a globular form and finally flattened into a circular table. Plate glass used saltpetre, and was heated for thirty hours before also being flattened. Flint glass needed forty hours of heating, while the production of bottles needed lime, wood ashes, iron surf and either sea or river sand.[16]

All glassmakers had to map their premises to indicate where all the furnaces, pots, pot chambers, warehouses and rooms were. A map of this was then kept at the front of the excise officers Dimension Book. The officer had to enter 'the Numbers and Dimensions of all your *Glass-makers* Pots for melting Materials for making of GLASS, *viz.* their Depth and Diameters, taken at proper Places, and from those Dimensions the Areas and content of each Pot must be truly calculated and tabled'.[17] Officers had to survey glass-houses four or five times a day. The gauge was made upon the weight of 'metal' (the fluid materials) in the respective pots.[18]

Glass petitioning seems to have increased again during the 1760s over the excise process of gauging and the thorny issue of accounting for waste during production. In April 1760 glassmakers from Stourbridge, Liverpool, Warrington, Dudley and Glassborough lobbied for the method of measuring glass tax to change to a process that simply charged the end product. Similarly, several manufacturers of crown glass, flint glass and glass bottles from the Bristol area complained over the procedure of drawback. The end product that the drawback was gauged upon, they claimed, was a great deal lighter than the original levy. This was because 'there is no Provision made in the said Act for any allowance of the Duty on Account of the Metal spoiled in preparing the materials for making of glass'. As usual the matter was passed from the Treasury to the Excise who dismissed both concerns.[19]

The issue over the incidence of waste continued to gain momentum, particularly after another rise in duties was placed on the necessary raw materials in the mid-1760s. The burden of debt generated by the Seven Years War was forcing excises up everywhere. The duty was now 9s. 4d. per hundredweight on all materials or metal used in preparation for making crown, plate and flint glass. A memorial of flint glassmakers was concerned at the loss of one of its former practices carried out to rectify waste. Typically, when the metal was gathered from the pots a significant amount 'is spoilt and rendered unfit for that time to be made into ware'. Traditionally, they had been allowed to return this waste back to the pots; however, such a practice had been recently banned by the Excise who claimed glassmakers were illicitly filling their pots.[20]

The flint glassmakers turned to 'age-old experiment' to justify their argument:

The manufacturers of flint glass find that the present Allowance is not equal to the loss sustained for upon the nearest calculations for many years past, and by Experiments lately made, the waste so far exceeds the allowance, that the Duty upon all flint glass really manufactured and finished for sale, amounted on an average to upwards of 14 s. per Hundred.

They also challenged the credibility of the Excise calculations, claiming 'there are some very material Errors in the Manner of Gauging Pots'. For example, one glassmaker from Stourbridge kept a record of measurements from 5 April to 10 May 1766, and claimed that the Excise had over-weighed the materials in his pots by a cumulative total of just over 36 lbs. The memorialists suggested that one-third of the glass materials be allowed as waste or the final product be weighed and charged duty. The latter, they argued, would remove all controversy over the problem of waste. However, the Excise dismissed the glassmakers' suggestion and the whole issue of waste continued to be a major source of controversy.[21]

In February 1773 the House of Commons received a report from a committee set up to examine a petition from Major-General Charles Fitzroy, Admiral Philip Affleck and eleven others to set up a glass company, aided by public money, for the production of casting plate glass in England. It was a bold, extremely expensive and risky venture; for at least eighty years the French plate glass works at St Gobain had lacked any serious competitor. In 1773 it was estimated that between £60,000 and £100,000 of plate glass was imported into Britain from France.[22] A key witness, Philip Besnard, on behalf of the petitioners, was a plate glassmaker from the global leader in this product. He argued it would be possible for an equally proficient industry to be developed in England to match that of the French. He estimated that the cost of setting up a plate glass manufactory would be £50,000, 'but that English glass would be cheaper to produce than the French and therefore advantageous to national trade'. His main argument was that all the primary raw materials, except barilla (the source of soda), were easily available. Moreover, the cost of production would be cheaper because the English used coal unlike the French who used timber. This was not because of a lack of French foresight – the St Gobain manufacturers certainly did experiment with coal; rather, the abundant availability of timber and absence of an adequate supply of domestic coal convinced the French to give up the idea.[23]

By contrast, the leading incentive to nurture a British plate glass factory at Ravenhead was the availability of cheap coal from the local Lancashire collieries. Further evidence promoting the plate glass project came from glassmakers engaged in the production of blowing plate glass, who confirmed that much larger panes could be made via casting than their method. The following month the House of Commons agreed to pass a bill to promote the company and thus commenced the introduction of the cast plate glass industry into Britain.[24]

The newly incorporated British Cast Plate Glass Company would eventually succeed in making this type of glass. One of the first things done was to import skilled French labour over and create a workforce of between 3,000–4,000 men.[25] A seemingly clear impetus came four years after its establishment when further assistance came to the domestic glass industry in general, after Lord North repealed the duties on imported materials used in production. And, just for good measure, further prohibiting duties were placed on the importation of wrought or manufactured glass. The catch, however, was a doubling of excise rates on material used in the production of most domestically produced glass later that year.[26]

The company were quick to protest over this massive tax increase. The allowance made in the new act was a quarter of the metal used that, they claimed, was hopelessly inadequate. Instead, they strongly argued it should be half. This would put them on a fair footing with all other types of domestic manufacturers of glass, whose method of production generated a great deal less waste than they did. It was also the case, they pointed out, that the law made no reference to the small pots used by cast plate producers since such pots were not used by those who made blown glass. The prevailing method required the large pots to be emptied into the smaller ones and thus an allowance should also be applied to these pots.[27]

In February 1779 the Excise sent their response to the petition to the Treasury. Their verdict was damning of the new glass company. They argued the problem of waste was less to do with the level of allowance and much more to do with the 'deficiencies' and 'the inexperience and improper management of the workmen'. This situation had to improve, the Excise commissioners claimed, and with it the loss of waste would greatly drop. In general, they concluded, the complaints of the plate glassmakers over the loss that occurred in the preparation of the plates for sale after being cast was not hugely different to other makers of glass. As such an additional allowance would give them an advantage over other types of domestic glass.[28]

Further excise rises upon glass came in 1779, 1781 and 1782. The British Cast Plate Company was again first to voice their concerns in the summer of 1782. The subject was, once again, over the issue of waste. The memorialists claimed to have carried out extensive experiments over the past three years to calculate the amount of waste they had sustained, all of which was done, they wrote, 'with the strictest attention, under the vigilant eye of an intelligent and experienced manager'. The results demonstrated, they concluded, that beyond doubt the waste 'is not to be imputed to the inexperience and improper management of workmen' as was suggested by the Excise three years earlier. The average waste after the pot had been gauged, they again underlined, was in fact half and not a quarter as the Excise claimed. By contrast, they added, a quarter was quite adequate for the production of blown glass, and thus by allowing them a half would simply be putting them on a level with producers of this latter type of glass.[29]

Once again, the Excise dismissed the memorialists argument claiming their own experienced officers believed that the allowance for loss in waste was on parity with other types of glass produced.[30] Meanwhile a parliamentary committee was created to examine the cast plate glassmakers' complaints and they reported in June 1784. The committee quoted the company's secretary, Alexander Black, who claimed that great advances had been made in the production of plate glass, which had 'become an Object of Envy and

Jealousy to the *French* Nation in that Branch of Manufacture, which in *France* has been upheld for more than a Century by peculiar Indulgences of Monopoly'. Nonetheless, by contrast the British plate glass monopoly was heavily taxed, which was a situation exacerbated by the unfair allowance for waste. This time the committee supported the Plate Glass Company's argument on the need to increase the allowance for waste from a quarter to a half. If something was not done, they claimed, the Plate Glass Company would have to stop production. In April 1785 the House of Commons agreed that the mode of collecting duties on cast plate glass should be changed to that of the weight of the plates when squared.[31]

The Excise, once again, was sceptical, arguing that 'by experiment carefully and cautiously made under our Direction by our most able and experienced officer we find that the loss and waste sustained' was what they had always stated, namely, a quarter. They also believed that by changing the duty by the pound weight on glass squared would neither be easier than or as secure as the current procedure. They reiterated their claim that gauging the fluid metal in the pots was the most 'convenient, effectual and just' method.[32]

Despite the Excise's reservations the House of Commons was on this occasion unconvinced and the Treasury, too, were clearly concerned at the flight of the infant cast plate glass industry. Relief, they concluded, was clearly urgent. Unusually for the Treasury, they also questioned the Excise's calculations: they were 'inclined to think from the Evidence given by Mr. Jackson [a leading Excise gauging authority] at the Bar of the House of Commons on Thursday last, that a fairer Experiment has not been made of the actual waste and loss incurred in the Manufacture of large Plate Glasses'. The Lords were of the opinion that taking the duty on cast glass squared should be extended to all makers of cast or blown glass that was 6 feet or more in length, although they also advised that glass below that length should be gauged in the usual manner.[33]

The Excise continued to oppose the proposed changes but to no avail. The Treasury finally told them that they 'have agreed to a proposal made by the Proprietors', namely, that 'on all glasses of 72 inches and upwards in breadth the thickness of which shall not be less than 5/16 of an inch, the whole computed duty on the weight of the same when squared from the annealing furnace shall be drawnback and allowed'. However, recognizing the Excise's fear of increased fraud, they also warned that 'care must be taken to prevent their making large Glasses in order to obtain the Drawback for the purpose of cutting them afterwards into smaller sizes'. The Excise subsequently sent a clause to the Treasury, and dispatched one of their most experienced officers to ensure 5/16 of an inch was thick enough for glasses 72 inches by 36 inches. In addition, they underlined their concern that they were relatively powerless to ensure duty-free glass – that is, that of 72 inches and over – would not be subsequently cut into smaller pieces.[34]

Meanwhile, the cast glassmakers continued to press for the need to increase the allowance for waste. This time they invited the Treasury to come and view a number of 'experiments' at their works to demonstrate 'the real waste incurred in their operations'. The Treasury, in turn, did what they always did and instructed the Excise to send 'such officers as you may think proper to attend the operations of both the casting and blowing

Manufacturers at that place'. The Excise dispatched their leading gaugers, 'Mr Sikes [Bartholomew Sikes] and Mr Jackson'. From their findings the Excise Commissioners concluded that any change 'would not only tend to the Diminution of the Revenue but would also give the said company a preference prejudicial to other manufacturers of Glass in this kingdom'.[35]

In January 1787 the Treasury instructed the Excise to send them all the details concerning the duties and allowances paid on all types of glass other than plate. They also wanted to hear from manufacturers and excise officers on this subject, with the aim of trying to understand the cost of waste in relation to tax. Complaints were also flowing in from flint glass and crown manufacturers that the legal allowance for waste fell far short of the real amount. By contrast, excise officers challenged their computations, but did admit that there was a 10 per cent shortcoming arising from the mode of gauging the metal in the pot. In particular, this failed to allow for the contraction of the pots and the expansion of the metal.[36]

In May that year Parliament significantly increased the duties upon all types of glass imported into Britain, while a bounty was given on all domestically produced plate glass that was exported.[37] However, the act also passed new methods for measuring the duty of various types of glass. For example, gauging cast plate glass by 72 inches squared soon caused uproar with the British Plate Glass Manufactory, who quickly started to complain over the term 'squared'. It seems the Excise was extremely strict over the exactness of the squaring, dimensions and thickness of the glass. The Excise responded by claiming they 'have given them every Relief that in our opinion the said Act authorizes us to do'. However, the Treasury, rather angrily, advised the Excise that until some superior way to measure the squaring of the glass is established, the product should 'be put in a proper place to be locked up by your officers, and there to remain until some future order shall be made relative to the same'.[38]

Despite this suggestion the term 'squared' remained and the British Plate Glass Manufactory agent sent an aggrieved memorial on the matter to the Treasury in April 1793. They complained that excise officers continued to interpret the 1787 Act literally and compelled the cast glassmakers to cut the glass at perfect right angles at the specified size and thickness. For example, if the glass plate was accidentally broken they would not let the manufacturer square the glass because it was no longer at the correct dimension. The company complained that this was highly detrimental to the future of their business and therefore result in a loss of revenue to the country. The monopoly company had taken the matter to court but failed to win their case and were now lobbying, once again, the Treasury. The company now suggested that the measurement 'revert back to the old method of gauging' but increasing the allowance for waste, as they had originally lobbied for, to half 'instead of a quarter and 4 inches in the bottom of the pot'. The Excise reported to the Treasury that they would now consider this request. In February 1794 it was decided by the Treasury to submit such a proposal to Parliament, with the footnote that makers of blown plate glass should also have their waste increased to one-third and 4 inches.[39] Circumstances, however, overtook compromise and the urgency of war put all such questions of waste on hold, while a large increase in tax upon all glass was made in 1794. Complaints over Excise gauging consequently intensified.[40]

The high wartime tax on glass was fuelling greater fraud. For example, manufacturers were substituting larger pots for those gauged by excise officers. The Excise told the Treasury it was absolutely necessary that all manufacturers submit new entries concerning 'his or her furnaces – Pots, Pot-chambers, warehouses, rooms and other places for the making or keeping of pots of glass'. If not they should be fined £200. Crucially, officers should be able to gauge and re-gauge pots at any time they thought important and place a mark upon it. If a manufacturer was caught forging the mark he or she should be fined £300. Thirdly, no filled pot should be allowed in the furnace until the officer had once again measured and ascertained its capacity and contents. There were a number of other suggestions, including a fine of £200 for anyone obstructing the officer in his official activities.[41]

Reversion back to gauging the excise for cast plate glass to the weight of the metal in the pot and allowing a reasonable wastage was eventually reintroduced. Above all, the company, under the management of Robert Sherbourne since 1792, had significantly reduced waste by 1801. This also indicated that labour inexperience had, as the Excise earlier suspected, been a problem in the past for the amount of waste created.[42] Further rises in the tax on all types of glass took place in 1805 and 1812. To put this into some perspective, the following reveals the massive increase in duties on materials per hundredweight (112 pounds) for glass from 1777 to 1812 (Table 1). Clearly, one of the largest concerns for any glassmaker was the level of tax, which was one of the biggest factors impacting upon production and therefore profit.[43] This pressure clearly forced manufacturers to innovate and, as in the case of Sherbourne and the Plate Glass Company, improve efficiency.

Consider, too, paper. The attempt to manufacture paper was probably first seriously introduced into England by a Bavarian goldsmith banker, John Spilman, under the patronage of James I. He erected his mill in Dartford in Kent but did not make much headway. Clearly, however, towards the close of the century an elementary papermaking industry had become established. By 1689 the newly established Company of White

Table 1 Tax in shillings per hundredweight (112 pounds) on glass between 1777 and 1812.

Type of glass	1777			1812		
	£	s.	d.	£	s.	d.
A. Plate, flint, and phial	0	18	8	4	18	0
B. Crown (Window) and German sheet	0	14	0	3	13	6
C. Spread window (broad)	0	7	0	1	10	0
D. Common bottle	0	3	6	0	8	2

Source: S. Dowell, *A History of Taxation and Taxes in England: From the Earliest Times to the Present Day* (1884, 3rd edn, 1888, New York, 4 vols, 1965), vol. 4, 299–300.

Paper Makers, run by French Huguenot refugees, lobbied Parliament for the creation of a charter allowing them to generate subscriptions to expand their manufacture of white paper throughout England. The lobbyists were an amalgamation of various papermakers that had been separately awarded a patent in the prior fifteen or so years. They falsely claimed to have reached a point where their product was as good as any made in Europe, including the leading producer of white quality paper, France. To prove their claim they wrote:

> The *French King* having notice thereof, did command his late Ambassador, *Monsieur Berillon*, to use his utmost Endeavours to ruin the Manufacture, who by himself, and others, with great sums of Money, seduced and carried away the companies workmen from their Mills, and raised other very great Oppositions against them, to their Detriment and Expense of several Thousands of Pounds, as was apparently proved before the late King in Council, and by a Trial at Bar in the Court of *King's-Bench*.

The company proposed that the raising of the necessary capital for expansion should be carried on from the home of the goldsmith banker, Sir Francis Child, at Temple-Bar and the company's own warehouse in Abchurch Lane.[44]

The petition triggered a hostile reaction from other papermakers and papersellers. For a start the idea that the company was the inventor of white paper in England was not just false but also simply ridiculous; moreover, to grant it a monopoly would be against the law. The Company of White Paper Makers were also lying, according to the petitioners, when they claimed to employ thousands of people and to supply the whole kingdom with white paper:

> That the same Grant was obtained through their specious pretences of supplying the whole kingdom, and imploying of Fifty Mills, which they have not performed, nor can, for that in fifteen years since they had their First Patent, they have imployed but five Mills; and if they had more, cannot procure Materials sufficient for making of a twentieth part of the quantity of White Paper used in England.

The petitionists concluded that if the company was given a further monopolist expansion it would destroy about a hundred independent paper mills, while the traders of paper would struggle to purchase home-produced paper.[45] The reality of paper production, especially white paper, was that it remained negligible and significantly inferior compared to France, Germany, Italy and Holland.[46]

Quite soon after the Glorious Revolution the Company of White Paper Makers now lobbied the new Dutch king to confirm their exclusive right. Again, this triggered and resurrected the arguments of opponents stemming from Kent, Surrey, Windsor and central London. One petition claimed that by the 'granting of particular persons the sole power of making paper will enable them to advance the price of paper as high as they please'. In contrast, if the industry was left free there would 'follow a greater supply of all sorts of white writing and printing paper for necessary use of this kingdom'.[47] This was part of a general attack upon company monopolies such as the East India Company, the African Company, the Hudson's Bay Company and, of course, the White Paper Manufacturers.[48] In general, the English attempt to nurture paper, like silk, spirits, linen and later cast plate glass, was part of a policy to undermine, as John Pollexfen from the Board of Trade put it, 'the great Staple commodities of *France*'.[49] A compromise was subsequently made where the company was confined to producing higher quality paper and the makers from the petition were allowed to make cheaper grades of paper.

An attempt to place an excise upon paper for four years was tried in 1694 to help raise money to fight the French.[50] However, a permanent duty was not established till 1712 when it was used to help fund the debt arisen from the War of Spanish Succession. Likewise, and in accordance with contemporary oeconomic policy, a corresponding rise in prohibiting duties was placed on all foreign paper. Paper was charged by the ream and varied depending on its quality, and just for good measure massive duties were also put on imported pasteboard, millboard and scaleboard.[51] Two years later, the excise was significantly increased but, as yet, still at a comfortable level. However, it was also the case that the quality of English paper was still relatively poor compared to that made on the Continent right up until the 1760s, when the Kent papermaker, James Whatman, in particular, established his manufacture at Maidstone. Much of Whatman's production process had been gleaned while travelling in Holland. By this point, due primarily to the quality of its water and climate, Kent had become the centre of England's papermaking industry.[52]

It was also during the mid-1760s, again after the hefty debt amassed by the Seven Years War put pressure upon the Excise to maximize revenues, that paper lobbying became more organized. A petition to the Treasury from the 'Committee appointed by a General Meeting of the Paper makers of Great Britain' was clearly upset by recent changes in the approach of the excise to gauging duty on paper, and wanted them to revert to their former process of measurement.[53] Such complaints continued to intensify across the spectrum of paper production over the next two decades.[54]

The gross revenues from paper in England had massively risen in the years between 1780 and 1785 from £13,439 14s. 7½d. to £56,091 19s. 3¾d. The government was requesting all sorts of information on the gauging and collection of paper revenues (and other products) in anticipation of the 1786 Trade Treaty with France and the subsequent Consolidation Act of 1787 (a reform of rates and procedures concerning taxes).[55] There was no respite for paper manufacturers in Britain, and Pitt doubled the duty in 1801 while, to simplify the gauging, paper classification was reduced to just two types in 1803. It was within this desperate situation, as Leonard N. Rosenband has shown, that British papermakers turned to Bryan Donkin's building of Fourdrinier's French papermaking machine as the only option for survival.[56] The burden of taxation in Britain, as Fourdrinier's fellow Frenchmen Jean-Baptiste Say and Jérôme-Adolphe Blanqui claimed, had acted as a significant spur to some of the important innovation occurring during this period.[57] Moreover, all the technological developments associated with the Industrial Revolution took place behind a protective wall whether the industry was taxed or not.

Consider, too, the example of soap. An attempt to excise the young soap industry was attempted in 1694 but failed. As with paper the first tax was successfully introduced by the Tories in 1712 to help fund the War of the Spanish Succession. However, since the product was so important to the woollen industry and other textile makers, a deduction of one third was allowed for these producers. Not surprisingly the 'Hard Cake and White Soap Makers' had fervently opposed the 1712 Act. A petition the year before underlined that the new duty was more than that upon green soap (an inferior and less popular soap). First, white soap was of much greater benefit to the poor and crucial to the textile industries. Secondly, unlike green soap, it was a potential valuable export. Not surprisingly, the days of green soap were numbered and the product was soon totally surpassed by the rise of white soap.[58] As with all excised articles the soaphouse was carefully mapped and gauged.[59]

The duty upon white soap was increased again two years later in 1714 to 1½d. per pound, followed some years later by a rise to help fund the War of American Independence. This time a distinction was made between hard soap and soft soap with the former charged at 2¼d. and the latter 1¾d. per pound. By this stage, the luxury status of hard soap had transmuted into a necessity at the expense and rapid demise of soft soap. From the mid-1760s, and especially the 1780s, the Treasury was bombarded with petitions from soap makers worried at the extent of fraud and the smuggling of the item. The next hike came in 1816 when the rate for hard soap was raised to help replace revenues lost by the repeal of the 1799 income tax. The duty paid for such soap now cost 6d. per pound, which made the tax on the article 100 per cent of its price. However, once the taxes on its materials such as tallow, barilla and turpentine were also included the actual cost of the tax was between 120 and 130 per cent of the product. The gross yield from soap in 1815 was £747,759.[60]

Like glass and paper, part of the new domestic textile printing industry was earlier targeted by Tories in 1712 to also help fund the costs of war with the French. The new excise imposed 6d. a yard on printed silk, 3d. for silk handkerchiefs, 3d. per yard on printed calicoes and 1½d. per yard squared on linens. However, calicoes, fustians and linens that were dyed with just one colour were exempted but, again, as with glass and paper, the 1712 duties doubled in 1714. In 1721 the wearing of British printed calicoes was banned but, as we saw earlier, it was soon discovered that fustians (stuffs made of linen and cotton yarn), when printed, looked very similar to prohibited printed calicoes.[61]

The importance of the Lancashire fustian and linen industry was underlined in 1751 when Parliament resolved to encourage it further by allowing foreign linen yarn to be imported under a lower duty, and thus putting 'the British Manufactures of Cheques and Stripes [the most important mixed cotton textiles competing in West Africa and the Americas] upon a more equal Footing with their Rivals, and enable them to regain and enlarge their Export Trade'.[62]

By the late 1760s textile printing had become established in Lancashire, primarily due to the region's ideal location for cloth manufactures; cotton, especially, benefited from the waterpower, damp atmosphere, the growth of the port of Liverpool and eventually cheap local coal.[63] By the close of the decade mechanization had enabled the production of pure cotton textiles, that is, the warp of fabric could now be made from cotton yarn. Pressure was now mounting to legalize the domestic wearing of British printed cottons. If so were these new goods, once printed, to be taxed at the 1714 rate of 6d. the yard squared? The issue was categorically resolved in 1774 when the lower 1712 duty of 3d. the yard squared was legislated and domestically manufactured pure cotton textiles could now be legally worn by British people. To ensure a distinction remained between domestic and the still prohibited Indian calicoes, each piece had to have three blue strips woven in the warp through the whole length. In addition, every piece of printed cotton had to be stamped at each end with the word 'British manufactory' to delineate it from prohibited foreign, principally Indian, calicoes.[64]

Petitions continued to flow into the Treasury and Parliament. In December 1779 linen dealers from Scotland complained over several alterations in the duties on pearl ashes, soap and small blue. First, pearl ashes were vital in the process of whitening linen and in the preparation of linen yarn, but since the war with the mainland American colonies the cost of importing the raw material from Europe had greatly increased by over a third. Previously, it was charged on importation at the same rate as pot ash

> so that whether the original cost was great or small, the duty was the same; but of late, the Commissioners of Customs have found that Pearl Ashes only of the product of Germany, may be imported as Pot Ashes; and that pearl ashes from all other parts of the Continent must be entered as unrated goods, and so pay duty ad valorem upon the oath of the importer.

The Scottish linen dealers claimed it was imperative to their industry and the nation in general, that the rate on pearl ashes should be the same whatever the country of origin. In addition, it was not a level playing field since Ireland had no duty at all on pearl ashes or soap. The Scottish linen dealers claimed that the excise of 1½d. per pound of soap used in linen production should be put on the Irish linen makers and British woollen makers.[65]

In 1781 the House of Commons agreed that a bill should be drafted to allow the importation of wood and weed ashes, pot and pearl ashes, barilla and the deep blue paint and ceramic pigment, 'smalts', to be duty-free. It was also ordained that bounties upon plain British and Irish linens should be extended to printed ones. Two months later, Parliament also agreed to establish a fund up to £15,000 per annum, to once again try and encourage the growth of hemp and flax in England. However, a petition two years later from the Nottingham manufacturers of linen and cotton to the Treasury implies that the said act was actually confined to Irish linen and cotton to specifically encourage their manufacture. Further petitions, sent at the same time, one by the General Convention of the Royal Borough of Scotland and another from those connected with calico production in Carlisle wanted all the import duties for these materials removed.[66] This was part of a wider debate involving Pitt's attempt to solve Britain's ongoing volatile political relationship with Ireland.

In 1783 the House of Commons continued its active encouragement of exporting linens along with pure and mixed cottons. The House agreed that items valued under 5 pence per yard (and breadth of 25 inches) be given a bounty of half a penny, while those valued at between 5 and 6d. per yard receive one penny, and that worth 6 to 18d. per yard get 1½d. (extended for a further period in 1787).[67] A few weeks later a memorial was received from the Manchester calico printers complaining of the legal requirement stipulating the need for having three blue threads 'in each selvedge [the edge of the fabric that is woven to prevent fraying], the first, third and fifth threads from the edge'. This, as we saw earlier, was legislated in 1774 to differentiate home-produced calicoes from Indian imports that were still prohibited. The problem had arisen because the aim of lifting the ban had been to allow domestic producers to imitate Indian printed cotton calicoes and allow them to be legally worn in Britain. As the memorialists at the time had put it, to 'resemble in Quality and Appearances, those imported from the East Indies'.[68]

However, the method of distinguishing the two cloths was proving deeply problematic due to the difficulty in making a suitable blue thread, which 'would bear the operation of bleaching the goods, by which means the manufacturers have sustained great loss'. They would have suffered more had it not been for the flexible 'Indulgence of the Commissioners of the Excise, who have allowed the reduced Duty to be accepted on goods where [only] one or more blue threads have been visible in the selvedge'. As a result, the petitioners wanted the law repealed.[69]

In 1784 Pitt tried to increase the excise duties on the growing cotton industry but, as we shall see in a later chapter, met a storm of protest and was forced to back down. Up until this point, too, the manufacture of quality British cotton textiles in imitation of Indian ones had proved relatively unsuccessful due to a lack of skilled labour and the necessary fine raw cotton. Mechanization solved the former but it was not till the final decade of the century, when 'Sea Island' United States of America cotton arrived primarily thanks to Eli Whitney's manipulation and improvement of the cotton gin machine used to separate cotton from the seed (Figure 2). Prior to 1790 no raw cotton was imported from the United States; however, by 1797 vast quantities of the raw cotton was being imported and the production of domestic cotton cloth (now legally termed calicoes) rapidly accelerated. By 1812 the cotton industry was considered mature enough to thrive without a bounty on exports and the incentive was removed that year.[70] It was from this last date that raw cotton prices also started to significantly decrease. Giorgio Riello concludes: 'This was an American "plantation revolution" on a par with the European industrial revolution.'[71] The subsequent meteoric expansion of southern cotton plantations hugely increased the slave population and became a significant part of the growth of nineteenth-century United States capitalism.[72]

This chapter has demonstrated that the intensification of the excise upon manufactures during the second half of the eighteenth century provoked an increase in technical challenges to the Excise process of measuring tax, and the subsequent level of industrial lobbying. In the following chapters we shall see how this led to increased pressure for deregulation, and the accompanying view that the market should be the arbiter of the quality and intrinsic nature of goods. For many in government this was simply the only

COTTON-GIN.—GINNING COTTON.

Figure 2 'The cotton gin machine', 1800.

solution to an increasingly desperate context in which the state was perceived as far too large, extractive (taxing), intrusive and corrupt, rather than any enlightened impetus. Eventually, this sheer urgency forced Pitt's administration to mould a new economic policy.

If this book so far has been concerned with the role of the state in forging Britain's interrelated fiscal, trade and industrial trajectory, the following two chapters will focus upon the role of the individual, knowledge and ecology. In contrast to the argument made so far, a large historiography underlines the emergence of a new philosophy as the key and unique component to Britain's industrialization. The following chapter seeks to explore the prevalent idea that a distinctive creative culture characterized Britain's industrial development. This widely held view maintains that this was defined by a freer and more liberal society compared to the country's main industrial rivals. This enabled Britain to embrace practical knowledge and successfully apply it to profitable industrial ends. In short, eighteenth-century Britain was a central driving force in the West's rise as the 'first knowledge economy'.[73]

CHAPTER 8
CULTURE AND INDUSTRY

A prominent view purports to ascribe Britain's Industrial Revolution and the subsequent rise of the West to their global economic supremacy, which was fuelled by the application of enlightened knowledge to technological development. There is nothing new in this argument. This belief has core roots in Austrian economics, most notably in the works of Carl Wenger, Ludvig von Mises and Friedrich A. Hayek. It then penetrated the thinking of prominent British economists and historians and, of course, the United States. Aspects of this argument, especially those claiming a distinct, Western culture of innovation, were given added muscle during the Cold War and in the face of the threat of communism through the work of American scholars, such as Walt W. Rostow and David Landes, and prominent British historians, among whom were Thomas S. Ashton and Ronald Max Hartwell, members of Hayek's Mont Pelerin Society. In recent years, however, the view that emphasis upon knowledge, ideal institutions and particular political context were the primary reasons for Britain's Industrial Revolution has enjoyed a renaissance.[1]

Vultures of production

The history of the rise of a distinct Western rational culture, ideally adapted for industrialization, typically begins in Elizabethan England with Sir Francis Bacon, who, the story goes, hatched the scientific method in his own head. In his *Novum Organum* of 1620 Bacon announced that the three inventions that had done more to change the world than any other were printing, gunpowder and the compass – all three originating from China.[2] Bacon emphasized the need in his *New Atlantis* (1624) for an elite body composed of those with the best experience to judge the utility of new knowledge and for a centre for facts to be deposited, tested and analysed. Even here, his suggestion for state-managed bodies to generate knowledge for commercial development was informed by the Spanish Consejo de Indias. This was an organization created in 1524 to gather information from the Americas to aid its exploitation of that continent's mineral and botanical wealth (Figures 3 and 4).[3]

It is conventionally claimed that the Baconian approach took root especially during the English Civil War and the Interregnum period and it was characterized by Charles Webster's notion of an 'invisible college'.[4] It subsequently became institutionalized with the Restoration and the founding of the London Royal Society in 1660. It was during this latter period that the key works of Isaac Newton, Robert Boyle and John Locke appeared. However, it is now predominantly argued that the diffusion of a

Figures 3 and 4 Andrés García, *de Céspedes, Regimiento de Navegación*, Madrid, 1606 and Francis Bacon, *Instauratio Magna* (*Great Instauration*), London, 1620.

practical experimental Newtonian natural philosophy was not primarily via the Royal Society or state institutions, but through the marketplace. It emerged in unregulated coffee houses and London public lectures and then diffused out to the provinces. It was here that the new philosophy informed and nurtured a culture of innovation and technological development that, it is argued, proved fundamental to the nation's eventual manufacturing dominance.[5]

Let us start, then, by looking more closely at the state of practical knowledge in the sixteenth century and the world Bacon would have been experiencing. For one thing, he would have noted that the origins of gunpowder, paper, the compass, printing press, an array of textiles and ceramics came from Asia. However, importing skilled Asians was simply not a viable option at the time.[6]

The deficiencies in English domestic manufactures had been increasingly pointed out as England sought ways to increase its European power. For example, 'letters of protection' for primarily foreign craftsmen such as 'weavers, saltmakers and glassmakers' can be found as early as Edward III's reign (1327–77). These were designed to encourage skilled Europeans to settle in England and stimulate new domestic manufactures. These letters did not, however, offer the person a monopoly. The incentive was rigorously revived during the sixteenth century, but this time drawing upon Italian practices in which exclusivity was awarded to the skilled foreigner. The policy was simple; namely, to encourage the manufacture of those products England currently had to import. Christine MacLeod writes: 'It was of great significance in the development of the patent system that the primary goal of [Lord] Burghley's policy was the introduction of entire industries or manufacturing techniques from abroad.'[7]

The Elizabethan era was also at the vanguard of administrative reforms within revenue collection, the Royal Navy, the Ordnance and the Royal Mint. Indeed, the Ordnance and the nation's military were considered weak compared to England's main European competitors. Not surprisingly, then, skilled foreigners were desperately sought after; for example, the experienced armourers at Woolwich Military Academy were from the German states. German experience was harnessed to make domestic cannon and saltpetre; it was also instrumental in creating a wool-card industry. The wool-card industry was fundamental to the production of woollen textiles and was made of brass and wire. The period also saw an increase in commercial missions – such as Edmund Fenton's voyage of discovery – and plundering missions – like the one to the Mulucca Islands (via South America).[8]

The encouragement of projectors was a practice first spearheaded by countries on the European continent; it was not emulated in England until 1552 when a patent was awarded for making glass. Six years later an Italian glassmaker set up a manufactory in London to imitate fine Venetian glass, which was then very fashionable among the aristocracy. In 1567 a patent was given to Anthony Dollyne and John Carye, two merchants from Antwerp, who brought over skilled glass makers from Vosges in East France. However, establishing a glass industry proved far more difficult due especially to a lack of skilled labour and energy (a factor that also dampened initial attempts to establish an iron industry). Timber, the primary source of energy, was perceived to be in short supply and prioritized for use by the Royal Navy, while knowledge about the use of coal as an alternative fuel was still negligible. The situation became direr in 1615 when James I banned the use of timber in the production of glass; unlike much of continental Europe, England never really encouraged a 'science' of forestry.[9]

Between 1558 and 1572, some 31 patents were granted to foreign projectors who brought new manufacturing processes over to England.[10] For example, prior to 1524 soft grey soap was being manufactured in Bristol, while superior hard white soap was imported to England from Castile in Spain. In 1561 a patent was awarded to the foreign producers Stephen Groyett and Anthony le Lewyer to imitate imported hard soap. The next patent went to a Dutchman for making saltpetre, while further patents were granted for producing alum and copperas – the raw materials needed for dyeing. In addition, there were patents for the manufacture of ovens and furnaces, and the production of Spanish yellow leather. England was playing vital industrial catch-up.[11]

Mining was recognized as crucial for a country's wealth and leading the way in Europe were the French, Dutch and, especially, the German states. As such, Frenchmen from Brittany were brought over to aid tin mining in Cornwall, while others were wooed over from across Europe to assist in the development of iron, lead and other metal mines. Dutchmen were also important in Cornwall while Germans were crucial, in general, everywhere. In 1528, for example, Joachim Hechstetter from Augsburg was made principal surveyor and master of all mines in England and Ireland. He was authorized to bring over six others from the German region to develop smelting houses.[12]

The year 1561 was a busy year with skilled workers from the German states brought in to run and manage a new company operating the mines in Northumberland and to search for copper in Keswick. Eric Ash writes, 'Digging, maintaining, and working such mines required an enormous amount of mechanical and mining expertise, both theoretical and practical. By this date the Germans had been working deep mines for generations; the English simply had no comparable experience.' Another German, Captain Gerard Horrick, was hired to cultivate domestic supplies of gunpowder, while his fellow countryman, Gaspar Seelar, was employed to manufacture salt in 1563.[13]

Other patents that were given to foreigners were for the dyeing and dressing of cloth in the Flemish manner (1568), for producing starch (1588) and for constructing mathematical instruments (1598). The decision to award patents to these items were often inspired by the lists of imports that were publicly condemned, with the accompanying cry that they should be domestically produced. Other patents included ones for engines that would dredge, drain, grind, raise water, pipe water and refine pit coal.[14] A policy of import substitution was already well on the way during the sixteenth century. The work being done here greatly relied upon imported skilled labour and was not inspired by domestic ingenuity. This was a crucial industrial catch-up driven by European competition, aggression and increasing global ambition.

Fen drainage and knowledge

There has always been money to be had from oil. A certain type of knowledge was quick to emerge that set out to legitimate the appropriation of land for such a product; as we will now see oeconomic colonization, rather than virtuous philosophy, helped forge a distinct notion of rationality. In this section, we look at the example of seventeenth-century Fenland drainage.

A huge problem was finding raw materials, at the right price, to aid England's fledgling industries. During the seventeenth century, there was a massive rise in prices for hops, madder, linen, cloth and pins throughout England. No wonder the growing of hops and madder, along with the manufacture of linen and pin making, were enthusiastically taken up as leading projects during this period. Trade prices and volatility expanded as other countries brought out heavy licences and increased tariffs. One such item affected was vegetable oil, which had increased by a third between 1542 and 1549. This was made even more alarming when Spain, a key supplier of alum, stopped the sale of this dye abroad in 1553 (except on licence). There was a subsequent frenzy of speculation that oil from Spain, already at a very high price, could go the same way. William Cholmely, a dyer in Southwark, London, spoke for every woollen manufacturer when he sighed: 'What if Spain did the same with oil? How should we then have oils to work our wool?'[15]

The prospect was industrial and commercial catastrophe since such oil was crucial in the carding and spinning of England's only really successful manufacturing industry, namely, woollen textiles. This fear led to probably the largest civil industrial project of seventeenth-century England. Where better to see an early example of a distinct English culture of ingenuity at work?

Clearly, as a pre-emption to this oil scarcity, one region in England around Lynn in Norfolk started growing coleseed in 1551. Enhanced action to promote coleseed increased as an influx of foreigners arrived during the 1560s; for example a patent was issued to two men from the Low Countries, Armigil Wade and William Herle, in 1565 for making oil from seeds, while a bill was introduced in 1572 to encourage the making of oils, in general, within England. As trade relations with Spain deteriorated, the reliability of oil imports greatly shrank and the price of oil soared. The government was actively lobbied to encourage the growth of hemp, flax and coleseed. Crucially, to the great delight of projectors, Herle underlined the huge potential profits to be made; these crops, he wrote, 'will be more gainful to the owners and farmers of land than any corn'. Rapeseed was soon added to the list and would, later, become the most popular choice. It was common knowledge that the best place to grow such crops was on Fenland, and as the coleseed oil project gathered momentum, so too did the projects to enclose and drain this area.[16] The promotion of domestic woollen textile manufactures became increasingly embedded in the encouragement of such aims. For example, the price of imported woad had also greatly increased and projects to develop this dye were also aggressively promoted.[17]

When the Dutchman, Humphrey Bradley, presented his detailed project to drain the Fens to the Elizabethan Court in 1589, the status of projects and projectors was at rock bottom. Projects had come to be perceived as a notorious way of gaining much needed revenue for the Crown by offering a patent monopoly for the successful advocate of such a proposal. This dominated a great deal of political debate and voices grew louder when the projects were extremely ambitious as in the case of draining the Fens.

Bradley was known in the Netherlands as a skilled dyker and was married to Anna van der Delft, whose uncle was a Dutch diplomat living in London. Bradley's scheme was rejected, probably for failing to attract the necessary financial investment. For the resourceful Dutchman, however, this turned out to be a blessing, as he quickly crossed the channel to become the key advisor to France over land drainage – working on extensive and lucrative projects in the Auvergne, Languedoc and Saintonge regions.[18]

The Fens, as well as being perceived by advocates of drainage as geographically inaccessible and generally environmentally unpleasant by those in social authority, was also seen as a popular refuge for outlaws and rebels. And, no doubt, those that saw the Fens as an ecological sickbed were thinking both in terms of its boggy and unruly terrain as much as its fiercely independent and uncompromising inhabitants. Stinking, unproductive, unhealthy bog land along with socially undesirable and unproductive labour could be removed through drainage reclamation schemes. The region was ripe for refashioning and settlement.

On the flip side, anti-Fen drainers, deeply hostile to the climate of greedy projectors and speculators, defended the Fenland as being fertile and perfectly suited to local needs. Bradley's scheme had been the first serious study on the feasibility of draining the Fens. He claimed that despite the sheer scale of the area it was less technically demanding than drainage projects in the Low Countries. However, in terms of English history, it still probably represented the most ambitious industrial project – even more than harbours and dockyards – to be considered to date.[19]

The first significant investor in Fen drainage was William Russell, first Baron of Thornhaugh, who was lord deputy of Ireland and one-time governor of Flushing. It was probably while he was occupied in the Lowlands that he took an interest in land drainage. In 1609 he brought over Dutch drainage engineers to attempt to drain the Fens around Thorney. This was the beginning of the family's involvement in such a project for the next two centuries.[20]

A plan by the Bedford Company of Adventurers to drain 95,000 acres was carried on with gusto by Russell's son, Francis Russell, who from 1627 became the fourth Earl of Bedford. The company allocated him 40,000 acres and convinced the king to come on board with an acquisition of 12,000 acres. The company spent a colossal £100,000 and the king £20,000. Work went on reasonably well and enough land was drained for use in the summer; however, after intense opposition lobbying and the interlude of the Civil War the work was halted. The project was eventually completed in the early 1650s, by which time the fourth Earl of Bedford had long since passed away.[21]

Throughout this period, the hostility towards fen drainage projects had increased and anti-projectors intensified their attacks. The anonymous author of the tract, *The Anti-Projector; or the History of the Fen Project*, first published in 1646, devoted a great deal of time describing the riches of the un-drained Fen Land, invoking nature to defend it in its 'natural' state. The author concluded with what he recognized as the motivating force behind the drainers' clamour: 'What is Cole-seed and Rape? They are but Dutch commodities, and but trash and trumpery' – they had nothing on the natural produce of the un-drained Fenland. Where better to see hostility towards projectors, especially the invasion of foreign ones, than at a project where Dutch experience and knowledge was the best in Europe?[22] Where better to see clashes between the proponents of land enclosure and those defending the traditional commons?[23]

The debate over the issue of 'naturalness' was multifaceted. At one level, the sense of these arguments, as just shown, are general and gain their meaning from pro- and anti-projectors. At another level, it would seem it was technically based and a debate between competing projectors and engineers to drain the Fens. In this case, observes Eric Ash, the argument revolved upon how seriously damaged the 'natural' system of drainage was and thence what degree of 'artificial' intervention was necessary to rectify it.[24] Despite English attempts, the necessary experience for draining the Fens was probably always going to come from the Netherlands. The general influx of Dutch projectors, entrepreneurs and financiers is entirely to be expected considering the technical and commercial position of the Dutch (and geographical proximity to England). In Europe they were at the vanguard of agriculture, certain manufactures, at the forefront of the carrying trade, pioneers of new financial practices and masters of land drainage.[25] The person who eventually became the architect behind the drainage of the Great Level or Bedford Level of the Fens was the Dutch émigré Cornelius Vermuyden, who was later utilized by Oliver Cromwell to try and solicit an alliance with the Dutch.[26]

Vermuyden came from a family of engineers with strong contacts in England and, after a period as a Dutch tax collector, came over to England in 1621. Instrumental in Vermuyden's early career had been the Dutch drainage authority, Joos Croppenburgh, who was stepfather to Vermuyden's wife, Katherine Laps. Croppenburgh employed him, along with a number of other Dutch workmen, to assist in the drainage of the Erith Marshes by the Thames. Croppenburgh was also instrumental in creating Canvey Island and a range of islets within salt marshes.[27]

In 1623 Charles I hired Vermuyden to drain Windsor Park and, in 1626, he started a drainage project in Hatfield Chase in Yorkshire much to the opposition of local inhabitants. Here, with an army of Dutch and English workmen, he straightened rivers and made artificial vents generally funded by Dutch investors based in London, Amsterdam and Dordrecht. The Dutch invasion occurred long before 1688–9. In September 1629, Vermuyden was in negotiation with the Earl of Bedford to drain the Great Bedford Level, but was not actually hired till Charles I intervened in 1639.

By the early 1630s, Vermuyden was tired of the continuing battle with locals over the Hatfield Chase drainage; his disagreements with one of the chief backers of the project, the second-generation Dutch-Italian Sir Philibert Vernatti, and dissatisfaction, in general, among members of the company led to his resignation. Consequently, Vermuyden was incarcerated in Fleet prison from May 1633 before being released for wrongful imprisonment in May 1634. As a result, he sold his interest in the land drainage project to a Frenchman called Monsieur John Gibbon. Gibbon, in turn, introduced new drainage men from Normandy and Picardy to work with the Dutch and English, with local opposition to land drainage becoming even more hostile. The work was deemed complete in 1637.[28]

Vermuyden subsequently put pen to paper and spent time promoting his approach to Fen drainage. The result was a detailed overview that he first wrote in 1639 but did not publish until 1642. In response, he was bitterly condemned by Andrewes Burrell, a self-titled gentleman who had lost money by the venture. He claimed Vermuyden was venting 'mystical discourse' and presented an alternative overview of what he considered were the Dutchman's shortcomings.[29] Four years later in 1646, the anonymous author of the *Anti-Projector* damned Vermuyden as foreign, and with one eye on the predominance of overseas, especially Dutch, projectors, penned: 'Is it probable strangers will do us more good, and study our profit more than we will do our own? Certainly we know how to drain ourselves better than they … and are better able.' Resentment to foreigners, projectors and Fen drainage ran deep – not least because of the impact it would have upon the common rights claimed by the 'bog' people. Not surprisingly, then, there were fierce riots and periodic attacks upon drainage work such as cutting embankments and, in at least one instance, the levelling of a foreign church in Axholme, part of the Hatfield project.[30]

Ash has shown in the ensuing battle how Vermuyden made a deliberate switch in his appeal to nature. He now claimed he was not producing anything unprecedented in the natural world and, in fact, was simply imitating nature. As he put it in his *Discourse Touching the Drayning of the Great Fennes* published in 1642: 'I resolve to imitate nature (as much as can be) in the Upland Counties.' Thus, in one swipe, the Dutchman dismissed accusations that he and his ilk would be producing something totally unnatural and artificial. He may have been producing new channels but they were based on nature's principles and not some abstract invention. One hostile commentator, Edmund Scotten, got wind of this new turn and scoffed: 'Whether instead of imitating nature ... doth he [Vermuyden] not in this and divers other darke passages rather imitate the popish Clergy, who keepe men as ignorant as they can, that they may the more easily deceive them, and leade them whether they list.' Nature, not for the first or last time, had been caught within a whirlwind of political conflict.[31]

For rival drainers this aspect of the debate offered the opportunity of offering natural solutions, namely, of enlarging and deepening nature's existing rivers – in other words, following the fenland drainage pattern as established by nature. Thus, one side of the argument, instigated by the Dutchman, Vermuyden, rested on the claim to be working to nature's principles to alter the drainage. On the other side, the argument pursued by the local English was that the only natural solution was to improve nature's existing drainage. On this occasion, Vermuyden's imitating approach – driven by the interests of capital – won. From Ash's account it seems, with the Dutch vindication of applying nature's principles, the licence was given to accelerate the 'rational' underpinning of this approach, which manifested in the subsequent geometrical carving up and privatization of the land.[32] A distinct commercial rationality had come to the fore; an early case of spatial destruction and reordering via the investment of capital combined with claims to an accompanying form of legitimating knowledge.[33]

For this chapter what is striking about the business surrounding Fenland drainage projects is the English reliance upon Dutch and French practical know-how and knowledge. This could be amplified throughout England. Wherever there was a technical project there was bound to be a foreigner – from Prussian miners and Dutch hydraulic specialists to Spanish navigators and French cartographers.

The case of Spanish navigators illustrates the situation well. Simply put, Spain, at this time, could trade far longer distances than England because it had more experience and skilled navigators. If England was to expand its trade it needed such know-how and, as such, the government seduced over two of Spain's leading navigators to try and pass on the necessary knowledge. It was also during this period that London started to gain a reputation for mathematical instrument-making. This, according to Robert Iliffe, was thanks in no short part to 'the arrival of an influx of Protestant refugees from Europe who had been highly skilled members of the printing and engraving trades.'[34]

England was playing frantic catch-up and was doing all it could to bridge the huge gap between its manufacturing status and its European rivals. The climax to Ash's recent survey of knowledge during the Elizabethan era comes in the work of Bacon's natural philosophy that, he claims, represents a systematized and crystallized fusion between practice and theory that had been gaining rapid momentum during this century.[35] For Mokyr the 'Baconian program' lies at the root of England's subsequent industrialization.[36] Ironically, as we have just seen, Bacon was simply theorizing the skilled experience of those continental Europeans that were spearheading England's 'program' of agricultural, military, industrial and trading projects. Bacon's work was an attempt to create an approach of creative emulation to catch up with best European and Asian practices; a desperate mongrel synthesis rather than an enlightened philosophical project. Imitation of nature's laws or imported products would come to serve the country well.

Clearly, when Margaret C. Jacob claims that 'Bacon saw more clearly than any of his contemporaries the extraordinary advances that had already been made by mechanical artisans in shipbuilding, navigation, ballistics, printing, and water engineering', he was not thinking of England's indigenous culture or population.[37] On the contrary, he would have been reflecting upon the method pursued by Dutch water engineers and ship builders, French, Swedish, Swiss, Prussian and Spanish approaches to army ballistics, Spanish and Portuguese skills in navigation, developments in continental printing and encounters with Chinese porcelain, silk cloth, fireworks and Indian cotton textiles. It was not English Protestantism that would pave the path for future industrialization but, initially, a whole transnational array of peoples and foreign things. What is also often forgotten is that Bacon emphasized the importance of industrial protectionism: 'This points at a true Principle, *viz*. Where foreign Materials are but Superfluities, foreign Manufactures should be prohibited; for that will either banish the Superfluity, or gain The Manufacture.'[38] Imitative innovation and industrial nurturing required, above all, foreign skills and state protectionism. England proved to be extremely adept at this project.

Typically, the prevailing historiography describes how the Baconian programme was subsequently propelled forward by English Presbyterians during the first half of the seventeenth century. The new philosophy became digested, deposited and given a prominent place in the revolutionary views of the Puritans, particularly as a tool for preparing this world for its divine conclusion. A group surrounding the Baltic emigrant from Elbing, Samuel Hartib, utilized the new philosophy as the means of improving practical subjects such as agriculture and mechanical projects. For Jacob, following Charles Webster, the English Civil War set 'modern science in its English guise' characterized by 'its social usefulness and linked to a larger vision of reform and enlightenment'. Experimental natural philosophy then became formalized with the establishment of the London Royal Society and the achievements of men like Boyle, Robert Hooke and, of course, Newton. Thereafter it entered the wider community via public lectures and the coffee houses of London.[39] However, was it really as straightforward as this and as crucial to Britain's industrial trajectory as so many have argued?

It should also be remembered that chemical studies were first taught at Oxford and Cambridge by foreign natural philosophers. Peter Stahl has been hailed as the first prominent teacher of chemical studies at Oxford, and was brought to England from Strasbourg in West Prussia by Hartlib and Boyle in 1659. He was wooed over due to his superior knowledge and experience of mining, mineralogy and metallurgy; some of his pupils included Christopher Wren, John Wallis and Locke. In Cambridge, chemical studies were first taught by John Francis Vigani, an emigrant from the Italian city of Verona, who started private lectures in 1683 and continued till 1708. He was said to have been one of Newton's few friends until, apparently, upsetting the philosopher with a rude story involving a nun.[40]

Even the official engineer of the Royal Mint, an institution that Newton became master of, was a Frenchman, Pierre Blondeau. He had been enticed over because England did not possess the skills and technology to produce coins of a standard weight and milled edge. Blondeau was part of an important objective of attracting over-skilled Europeans due to the indigenous poverty in England of such practices and knowledge. He was clearly recruited as an experienced person vital to preventing the depreciation of England's coinage from illicit clipping.[41] Elsewhere, the Royal Laboratory at Woolwich Dockyard, established in 1696 and used for the development of weapons, was managed by the Swedish Chief Engineer for England, Martin Beckman. Also in the Woolwich complex was the Royal Brass Foundry, which was created in 1716 for the production of guns and cannons, and run by the Swissman, Andrew Schalch, until he was replaced by the Dutch Master Founder Jan Verbruggen, in 1770.

Far from having a unique inventive culture, Britain needed to first import much of its creativity. The country's ability to usurp foreign trades via its wooing of European skilled labour was recognized by many on the continent, none more so than Georges-Marie Butel-Dumont and his two-volume translation of John Cary's 1695 tract, *Essai sur l'etat du Commerce d'Angleterre* (1755). Those enlightened philosophical pioneers of the late seventeenth and eighteenth centuries celebrated today were not, as Sophus Reinert has recently emphasized, necessarily those of contemporaries.[42]

The foundation of the Royal Society of London in 1660 was once seen as an important component to Britain's eighteenth-century oeconomic development. However, as Steven Shapin has shown, despite initial statements, members of the institution held deep reservations about getting their hands dirty and associating with lowly technicians, paid philosophical demonstrators, artisans and craftsmen.[43] In fact, argues Larry Stewart, it was not the privileged and private space of the Royal Society that transported natural philosophy outwards but, rather, the technicians and philosophical demonstrators of Restoration England. Indeed, he claims, it was almost in spite of the Royal Society that natural philosophy entered the public arena of pre-industrial England.[44] The Royal Society may have spoken about the practical utility of natural philosophy but very little value emerged from it. Practical knowledge was never really the target of the society.[45] As John Henry writes: 'When Robert Boyle and others talked about the usefulness of their new natural philosophy … it is quite clear that what they had in mind was its usefulness for combating atheism' and not promoting industry.[46]

In spite of the assertion by the Royal Society that it was composed of a whole gamut of the social spectrum all working to help each other, it was in practice far more closed. From the outset the relationship between philosophers, merchants and manufacturers among the society's ranks was problematic, in particular, on the question of who was eligible as a member and who was not; there was an extremely limited exchange between Royal Society gentlemen and artisans. Moreover, those bridging the two worlds, most notably Robert Hooke, sat uncomfortably within the space of the society. He was, it would seem, far happier meeting fellows at coffee houses. For Stewart this 'anticipates a time when discourse over a bowl of coffee would be transformed into experimental demonstration before mechanics and merchants'. In other words, a sign of things to come when experimental natural philosophy, from a trickle, flooded out from the preserve of the Royal Society and entered public dwellings. It was at this moment, according to Stewart and others, that experiment became truly concerned with being useful.[47]

The legitimacy that would underpin the new philosophy, Stewart claims, would be the belief that it could be useful and bring great benefits. The proponents of this view aggressively pedalled Newtonianism, a notoriously vague term, driven by the social forces of the marketplace. For Stewart it was by making science public that its practical use for mechanics, mining and hydraulics was demonstrated.[48]

The primary evidence Stewart provides to reveal the rise of Newtonianism in the marketplace is through the promotion of experimental natural philosophy via public lectures. He supports this argument by giving a few case studies such as James Hodgson. Hodgson stopped working for the Astronomer Royal, John Flamsteed, in 1702, and started employment with Francis Hauksbee, then demonstrator to the Royal Society, in public lectures on natural philosophy. Hodgson lectured on philosophical subjects to a public audience, and thus reached a wider and less exclusive social strata than the elite and private world of the Royal Society, although there does not seem to be any records of the social anatomy or the size of this audience.[49]

In December 1704, Hodgson announced that he was to put on classes in natural philosophy and astronomy to 'lay the best and surest Foundation for all useful knowledge'. He made a great deal of the fact that his programme of experiments was conducted with equipment that had hardly been witnessed outside of the Royal Society. The course was to be held in the City at the Hand and Pen in St Paul's Churchyard. Hodgson was, claims Stewart, at the top of an emerging group of Newtonian teachers who were also expanding the reach of experimental philosophy beyond the confines of the Royal Society.[50]

However, how extensive these lectures were, how much new or – crucially – practically useful natural philosophy they contained and what the background anatomy of the lecturer's audience was is hard to ascertain.[51] Certainly lectures on gauging taxed goods, like those provided by the astronomer and former excise officer, Charles Leadbetter, would surely have been for revenue officers and manufacturers or merchants who were levied. To make money these must have been practical lectures designed to teach those people immersed within the mechanics of the fiscal state how to measure and count like the state. On closer scrutiny of Stewart's examples, they tend to also concentrate upon the more immediate commercial concerns of navigation and insurance rather than innovation in industry.[52] A good argument can be made that the demands of the state and a fiercely regulated trade were the key vectors of knowledge diffusion and the creation of a calculating people.[53] From this stance Stewart's argument takes on added importance.

For Stewart the explosion of finance surrounding the government's need for short- and, increasingly, long-term loans during the 1690s created a gambling spirit and mania for investments in technical joint-stock projects. The spate of these schemes being pedalled in and around Exchange Alley needed, he claims, both technical justification and refutation. Newtonian experimental philosophy therefore stepped into this space to fulfil both roles. Thus 'lecturers, mathematical practitioners and instrument-makers' offered technical knowledge to the increasing population of commercial men ready to exploit any knowledge that could increase their wealth. As a result, Exchange Alley became a centre of both financial and intellectual knowledge exchange – both traded for the right price. This seems entirely plausible but not necessarily of a Newtonian or industrial bent.[54]

Nonetheless, John Harris seems to fit the profile of a Newtonian market-driven exponent of practical industrial knowledge. Harris was certainly an admirer of Newton, a Whig and a Protestant religious dissenter. He delivered his lectures between 1698 and 1707 in a series founded by the heavily excised Southwark brewer and entrepreneur Charles Cox, who went on to become an MP for said London borough. However, most of Harris's work seems to actually be focused upon navigation and not the application of experimental natural philosophy to industry. In general, Harris seemed more concerned with projecting financial instruments; for example, along with his patron, Cox, and several others, he obtained a charter for the Amicable Society and became deeply involved in numerous other insurance ventures, although he declined to become one of the managers of the new Sun Fire Office in 1710.[55]

It seems likely that public lectures were primarily concerned with teaching people to count like the state as, for example, the case of taxed manufactures, financial instruments connected to the national debt such as actuary tables, lotteries and tontines, and to master new fiscal instruments associated with the rise of trade like navigation skills, bills of exchange and marine insurance. Stewart implies this when he concludes, 'The whole notion of mixed mathematics led to the existence of a community of learned practitioners who were more likely to be found on the *London docks* than in the common rooms of Cambridge or at Whitehall' (my italics).[56]

Even if a lecturer spoke of the role of experimental natural philosophy to aid industry, 'it seems unlikely', claims Alan Morton, 'that the lecturers themselves had a direct and significant effect on the development of industry: in the 1740s there were only 13 lecturers in the whole of Europe according to Desaguliers', while in England only Desaguliers and James Stirling had any direct input into industrial projects. It is also, as we have seen, extremely difficult trying to define the audience for such lectures.[57]

The link between natural philosophy and technologically-induced industrial development, for Morton, comes via the use of the models used by lecturers and certain other practical men to demonstrate the making and functioning of machines. To support his argument Morton gives the example of Benjamin Robins and his work on ballistics using a pendulum to estimate the effect of air resistance on a cannon ball. Similarly, John Smeaton, drawing upon parts of Robins model, designed a way of examining the efficiency of windmills and waterwheels via models. Lastly, Watt used a model Newcomen engine to investigate heat loss in a steam engine, which culminated in the development of the separate condenser. Models, of course, had been used for a very long time and were probably most important in improving state maritime technical issues and revealing excise fraud in court cases.[58] This is not surprising since the costs of building a war ship was huge with dockyards dwarfing all other eighteenth-century industrial complexes, while demonstrating tax evasion in a court room often required a model of the manufacturing process.[59] Warfare, in general, has been seen by some scholars as the key source of innovation during this era of Britain's growing fiscal–military state.[60] In this sense it came within the context of what Sven Beckert has recently coined 'war capitalism'.[61] Another vital area to Britain's industrial prospects was in the realm of textile design and printing.

Textile design

Fundamental to industrial success in textiles was design. The Quaker, merchant and staunch protectionist Joshua Gee, writing in 1729, was in no doubt about the vital importance of good design: 'It was certainly a Master-Piece in the *French* to keep this Nation [Britain] dependant on them for their Fashions; how little so ever some may think of this, it has drawn many Thousand Pounds yearly into *France*, and lessened our Trade with Foreign Nations.'[62] By 1738 Gee's treatise, *The Trade and Navigation of Great-Britain*, was in its fourth edition and being translated across Europe.

British design compared to its French and Asian rivals was a constant source of frustration for eighteenth-century commercial and industrial reformers. One obvious issue was knowledge and access to dyestuffs, which was a particular problem for the young textile printing industry. Indian developments had long ago produced an array of world-beating dyes. Despite dedicated attempts, eighteenth-century British printers – with all their apparent access to new philosophical experimental ingenuity – failed to imitate or understand the Indian process of cotton dyeing. It was also the case that the cost of importing gums (a vegetable sticky substance that hardened) and dyes was very expensive. As well as failing to find a durable way of setting the dye on textiles via the mordanting process, the use of all these expensive materials and tedious techniques greatly frustrated the British textile printing industry. These manufacturers struggled to compete with the Indian process of printing and increasingly tried mechanical contrivances to aid them in their quest for a solution. For example, William Sherwin, very early on, took out a patent in 1676 for a double-necked rolling press that was modelled upon the German method of mezzotint printing, and was very likely an early version of the later cylinder-printing process.[63]

However, despite some of these initial setbacks, Audrey W. Douglas and, more recently, John Styles make the convincing observation that a major advantage the British domestic printers had, quite early on, was their ability to make a quick response to fashionable demand. By contrast the East Indian Company would have to wait several months to act upon changes in taste. The slow flow of information from England to South Asia and the return of such Indian printed cotton textiles was a great advantage to the growing home industry. Domestic calico printers were initially nurtured by Huguenot immigrants who, in turn, probably learnt their skills from Near East Armenian calico printers. To begin with, they were primarily based at the heart of English fashion in London and the Home Counties. The extraordinary growth of English textile printers and their competitive impact upon the European market, clearly weighed heavily on the East India Company after the first Calico Act of 1701. The increasing quality of domestic printers was a threat to the company that was only going to get greater. Developing a finishing textile industry was the initial platform for English cotton cloth.[64] From this base imported plain Indian cottons could be printed and penetrate the international market – a move greatly aided by protective legislation.

Maxine Berg has theorized this process of manufacturing emulation and emphasizes the role of innovation through imitation.[65] The introduction of Asian products helped fuel the desire for diversity and the impetus to find ways to copy such items via new techniques, materials and production processes. Three of the key manufactured imports that triggered European emulation and material culture were porcelain, chintz and lacquerware.[66] Of course, many of these luxury products would subsequently diffuse down and become much more accessible everyday items.[67] Berg situates the Society for the Encouragement of Arts, Commerce and Industry as, partly, Britain's answer to the French Academy, which was seen as the engine of this country's lead in fashion. An alliance between *marchands-merciers* based in Paris and textile producers in Lyons combined to produce textile designs to feed a fashion cycle. Since the seventeenth century, a great deal of money in France had been invested in design studios to aid this process.[68]

In Britain, particularly from the 1720s, there was a widespread recognition that the country lacked freehand drawing skills, resulting in a concerted movement to improve the situation along with backwardness in modelling. Between this decade and the 1760s, there was a general fear that Britain was uncompetitive in the production and design of luxury goods stemming primarily from France (Figure 5).

Figure 5 'The Imports of Great Britain from France' by Louis Peter Boitard, 1757.

As a result, there was increased effort to cultivate import substitutes for such items by improving domestic design. A key to aiding the situation in Britain was to improve the country's process of training draughtsmen. Not surprisingly, then, another of the early objectives of the new Society of Arts was to improve British drawing skills. This was not simply imitation of, say, Chinese porcelain with bone China but the craft skills needed to decorate them. For example, Josiah Wedgwood employed about seventy designers and modellers from the 1770s, as well as commissioning famous foreign artists and domestic talents such as William Blake and Joseph Wright.[69]

French design, then, was seen as far superior to the British and something needed to be done to rectify this situation. The Society of Arts programme in 'polite arts' was initially aimed at providing monetary awards for drawing and to promote the need for skilled designers among the young. However, in the end, the society's attempt to nurture native designers was not a great success. Certainly by the 1780s the struggling silk industry increasingly reverted back to copying French designs. In fact, the society had already given up offering awards for silk patterns in 1776 and focused its prizes for calico designs to aid the newly emancipated pure cotton textile industry.[70] However, even here, the society stopped giving prizes two years later, probably because legal protection of original designs was very poor in Britain. Defence and protection of designs gained much more attention in France than in Britain.[71]

French superiority in this field was reflected in Britain by the fact that the two primary design manuals in the 1750s were translations of French texts originating from the mid-seventeenth century, and promiscuously plagiarized by British design writers. A lucrative trade in optical drawing aids also took off in London to aid draughtsmanship in drawing three-dimensional structures. This promotion of various aspects of design was also aided by the vast increase in the array of possibilities triggered by the arrival of new materials from global trade and colonization. All of which continued to fuel an elite appetite for diversity and exotic design.[72]

Between 1730 and 1760 concerted attempts were made, especially in London and the Midlands, to improve creative freehand drawing. This was spearheaded by the expansion of private schools of design, predominantly managed and staffed by continental Europeans like Jacob Bonnean. There was also a widening of subcontracting work to specialized shops, with the larger manufacturers benefiting most from the practice. A key aspect of success for a significant producer like Wedgwood was the employment of a gifted team of designers that were capable of dominating the market.[73]

Once the restrictions upon the domestic sale of cotton cloth were lifted in 1774, the textile printing industry started to lobby Parliament for protection of all its designs. This politicizing intensified during the 1780s. For example, early in 1785 the House of Commons received a petition from a number of 'Callicoe Printers, Artists, designers of Drawings, Engravers, and others, Proprietors of original Patterns for printing Linens, Cottons, Callicoes, and Muslins' wanting greater protection. A calico printer, William Kilburne, based at Wallington in Surrey, drew his own prints but complained that a number of them had been copied: 'That a thousand Pounds worth of Prints have been obliged to be laid by as useless, on Account of the Imitations.' Another calico printer and draughtsman from Mitcham in Surrey, Thomas Hatcher, shared Kilburne's grievance. He too had his pattern for a lady's dress copied and reproduced 'upon a very course Linen' and sold cheaply. Francis Moore, a London linen draper based in Cheapside, confirmed that he had purchased a pattern from Kilburn but after just a month of selling his printed cloth, 'a base Copy, at a reduced Price, and of inferior Cloth and Materials, was produced for sale'.[74] A particular focus of the petitioners was over the 'proliferation of designs manufactured by Northern printers on inferior cloth, which also attracted a lesser duty'; they wanted protection based on the kind of copyright authors' of books received.[75]

An act was passed in 1787 but only granted protection for two months – later extended to three. This compared really poorly with the length of time awarded to other copyright protection, such as fourteen years for a book and a further fourteen years if the author was still alive (1710), while engravers were also entitled to fourteen years (1735). Part of the discrepancy, argues Kathy Bowrey, seems to have been a lack of direction over dealing 'with artistic works of an industrial character' and, possibly, 'a reflection of northern discontent with the granting of monopoly rights in connection with textile inventions'. Moreover, designs changed relatively rapidly due to different fashions, and thus a short-term protection serving a fashion season may have seemed adequate. Bowrey concludes: 'Originality in design referred to a commercial, rather than an artistic context.'[76]

Printing once again drastically changed in the late eighteenth and early nineteenth century with the advent of textile roller printing – a process drawn from book printing and patented in Scotland by Thomas Bell in 1783. Once the design had been engraved the pattern could continually be reproduced; where once only six pieces per day could be made upon a single table, a steam-powered roller could toss out 500. It is certainly the case that the production of printed textiles increased from 1 million to 16 million pieces per annum between 1769 and 1840. In addition, a massive impetus was given in 1831, especially this time to cotton cloth, when the excise on printed textiles was significantly reduced. With no global rivals anymore cotton textiles neither needed any tariff protection or bounties to encourage export.[77] *The Penny Magazine* reported in 1843 that the printing cylinder machine could produce three-quarters of a mile of cloth in an hour. 'Few things', the magazine concluded, were 'more extraordinary' than the 'substitution of miles for yards'.[78] However, the arrival of cylinder-printing was far less decisive than *The Penny Magazine* implied or subsequent historians once thought. It cost a great deal more than block-printing and thus was not cost-effective for short-run printed textiles. As a result block-printing remained very important throughout the nineteenth century.[79]

On the whole, those printers catering for a small high-quality market tended to support copyright extension, while those serving Britain's majority classes and an extensive export market tended to oppose extension. The protagonists of greater copyright underscored the value of the skill needed to produce original designs and the need to protect them. In addition, the copyright issue became entwined in anti-corn law debates and the politics of free trade versus protectionism, with 'the so-called pirates' accusing the campaigners of extension deliberately promoting a monopoly. 'As they saw it,' writes Lara Kriegel, 'it was not copying, but the copyright itself that harmed market health. Its extension would raise prices, increase litigation, and generally stymie the printing trade, not to mention the spinning and dying connected to it.' In many ways it was a battle between the pre-industrial metropolitan printers' preservation of this world and the new mechanized mass-producing view of the northwest. It was the copy, rather than the original, that satisfied the newer dynamic market of fashionable bulk production.[80]

Textile quality

Equally important to design was quality. British linens in the early eighteenth century were frequently poorly finished with superior linens having to be bleached in Holland (known as 'Scottish Holland's'). The Dutch, in general, during this period were still considered the leading European dyers and finishers of cloth. In addition, such was the quality of finished Indian textiles that Manchester merchants could often only sell their cloth in Africa if such Asian cloth was unavailable. The expense, as opposed to simply skill, of finishing cloth was a major factor. For example, purchasing the dye cochineal could surpass the price of unfinished cloth, and the orchilla required to dye silk violet could weigh four times the undyed fabric. Trying to match the quality of Indian dyes, in general, took almost the whole century to achieve. In addition, bleaching linens and cotton was a very lengthy process, let alone applying the dyes.[81]

Textiles varied greatly in their colouring treatment with wool being the easiest using vegetable dyes, then silk, followed by cotton and finally linen; this ranking was primarily to do with the level of impurities within the cloth itself. The only dye that worked on all four textiles was indigo, while cochineal could only be applied to wool and silk. The amount of dye needed also varied, depending upon the nature of the cloth; for example, 1 pound of silk needed 2 ounces of cochineal while 1 pound of wool required just 1 ounce. Textiles also needed fixatives, known as mordants, for the dye. There were a wide availability of these with the most common being '*alum*, crude *tartar* (or argol) and *cream of tartar* (potassium *hydrogen tartrate*) often used together'. Other materials used for this purpose included vegetable ashes like pearl and potash, kelp and barilla, copperas (i.e. ferrous sulphate or green vitriol), gall nuts, shumack and lime.[82]

In addition, materials were needed to clean and bleach the cloth. The alkali was often ashes and soft soap, while the acid was butter milk and in some places, especially Ireland and parts of Scotland, sour water derived from bran or rye flour. The properties of lime as an alkali and vitriol as an acid were known, but considered harmful to the cloth, although cotton was washed in a weak vitriol if it was going to be dyed.[83]

Despite concerted attempts to domestically nurture many of the above materials, ultimately, Britain was dependent upon imports (although a certain amount of kelp was cultivated in Scotland and Ireland). Perhaps the most important player in all this was Spain. The country had a monopoly in the supply of cochineal, and dominated trade in indigo, dyewoods, barilla, olive oil, yellow berries, orchilla, madder and shumack. It is also the case that all these items were subject, even by contemporary standards, to a high degree of regulation. It should be remembered that cochineal was the second-most valuable export from Spanish Mexico after silver.[84] With the exception of a few substitutes, like kelp for potash, attempts to replace imports with British substitutes typically failed. For example, a trial to replace the red dye, cochineal, with dried ladybirds proved messy and unsuccessful.[85]

Much more success came from growing the materials in the colonies. In particular, North American potash became standard from the 1760s, while indigo had been semi-successfully cultivated there since the 1740s. The emergence of indigo from South Carolina became a very important source to Britain from the mid-century, after planters in this colony turned to it during the 1740s due to the depression in its predominant staple, namely, rice. Prior to this Britain relied upon supplies of such dye from Spanish and French colonies in South America and the West Indies. Although the Carolina planters never truly mastered a consistent mode of production, the final product was found adequate for the leading sectors of Britain's textiles (linens, cottons and coarse wools).[86]

Nevertheless, the supply of imported natural products used in the process of bleaching and dyeing textiles had reached its maximum. Trials to find alternative chemical substitutes had been taking place since at least the sixteenth century. One problem was the belief that an acid, frequently the private recipe of a dyer, was seen as harmful to the cloth. Indeed, legislation was passed in Britain against the use of 'acid blacks and lime and vitriol for bleaching'. Leading the way in researching dyes and bleaching during the eighteenth century were the French; in the 1730s Charles-Francois de Cisternai Dufay tested dyes to ascertain their fastness. Jean Hellot experimented with red dyes but failed to make any significant breakthrough, but Pierre Joseph Macquer created an artificial 'Prussian blue' for wool and silk. Nicolas Leblanc helped devise a process that used limestone to convert sea water into soda or, in present terms, converting sodium sulphate to soda. Most famously Claude-Louis Berthollet provided a chemical explanation for mordants, furthered soapmaking and, most importantly, observed the bleaching qualities of chlorine.[87]

Meanwhile, the expansion of linen cloth and the extraordinary rise of cotton textiles during the final third of the eighteenth century was adding pressure on the traditional methods of bleaching.[88] Several thousand square feet of fabric was typically spread on land and naturally processed by sunlight, which was not one of Britain's greatest resources. Even prior to exposure to scarce sunshine, the cloth had to be boiled in an alkali several times, dried and hot pressed followed by a number of other operations. All of this required a great deal of fuel, which explains Scotland's long-term success in linen thanks to abundant supplies of coal. After this lengthy process, the cloth was immersed in a mild acid to remove some of the salts congealed within the fabric deposited after the alkali detergent washings – a process known as the 'sour'. The material used for this purpose was sour milk or whey, although, as already noted, in Scotland – following the Irish method – bran was the primary ingredient. Bran was much cheaper and found adequate for the more common courser linen made in such areas. The superior linen required the use of milk or whey which partly explains why the Dutch Harlem bleachers were so successful, since they lived in the heart of rich dairy country. Both methods required extensive land and took weeks to complete. From the second half of the eighteenth century many linen producers started using vitriol (sulphuric acid) for this latter operation.[89]

The use of vitriol in the sour process was made possible in Britain after the establishment of its large-scale production. A similar switch was also taking place in France, Germany and Austria. Interestingly, however, the impetus to the production of this acid came originally from the demands of refiners of precious metals as a cleaning agent. Consequently, major producers of sulphuric acid were established during the 1740s in the heart of Britain's fast-expanding metal-working regions, namely, London and Birmingham. The substance was put into lead containers to ensure it could be safely and efficiently transported. It was really not until the mid-1750s that it was recognized as a way of radically speeding up the bleaching process of cloth by as much as 50 per cent (from eight to four months), although there is evidence that the Scottish linen industry – under the encouragement of the Board of Trustees for Fisheries, Manufactures and Improvements – had already been importing the bleach from the English and Dutch as a substitute for the old process. This also probably explains why the early pioneer of its production, the medical doctor John Roebuck, established a second vitriol plant near Edinburgh.[90] Consequently, it was thanks to a process developed within the metal industries, which subsequently diffused out into the arena of textile production, that cloth bleaching greatly improved.

Closely related to the use of vitriol as a bleaching agent was the arrival of chlorine. Although chlorine was identified in 1773 by the Swedish apothecary Karl Wihelm Scheele, it was not taken up by textile bleachers till Berthollet published an account of its bleaching properties in 1785. Despite the problems in trying to use it, bleachers sensing the profits to be made, doggedly continued with their attempts culminating in Charles Macintosh and the handloom weaver Charles Tennant's bleaching powder in 1799. Prior to this it had been aggressively promoted in Liverpool by two recent French immigrants, namely, Anthony Bourboulon and Matthew Vallet. A clear impetus for this perseverance was down to the lack of cheap British meadowland available for laying out the cloth to bleach via the scarce sun, coupled with the difficulty in gaining supplies of sour milk; land rent had also shot up during this period.[91]

Equally important for this development was the central issue of speed demanded by a fast-expanding cotton textile industry. The full bleaching method cost a great deal of money and was dependent upon limited British sunshine. In addition, while the cloth lay on the field it was vulnerable to theft that led to the creation of elaborate and expensive man-traps coupled with the hiring of guards. It was climatic limitations, growing land rents, expensive policing and, especially, the length of time to actually bleach that was the prime motor to the development of user-friendly chlorine bleaching. This had significant implications for financial savings at a time when there were so many competing sectors for capital.[92] Without this development Britain's leading manufacture of the Industrial Revolution, cotton textiles, would not have been possible.

It was not just the bleaching process that invited changes in textile production but the operation of cleaning the cloth. The natural sources used for this such as barilla, potash and kelp were either becoming increasingly scarce or were becoming more and more expensive. Manufacturing potash was enormously wasteful and Britain's domestic supply of timber was inadequate to meet the demand. Consequently, from the mid-eighteenth century potash production in the American colonies was actively encouraged. Despite the supply of American potash remaining relatively abundant, even after the War of American Independence, it almost doubled in price between 1785 and 1815.[93]

As such the search intensified for an alternative alkali. Spearheading this quest were the French. The Marseilles soap industry's dependence upon Spanish barilla was becoming deeply problematic, and the French Academy of Sciences in 1776 offered a lucrative prize for someone to find a method of producing soda from common salt. The eventual winner was Leblanc's process. However, it was not until the Napoleonic Wars spread to the Iberian Peninsula in 1808, leading to a severe shortage in the supply of Spanish barilla, that the production of Leblanc's soda commenced in Marseilles.[94]

In Britain, the primary impulse to adopting the Leblanc process came from the Liverpool soapmakers. Along with textiles, the partly associated soap sector was rapidly expanding, and the relatively new Merseyside soap industry was approaching the production levels of London by the close of the Napoleonic Wars. The Liverpool producers used kelp as their alkali and the London makers used barilla. In 1822 the duties on the latter were halved giving London soapmakers an enormous advantage over their Liverpool rivals. The Merseyside equivalents urgently needed a solution and the answer came with a replacement synthetic alkali. This became feasible later in 1825 when the British government abolished the £30 per ton duty on salt, making the production of Leblanc soda much more attractive. Also important was the abundance of salt from Cheshire and coal supplies to Liverpool as key materials in its production; once again the region was blessed with the right quality of both items.[95] At the vanguard of the British production of soda was the Irish pharmacist and soldier James Muspratt who, although not the first in Britain to make it, produced it on an unprecedented scale.[96]

Muspratt began by manufacturing the cruder, smelly and weaker black ash. After a period of distrust over the substance, the soap boilers in Merseyside abandoned their traditional use of potash and turned to the new synthetic alkali. This enabled the Merseyside soap industry to outproduce London. In addition, the demand for Leblanc alkali led to a rapid establishment of factories to produce the substance. The strong white ash could be easily transported and stored for lengthy periods without deteriorating. The process also enabled the use of palm oil, rather than the more expensive use of animal fats, in the production of soap. Merseyside soon became the leading exporter of British soap and supplier of the domestic market. By this stage, Muspratt was producing his alkali in St Helens after being evicted from Liverpool for polluting the atmosphere.[97] The northwest now had a crucial supply of soap to aid its world-beating textiles. In the following chapter, we continue the theme of innovation and focus on technological developments in the key industries that define Britain's Industrial Revolution.

CHAPTER 9
TECHNOLOGICAL INNOVATION AND INDUSTRY

Cotton textiles

The focus of this chapter are the four sectors most associated with the British Industrial Revolution. Consider, first, the fundamental role state protection played in the emergence of cotton textiles. Printed or painted calico from India was banned from English consumption in 1701, followed by a total prohibition of domestic sales of Indian unprinted cotton in 1721. This was the case till such legislation was removed in 1774.

Despite the 1721 ban on wearing pure cottons, a robust and successful textile printing industry had emerged. It was the printing that was, at first, the most successful process in imitating Indian calicoes; Indians on the whole preferred painting the design on the cloth whereas the British used a block or plate.[1] Consequently, everything was in place to continue printing upon alternative cloths that could imitate and replace the demand for pure cotton textiles. For example, the production and consumption of mixed cotton fabrics, most notably cotton–linen fustian cloth, was permitted for domestic consumption; in addition, Indian plain pure cottons were also still allowed to be imported if they were subsequently (after being domestically printed) re-exported. Thus, those textile manufacturers working with some aspect of cotton were protected from Indian competition in the domestic and colonial market (but not, of course, in other places such as Africa). By contrast, most other European countries, apart from the Dutch, placed a *complete* ban on importing pure cotton cloth and wearing such items. This provided a major impetus to the subsequent expansion of the British cotton industry over the rest of Europe. For example, while Holland kept its domestic market unprotected from dyed and printed Asian textiles imports, its hitherto European lead in bleaching, dyeing and printing declined. In general, as Ian D. Colbin once put it: 'The easy wealth begotten of trade tempted her to forsake the more laborious course of a national manufacture.'[2]

Most of the initial calico and mixed cotton technology – for example, the early Dutch engine loom and the stocking frame – was first utilized in London before diffusing out to Manchester.[3] Prasannan Parthasarathi has clearly shown how British attempts to match the quality of Indian cottons fuelled its technological innovations in spinning and later weaving. Indeed, he emphasizes, such contests and confrontations were the key factors driving the intellectual and technological advances of Europeans. It is 'striking that the most revolutionary technological breakthroughs of eighteenth-century Europe were in two areas, textiles and energy, which worried Indians little'. It is also important to point out, as Giorgio Riello does, that cotton did not become a global commodity due to British mechanization, but rather Britain industrialized because cotton was already a global good.[4] Moreover, such innovation all took place behind protectionist tariffs and was subsequently encouraged via export bounties.

Meanwhile the Irish, who had been forcibly encouraged to nurture their own linen industry, were successfully doing so by the early eighteenth century. Since the banning of all East India calicoes imported for domestic use in 1721, the production of linens and mixed cottons had all greatly expanded. The supply of necessary linen yarn for such textiles in Lancashire continued to come from Ireland and Scotland – with 70 per cent emanating from the former. However, by the second half of the century Irish and Scottish yarn prices were greatly rising. Consequently, there was a massive impetus to find alternative suppliers and to improve the spinning of yarn. Despite the legislation, could a way be found for cotton yarn to be used to make the warp? This was something that came to be solved by technological innovation.[5]

An early attempt at improving weaving was John Kay's flying shuttle (1733), which basically freed one hand of the weaver, allowed the manufacture of much wider cloth and increased the speed of the production process.[6] The other fundamental development was patented in 1738 when Lewis Paul, of Huguenot descent, and the carpenter John Wyatt mechanized the twist given to the raw material to make yarn. This was achieved by replacing the use of the spinner's finger and thumb by the use of rollers. Paul persisted with his attempt to mechanize the process and twenty years later patented a roller and bobbin machine in 1758. It was a combination of the flying shuttle and twisting the raw cotton that would inform subsequent technological changes.[7]

The environment was now set for the industrial mechanization of textiles. Thomas Highs, an experienced reed maker from Leigh in Lancashire, tried to operationalize the Paul and Wyatt innovation. However, he soon realized he needed a skilled clockmaker to try and make the rollers work and so he formed a partnership with the Warrington clockmaker John Kay. The project was not successful and the two parted company. Despite this setback, Highs persisted and eventually created a machine he called a spinning jenny in 1764.

However, it would take the Lancashire-born carpenter and weaver, James Hargreaves, and the barber and wig maker, Richard Arkwright, to improve and commercialize the machine. Cotton had long been used for the weft but social labour had failed to master the warp from cotton yarn. The answer was to mechanize the process. This would solve the problem of both matching Indian skilled labour and as a substitute for reliance upon Irish, Scottish and European sources of linen yarn. It took Arkwright a few years to mechanize the production of an appropriate cotton yarn for the warp but, once this was achieved, it paved the way for the rapid rise of cotton factories. A major development was the carding engine that allowed the carded cotton to be removed without damaging it (Figure 6).[8] These key innovations of the Industrial Revolution were not born from Newtonian experimental natural philosophy and the work of public lectures.

The next obstacle to overcome was the 1721 Calico Act. The prohibition of printing domestic manufactured cottons for home consumption was lifted after intensive lobbying

Economic Botany — The Cotton Manufacture. Plate II. See page, 608. Vol. II.

CARDING, DRAWING, AND ROVING.

Figure 6 'Carding, drawing and roving cotton', c. 1830.

led by Arkwright and his Northampton partners in 1774. The result was a huge increase in the use of raw cotton, although it would take another ten years before domestically produced calico cloth would truly match Indian cotton textiles. To underline, these technological innovations were not primarily a reaction to the increasing costs and scarcity of linen yarn or labour costs, but the desperate attempt to match Indian quality of pure cotton textiles, versatility and turnover of designs; it had taken several decades but British cotton cloth was now on a par with Indian calico (still prohibited from domestic consumption). This, in turn, provided the means to satisfy an increasing demand for such diverse textiles from domestic demand and, especially, export markets (where British cotton textiles had a bounty). By this point, Britain and Europe were dominating global trade through the ability of its merchants to trade in a variety of markets between both Eurasia and the Americas.

It was also the case that the nature of raw cotton made it ideal, compared to wool and other fibres, to mechanized spinning – with further momentum from the lucrative rewards available from the global cotton textiles market.[9] A petition in 1790 underlined the key role of technology to British cotton quality, 'until the year 1774, when, in consequence of the invention of cotton mills, yarns were produced of a quality fit for warps, so as to admit of the manufacture of calicoes similar to those imported from India, by making a species of cloth wholly of cotton yarn'.[10] The mechanization of weaving took a little longer with the subsequent innovation being Edmund Cartwright's first power loom in 1785, although it took roughly another thirty years before it worked well.[11]

By the mid-nineteenth century the power loom had finally eroded the competition from hand-weavers and the costs of power had significantly reduced. There had also been a general economic slump during the 1840s and the reduction of social labour to a legislated 10-hour day. All this combined to promote a switch from human labour to the new weaving technology.[12]

Sven Beckert and Giorgio Riello also emphasize the crucial supply of raw cotton Britain eventually monopolized from the Americas. It should be remembered that it takes approximately twelve times more land to produce a unit of woollen fibre compared to cotton. This has a parallel argument to the ecological argument by E. A. Wrigley regarding the British advantage over coal, as opposed to the large amount of land needed to cultivate timber. The solution to solving a fast-growing population needing to be clothed, writes Riello, lay with a 'switch from a high energy-intensive fibre (wool) to a low energy-intensive fibre (cotton)'.[13]

If you combine these facts with the aggressive competition British cotton-based textiles had with superior Indian calicoes in Africa, the increasing demand for the cloth in the fast-expanding British American colonies, and the fact engineering skills were available in the nearby Midlands along with skilled clockmakers in the Lancashire city of Preston, then you have a convincing argument to the impetus behind technological innovation in cotton in the northwest.[14]

Crucially, this innovation required a high degree of state protection from competition. The result was, as Beckert puts it, the creation of 'a world radically different from anything ever seen before without recourse to theoretical science, often without much education'.[15] The ideas adopted for the spinning jenny drew from an array of other manufacturing processes such as the rollers involved in shaping metals and pressing paper, while the use of gears derived from the workings of a clock. Not surprisingly, then, Arkwright employed clockmakers to produce the gears and cogs involved in the new textile machines. Robert C. Allen estimates that something like 800 skilled watch- and clock-making artisans were employed in 150 Arkwright mills by the early 1790s. By 1830, 70 per cent of all Britain's cotton workers were based in Lancashire. By contrast eighteenth-century continental Europe, for example, lacked such an extensive and ideal geographical pool of skilled artisans and textile labour.[16] Nearby, too, was Britain's most important Atlantic port, Liverpool. The latter, by the close of the century, was the hub for a monopoly of imported raw cotton from American southern slave plantations and the export of northwest cotton textiles; all these domestic centres were relatively close and now linked by an extensive canal system.[17] This last point was also crucial to the question of metals, energy and steam.

Metals

Seventeenth-century England was clearly concerned at the level of its domestic timber supplies and, as a relatively small land mass, it only has a limited area of cultivable land (the surface area is roughly a third of France). As such, James I felt compelled to actually ban the use of timber as a source of energy in glassmaking as early as 1615. One way out of this was to extend its terrain via colonization of the Americas to produce scarce items such as timber; however, this proved disappointing. Another solution, much closer home, soon beckoned. The island could tap into its own uniquely accessible rich domestic deposits of the right type of coal (bituminous) as a substitute. This, for a number of historians, was crucial to Britain's Industrial Revolution. For E. A. Wrigley the switch from an organic to a mineral economy was the key factor in explaining Britain's Industrial Revolution. As Rolf Peter Sieferle has calculated, by 1820 it would have taken a forest the size of England to have supplied as much energy as it was now using per year from coal. While Allen recently concludes: 'The diffusion pattern of the Newcomen engine was determined by the location of coal mines, and Britain's lead reflected the size of her coal industry – not superior rationality.'[18]

The switch to coal was adopted by a number of Britain's infant industries that, in turn, fuelled the evolution of technologies connected to coal-burning. All this was developed ad hoc over a long period of time. Its use in soap, malt, salt, sugar, glass, iron, dyeing and bleaching textiles commenced long before the institutional establishment of applying formal knowledge to industry. In 1675 the German immigrant Frederick de Blewstone tried to smelt iron using coal at his workshop in Stafford, but failed due to his inability to remove impurities from the coal. The technique of altering coal into coke was first used by English malsters in their kilns, and was later copied by men like the malster apprentice and subsequent iron producer Abraham Darby. In 1709, using the malster method, Darby decarbonized coal at his manufactory in Coalbrookdale to make coke by baking the bituminous coal to remove impurities such as moisture, sulphur, tar and ash.[19]

The actual finery process was initially established by workmen from Pays de Bray in Normandy, France, between the late fifteenth century and mid-sixteenth century. Over five hundred furnaces were introduced by these foreigners in Kent and Sussex in southeast England. To make wrought iron, however, required the coke pig to be further processed. This only made commercial sense when the cost of charcoal increased and greatly exceeded the price of coal from the mid-eighteenth century.[20]

Coke-produced pig iron remained inferior to charcoal pig iron for most of the century due to its higher carbon and silicon content. Solving these problems at the forge by developing the necessary refining techniques proved hugely difficult; both smelting ore and refining the pig iron needed a great deal of heat and the right purity of fuel. Getting the heat was not the problem, rather, it was removing the impurities from the coal that proved the stumbling block; in particular, extracting the silicon was really hard and expensive. This had to be overcome before wrought iron could be produced. Coke-produced cast iron could be used to make pots, ovens and cannons but not things like machine parts, locks and precision tools. In terms of understanding the technicalities of converting cast iron into wrought iron and iron into steel, it was the French and savants like Rene Antoine Ferchault de Reaumur who led the way. However, despite opening a manufactory, the French never pursued the process with the vigour of the British.[21]

This, of course, also had something to do with Britain's comparative poorly wooded countryside, its monopoly of Swedish Orground iron, rich deposits of the right quality coal and subsequent protectionist tariffs. However, British developments in iron were not fast. In 1750, 95 per cent of pig iron was still being produced using charcoal, with imports from Sweden and Russia remaining hugely important. Only 1 per cent of mined coal in 1750 was used in domestic iron production but by 1830 this figure had risen to 20 per cent.

Between 1750 and 1771 twenty-seven new coke furnaces were started while twenty-five charcoal furnaces closed; ironmasters had greatly improved the efficiency of the furnaces while the price of coal had hugely dropped. A technological breakthrough came during the early 1760s when Charles and John Wood in Cumbria (1763) and various manufacturers in the West Midlands found a way of re-melting the coke pig iron in a foundry furnace to remove the silicon. After this the de-siliconed pig iron was re-heated in small pots to further remove sulphur and carbon using a lime flux to produce wrought iron. Further developments continued when a method was found to substitute coke with coal for the initial process of heating, while mechanical stamps were introduced to break the iron up and then put in pots.[22] This was shop-floor innovation centred around coal-produced iron and not any new enlightened knowledge.

The urgency of war and Britain's place at the vanguard of European military expansion led to crucial innovations in this field. Significant developments were made at military state complexes such as the Royal Artillery facilities at Woolwich. It was here that an amalgamation of the Royal Laboratory (1696), the Royal Brass Foundry (1716) and various other establishments were located. This important complex was called the Woolwich Arsenal in 1805 after, apparently, the suggestion of George III. From its location in Woolwich foreigners were pivotal to its development. For example, the Royal Laboratory used to develop new innovative weapons was devised and managed by the Swedish Chief Engineer of England, Martin Beckman. The Royal Brass Foundry, used to build guns and cannons, had as its first Master Founder another Swissman, Andrew Schalch, who had learnt many of his skills and know-how at the famous French foundry at Douai. However, the foundry at Woolwich slowly decayed over the century and Schalch was replaced by the Dutch Master Gun Founder, Jan Verbruggen. The new master was important in bringing with him the latest machine tool techniques and technology from the European continent to Britain. He had been Master Founder for the Admiralty of West Friesland where he learnt new boring cannon techniques, originally devised by Johann Maritz, Master Founder at Burgdorf in Switzerland. This new boring technique at Woolwich was later copied by John Wilkinson, a leading British ironmaster, which he subsequently patented four years after it had been introduced in London.

A really important innovation came in 1784 when the Royal Navy agent Henry Cort devised the puddling and rolling process. For this he adopted the coal-burning reverberatory furnace used in glassmaking and the rolling of heated metal using grooved rollers, which removed the need for pots and lime. The furnace simply applied the heat from above therefore exposing the iron to an oxidizing current of air rather than forced air from below. The actual puddling process was where the iron was stirred to separate impurities and extract the higher quality wrought iron. The furnace effectively lowered the carbon content of the cast iron, while the 'puddler' extracted a mass of iron from the furnace using a rabbling bar (an iron rod with a hook at the end).

The extracted ball of metal was then processed into shingle by a hammer that beat out further impurities, after which it was squashed in the rolling mill to push out the final unwanted matter. The rolling allowed the production of malleable wrought iron with a speed and uniformity of finish that was unattainable with just the forge hammers. This whole transformation was based upon techniques devised by other manufacturers, such as the Shropshire-based workmen Thomas and George Cranage (they gained a patent for producing wrought iron via a reverberatory furnace in 1766), and Peter Onions between 1783 and 1784, rather than any knowledge stemming from new natural philosophy.[23]

Ecological factors, military demands, innovative copying and shop-floor ingenuity from other domestic and transnational industries thus played a major role in the trajectory of Britain's iron industry. However, Baltic iron remained the most important source for this metal in Britain right up until the close of the century. Chris Evans and Göran Rydén have persuasively shown the crucial place of Baltic iron during this period in the Atlantic world. They masterfully trace the path of this fundamental metal from the ore in the Baltic, especially Sweden, to the iron produced at the forge, and then on to key Atlantic markets. Without the rich supplies of resources from the Northern European hinterlands, which the Dutch and especially the British lacked at this time, the world oeconomy would have been a very different one. Indeed, right up to the 1790s a great deal of the iron used in Britain still came from Sweden and to a certain extent Russia. This crucial fact has, on the whole, got lost in the hurry to emphasize the domestic production of iron in Britain's Industrial Revolution.[24]

Swedish and Russian iron was shipped to Britain's western ports, then on to the Midlands where it was converted into metal goods and traded, especially to Africa. This iron was fundamental to the supply of nails, the steel machetes used by African slaves, and hoes that were then exported to aid the westward march of the plantation. With a perceived lack of indigenous timber and charcoal to fuel iron production in Britain, and the traditional supplies from the Basque unable to quench demand, a determined switch to the Baltic was made. By the 1720s demand for Swedish iron was putting a strain on supply, which is when eyes began to also turn to iron from the Urals in Russia.[25] Thus, by the 1730s Britain had a variety of iron (of very different qualities) from Sweden, Russia, its own domestic supplies and some still from Spain.

Crucial to the development of British steel was its monopoly of Swedish Orground iron (and large supplies of domestic coal): 'French industrialists, savants and state officials were intent on developing a steel sector to match Britain's but misplaced economic nationalism led them to forswear the use of Swedish "Orground" iron.' French savants certainly had a much greater understanding of the properties of steel but this, again, did not aid them.[26] Steel is a difficult metal to produce; it is an intermediate product lying halfway between almost carbonless wrought iron and high carbon pig iron (it is an alloy of iron and carbon). The most popular way of making it was by adding carbon to low carbon wrought iron. This was done in something called a cementation furnace, technology imported from the Netherlands in the seventeenth century, where carbon was infused into bar iron. This was an extremely expensive process but the end metal, steel, is vital for machine parts, tool making, exact joints, cylinders, pistons, springs for clocks, razors and anything requiring a durable precise form.[27] The process was greatly improved in 1740 by the first-generation German and Yorkshire clockmaker Benjamin Huntsman, who used coke and reverberatory ovens to create the necessary high temperatures to melt steel and produce cast or crucible steel.[28] Ultimately, however, it was by monopolizing the top quality Swedish Oreground iron that British steel-making was given the all-important boost.

The ultimate demise of Baltic imports, eventually, came from Britain's own iron industry via its technological transformation and through state protection. British iron masters had been unable to compete with Baltic iron because it lacked the available skills and right form of energy. The answer, partly, was a technological one through the adoption of coal-fired refinery methods. So, like innovations in cotton textiles, a key solution for the British iron industry to match foreign quality was via urgency and the development of new shop-floor technology. After decades of work a major breakthrough came with Cort's puddling technique. This was anything but an overnight solution and it was only really during the 1790s that the iron industry turned fully to mineral fuel. However, even here as Evans and Rydén show, this was not without the aid of state protection: 'Baltic iron, it should be recalled, did not reach its peak on the British market until 1793. It was only in the years after 1800, when tariff barriers against foreign iron were ratcheted up, that the fate of Russian and Swedish iron was sealed.'[29] Consequently, a crucial aspect in the success of this transformation was, once again, the key role of government protectionary policies.[30]

Britain's development of its metal industries was therefore not through the application of systematic knowledge. Elsewhere, however, other nations did attempt to create an indigenous iron and steel industrial base drawing upon the latest chemical studies. Consider the case of Frederick the Great's disastrous attempts to do so via the application of formal knowledge in Prussia. The idea was to substitute large imports from Sweden, Saxony and Russia with home-produced supplies. The man put in charge was the Prussian Inspector of Mines, Glass, and Steel Works, Johann von Justi, who seduced everyone with his confidence and apparent mastery of the relevant knowledge. After it was clear he had deceived everyone and the project had failed Justi was sentenced to prison in Küstrin.[31]

Energy and steam

Joel Mokyr dismisses the argument that Britain switched to coal because of an energy shortage. He claims it suffers 'from the logical difficulty that the scarcity of natural resources and their abundance cannot *both* be regarded as stimulating factors for technological progress', that is, raw cotton (imported) and coal (indigenous). Elsewhere, he claims the role of coal is a 'simplistic model' of the British Industrial Revolution that has 'long been abandoned'. This loose play with logic was cogently dismissed by J. R. Harris in his review of Mokyr's *The British Industrial Revolution*: 'On resources, there is the usual playing down of the importance of the coal endowment and the fanciful idea that Britain could have imported coal if necessary. Where from, one may ask, in the classical Industrial Revolution period?'[32]

Britain's unique access to the right sort of coal became less and less expensive throughout the eighteenth century, thanks to improvements in extraction and transportation. There is no doubt the surge in canal construction was originally driven by the need to reduce costs of moving coal; the output of coal between 1560 and 1800 increased sixty-six-fold by which date Britain was mining most of the world's coal. The industry to benefit the most was coal itself and iron (although malt, brewing, lime burning, alum boiling, sugar, dye industries, metal processing, smithing, brick and tile making, glass, soap, salt and much later cotton also utilized it). Within a commercial and industrial context Britain had stopped importing any iron by 1804 and, by 1815, nearly a third of domestic production was exported. Such an expansion had an important knock-on effect in other industrial processes, most importantly, machine tool making and steam engines.[33]

The demand for digging out coal was fundamental in the development of steam technology; coalmines were dangerous places and vulnerable to floods. Not surprisingly mine owners, not just of coal but valuable tin and copper from Cornwall, sought a way of solving this problem. In 1698, the Devonshire-born army engineer and fellow of the Royal Society, Thomas Savery, with his gaze locked upon Cornwall's rich tin and copper mines, marketed his engine as 'the miner's friend'. However, it was another Devonshire man, Thomas Newcomen, an ironmonger from Dartmouth, who successfully operationalized an atmospheric engine in 1712 that provided the first real solution (Figure 7). The bulk of these new engines would be utilized at coal, rather than metal, mines. Interestingly the

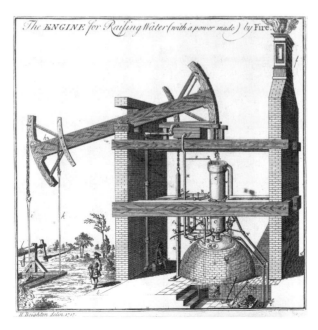

Figure 7 'Early Newcomen water-pumping steam engine, Oxclose, Tyne & Wear' by Henry Beighton, 1717.

leading protagonist associated with promoting the spread of Newtonian experimental philosophy, the French refugee John (Jean) Desaguliers, referred rather dismissively to the ironmonger, Newcomen, and his partner, the local glazier John Calley, as having 'very luckily by accident found what they sought for'. For Desaguliers they must have just stumbled across their atmospheric engine since they were neither philosophers nor mathematicians and thus incapable of understanding how it worked.[34] This is a demarcation taken too literally by an array of recent historians.

Savery and Newcomen did, however, use one piece of formal knowledge in their work, namely, that the atmosphere had weight. This had been widely known for a long time and earlier attempts to create a working engine had been made by the Dutchman Christian Huygens and Frenchman Denis Papin. The latter had tried to create a vacuum below the piston by igniting gunpowder, but this proved too volatile and dangerous leading to Papin attempting to use steam instead. The cylinder beneath the piston was filled with steam and then sprinkled with cold water to create a partial vacuum. The atmosphere, attracted to the vacuum, would then do the work by pushing down upon the piston that was attached to a beam; the weight of the beam would then pull the piston back up. The first Newcomen engine to use this principle was some 50 feet high. To build such an engine required skilled mechanics and engine stokers, who had to be created as much as the machine.[35]

The steam engine had also made an early appearance in the Habsburg hard-rock mines of lower Hungary. However, no one took it seriously as a productive tool since it was viewed as too cumbersome and inefficient there. It was common knowledge during the seventeenth and eighteenth centuries that if you wanted to view the latest and best mining technology, especially water-pumping equipment, you went to the Harz Mountains, the Erz Mountains or the Habsburg mines in the Carpathians. Moreover, these regions developed energy systems around water power so resilient that some of them continued to be used into the twentieth century. It seems a combination of fierce and expensive legal battles to obtain river and stream rights to power waterwheels for draining coalmines, coupled with the unique easy access to coal at the mines persuaded owners in Britain to gradually turn towards the Newcomen Atmospheric Engine. Unlike Britain, however, the European continent lacked such accessible coal or strict legal rights to water.[36] Nonetheless it should be underlined that, in the case of cotton spinning, waterwheel power was by far the most important source of energy well into the nineteenth century.[37]

The case of Sweden serves as another good example of how the local ecology and infrastructure informed technological development. Like the German states, Swedish technology during the eighteenth century was mainly based upon timber. The Newcomen engine seemed an attractive option to solve the need for an alternative energy to traditional ones such as muscle, water and wind. However, Sweden had little coal and the amount of wood required to fuel a Newcomen engine was huge compared to coal due to the former's much lower heat content. This triggered a major source of conflict. For example, a scarcity of timber was perceived to be a threat to the country's most important industry, namely, the production of bar iron (constituting 70 per cent of all exports) as well as other manufactures and, of course, an embedded timber-based culture (for example houses and general building infrastructure). The use of steam would thus have significantly depleted Sweden's timber supplies and, therefore, was one of the initial concerns expressed by the Swedish Board of Mines over the attempt to introduce the engine in 1725. As Svante Lindqvist writes: 'The Newcomen engine was economic in the context in which it had been developed i.e. the British coal industry…. . The basic economic reason for the failure of the Dannemora engine [the mine that trialled a version of the Newcomen engine] was thus the *difficulty of reproducing the cost-effectiveness of the technology in a new environment* [italics in original].'[38] The development made sense in Britain precisely because it was used primarily to pump water out of coalmines where there was an abundance of local free energy.

The Newcomen engine continued to improve throughout the century, but it was still too inefficient to be used on an extended scale in other potential areas such as the Cornish tin mines because getting coal there was too expensive. Nonetheless, there was a great deal of money to be had if this could become possible, and one way to achieve this was by making the engine much more efficient and obtaining energy far more accessible via better transport routes. Consequently, there was an incentive to try and reduce the waste of the engine and build canals to improve energy supplies.

It was a Scottish instrument maker to the University of Glasgow, James Watt, who was important here. The university had a model Newcomen engine that did not work as well as the full-sized working engine and kept running out of steam. Certainly, it was well known that small bodies lost heat much more quickly than larger ones since, proportionately, they had a much larger cooling surface. But Watt was convinced other things were also at work such as the brass used to make the cylinder rather than cast iron – indeed should it be made of wood? How could steam be so efficiently used that none of it was wasted? It certainly took less time to heat a wooden cylinder, but it was much slower to cool down and create a vacuum, while cooling the steam within a metal cylinder took more cold water than was expected. Surely boiling water and steam contained the same amount of heat? Yet the condensing steam actually gave the cooling water heat that could in turn produce steam – what Joseph Black independently defined as latent heat. Watt had no idea why this happened but found by creating a separate condenser outside the cylinder this could be avoided. This dealt with the crucial issue of having to solve the cylinder temperature problem.[39]

Watt's engine was also now truly a steam engine in the sense that it did not use the atmosphere but, rather, harnessed steam to push the piston down and up. All this required was the same steam to carefully flow from above to below via a pipe and valve. The process would then be repeated. The subsequent building of an operational steam engine would not have been possible without the financial support of the industrialists John Roebuck and, subsequently, Matthew Boulton. Importantly, both men provided the capital, space, tools and skilled labour required to build Watt's engine.[40] It was local financial incentives, ecology, capital and shop-floor ingenuity rather than any new philosophy that was crucial to its development.

A major problem faced by Watt and his skilled men was the issue of leakage and waste due to the inexact fitting between the cylinder and piston. The solution came from the machine-making industry and, in particular, John Wilkinson's new boring mill for the production of cannons to sell to Britain's military complex. Thus, without the Dutchman Verbruygen originally bringing this technology over from the continent in 1770 to the state's Royal Brass Foundry, there would not have been Wilkinson's boring machine and thus no improved cylinders for Watt's steam engine. Wilkinson's mill was consequently able to produce the necessary precision for a near perfect seal between the piston and cylinder.

The main non-coal mining markets initially targeted by Watt and Boulton's engines were the tin and copper mines of Cornwall. Between 1779 and 1794 Watt's most skilled and trusted mechanic, William Murdoch, was dispatched to the region to ensure the engines were correctly erected and maintained. Further tinkering with the engines led to it being given greater regularity via the aptly named 'governor', which enabled the steam engine to be rated in terms of 'horsepower'. The next key development was the creation of uninterrupted power via two single-acting engines working out of sync that, through a set of so-called 'sun and planet' wheels, connected to two toothed wheels enabling continual rotary power capable of connecting to textile machines.[41]

Clearly, the place of coal in the British oeconomy was an extremely important source in developing some of its central technological achievements in furnaces, metals and the steam engine. Through this close relationship Britain obtained a lead in tacit, unformalized knowledge in the development of coal as a source of energy and artisanal knowledge in general. This understanding could not be written down and could only be imparted via skilled engineers.[42] Ultimately, it was coal for Wrigley, Harris, Allen, Brinkley and numerous other historians that separated Britain from the rest of the world.[43]

Britain's natural resources were obviously crucial to its industrialization, which, in addition to coal, eventually included easy access to deposits of iron ore (much more obtainable and of a better quality than that found, for example, in France), rock salt and non-ferrous metals. By contrast, most of Britain's primary European competitors still had easy access to forests and timber. Moreover, it was not till the rich coalmines of the Pas de Calais and the Ruhr were developed in the mid-nineteenth century that coal close to iron ore was found, while the Scandinavian countries and Italy had even fewer sources of coal. Britain's access to this mineral and its intrinsic association with key technological innovations has also been underlined by Kenneth Pomeranz as a defining factor in the 'Great Divergence' between Britain and China's industrial development from approximately the mid-eighteenth century.[44]

The skills needed for all this were not conducive to formal philosophical descriptions – despite the concerted attempts of French encyclopaedists to do so. In other words, reducing them to scientific, prescriptive or formal knowledge was not the impetus to the development or transfer of such technology as a current and popular historiography implies. Meanwhile, the educational institutions we now take for granted to train people in such skills were not around. Instead, a person would depend upon an apprenticeship at a few places such as Boulton and Watt's foundry, Wilkinson's boring mill, the military arsenals and dockyards or Henry Maudsley's London workshop. This was not industrial development driven by knowledge disseminated via coffee houses and regional philosophical societies; the British Industrial Revolution was not triggered by a scientific revolution and a peculiarly liberal environment.

Ecological factors, regional industrial development and commercial urgency fuelled by debt born of war and imperial expansion, rather than a unique inventive culture, clearly drove the early development of the atmospheric steam engine. It will be recalled that Newcomen, as Desaguliers was quick to remind his readers, had no close connections with the leading savants of his day. Likewise, Watt's work depended far more upon age-old practical trials and the skills of the artisan working the metal or fitting a piston than any formal knowledge. This was a trajectory that, Peter Mathias concluded, continued with those developing high-pressure steam remaining 'innocent of scientific fundamentals and were not seeking to create their improvement in the light of awareness of such fundamentals'.[45]

So what can we conclude about innovation and British industrialization surveyed in this and the prior chapter? Cotton textiles, metals, coal and steam engines are the four leading sectors that define the Industrial Revolution, and all were characterized by key technological developments. However, this was not the primary result of any indigenous superiority in relevant knowledge. Rather, it was the outcome of other factors: state protection and regulation, the wooing of transnational skills, ecological good luck, labour exploitation (slavery, women and children), aggressive European commercial competition, institutional imperatives and shop-floor know-how. In addition, a vital component in all this was simply urgency born of war and enormous fiscal pressure. By the final third of the eighteenth century, as we shall see in the next chapter, the challenges of a huge national debt and increasing social unrest was going to force a new 'economic' approach and radical reform of the state. This would have an added and profound impact upon Britain's Industrial Revolution.

CHAPTER 10
FISCAL PRESSURE AND INDUSTRY

In 1779 William Eden, Member of Parliament for Woodstock and first Lord of Trade (1776–82), succinctly explained how current fiscal and commercial policy had reached its maximum limit: 'It has hitherto been found in most instances, that our general consumption has gained ground under the pressure of increased taxes; but there is a point beyond which particular duties cannot advance, without the hazard of a fall, from which they may never rise.'[1] The Scottish philosopher and historian, David Hume, would have concurred. He had prophesized in 1752 that 'either the nation must destroy public credit, or public credit will destroy the nation'. Central to his thinking was the predicted dire consequences to the country via the apocalyptic debt born of war. The only solution was, he argued, voluntary bankruptcy.[2]

The state was now on the verge of consuming the people more than the people were consuming and a new 'economic' policy was desperately needed. The War of the Austrian Succession (1740–8) and, especially, the Seven Years War (1756–63) had greatly increased the national debt with blame falling upon a perceived corrupt government and state that was deeply in need of reform. The situation became dire in 1776 after the outbreak of war with the mainland American colonies, followed quickly by a maritime clash with France and Spain. To add to the woes, it now seemed that there was a real possibility that the West Indies and Ireland would soon follow colonial North America. In general, the state finances were seemingly in an extremely precarious situation – with yet more money urgently needed for the Royal Navy to modernize.[3]

By 1780 the British state was at bursting point and had, somehow, to be radically reduced. This would entail a major dismantling, restructuring and withdrawal from regulatory functions, particularly at first, within the domestic economy. To eventually achieve this would require a supporting creed that would come to be filled by a new political economy. The onus, predictably, would increasingly emphasize the opposite of past experience and stress an idealized market free of 'unnatural' regulations with individuals efficiently producing, selling and buying. It was during this decade that a discrete industrial policy took shape on the ground and in the halls of power, which framed the relatively rapid maturation of Britain's industrialization during the 1780s. It was this set of policies and practices that gave shape to an emerging political economy rather than the reverse. This tension and restructuring can clearly be seen in the clash between the old and new industries that manifested in the negotiations in the 1786 Anglo-French Trade Treaty.

This and the following chapter will trace how such a different stance came to be implemented particularly within the key spheres traditionally managed by the state. The solution to tried-and-tested policies would come to be the opposite.

Degeneration and reform: The state and the new industries

The 1780s was a critical decade for British trade and industrial policy. It was a time of forced reform driven by fiscal urgency and fear in the wake of losing the mainland American colonies. This was an event, after all, partly aided by the excruciating weight of the national debt that had accumulated greatly by this decade. The various publications of the influential reports made by the 'Commissioners Appointed to Examine Public Accounts' spared nothing, and were damming in their conclusions of administrative waste, cronyism and malpractice. On top of all this, events in Ireland were looking ominous with growing radicalism inspired by the recent revolution across the Atlantic. In 1782 a semi-independent Irish Parliament was introduced, and three years later William Pitt the Younger attempted, but failed, to liberalize trade with the country. If there was political and social trouble abroad, things were equally bad at home. As Edward P. Thompson once wryly remarked: 'There are times during these decades when one senses that a good part of the English people were more ready to secede from the Crown than were the Americans; but they had the misfortune not to be protected from it by the Atlantic.'[4]

As always, revenue was at the forefront of government concerns and finding new, as well as increasing traditional sources was the chief objective. The latter emphasis upon indirect taxation, however, had now seemingly reached a dead end. The French populace typically paid two to three times more *direct tax* over the course of the eighteenth century than Britain. Attempts to target elites, especially those exempt from tax in France, accelerated during the final years of the monarchy prior to the French Revolution.[5] Indeed the incidence of direct taxes fell more heavily upon the wealth and incomes of the affluent ranks in France than they did in Britain. In terms of French revenue generated from indirect taxes these came from royal monopolies concerned predominantly with salt, tobacco and levies on the transit of commodities – with wine being the most lucrative. These internal tolls, in turn, created risks, costs and delays upon commerce, and undoubtedly had a negative impact upon the unification of the French domestic market. It is also the case that the cost of collecting revenue was a great deal cheaper in Britain.[6]

In addition, then, to having a nationalized, relatively efficient (at least, in the case of the Excise) and more accountable system of revenue collection, Britain also had a far more integrated national economy to tap. It was not burdened with regional tariffs, as many of the strong independent-provincial identities and, specifically, the array of local taxes as France.[7] By the 1780s, the oeconomy of the Old Regime was unable to generate the revenues needed to service the country's debt. This was clearly one factor in the trigger to the French Revolution.[8] It was the case that Britain also faced dire fiscal straits but within a very different context. On both sides of the channel issues related to the wealth and governance of nations were being vigorously debated. Throughout the century, officials from the French Bureau of Commerce battled to implement a single duty, knowing that the free flow of internal goods was one of the key strengths of the British domestic market. The latter greatly benefited from having no internal customs and frontier duties adjusted in favour of domestic trade and industry.[9]

Hanoverian ministers and creditors greatly valued the relative predictability of excise revenue, and recognized this was partly due to the better organization of the Board of Excise in comparison to the Customs. As a leading British oeconomist, Sir James Steuart, wrote in 1767:

> In France, the collecting of the branches of cumulative taxes, such as the general receipts, comprehending the taille, poll-tax, &c. costs the state no less than 10 *per cent*, or two sols in the livre, which is superadded to those impositions, in order to defray that expense. Whereas in England the expense of collecting the excise administered by Commissioners, who act for the public, not by farmers who act for themselves, does not cost above 5£. 12 *s*. 6 *d*. in the 100£.[10]

In this sense, French privatization of much of the revenue, coupled with social and regional tariff variations, was inefficient and British state nationalization the opposite. The system of excise officer removes, by which they were periodically transferred to new stations, not only meant they were less likely than customs men to be complicit with local traders and smugglers, but they also avoided local political entanglements. Moreover, excise officers were given a comparatively attractive and, crucially, regular wage. The price of this security came from being subject to a much closer scrutiny than their colleagues in the Customs. This was one of the reasons Robert Walpole's administration had earlier wanted to switch the supervision of certain lucrative imported goods to the Excise. The Scottish Customs Commissioner, moral philosopher and oeconomist Adam Smith confessed in 1776: 'In point of perspicuity, precision, and distinctness, therefore, the duties of customs are much inferior to those of excise.'[11]

Over the course of the War of American Independence, the national debt had grown from £131 million to an approximate figure of £245 million. Pitt had a limited number of options to draw upon: the first was simply to cut back on expenditure; the second was to increase the yield from existing taxes; the third was to ensure interest rates stayed low; the fourth was to smash illicit trade and, finally, the fifth option was to introduce new indirect taxes. The creation of an income tax was still politically out of the question. This would all take cautious planning, administrative improvements and careful timing. There was, however, an area that could be addressed sooner rather than later, and that was a well-advertised gesture at severing administrative waste, cronyism and corruption.

With the loss of the American colonies close by 1780, the expense of the war unbearably high, attacks upon 'Old Corruption' intensifying, and political radicalism fuelled by the weight of high taxation ever louder, the government had to at least look as if it was seeking ways of economizing to subdue the volatile situation. Perceived incompetent administration – especially placement and sinecures, greedy moneyed men and political non-representation – had all combined to leave people feeling powerless. Eden wished for a time 'when all the junto caballing system, which, at the present however, completely triumphs, will wholly be overthrown'.[12]

Frustration started to escalate and collect into a potentially explosive situation. In an attempt to dilute growing cries for parliamentary reform, politicians started targeting the issue of placemen and abuse of the Civil List. During the early 1780s this list had its independence removed and was brought under closer parliamentary scrutiny (frozen in 1782). This, however, was more of a distraction from the really serious task of solving the government's dire financial difficulties and sustaining public credit. Charles James Fox called for a large increase in the land tax, while Lord North with Lord Shelbourne persistently hounding him, appointed a Board of Commissioners to investigate the state of public accounts and allay 'public' fears that their money was being wasted. Their objective was to cut waste and promote a prudent public ethos in an attempt to improve the efficiency and safeguard the legitimacy of state institutions.[13]

The role of the British Parliament in discussing and legislating upon financial matters, using state-collected economic information, tended to make the details accessible to a wider public.[14] By contrast, in France, the Crown and his minister's decision-making were not subject to parliamentary scrutiny and thus tended to remain far more private. Although, in theory, this gave French ministers more power to regulate commerce, in practice the French government greatly struggled to impose its authority to restructure the oeconomy. Consequently, legislation attempting to totally liberalize trade, agriculture and industry tended to fail, whereas the British government was able to use political and legal methods far more effectively in such matters.[15]

Despite this advantage and Pitt's initial success in casting himself as trustworthy and a capable politician, along with a greater public awareness of commercial matters and parliamentary discussion, Britain was still facing financial disaster. Not surprisingly, a new commercial, industrial and fiscal strategy was paramount and would be defined under Pitt's reign. The policies that had roughly carved the track from the mid-seventeenth century to the 1780s had served the nation well, but were now severely straining under the ballooning national debt. An environment of degeneration rather than enlightenment was the main trigger for reform; this was the primary force in the British move from oeconomy to a new political economy.

Throughout the early 1780s, Pitt, like Walpole earlier, concentrated a great deal of his attention on tackling the problem of the illicit 'common economy'. During the War of American Independence, the manpower of the revenue service and the home forces had become depleted and smuggling activities had taken an even firmer hold. A dramatic pitched battle took place with the Deal smugglers in Kent, involving a large group of excise officers and a significant number of troops fighting them on a wet day in February 1782. The officers reported that they 'had not been there many minutes before they were fired upon' by a body of people. The troops shot back but, because it was so damp, many of their guns failed to go off – 'otherwise it is probable many lives might have been lost'. Meanwhile, shots were fired from various houses and rope was drawn across the street to prevent the troops advancing. Such was the local ferocity, the soldiers eventually had to retreat having only been able to seize 22 gallons of illegal French brandy, 304 gallons of Dutch jenever and 224 lbs of coffee.[16]

The Excise was extremely worried at the extent and sophistication of this large alternative 'common economy'. Smugglers, for example, were forging excise permits for the duty paid on the movement of large amounts of goods. One group based in

Surrey had obtained some sixty-one counterfeit permits enabling them to transport 52,425 gallons of smuggled brandy and jenever. In Essex, fifty-six counterfeit permits were used to transfer 40,800 gallons of brandy, rum and jenever. These were just the tip of an iceberg with, perhaps, the worst culprits once again being dealers in Deal. The Excise claimed smuggling here was 'carried on to a very great degree and at this time we have reason to believe that not less than a Million of Gallons of smuggled foreign spirits are in circulation which have been introduced into the stocks of divers Traders under the sanction of the like counterfeit permits'.[17] According to excise returns for 1782, apparently something like a quarter of all smuggling vessels operating around the British coast were based in Kent and Sussex.[18]

The parliamentary report of 1783 investigating national illicit activities highlighted Deal as an 'emporium' of duty-free goods, with almost the whole of its population, including the mayor, seemingly aiding smugglers with their work. Events reached a climax in early January 1784, when the government got information that the free-traders had drawn in a large section of their fleet into various creeks and harbours around the vicinity of Deal. They quickly dispatched several hundred soldiers and a number of well-armed cutters culminating in the capture of the whole 'smuggling navy'.[19] Also that year complaints were being made by the Lancashire and Glasgow calico printers (John Livisey for Blackburn, Lawrence Peel for Manchester, John Watson for Preston and Patrick Colquhoun for Glasgow) that serious pilferage and damage to their goods was occurring along the wharf quays. As a consequence, they wanted all goods for exportation to be checked in Manchester and Glasgow before going to the port. Colquhoun, of course, went on to become one of the key instigators of the Thames River Police at the turn of the century.[20] In addition, he was a staunch protectionist of the growing British cotton industry.[21]

The most popular illicit commodities in the common economy were brandy, tobacco and, especially, tea. The success of free trade in tea was also undermining the finances of the powerful East India Company that resulted in concerted lobbying from this powerful organization. The size of illegal trade had recently been investigated under the auspices of Lord Shelbourne's ministry prior to Pitt's period of power. However, the most extensive investigation was conducted in the summer of 1783, when the coalition government appointed a Commons committee to investigate illicit practices.[22] Following Steuart, Smith and Walpole (nearly fifty years earlier), Eden spoke for many policy advisors in 1780 when he advised that such commodities be transferred from Customs to Excise: 'It certainly appears too, from experience, that the Excise laws confound the operations of the smugglers much more than those of customs.' In addition, he advocated what was fast becoming a primary objective, namely, the removal of drawbacks with an expansion of bonded warehouses and the simplification of duties.[23] All these policies would be successfully introduced under Pitt's regime.

Pitt estimated that a mere 42 per cent of the tea and 14 per cent of the brandy consumed in Britain had been taxed. These investigations prepared and laid the path for two of Pitt's most celebrated tax reforms, namely, the Commutation Act of 1784 and the signing of the Anglo-French Trade Treaty of 1786. The primary objective of the former act was to destroy widespread tea smuggling, and instigate a total monopoly of tea imported by the East India Company through the reduction of duties on the item from 119 per cent to 12.5 per cent *ad valorem*. To enable Pitt to do this required the retail prices of tea to be reduced to a figure that could be compensated by a new window tax. This was no easy task since the price of such tea was mainly based on its unpredictable availability.[24] Nonetheless, for a time the Commutation Act achieved what its instigators had hoped.

The final third of the eighteenth century witnessed a number of new taxes on luxuries. Despite this expansion, however, it was nowhere near enough to quench the required revenue. As a result, taxes on popular items were all increased. For example, malt rose in 1779, 1780 and 1790; salt in 1780, 1782 and 1798; soap in 1782, and the candle tax in 1784. Pitt also, once again, increased the tax on tea in 1795 and exploited the great demand for sugar among the masses by also increasing its duties. The leader of the opposition, Charles Fox, protested, 'Tea and sugar were now in such common use that he feared they were necessaries of life.' The next year Pitt proposed to increase the tea duty again, but this time exempted the coarser kinds of tea drunk by the lower orders in an attempt to dilute Fox's criticisms.[25]

Following on from the brief success of the Commutation Act, Pitt slightly lowered the duties on rum and British spirits. This was followed, after the Anglo-French Trade Treaty, with the significant reduction of duties on French wines and brandies and, soon after, on other European wines in general. Official British statistics at the time revealed that prior to this treaty, imports of duty-paid French wines hardly ever passed 100,000 gallons but by 1787 it surpassed 969,856 gallons. This great increase clearly demonstrated that French wines, which had formerly been smuggled, were now being legally imported into Britain. In other words, the market was already there but it was now being filled by legitimate wine. Pitt's above moves were still primarily aimed at the smuggler, but were also fuelled by a more general process of revenue restructuring and financial reform.[26]

Like many of his predecessors, Pitt wanted the task of revenue collection to be put, as much as possible, into the hands of the Excise. Most of the duties on wines were transferred from Customs to Excise in 1786, some fifty-six years after the humiliating defeat of Walpole's tobacco and wine excise bill of 1733.[27] Pitt had finally managed to pass most of Walpole's scheme, while the duties on 'sweets' (used to adulterate spirits and beer) were raised. In general, the above reforms were a success with the revenue on wines increasing from £625,000 in 1783 to £804,000 in 1790; on spirits from £561,000 in 1784 to an average of £915,000 per annum between 1787 and 1790; and on tobacco from an average of £424,000 in 1789 to an average of £590,000 per annum by 1792. Taxes were also increased in 1784 on retail licences for certain excisable goods, on shooting certificates, on bricks, tiles, failed attempts on coal, linens and calicoes; new levies were placed on gold and silver plate, on imported silk and exported lead, and the postage rates were also raised. New taxes also appeared on men's hats and another one on ladies' ribbons. Also that year Pitt made structural changes by transferring some of these taxes from the Excise, mainly on carriages and male servants, and putting them in a category termed 'Assessed Taxes' (along with taxes on horses and saddles). This new classificatory group was to be collected by the Board of Taxes modelled on the Excise administration. The flood of taxes continued with new duties on attorneys, female servants, gloves and perfume.[28]

In addition, Pitt continued to keep the pressure on the common economy by substantially increasing the legal weaponry against such free trade. For instance, the Hovering Act of 1780, in which vessels within two leagues of the coast could be seized, was extended to four leagues in 1784. Further, vessels being built along known smuggling routes could be stopped at any stage and, lastly, forfeited vessels were to be destroyed if the Customs had no use for them.[29] Free trade was an expensive thorn in the side of Pitt's government and occupied a great deal of their time. It would soon, however, emerge as the perceived solution to socio-economic problems rather than the problem.

Despite an ill-fated attempt to implement a new tax upon shops and a concerted attempt to crush smuggling, in the end the only policy Pitt could really pursue was to either introduce new indirect taxes or increase the revenue from existing taxes. This could be achieved either by raising them, or improving methods of assessment and making revenue collection more efficient. Ultimately, under this approach, the most effective way to increase the yield was to nurture the necessary conditions for greater prosperity. Not surprisingly, such an expansion of indirect taxation provoked a number of confrontations. Indeed, the extension of excise taxes led directly to the formation of new interest groups that soon impacted on financial, industrial and trading policy.

Manufacturing interests were beginning to combine together in an attempt to produce a united manufacturing front. For example, when the coal tax was increased, British industry flexed its muscle in such an unexpectedly powerful way that Pitt was forced to drop it after just ten days. The iron masters bitterly complained that the increase in coal duties would make it extremely difficult for them to compete with the Swedish, while James Watt and Matthew Boulton were furious over the possible impact this could have upon their steam engine business and vented their opposition to the tax proposal. Another incident was over the government's policy towards linens and calicoes, when the Manchester and Glasgow cotton manufacturers unleashed their anger over the government's proposed plan of levelling the duties for Ireland. They were willing to accept competition but only if both countries were subject to the same regulation. The Manchester and Glasgow cotton interest, the iron founders of the Midlands and west of England, and the Midland pottery makers combined to establish a General Chamber of Manufacturers, with the objective of being a national body representing industrial interests and influencing Parliament on behalf of all domestic industry.[30]

The impact of the new manufacturers on economic policy is extremely significant. Already the cotton industry, led by a petition from 'Richard Arkwright and Company of Nottingham spinners of cotton stuffs', had been given important concessions in 1774, including the removal of prohibitions and, soon after, the go-ahead for British people to legally wear or use goods wholly made of cotton. To distinguish the domestic textiles from illegally imported calicoes, three blue stripes of one thread were woven in the warp in both selvages and through the whole length. In addition, if printed it had to then be stamped at each end with an excise mark, and imprinted with the words 'British manufactory' rather than 'calico', since the latter still referred to banned foreign calicoes. By this point, too, the government was not so worried about protecting the Scottish and Irish linen industry.[31]

Ten years later, in 1784, an attempt was made to add an additional excise duty upon printed linens, dyed stuffs of cotton and mixed cotton textiles, while bleachers and dyers would now have to purchase licences. The result was an angry petition to the House of Commons by an impressive list of vested interests from the northwest that included both manufacturers and landowners. In April 1785 the House ordered a bill to be drafted that would explain and amend the said act.[32] One petitioner from Lancashire, John Wright, claimed the increased tax would discourage the growth of the domestic cotton industry and simply encourage Indian cotton textiles. Moreover, the act would greatly aid Ireland and 'do more harm to England than the persecution of the Huguenots did to France'. Britain's cotton industry had become the country's goldmine and a huge employer of people 'who pay many taxes in the consumption of many articles'. This last point was underlined as a crucial component to the success of the British state: 'If our artists are kept unemployed, can they afford to consume an equal quantity of either the necessaries or luxuries of life, which by various taxes raise the revenue of the State?'[33]

Despite being untaxed, the pottery manufacturer and entrepreneur Josiah Wedgwood wanted to see the excise tax 'annihilated'. He warned: 'Excise laws are the bane of manufacturers: the officers are spies upon all the operations of the artist: discoveries, which have been the fruit of great labour and expense to him, they convey to his rivals, perhaps foreign nations.' In well-known language, Wright claimed all excise laws struck 'at the root of our freedom, and the basis of British liberty'.[34] This could equally be seen as a demonstration of just how successful the Excise had been in achieving a nationwide standardization of production approaches and goods. It should also be remembered that patenting in the pottery industry was near impossible and the key was keeping techniques and recipes secret. These industries still demanded protection from foreign rivals, but they now also wanted to ensure freedom from domestic manufacturing regulation. With Pitt busy trying to tax anything he could the threat of a national excise was a real one. In addition, the pottery industry and new textiles were not subject to forms of apprenticeship but did initially support the old Poor Law, as it provided a source of cheap labour and a safety net when they needed to dismiss employees.[35]

Although the Excise was willing to accept changes concerning the manufactory process if it did not impact the amount of revenue generated, it was now considered far too intrusive by the lightly taxed or untaxed new industries that faced less foreign competition. The new manufacturers, both those excised and those who feared being so, claimed the Excise adversely interfered with the production process. In a familiar tone, it was declared by the lightly taxed cotton manufacturers in April 1785, 'Such an influx of those gentry [the excise officers] to disturb the harmony and arrangements of their manufacture, to deprive them of personal liberty and the free exercise of their property, is unwise, impolitic and unjust.' In the words of Witt Bowden: 'The administrative features of the law [excise upon cotton], minute and inquisitorial, were similar to those of earlier excise laws. These older methods were no longer applicable to the more complicated and advanced technique of manufacturing then being introduced.'[36]

Other industries, also fearing a general extension of the excise, joined the attack, most notably the iron founders and manufacturers in the counties of Salop, Worcester,

Stafford and Warwick. So too did the Birmingham Commercial Committee who sought the cooperation of other manufacturers. Thus, despite the incredible pressure upon Parliament to find additional revenues, MPs refused to support taxes made upon Britain's well-performing export-oriented newer industries, namely, textiles, potteries and metals.[37] In addition, key imports of certain raw materials, on the whole, remained untaxed or lightly taxed, and new labour competing technology also remained free from taxation (and banned from exportation). The latter being an issue that would be hotly contested by political leaders of the working classes.

Irish industry and trade

It was not just the excise that was receiving the wrath of the new industries but, equally, Pitt's policies towards Ireland. By 1779 the situation here seemed to hang in the balance with Irish merchants and gentry arming, furious riots erupting in Dublin and the oeconomy descending into dire straits. The country's main industry, linen textiles, was on the brink of collapse. Public finances were depressed with tax revenues unable to meet expenditure, while the loans that could be raised were all on crippling prohibitive terms. The only way the Irish Exchequer could be saved from bankruptcy was through an advance made by the Bank of England. The Irish Lord Lieutenant Lord Buckinghamshire (John Hobart) warned the government that ameliorative legislation was vital. The whole situation was further fuelled by radical political inspiration flowing east across the Atlantic; in particular, drawing upon colonial American consumer protest methods, the Irish also instigated a movement to shun British goods.[38]

Sir Lucius O'Brien, the parliamentary member for County Clare, stated that Ireland's troubles boiled down to prohibitary legislation passed under Charles II; this included restrictions excluding Ireland from England's colonial trade and crushing the lucrative part of its woollen textile industry (the new draperies). The Irish political elite also pointed to the 'great Drains by Pensions and Remittances to Absentees and considerable Appointments to useless nominal Employments, High Rents, Local and Grand Jury Assessments, which are now grown, and that of late Years, to so large a sum as one hundred and thirty thousand Pounds per Annum'. The only solution for the Chancellor of Ireland, Lord Lifford (James Hewitt), was to place the country upon an even footing with Britain.[39]

Edmund Sexton Perry, Speaker of the Irish House of Commons and fervent critic of Britain's restrictive trading and industrial policies towards Ireland, also agreed with Lord Lifford that the only remedy was for much greater assimilation of Ireland into Britain's oeconomy. He claimed that the 'general Cause of Distress is undoubtedly the restraint upon the Trade, and consequently upon the Industry of the Kingdom'. Such views, at least over the repeal of trade and industry restrictions, were repeated by an important barrister and leading Irish politician, Walter Hussey Burgh, along with John Foster, MP for County Louth and, in all but name, Irish Chancellor of the Exchequer (made official in 1784) and, finally, all the Irish commissioners of revenue.[40]

The Irish revenue commissioners also pointed to the mass emigration, prior to the War of American Independence, of skilled Irish workers to the Americas: 'In America every Handicraft is sure of Employment, and every Religious Profession finds an established communion in some of the Colonies.' The commissioners warned that once the situation in America settled, emigration from Ireland would reach unprecedented levels and greatly depress the possible establishment of manufactures in Ireland. It was now time, they argued, to lift all trade regulations from Ireland.[41]

Foster pointed out the importance of the Irish market for British exports and warned that the Irish associations formed to boycott British goods 'have done us more service than the whole of the Free Trade will do these fifty years'. After North America, the British West Indies and parts of Africa, Ireland was Britain's most lucrative overseas market. Its importance was thus even greater during the War of American Independence, but with Ireland's oeconomy in such a poor condition, British exports had dropped in 1778 by £600,000. Moreover, since the Irish could no longer afford to purchase such goods (or decided to boycott them), Foster claimed, they would be forced to try and nurture their own substitute industries.[42] This, of course, was precisely what American colonial radicals in the build-up to the War of American Independence had done.[43]

Most of the above commentators tried to reassure and pre-empt any arguments that removing regulatory legislation would have a negative impact upon British manufactures. Foster claimed: 'First we have neither the settled Habits of Industry, the knack of Manufacture, or established credit which attends a Country long confined in any particular Trade'; while borrowing in Ireland was much more difficult since the interest rate was higher than in Britain. Elsewhere, however, Lifford underlined the power of the Irish boycott movement and threatened: 'The Resolutions of the people not to wear or use British manufactures will increase to a degree much beyond … any kind of disadvantage that can happen from any Rivalship of Trade.' Like the revenue commissioners, he emphasized the repercussions to Ireland of lost skilled labour once the American war was over.[44] Meanwhile, the Dublin Society in 1782 offered generous premiums for numerous Irish manufacturers to further their textiles such as silk, woollens and cottons. The society was also keen, like the equivalent English society, to nurture the quality of domestic design.[45]

In general, 1782 was an important one for Ireland. A degree of self-government was granted to the Irish Parliament with the repeal of Poyning's Law, giving independence back to the Irish Parliament (although it was still subject to the British Privy Council). In addition, the Irish judicial process was also severed from British supervision and courts. These reforms were passed under the Rockingham government and confirmed by Shelburne's Renunciation Act. The latter was the result of various doubts being cast on the commitment and application of Rockingham's initial measures. Ireland, however, was once again struck down by two dire harvests in 1783 and 1784 – something more immediate was needed to aid the Irish oeconomy.[46]

Although legislatively independent from Britain since 1782, the commercial and political relations between the two countries was still obviously far from fair. In 1785 Pitt set about trying to formalize Ireland's place in the British Empire. The aim was to give the country many more trading concessions in return for a change in their constitutional relationship. The idea was to build upon Ireland's increased internal self-government, expand the access of Irish traders into British markets, and for the subsequent increase in Irish wealth to be taxed to aid the defence of the British Empire, especially, in shipping. It was this last factor, however, that caused further uproar in Ireland.[47]

Meanwhile in Britain, manufacturers combined, supported by the Foxite opposition, to prevent the possible threat of Irish competition. The attack in Parliament was spearheaded by Eden, now Irish Chief Secretary as well as first Lord of Trade, and John Baker-Holroyd, MP for Coventry and recently made Lord Sheffield in 1782. The latter published a long tract entitled *Observations on the Manufacturers, Trade and Present State of Ireland* in 1785 that examined Britain's commercial policies with Ireland in great detail. A fresh momentum was also given by the establishment, touched upon earlier, of the General Chamber of Manufacturers that met for the first time on 8 March 1785. Its chairman, Wedgwood, was in regular contact with Eden and Sheffield. A major mistake by Pitt was not to have first gauged the concerns of British manufacturers. Indeed, argues Bowden, such was his desire to pass a set of Irish resolutions and avoid conflict in the Irish Parliament, he pursued a policy 'of needlessly antagonizing the manufacturers and ridiculing them, based as it was upon a failure to recognise their united power of resistance', which culminated in strengthening 'the union of the industrialists against him'.[48]

Whereas the British woollen textile industry had a monopoly over raw materials, the cotton cloth manufacturers had to compete with Ireland over, at this point, limited supplies. Prior to the sudden huge influx of southern North American raw cotton during the 1790s, most supplies were from the West Indies, Guyana and Brazil.[49] Many English cotton producers seriously considered moving their operations to Ireland. Water was, as it would be well into the nineteenth century, still the most dominant power source in the industry and Ireland had the ideal rivers and streams. In addition, the country provided the perfect damp climatic conditions for cotton, it had cheaper labour and, of course, was without the burden of an excise inquisition. Very attractive offers were made from powerful Irish figures to woo English manufacturers over. Despite an attempt in England to level the playing field by putting countervailing duties on Irish imports, it was the mode of tax collection that the domestic cotton manufacturers were primarily against.

What was also new in this debate, spearheaded by the new export-oriented industries (cotton, potteries and iron), was the view towards the market. Unlike older industries bred upon a culture of preserving and protecting markets, the cotton manufacturers, in particular, wanted to acquire new ones currently occupied primarily, Indian cotton textiles. Unlike the traditional excised industries, British cotton cloth was on the verge of eclipsing its Indian rivals and therefore would soon no longer require a protective barrier. This was a unique occasion – although protective duties and bounties remained into the nineteenth century. The stakes grew and the difference between the Irish and British tax systems took centre stage.

At a meeting in Manchester of the top eighteen British manufacturers, it was resolved that 'the destructive system [of taxation] adopted towards the manufacturers of this kingdom, and to this town and neighbourhood in particular, renders it incumbent upon them immediately to appoint delegates to go to Ireland for the purpose of treating with any public body, or individual, nobleman or gentleman, respecting a proper situation for conducting an extensive cotton manufacture'. As for their reasons they underlined the 'evil' excise system and compared it to the far more advantageous system in Ireland. The cotton manufacturer, Robert Peel, father of the later free-trade reformer and nineteenth-century Conservative prime minister, claimed the excise tax would mean the end of the British cotton industry. The threat worked. On 20 April 1785 Pitt told the Commons that the additional excise on plain cottons and fustians would be repealed.[50] Unlike other traditional excised industries, cotton had been nurtured under a protected system but had never become an important source of revenue. This textile was the world's favourite and, after mechanization and access to raw cotton from the West Indies and, crucially from the 1790s, the southern slave plantations of the United States, the British quickly gained a global monopoly.

Peel's threat may have seemed like the decisive factor but, perhaps, more important was the fear of social suffering and disorder among the cotton workers. Thomas Pelham declared in Manchester in August 1784: 'The Tax upon Cotton is very severely felt in this Place & I fear that it will be attended with the worst of Consequences. Many of the Principal Manufacturers declare their Resolution of going to France, & I understand that some of them have made application to Paris to know upon what terms they may expect Protection.' Although some claims, such as 100,000 jobs would be lost, may have been exaggerated, it was also true that many dyers and bleachers had closed down. In March 1785 Thomas Stanley, one of the MPs for Lancashire, presented a petition to the House of Commons with 80,000 signatures. This was followed by another petition from Glasgow. If the cotton employers were primarily concerned over the Excise method of collection, the employees were angry over the impact an increase in the tax would make on their purses. The House of Commons received some sixty petitions opposing the attempt to liberalize trade with Ireland and condemning the hike in the excise tax. It was the workers agitation that primarily forced Pitt to repeal his policies. As he admitted,

> the addition of 30 or even £50,000 was not in the present state of the revenue to be looked on as so indispensable, as not to give way to the very desirable purpose of quieting the minds of a large body of the people who contributed by their labour so great a proportion of the national strength, and on whose satisfaction the public tranquillity so much depended.[51]

It should be remembered that these textile workers were important consumers of other excised items and thence to the national revenue.[52]

Pitt's relationship with Manchester had an equally adverse impact upon his proposed Irish Propositions of 1785. The Manchester cotton merchant Thomas Walker and his associates had already been humiliated in January 1785 when, as we have seen, the Committee of the Privy Council on Trade had interviewed manufacturers, apparently, not for their opinion, but to discredit them. The result was a greater intensity of opposition to

Pitt's Irish plan. Numerous manufacturers, especially the newer ones, sought protection from the proposed easing of trade regulation with Ireland. The result was an official declaration by the General Chamber of Manufacturers on 8 March 1785 to coordinate opposition against the Irish policy. The primary fear of British manufacturers was the threat of competition from Ireland and, once again, Pitt was forced to drop the scheme.[53] The enlightened minds spearheading Britain's Industrial Revolution were liberal free-traders as long as there was no competition.

By 1773 Britain imported over 90 per cent of Irish-produced linen, which by any standard was a dangerous situation for any important industry to rely upon. It was also now a decentralized industry produced by small farmers hedging their bets against a total reliance upon agricultural produce, and found it increasingly difficult to secure adequate amounts of the world's limited flax. It was within this context that the semi-independent Irish Parliament had set about nurturing a cotton industry. The plan quickly took off and the Irish industry rapidly expanded. Between 1782 and 1801 the British cotton textile industry, for example, grew at 6 per cent per year while the Irish industry grew at 5 per cent per year.[54] This expansion of the industry clearly provided the impetus to the opposition against Pitt's proposals in 1785 for limited free trade with Ireland. Yet, fifteen years later, this fear had evaporated; indeed the British manufacturers wanted Irish cotton duties to be repealed and now lobbied hard for free access to Irish markets and were now no longer concerned by competition. Irish duties on cotton yarn were eventually repealed in 1816 and on cotton cloth in 1824.[55]

It was particularly the rapid localization of innovation in cotton around Lancashire that was instrumental in peripheralizing the Irish industry. Not only had northwest England developed new technology but the region also exploited new forms of centralized production and commercial organization. In contrast, Ireland had simply intensified its labour forms of putting-out that increasingly concentrated on weaving. This was certainly not helped by the fact that it also suffered from a lack of access to raw cotton as most of it now came directly to Liverpool; this was a trajectory that would soon make Ireland a subsidiary sector to English spinning. Moreover, because Ireland also failed to innovate in weaving it subsequently suffered from mechanized British weaving during the 1830s and especially the 1840s. Cheap labour in weaving could no longer compete. By this point, the Irish cotton industry had more or less collapsed.[56] A decisive moment in Britain's confidence in its new manufacturers, and what would later be termed its Industrial Revolution, was the Anglo-French Trade Treaty of 1786.

The 1786 Anglo-French Trade Treaty

The young British Prime Minister was hugely optimistic a few months after the signing of the Anglo-French Trade Treaty in 1786: 'I am persuaded that our power and greatness will be extended and increased, and new sources of opulence laid open to the industry, activity, and exertion of this country, which will raise both individuals and the nation to a very high degree of prosperity, such as we have not hitherto known.'[57] The power of the British cotton industry and the other new export-oriented industries, most notably potteries and increasingly iron, were surging forward. This was particularly evident in this significant trade treaty with France. Between 1785 and 1793 trade treaties were also attempted with Portugal, Spain, Russia, Poland, Prussia, the two Sicilies (Kingdoms of Sicily and Naples) and Holland. The primary impetus for much of this commercial activity was the loss of the 13 mainland American colonies, with many European countries seeking better trading opportunities with a greatly weakened Britain. Treaties were also considered with Sweden, Turkey, the Austrian Netherlands, China and the new United States of America.[58]

The 1786 Anglo-French Trade Treaty split British manufacturers roughly in half. Those older industries that had grown up with protection, relatively monopolistic conditions, an emphasis upon the domestic market and the Excise, were against the treaty. By contrast, the newer industries that also developed under protectionism, but which would benefit from freer trade with France, generally supported the treaty. As the pro-monopoly organ the *British Merchant* claimed, one group were keen to conserve control over the domestic markets, while the other faction sought an open trade since 'their present ascendancy of skill, have nothing immediate to fear from competition, and everything to hope from the speculation of an increased demand'.[59] This and other publications identified cotton, pottery and iron as representative of this latter group; other industries such as the silk makers, certain woollen textile producers, ribbon makers, hat makers, paper manufacturers, clock and watch makers, leather manufacturers and glass producers felt they would lose their domestic markets to the French.[60]

The division between the traditional and new industries was stark within the General Chamber of Manufacturers. This body was dominated by cotton, iron and potteries – all of which fervently supported the 1786 treaty. The leader of the Chamber, Wedgwood, was energetic and vocal in his lobbying. These exponents were also hostile to the Corn Laws, with the quickly expanding northwest of England needing access to more grain to feed its fast-growing workforce. A clear case of the landed interest clashing with the increasingly powerful provincial manufacturers was rearing its head before the Napoleonic Wars. The cotton industry, especially, was also desperate for raw cotton since the West Indian colonies could not quench its demand. Hence, it now looked beyond the restrictions of the Navigation Acts and would soon rely upon the southern slave plantations of the new United States of America.[61]

Spearheading the negotiations with the French was Eden. He was educated at Durham School, Eton, and Christ Church College, Oxford, where he was greatly informed by the lectures of the leading legal authority of the time, William Blackstone. Eden had been chosen by Lord North as one of the five men seeking conciliation with British North America in 1778. In 1780 he was appointed chief secretary to the newly appointed Lord Lieutenant of Ireland, the Earl of Carlisle. Eden was also returned to the Irish House of Commons for Dungannon. It was here, according to one of his biographers, that 'he developed an expertise in commercial matters and was involved in the foundation of the Bank of Ireland'.[62] As we have seen, he had fervently opposed Pitt's attempt at establishing favourable Irish resolutions in 1784, and was an important supporter of the new industries in general. In the Anglo-French trade negotiations Pitt made it clear to Eden that he was willing to make concessions on glass and other products to aid cotton, some woollens, hardware, earthenware and the Irish linen industry.[63]

Joel Mokyr describes the treaty as 'the first unambiguous sign of Enlightenment influence' and later 'a model of Enlightenment thought'.[64] However, the truth was far more mundane, pragmatic and born of necessity. All that Pitt was advocating were the failed Tory policies of the 1713 Anglo-French Treaty, while the arguments spearheading the attack upon Pitt in Parliament, led by Fox, were simply a reiteration of the Whig's outlet, the *British Merchant*, also made some seventy years earlier. However, Britain's industrial base had now significantly changed and European competition in the new industries was not a huge source of fear; these industries would now benefit from freer European trade. Likewise, Ephraim Lipson had long argued that the impetus to the treaty 'was not any theoretical demonstrations of free trade, but the confidence which English industrial interests now felt in their ability to meet foreign competition'. The origins of the free-trade movement in Britain was fuelled 'by practical considerations in which abstract doctrines of economic freedom did not have the influence commonly assigned them'.[65] For the British government it was hoped the treaty would raise more revenue from import duties and greater opportunities for manufacturers to export.[66]

Britain was already disturbed by the recent signing of a French-Dutch treaty of alliance, which promised to bring the United Provinces both politically and commercially under French influence. Moreover, the French East India Company was becoming more aggressive in South Asia. The combined naval power of the Dutch and French could challenge Britain's superiority at sea, and possibly lead to the expulsion of the British from India. Certainly, too, the French Minister of Finance, Marechal de Castries, fought hard for the French to match the British Navigation Acts and put them on a par. These factors, no doubt, added further incentive for the British to sign a trade treaty with France as committed to in a clause to the treaty of Versailles back in 1763.[67]

In many ways the 1786 treaty was predominantly about cotton textiles, on which Eden secured a hugely reduced tariff from the French of a mere 10 per cent duty.[68] The British government knew cotton cloth had no European rivals in terms of technology and production methods, while the French also knew this but thought they would quickly catch up. Pitt confidently told the Commons:

> I believe it is a fact that will not be denied, That in many of the greatest and most leading manufactures calculated for general consumption, the situation of this country is more flourishing than any other country of Europe. There are many in which our actual superiority is confessed. In all of what is clear and obvious, that at present the advantage will be on the side of this country, and that France cannot pretend to hold any competition with us in these leading articles.[69]

However, prominent French advisors to the treaty, such as DuPont de Nemours, were convinced the French would soon match and surpass these technological advantages.[70] Moreover, both countries saw the treaty as an opportunity to secure long-lasting revenues to help service their country's huge respective debts. France now, ironically, appreciated that the key to Britain's industrial might was a state-led national approach that had been far more successful than their prevailing practices; in particular, their so-far-unsuccessful quest to establish a unified domestic market with a single duty.[71]

The emphasis by the British in the treaty was upon cotton textiles, iron, steel, metalwares, hardware, pottery and earthenware. By contrast, French superiority in areas such as wine, brandy, vinegar, oils, paper, glass (especially plate), and certain textiles such as cambric and silk were acknowledged. Not only would the treaty thus allow certain British goods to enter France at much reduced duties, but highly smuggled French goods (particularly wine and brandy) would now enter Britain legally and thus help smash illicit trade while increasing custom revenues. In this sense, the treaty was also a way for Pitt to put another mighty dent in the common economy and national debt.[72] This was an objective close to his heart and he boldly predicted that 'the destruction' of this 'pernicious' trade would create an entirely 'new source' of revenue.[73] Crucially, both countries hoped the treaty would prevent future bankrupting war by bringing the countries closer together.[74] Fear of foreign imports was also being replaced by a confident belief in British exports. This was thanks to the success of the newer, less domestically regulated but still highly protected export-led industries. This selective proto-laissez-faire policy, of course, would reach full fruition later in the nineteenth century. The period of nurturing predominantly non-exporting industries was being eroded and, instead, was now being squeezed into an extremely high level through fiscal demands, which was pushing them to the level of protective custom tariffs; it was now believed they would be mature enough to cope with increased competition.

The outcome of the Anglo-French Trade Treaty of 1786 had been far from certain. Just as in 1713, increased trade with the old enemy was not going to be welcomed by everyone. Not surprisingly, then, these older arguments were once again rehearsed.[75] Fox claimed the trade treaty would be a disaster, 'they may gain our skill, but we can never gain their soil and climate'.[76] However, this time Britain's industrial base and confidence was far more robust; 1786 was a very different world to 1713.

Eden had the support and an excellent relationship with the new industries, which he had built up during his campaign against Pitt's Irish Propositions. By contrast, the relationship between Pitt and the new General Chamber of Manufacturers was far from good. Pitt was keen that as little recognition to the chamber, as a collective voice, should be given. As he wrote to Eden:

> It cannot be too generally understood, that our sole object is to collect, from all parts of the Kingdom, a just representation of the interests of all the various branches of trade and manufacture which can be affected by the French arrangement, and that we are perfectly open to form an unprejudiced opinion on the result. I probably need hardly add, however, that there are many reasons which make it desirable to give as little employment or encouragement as possible to the Chamber of Commerce taken collectively.

Pitt's appointment of his old adversary, Eden, as negotiator for the Anglo-French Treaty was a shrewd decision.[77]

In the end, the treaty split the old and new industries and the chamber quickly dissolved. This division would prevent there ever being a unified manufacturing voice during this period. The British woollen textile interest were on the whole furious with the treaty and sarcastically wrote: 'This *wise* scheme is to give power and license to the French to bring in ALL their *woollens* to our market, on proviso of our Manchester Merchants having the same privilege to sell the *French* and their *cottons*, and the Birmingham and Sheffield trades, and the iron branch.' Portugal was also to be sacrificed for French wines and the West Indies rum (as well as domestic-produced gin) for French brandy.[78] In short, this rehash of the defeated Tory commercial treaty proposals of 1713 was simply 'a shameful sacrifice of the best trades of Old England, for the worst luxuries of France'. Moreover, the French labour force was, according to opponents, much better off than the British due to paying less tax and having cheaper provisions.[79]

If British manufacturers were split over the treaty, the situation among the French was, if anything, more hostile. When the treaty was signed many manufacturing towns were dismayed; in particular, those areas that produced silk and cotton goods. The Normandy Chamber immediately dispatched two of its members to Britain to compare the country's cotton manufacturers with their own. The result was the printing and diffusion of a large number of copies of a memorandum entitled *Observations sur le Traite de Commerce* by the chamber. It begun by announcing that the French Chambers of Commerce and Manufactures had not been consulted in the build-up to the treaty. This, they complained, was in stark contrast to producers in Britain. Pitt had, as we saw earlier, learnt his lesson. More specifically, the two observers first underlined the British advantage in raw wool, which they claimed was an indigenous stock of 12 million sheep (of which the woollen manufacturers had a monopoly). Although France currently produced brighter and softer woollens from Louviers, Abbeville and Sedan, the price of their woollen textiles was too high and the finish not particularly good. Moreover, if Britain gained imported raw Spanish wool more cheaply and on a par with France, 'they will soon succeed in imitating them perfectly'.[80]

By far the largest concern of the Normandy Chamber was the cotton industry, which was the most important manufacture in Normandy. For a start, they warned, some of the articles produced in Manchester were up to 30 per cent cheaper. The reasons for this, they rightly claimed, was Manchester's advantage in access to imported raw cotton, the region's rampant introduction of new innovative machinery and centralized production. This, they continued, had also had a positive impact on the quality of Lancashire cotton: 'The mills and Jennys for spinning cotton are brought to so great perfection that Manchester flatters itself that it will soon be able to equal Indian muslin.'[81] This objective had been the overriding drive to mechanization in the first place. This is in contrast to the traditional view that it was a shortage of human spinners and expensive labour; hitherto British textile labour had been unable to produce cotton warp.[82]

The Normandy Chamber report also stressed the importance of coal in fuelling British industry and contrasted its importance with its scarcity and negligible use in

France. This, they claimed, had greatly aided English industry such as potteries and iron. As yet cotton textiles were still predominantly reliant upon waterwheel power and would continue to be well into the nineteenth century. Of even more immediate concern was the deliberate seduction of skilled French workers into English manufactures:

> English travellers are already among our manufactory towns, and are much busier about picking up hints than about getting orders. Manchester has not yet been successful, as we have, in obtaining the fine Indian scarlet dye on cotton, but twenty French dyers have already gone there and from the generosity which has already given 2,000 guineas to a German who produced only a very faint shade, we may rest assured that before a year is out this fine rich colour will be known throughout England.[83]

This is in contrast to much recent historiography that simply underlines the opposite flow of skilled labour.[84] Thus, this represented yet another English gain embedded in the treaty. Whatever way you look at it, the treaty was a huge success and vindication for the new British industries, particularly, cotton textiles.

Anglo-French war and taxation

As well as the Anglo-French Trade Treaty, 1786 was also significant for Pitt's reintroduction of Walpole's earlier Sinking Fund, established with the aim of paying off the national debt through surplus revenue. This, for Pitt, was a key policy and one fervently urged by the commissioners examining the public accounts. It had been, of course, for precisely the same reason Walpole had first introduced a Sinking Fund in 1716. This surplus was to be generated by further tapping domestic industry and especially foreign trade. For a time it seemed a feasible plan with the public revenue increasing by a staggering 56 per cent between 1783 and 1792, and government spending slashed by some 30 per cent due to the huge decrease in military spending since the War of American Independence. In addition, despite the fact the national debt had almost doubled during the war, the cost of servicing it had only grown by 20 per cent. Pitt's government was riding high – but all that was about to change due to events just across the channel.

Over the next twenty-three years, the government would have to raise some £1.5 billion in taxes and loans to enable the country to effectively fight revolutionary, and subsequently Napoleonic, France. According to Patrick O'Brien's figures, something like 63 per cent of all the *additional* taxes raised between 1793 and 1815 fell on the consumption and income of the wealthy. This, however, simply reveals there were no other choices since the overwhelming burden still fell disproportionately upon the labouring ranks. On one hand, the government showed it could raise such a colossal level of revenue, but it could not prevent the mass mobilization of a powerful backlash. This political opposition now intensified as the pockets of the middling ranks were hit and they accused the government of misappropriating funds and failing to spend the revenues from the people's hard-earned money on the defence of the nation. Instead, the government was denounced as corrupt and rewarding idle private interests.[85] The national debt in 1792 was approximately £237,400,000. The costs, however, of all former eighteenth-century wars combined would not even add up to a third of the total cost of the great war now embarked upon with France. The final price was to be something like £831 million, of which £622 million would be added to the national debt.[86]

The argument that necessaries should only be lightly taxed, if at all, still carried a powerful moral punch. However, when the fiscal demands of the state were desperate such concerns were quickly forgotten. The equitable view that everyone should pay tax had increasingly become absorbed into the sponge of British political life through the demands of war and fiscal necessity. The sympathetic Pittite newspaper *The Times* waded in to justify Pitt's policies in April 1790. The paper acknowledged all the adverse aspects of the excise, namely, the traditional argument that it was an assault upon 'political, civil, and domestic freedom'. However, the editorial underlined the dire nature of the era and the urgent need for greater revenues. As such Pitt's continued emphasis upon the excise was not only right but 'MERITORIOUS'.[87] The newspaper continued its defence of Pitt's tax policy the following month with some carefully worded comments: 'But, admitting that the system of Excise is unconstitutional, we contend that Mr. PITT would be a *traitor* to his country if he rashly abolished a system productive of six millions and a half per annum and upwards. It would reduce the nation to immediate bankruptcy.'[88]

Pitt reiterated the equitable view of the excise in 1798 in an attempt to double the salt tax:

> I am still more confirmed in the justice of this tax, and I am still more persuaded that the very order of people I am speaking of will be satisfied of that truth, when they are informed that persons of the highest rank are not, either with respect to their property, their liberty, or their happiness, so interested in the preservation of this country and the happy constitution under which they live as the lower and labouring classes of the community. If they want to be convinced of this truth, let them look to the situation of these countries which have been overrun by the French.[89]

Pitt's evangelical pursuit of trying to redeem the national debt via the Sinking Fund, when there was no budgetary surplus and the nation was at war, seemingly added greatly to fiscal problems. Importantly, however, it had hitherto helped secure financial credibility and thus reasonable interest rates that saved a great deal in costs servicing the debt.[90] This is why the Sinking Fund was so important and Pitt doggedly hung on to it for so long (Figure 8).

It is fair to say that under the extraordinary pressures of the ongoing war, Pitt and his administration had so far proved they were less tax innovators and more tax multipliers. However, by the close of 1797, Pitt's tax policy had basically hit its maximum reach and a new direction was urgently required. In addition, the huge growth in loans was now depressing the price of government stock; interest rates – despite the Sinking Fund –

Figure 8 'John Bull and the sinking fund' by James Gillray, 1807.

now rose, and the government had to suspend convertibility of British currency after a run on the banks. It was against this dead end that Pitt turned decisively to those people who possessed property, culminating in the introduction of the short-lived Triple Assessment, which Holland Rose described then as 'a rather cumbrous form of graduated Income Tax'. This was quickly replaced the following year by an emergency income tax of 2s. in the pound. A major shift was made from the traditional axiom that taxes should ideally occur on expenditure to one that now included direct assessment with the supplementing of the land tax with an income tax. The initial targets of this approach were the middling ranks and the rich, namely, those with incomes over £60 per year. Incomes below this figure were exempt, while those situated between £60 and £200 were graduated, and those over £200 paid a flat rate of 10 per cent.[91]

The introduction of the income tax was only made possible by the national emergency of the Napoleonic Wars, dire financial straits, and an unstable socio-political context framed by fear of revolution. All this combined to allow Parliament to convince the propertied public that they should have their incomes taxed. This move was further fuelled by three events that all closely coincided. In February 1797 one thousand French troops landed at Fishguard, thus exposing the vulnerability of Britain; in April sailors mutinied off Spithead and, as we have just noted, the Bank of England suspended the convertibility of paper currency into gold. After five years of war, the national debt had almost doubled, reaching an astounding £407 million. Within this context, Pitt really had no option but to raise more revenue from a new form of taxation, which also included a tax on those making money from the interest made via loans to the government. Crucial, too, was the wartime need of cultivating increasing acres of marginal land that improved its value via rents, thus boosting the income tax.[92]

This new direct tax generated 28 per cent of the additional revenue needed to prosecute the war. It was also a more flexible tax in the sense it would rise in conjunction with the country's income. However, as Martin J. Daunton points out, it also represented a switch 'from a voluntary income tax which appealed to the taxpayer's self-interest [the land tax] to an intrusive, compulsory tax' that would make it more difficult to enforce and legitimize.[93] The pressure Pitt and the country were under was quite extraordinary. Shortly after the Act of Union with Ireland in 1801 and set back concerning Catholic emancipation, an exhausted Pitt left office and Henry Addington took over as prime minister. Addington set to work on trying to address the increasingly widespread public perception that the state's administrative structure was riddled with corruption, waste and negligence. He was able to put the reform of administration back on centre stage thanks to the Treaty of Amiens signed in March 1802; in particular, improving the process of collecting the new income tax, reforming the Royal Dockyards and destroying the notorious abuses characterizing the Irish administration.[94]

Consequently, when Pitt returned in May 1804 administrative reform was firmly reinstalled on the political agenda. At this point, too, just about the whole of continental Europe was against Britain. The commercial, industrial and fiscal cost to these mainland countries, especially those reliant upon overseas trade, was actually greater due to the sea blockade by the British. This, of course, cost a huge amount of money to service but was made possible by the British monopoly of the lucrative Atlantic trade and the state's incredible ability to tax its people.[95]

However, despite Pitt's personal reputation, many of his ministers soon regained their standing as parasites living off the spoils of war. This came to a dramatic climax when Lord Melville (Henry Dundas) was accused of misappropriating funds from the navy. Popular radicals were now, more than ever, convinced that the only way to cleanse the state's administration was through constitutional reform. By the time Pitt died in January 1806, the system of government associated with him had become synonymous with a form of government now widely despised.[96]

The Excise increased its intensity and successfully intervened in various towns and cities in the fight against fraud. For example, a team of excise officers including three surveyors and six clerks descended upon Ipswich and obtained £100,000 in defrauded revenue, while it was estimated that £80,000 would soon be claimed back from Plymouth.[97] And in 1815 the government organized an aggressive attempt to apprehend some of the most notorious smugglers by mobilizing the Bow Street Officers.[98]

Despite Pitt's pre-war attempts at deregulating and shrinking the state, the huge administrative expansion and expense of the Napoleonic Wars had expanded it to the point of bursting. The public was angry and no longer willing to shoulder such a burden through taxation. This was coupled by a strong sense that much of the revenue was being squandered and that most taxpaying people were powerless to rectify the situation since they had no political representation. A whole array of folk from diverse social backgrounds started voicing their concerns. This groundswell had far-reaching political, economic and institutional implications. It was this widespread public hostility that fuelled one aspect of the post-war Liberal Tory rationalizing of the state. Ultimately, their administrative reforms would stop government growth and subsequently shrink the state through a pragmatic pursuit of deregulation and free trade. In this sense, too, the emphasis and implementation of values of efficiency and professionalism probably served to secure and merge landed interests into this new guise.[99]

During the French wars, over half of all public statutes were connected to the issue of revenue, with a further 8–12 per cent regulating the practice of trades and industry; in other words, as we have so clearly seen, the urgent demands of sustaining the fiscal–military state-dominated parliamentary business. However, this deflects from the major withdrawal of the state that had already taken place – particularly under Pitt – in the food and labour markets. This deregulation, born of desperation, was a profound change that occurred during Britain's Industrial Revolution.

CHAPTER 11
THE LIVED EXPERIENCE: FOOD AND LABOUR

In 1795, a year after he had been tried for treason, the political radical John Thelwall reflected upon the state of France and Britain:

> *Robespierre* unjustly oppressed the rich, that he might support his popularity among the poor. *Pitt* has neglected, and by his wars and consequent taxes, oppressed the poor, to secure his popularity among the rich … *Robespierre* set up a free constitution, and tyrannized in direct opposition to it. *Pitt* praises another free constitution and tramples all its provisions under foot.[1]

For most people the latter meant the amount of food in their belly and the security of work.

The subject of this chapter is the reduction of the size and activities of the British state within the crucial arenas of the food and labour markets during the late eighteenth and early nineteenth centuries. This subsequently perceived act of liberalism was seen at the time as actually very illiberal by many contemporaries. Among other things, the process entailed the replacement of the legal and customary paternal regularization that had characterized these spheres for the past two and a half centuries. The momentum behind this eradication, often pitilessly carried out, had been primarily triggered by the hugely expensive Seven Years War (1756–63) and greatly accelerated in the aftermath of the War of American Independence (1775–83). Moreover, a rapidly growing population and swelling urban areas were putting pressure on the supply and distribution of grain, although like other bulky goods such as coal, limestone and salt, this was all greatly aided by the growth of inland waterways.

The dismantling of the food market has typically been situated as a prominent feature accompanying the changes associated with the Industrial Revolution. E. P. Thompson long ago captured the implications of state withdrawal:

> To demand an absence of State regulation meant simply giving their larger competitors (or market forces') fuller reign. And this was so evident that Carlile [Richard Carlile], no less than Cobbett [William Cobbett], was forced to make a demonology of sinecure's, placemen, and tax-eaters. The great evil afflicting the little [labouring classes, small producers, traders, farmers etc] must be seen to be taxation. There must be as little Government as possible, and that little must be cheap.[2]

Despite numerous critics, the work of Thompson on the history of food provision and the culture that grew up around it has weathered very well. However, the impact of high indirect taxation has, despite Thompson's remarks above and the important exception of an essay by Gareth Steadman Jones, been rather neglected when it comes to the growth of popular radicalism.[3]

Food fuelled the majority of popular unrest in the eighteenth century, with some historians estimating that two out of every three riots were the result in supply and price changes in food. The corn harvest was without doubt the single most important factor in people's everyday lives. A poor harvest was an absolute disaster while, not surprisingly, any fiddling with the process of market provisioning and practices was liable to provoke popular protest. Uprisings over food had deep historical roots dating back to the medieval period and beyond. Thompson concluded his important essay on the 'Moral Economy of the English Crowd' by claiming the 'breakthrough of the new political economy of the free market was also the breakdown of the old moral economy of provision'. As we have touched upon in the last chapter and will now examine in detail, this was not the result of some industrial enlightenment or dignified middling polite culture.[4]

The British labouring ranks did not possess some monolithic attitude towards the market, indeed, what they sought was simply protection for the value of the labour they expended and to secure accessibility to market goods at a fair price. This, as Adrian Randall puts it, was not 'an "anti-market" mentality'. On the contrary, they 'were all too aware of the market … their whole lives were lived within market economics: as consumers in an increasingly volatile food market; and as producers in a labour market that they well knew fluctuated both in demand for and in the supply of labour'.[5] However, by the late eighteenth century, during the height of the Industrial Revolution, the food market moulded by years of local understandings and regulations was under unbearable pressure to change. This was compounded by an intensification of land enclosure; to be sure this process commenced far earlier but the appropriation of common land hugely accelerated during this period. Key moments included the Enclosure Act of 1773 and the General Enclosure Act of 1801. The latter act speeded up the process by enabling enclosures to bypass parliamentary sanction.[6]

In general, the regulated and protected system that has so far been the concern of this book, of which the moral economy was part, had reached its zenith and had become seemingly unsustainable in its prevailing form. Consequently, the government's only way out was just that – to shrink from playing a part in adjudicating the interests of the land owner, merchants, everyday people and industrialist. The disintegration of a protectionist and paternalist model of food marketing was mirrored by the retreat of the state, in general, from its close regulating activities in an array of spheres. The overriding fiscal pressures upon the state demanded urgent action, and this invited certain economic interests and political reformers an excuse to step in and radically reform the prevailing socio-economic structure.

The regulated food market and workplace was based upon a body of old customs and legislated law, which worked in equilibrium between the labouring masses and the landed ranks. However, as we saw in the last chapter, commencing during the early 1770s, the state was straining under the weight of debt and accompanying social agitation. The result, particularly under Pitt, was a pragmatic switch in commercial, industrial and fiscal policy that favoured the newer, export-oriented and less regulated industries; a situation that invited the need for an alternative doctrine, namely, free trade and a new political economy. Accompanying this was a redefining of the state's role in regulating the economy and, thus, the food and labour market. The result was a volatile arena, sometimes teetering upon revolution, which would finally end with the victory of an invented notion of an anonymous, supposedly free and neutral market. The creation of this ephemeral utopia would serve successive governments and certain interest groups up to the present day very well. The argument was not new but the seduction and growing theory that surrounded it was.

Thompson is cautious about the initial role of the middling ranks in fuelling this shift; although as the significant benefactors of the new commercial society, their subsequent part is important. It was not until the food and labour market became more and more distant from local view, and political survival forced the extension of the franchise that the middling ranks could cultivate the confidence and power to assert themselves. It was also the case that the government, primarily composed of landed gentlemen, had reached a dead end. As such, there could be no more careful manoeuvring between the plebeian and patrician classes because all room for concessions had been exhausted. In short, the demands of the debt-ridden state had finally filled all such possibilities. It was at this point that the voice of the growing middling ranks really stepped in to significantly impact on the threat of social collapse. What some claim was a victory for Enlightenment thinking was, on the contrary, a product of desperation and opportunism.[7]

This disillusion became all too clear in the aftermath of the French Revolution and the hugely expensive Napoleonic Wars. It was this that dissolved any pretence that the working classes were independent and free. Thompson writes, 'In the wake of the experiences of these years the relationship of reciprocity snapped. As it snapped, so, in the same moment, the gentry lost their self-assured cultural hegemony.' This dead end demanded a strategy for social, political and economic survival; within this vacuum the growing commercial middling ranks wasted no time in taking their chance to fill it.[8]

So what had snapped? Social customs among the common people, especially over food rights, were probably stronger during the eighteenth century than at any other time. Such customs were defined by both legislated laws and age-old practice (customary law). During the first half of the eighteenth century, both legal customary definitions and popular practice existed within a complicated but mutual understanding. Douglas Hay and Nicholas Rogers explain the environment: 'The fact that law recognised custom helped extend a more generalised legitimacy to any practice that could be convincingly presented as customs.' These customs by the end of the century were propagated as 'rights', much to the increasing suspicion of a vulnerable landed social authority and a growing commercial middling rank. Drawing upon the language of the ruling ranks and constitutional notions of a 'free-born Englishman', many of the working masses realized that if law and prescription underpinned the rights of the ruling landed elite then they had little legitimacy in ruling over their particular customs and rights.[9]

The gentry's power may have set the boundaries to their relationship with the working classes, but it did not determine the character of the culture that grew up around it. The customs of the common people were invoked if they deemed this relationship was not functioning correctly. During the eighteenth century the landed gentry – despite the rapid increase in the new moneyed, industrial and commercial interest – still dominated power (especially judicial) that was traditionally erected upon land. The authority of the gentry was still, on the whole, seen as embedded in the very course of nature. The working people did not confront or see the gentry as employers and thus depict them as responsible for the conditions of their life. When the price of food rose the population's rage fell not on the landowners, but upon middlemen such as the forestaller who bought grain before it got to market; the regrater who purchased grain in the market and then subsequently sold it for a profit elsewhere; the engrosser who bought large quantities and sold it on; and millers if they were found adulterating grain with chalk or other substances.

The paternalist gentry were expected to police such illegal actions and ensure market regulation preserved a fair market. 'Therefore,' as Randall explains, 'the great majority of consumers, not merely the poor, agreed that regularisation of markets against such practices were an absolute necessity.' Such a view of the market started to come under particular pressure as the population, particularly within fast-expanding urban areas, greatly increased. Morever, the efficiency of the national market through the building of canals and superior turnpike roads during the second half of the eighteenth century made the flow of goods, like grain, much easier. These were developments that enabled the ever-growing number of people enclosed in urban areas to consume. Large farmers and very wealthy landowners were the ones to especially benefit from such a move as they found a greater demand (and price) for their produce. Crucially, too, it significantly enhanced and bolstered the power of dealers and middlemen.[10]

Everyday people at this time exhibited no widespread shared levelling spirit or political consciousness, and did not believe they were subverting the authority of the magistrate's role in regulating markets when they protested. Rather, they thought they were enforcing a control that the magistrates should be doing, with food riots ending when the grain returned to the crowd's notion of a fair price. These local groups consisted of an array of urban and industrial workers but seldom any farm labourers, which was probably because the latter often received part of their wages in kind during times of scarcity. Some manufacturing and mining areas were communities where a stronger collective labour consciousness had been forged; these places had experience of large-scale conflicts over not just food prices, but rather over a wider range of issues. They were communities embedded within a whole diversity of forms of protest. This culture of customary defiance seemed to justify and reinforce belief in the 'moral economy'.[11]

Most people during the eighteenth century lived on a diet dominated by bread. Riots could occur at various stages in the journey it took grain to become bread. The paternalist model of the market and, indeed, the manufacturing process, existed in an eroded body of Elizabethan Statute law, common law and custom. It was an array of regulations that very often informed the magistrate's decisions during times of desperation. It reproduced emergency measures made in times of scarcity and codified in the *Book of Orders* between 1580 and 1630. Under this old legislation, the magistrates were required to attend the local markets and where there was insufficient corn, resort to the home of the farmers and view what store and provision of grain they had remaining either threshed or un-threshed. Not infrequently, the result would be to order the farmers to send suitable quantities to market at a reasonable price. The justices were not ordered to set down a price upon the bushel of every kind of grain but, simply, to ensure the poor received enough corn. Although the legislation became neglected during the English Civil War period, it remained in everyday folk and paternal consciousness. As far as possible marketing was meant to be direct from the farmer to the consumer. The farmer was expected to bring his corn in bulk to the local pitching market and not sell it while it was still standing in the field, nor indeed withhold it in the hope of rising prices. Pitched markets were controlled with no sales allowed to be made before stated times. Despite the rise of selling by sample among the large farmers in the latter half of the eighteenth century, the old pitching markets still remained a common sight throughout the century. And although they were in decline they remained sunk within people's minds as the new marketing procedures were contested.[12]

Dealers, farmers and millers were often accused of colluding together; grain would be taken to market to fulfil a legal requirement, only for the farmer to tell anyone who intended to make a purchase that it had already been sold. Such practices could cause a riot. For example, a crowd rose at Oxford in 1757 and within a few minutes seized and divided a large amount of corn suspected of having been bought by sample. During these riots they would set the price of corn at what was deemed a fair price. The crowd moved from the marketplace outwards, as in the *Book of Orders*, to farms where stocks were inspected and the farmers were ordered to send grain to market at the 'fair price' stipulated by the crowd. Even though they were protected to some degree from popular wrath by the Assize of Bread (state officials determining the fair price of a loaf), many bakers were also found guilty of using false weights and measures in the size of the bread or adulterating it with cheap and spoilt flour.[13]

Both the landed classes and the poor continued to complain at the extension of unregulated market practices. However, middlemen were particularly necessary to supply rapidly growing urban markets outside the main corn-growing districts, and paternalists recognized much of the change but referred back to the old model whenever an emergency arose. The Privy Council authorized the posting of proclamations, threatening dire penalties against forestallers throughout the first seventy-two years of the eighteenth century.[14]

The zenith of the 'moral economy' took place three years after the Seven Years War in 1766, when a series of national protests against the exportation of English grain took place, resulting in a rigorous implementation of the old regulatory paternal management of the market. However, it also marks a moment when a significant change towards the future of a regulated food market took place. In particular, a growing population, the continuing shift in the oeconomy from agriculture to industry and rapid urbanization were raising increasingly urgent questions concerning the distribution of grain; this was all compounded by attacks upon a perceived bloated state. Within this context, the role of middlemen and easing the free flow of grain seemed to be increasingly, for many, the only practical solution rather than any ideologically-driven notion of a free market.[15] To be sure, however, this certainly speeded the appropriation of customs people held in common and their access to common land via enclosure.[16] Carving up the landscape with artificial waterways was about fuelling industry, commerce and feeding growing industrial clusters in Lancashire and the Midlands.

For exponents of unregulated trade in the domestic sale of grain, the moral economy restricted and prevented a more equitable and efficient system; that far from being a popular value system was characterized by a selfish localism at the expense of the wider consumer. Moreover, regulation seemed to support a corrupt, fat and interfering state. Thompson claimed: 'Few intellectual victories have been more overwhelming than that which the proponents of the new political economy won in the matter of the regulation of the internal corn trade.'[17] The new model set out to repeal all the domestic Corn Laws and let grain operate within a free national market. The supply of grain, it was increasingly argued, should be left to regulate itself free from all legislative and local interference. In such a model the middlemen played a natural and necessary role in helping the flow of corn from areas of surplus to scarcity. This played well into the hands of the government's forthcoming emphasis in 1786 upon the new export-oriented industries that defined the Industrial Revolution and the urgent need to shrink the activities of a hugely expensive state. Indeed, it crystallized into a generalized potent new political economy characterized, eventually, by deregulation and an ideology of free trade.

By contrast, traditionalist writers claimed that an unregulated trade in domestic grain gave the farmers and dealers a monopoly. They, in turn, were condemned by the apostles of the new political economy as being illogical and out of touch with the new demographic, industrial and urban conditions. The point of the traditionalists was simply that the farmer and the dealer could now exploit their advantage over a pure necessity of life; farmers did not have to sell in an open pitched market, while dealers or millers were in a better position to hold stocks and keep the market high. The post-harvest price was set on the expectation of the harvest yield and, typically, the growing farming lobby estimated that there would be a shortage, which suited them to do so in order to keep prices high.[18]

The exponents of the new free-market model often complained at a certain section of the gentry activating the muscle of mob discontent. Certainly many of the gentry persisted in their dislike of middlemen and underlined the need to retain their traditional relationship with the bulk of the population to preserve the social order. Their anger towards the dealers was expressed by many magistrates, some of whom remained inactive when popular disturbances swept through the areas under their jurisdiction.[19]

In this way the key period associated with the British Industrial Revolution was the background to the destruction of the authority of customary expectations. And it was this, for Thompson and others, which demarcates the 'pre-industrial' or 'traditional' from the modern industrial era. This was sealed in the mid-1790s and early 1800s, the war years with France, when the equilibrium between paternalist authority and the crowd was rapidly eroded. First, the acute anti-Jacobinism of the gentry led to a new paranoia of any form of popular self-activity propelled by the French Revolution, which was now feared far more than the insurrection of the masses over food; price-setting actions were increasingly branded as subversive. There was also the fear of invasion that raised the volunteers, and thus gave the civil powers much more immediate means for confronting the crowd – this time without negotiation and concession but with repression.[20] This was the great era of enclosure – from land and, during the early nineteenth century, prison building to bonded warehouses, urban expansion, asylums, barracks and factories.[21]

Nonetheless, the outcome was still not inevitable with provincial paternalism still persisting. Rather than repressing the moral economy, many justices sought to strengthen it as the best remedy to dangerous radicalism. In contrast, the government had a very different view and conflicting approach. For the first time, under the leadership of the Duke of Portland at the Home Office, there was public criticism of magistrates who sought to prop up the regulated model. There emerged a stark split between localism and central government. Some of the former authorities may have been sympathetic to aspects of the government's view, but local survival still pointed towards the old paternal model as the best route. This may have been partly pragmatic but it was also true that they viewed the idea of a free market with great scepticism.[22] Consequently, the old regulatory moral economy did not die quietly or totally disappear.

It was not the period between 1795 and 1801, as Thompson argued, that witnessed the demise of the moral economy, but erosion over a longer and later period of repudiation. Hay, Roger Wells and Randall have shown that the realities of these harsh years meant that the old moral economy could only aid things so far, but if there simply was not enough food to go around no amount of regulation could help. 'This revelation', writes Randall, 'was to prove the most powerful argument against the old ideology'. The power of the large farmers and middlemen were the ones to benefit from this reality. 'This experience', he concludes, 'more than any ideological struggle or fear of Jacobins demonstrated the fracturing of the old moral economy.'[23] However, this was just one part of a larger movement with far-reaching ramifications for all aspects of state activity and the socio-economic structure in general. An equally radical change was taking place in the regulation of Britain's industrial labour. As in the food market power would shift from the state to the employer and an unregulated economy.

'Broken in upon and violated': Industry and labour

Customs and regulations in Britain's various industries were, like the food market, also deeply embedded. There was a relationship between manufacturers and workers that, on the whole, both sides understood. At the forefront of extending Thompson's notion of a moral economy to the workplace during the eighteenth century has been the work of Randall. Like the food market, this relationship was defined by both custom and the existence of old regulatory legislation.

Overcoming nature was often a much simpler challenge than changing embedded work practices and making workers amenable to new machines, tools and practices. The solution to both was frequently a dialectic relationship; this was to prove vital in defining the future trajectory and political place of the machine, factory and division of labour in British history. Fundamental to the successful application of these factors within the workplace of domestic industries was the repeal of old legislation built upon mature protectionist policies. The traditional role of the state in maintaining a standard of living, including the level of wages among the working ranks, was fast dissolving towards the end of the eighteenth century before being completely severed in the nineteenth century. In his book *Before the Luddites*, Randall has described how practices built around long-standing state regulatory legislation worked within England's oldest industry, namely, woollen textiles. He traces this until the final demise of these laws in 1809 and with it the customs and community that had grown up around them. One of the defining features in this breakdown was the green light for the introduction of new machines and production methods that, in turn, provoked a varied regional reaction to their arrival.[24]

The bulk of this regulatory legislation had been clarified during the Elizabethan era, which confirmed an old act of 1390 ordering justices of the peace to regulate workers' wages. The Statute of Artificers, passed in 1563, was presented as a codification of prevailing measures, although it was designed to be durable and flexible. Its primary aim was employment, particularly to ensure there was enough agricultural workers who, if necessary, could be compelled to work. The law also attempted to specify a seven-year apprenticeship for all rural and town artificers, although it excluded crafts arising after the 1563 statute. In attempting to legislate for this period it was, in many cases, greatly extending the period of training found in different regions; in short, the law was attempting to introduce uniformity to all crafts across the country.[25] The state was doing what guilds once did to ensure a standard of skilled labour. The west of England Coggeshall wool combers described the legislation as 'the law Queen Betty made'.[26]

The legislation was also very different from the former specifications in the sense that there were now no limitations to the number of apprenticeships an employee could undertake; this was of great relief to the earlier highly regulated cloth trades. After initial hostility to the enforced seven-year apprenticeship time-scale, it was eventually accepted and became custom throughout the country.[27] This period of time was probably legislated, as John Rule argues, 'to protect the quality and reputation of English manufactures by ensuring that only the properly trained produced them'.[28] The statute also dealt with terms of employment and wage rates. For example, the maximum limit someone could be paid was removed and now left ultimately to the decision of the justices of the peace (authorized by the Privy Council and proclaimed by the sheriff). Attempts to set a minimum wage in the woollen industry were introduced in 1593, 1598 and 1604.[29]

Stephan R. Epstein claimed that at a time where there was no schooling or places of training, such apprenticeships under craft associations were 'the best possible solution'.[30] However, the enforcement of apprenticeships was flagrantly ignored by many trades. For example, shortly after the introduction of the 1701 Calico Act, a petition from serge, worsted and other woollen weavers estimated there were about 1,500 weavers in Taunton, and a further 2,000 more in the surrounding vicinity, who had not served apprenticeships, with most paid in kind rather than a coin wage. The House of Commons Committee to which the petition was referred agreed that the petitioners did indeed 'labour under very great Difficulties and Discouragements in their Trade; for that many intrude themselves into the weaving Trade, who never served an Apprenticeship thereto, contrary to the statute made in the 2d and 3d Years of the Reign of Philip and Mary', along with another act made in 'the 5th Year of Queen Elizabeth'. The committee resolved that the statutes should be enforced and that all workers be paid in coin and not in kind. Nonetheless, they also acknowledged manufacturers' concerns over embezzlement, and advised that 'all serge and worsted weavers, wool-combers, spinners, and other workers in the Woollen Manufactures, be effectually restrained from embezzling, selling, or detaining, any Wool or Yarn, delivered to them by any Clothier, or other Person'. The House passed the issue of embezzlement and payment to be made in coin, but were less sympathetic to better enforcing apprenticeships in such trades.[31]

The term 'combination' was first used in the Tailors' Combination Act of 1721, which was the same year as the 1721 Calico Act. This 'extended the common law of conspiracy to include collective actions by workers if taken in pursuit of trade claims'; individuals could take actions but collective actions were now illegal. Subsequently, if a conspiracy involving a combination of workers was suspected as having caused an industrial dispute they would be punished. Another eighteen related statutes prohibiting trade combinations were passed between 1721 and the well-known general Combination Acts of 1799 and 1800. Importantly, the 1721 Act also attempted to introduce a way of independently regulating wages. This role was given to the quarter sessions that, like the old Tudor legislation that regulated wages, now had the task of setting annual maxims. As with so much legislation it was generally flouted by manufacturers who often paid over the price to woo the best workers, leading to protests from other journeymen to be similarly remunerated.[32]

In all of this the state played a prominent role in both trying to settle industrial protests and to regulate the workplace. Workers frequently petitioned Parliament to intervene, while magistrates were often told directly to enforce laws against combinations and arbitrate employer/employee disputes. Organization was a matter for employees and employers but protests, when it threatened social peace and national revenues, became a matter for the state. There was a huge diversity of industrial protest that was subject to geography, the size of the trade, and the particular customs of the trade; in other words, an array of variations that defy any simplistic all-fitting models. Perhaps the most frequently disruptive trades were the textile industries which, with their different organizational structures, led to divergent patterns of industrial relations.[33]

The problem was constructing piece rate lists for textiles since most of the justices lacked a technical knowledge of the skill and procedures involved in production. The price was simplistic and based primarily upon the number of threads contained in the warp, weft or chain of the cloth. This ignored the 'size of threads, the weight of the chain, the fineness of the weft, the breadth of the cloth, and the mode of manufacture – the qualities and kinds of cloths being "too various to be reduced to any regular fixed standard". The legal rates also made no allowance for degrees of technical skill'.[34] In particular, different textile trades were reluctant to abandon their own customary measures of yarn, while spinners, weavers and clothiers judged the fineness of yarn in different ways.[35]

In general, 1756 was a dire year in Gloucestershire with some 25,000 unemployed weavers protesting and the potential of this spreading to surrounding counties.[36] In that year the woollen broadcloth weavers of Gloucester petitioned Parliament, complaining of the lack of legal rigour in the enforcement of wage rates in the county, and the unacceptable number of them paid in truck. Clothiers, they protested, 'often oblige them to stay for their wages till they amount to considerable sums, and then oblige them to run in Debt for their Subsistence, and that, when they are paid Notes in manner aforesaid, they are obliged to make great Allowance to Persons to discount the same'. The problem of prosecuting such clothiers stemmed over the sheer cost of trials at Westminster Hall. As a result, Parliament agreed that an act should be passed to rectify the issue of wages and legal costs and double the fine applicable to employers.[37] The justices of the peace were to set the wages and pin such rates in public places such as upon church and inn doors. However, it was also agreed that more efforts should be made to prevent the unlawful combination of workmen – the state officially worked hard to achieve a balanced front.[38]

Despite the weavers' success, the clothiers chose to ignore the set rates. As a result, the weavers took two prominent clothiers to court and won. The clothiers, however, continued to aggressively lobby Parliament and eventually managed to win a repeal in March 1757. The whole process reveals the key role of regional authorities in moulding labour relations under an umbrella of neutrality. The Gloucestershire bench was open to both weavers and clothiers, and independent enough not to allow clothiers complete power to subjugate their workforce. Local ratepayers 'feared the consequences of prolonged industrial warfare', and it was this that created 'a pattern of textile workers applying to the bench for support in times of conflict'.[39]

In 1773 came the first Spitalfield Act. This was passed in an attempt to rectify the increasing problem revolving around an agreed list of piece-work rates within the silk industry. An elderly foreman, Edward Jones, claimed it was a list 'that had existed long before I had existence', and one that was 'broken in upon and violated', he thought, in 1767. This would make sense since it was a period of falling demand and profits for many silk masters, therefore, forcing them to undercut the official wage rates. In turn, such action had triggered a spree of intense rioting and organized sabotage. A practice called 'silk-cutting', for example, became quite common; a weaver who accepted a lower rate of pay would have his work literally cut up and destroyed (the sabotage had been made a capital offence two years earlier). The weavers were mainly of Huguenot decent or Irish immigrants frequently at each others' throats. However, during the riots ethnic prejudices were forgotten and many fought together and when the disturbances reached a zenith in 1769, two weavers, John Valline (of French origin) and John Doyle, probably Irish, were hung in front of the Salmon and Ball Public House in Bethnal Green. The state could also be balanced when it came to punishment. To fight the breaking of the agreed Book of Rates the journeymen silk weavers had formed an illegal combination to pressurize employers.[40]

The 1773 Act was designed to prevent these disturbances from reoccurring. It gave power to the justices of Middlesex, the Tower Hamlets and the City of London to negotiate and regulate the silk weavers' wages. The rates were published three times a year in two daily newspapers, and if owners paid less or more than the fixed rate they would be fined forty shillings. A much higher penalty of £50 was applicable if the employer used workers from beyond the regulated area. Most of the subsequent disputes occurred during times of high food prices with the magistrates normally favouring the weavers. List prices were formalized into a book of fabrics in 1774, a revised one in 1795, and again in 1800, 1802, 1804, 1806 and 1818. The 1773 Act also legislated that employers could not hire people outside their respective trades, while no weaver was allowed more than two apprenticeships. The law was subsequently copied and introduced in Dublin, and extended in London to include fabrics of mixed silk and other materials.[41]

Meanwhile, problems continued over the issue of enforcing apprenticeship regulations. A petition from master dyers and calico printers in Middlesex, Essex, Surrey and Kent complained about the enforcement of certain Elizabethan legislation. The petitioners were angry that they were unable to employ forty men of whom only four had served a regular apprenticeship: 'That they can't find Men of the Trade to do their Business, for which Reason he is under a Necessity of employing such labouring men, or could not go on with his Trade.' As a result, the House of Commons voted to bring a bill out to 'allow the Master Dyers and Calico Printers' within the Home Counties 'to employ Journeymen, in their respective Trades, who have not served Apprenticeships thereto'.[42] Despite the legal onslaught upon guilds, they proved flexible and, in many ways, came to anticipate trade societies, or what later came to be termed in the nineteenth century as trade unions.[43]

The silk and mixed silk industry had spread way beyond Spitalfield, where typically only two-thirds of the Spitalfield wage was paid to weavers. London manufacturers were evading the 1773 Act by farming work out of the capital to expanding provincial areas. Despite some convictions the practice remained, while competition from new fabrics and an increasingly quick change in fashion was exacerbating the situation. By the time adjusted peace-rates could be worked out for new fabrics it was too late, leading to rates being illegally made between individuals contrary to the act. A number of wealthy City of London masters, no doubt inspired by the repeal of the wage-fixing claims of the Elizabethan labour code, lobbied to have the Spitalfield Act abolished. Smaller London and regional weavers along with a great number of masters, however, counter-lobbied to keep them. Indeed, the Coventry weavers in 1818 wanted the Spitalfield Acts to be extended to their area, while those London masters who wanted the legislation to remain claimed it helped prevent disputes.[44]

The split in the perspective of silk masters had become patently obvious by the time the 1818 select committee was set up to investigate the industry. It was clear that the large silk masters, typically City rather than Spitalfield men, were against the acts, while the smaller concerns still 'thought in Spitalfield terms'. They were predominantly in the staple trade and less concerned with outside competition. By contrast the big City capitalists, claimed J. H. Clapham, 'thought the Acts a relic of barbarism, an interference with capital and political economy, and a nursery of combination'. As well as emphasizing the role of the acts in fostering combination, one of the 1818 witnesses, Stephen Wilson, claimed they blocked labour-saving mechanization: 'Masters had to pay the same rates whether labour-saving appliances were used or not ... so, of course, labour was not saved. Such a law in the cotton trade, said Wilson, would have ruined Arkwright.'[45]

The opposition to the acts continued to gain momentum, especially when a Lords Committee examining the silk trade and the question of tariffs was set up and concluded that the acts were adverse to the industry. On 9 May 1823 a petition against the acts was sent to the House of Commons, followed by a counter one a few days later from the Sudbury weavers. The latter were clearly worried that if the acts were repealed then their customary rate of two-thirds that of Spitalfields would be threatened. In June, however, a bill drawn up by the new President of the Board of Trade, William Huskisson, to repeal the acts was narrowly passed by the Commons with a split of 53 to 40.[46] 'Henceforth,' as Joanna Innes writes, 'the state was not to arbitrate: employers and workers were to work out their own future.'[47]

The repeal of the acts may seem in hindsight to be another example of the government being enlightened by the new political economy or simply the result of lobbying by large capitalist silk manufacturers, but it was clearly part of the momentum to shrink the state and withdraw the government from the oeconomic arena in general. Nonetheless, legislation such as this was viewed by social labour as the final guard against the unimpeded march of a new economic system and erosion of workers protection. In this sense, the statutes operated in much the same way as the legislation controlling the marketplace for food did. This thwart debate and controversial development had already, as we have seen, come to a head a few years earlier with the final repeal of most industrial regulatory laws in 1809.

One potent symbol associated with the new deregulated world was the machine. Breaking machines was made a capital offence in 1769 after a saw mill along the Thames in Limehouse had been destroyed. However, this did not prevent disturbances in Lancashire ten years later when cotton textile machinery was targeted. Josiah Wedgwood reported meeting several hundred people damaging such machines on his journey north. Two of this crowd were shot dead while attacking a cotton mill. The angry textile workers were subsequently joined by colliers employed at the Duke of Bridgwater's coalmines and numerous others until they approached 8,000 people marching to the beat of a drum. They returned to the mill where the two men had been killed and levelled it to the ground. The drum started again and the crowd set forth to do the same to mills in Bolton, Manchester and Stockport. A worried Richard Arkwright had already prepared for the worst and set in place measures to defend his mill in Cromford. The government sent the army in from Liverpool and dispersed the protestors. However, some were caught, tried and hung. If things were bad in the cotton textile industry, it was even more thwart in the woollen textile industry.[48]

Randall shows how purely economic determinants cannot account for regional variations when comparing the woollen industries in the west of England with West Riding. In particular, the 'craft consciousness and solidarity' of the West Country woollen textile workers was a major obstacle to mechanization. Britain's oldest industry was not simply a world without roots that could be easily overhauled but was a way of life. The machine innovators were frequently viewed in the same way the forestaller and regrater were in the marketplace. This is why, Randall claims, their actions also constituted an industrial moral economy. His argument is made even more convincing by the use and appeal to old legal regulations encoded in law and practice. Not surprisingly, then, the new mill and factory owners sought aggressively to repeal the old legislation.[49]

Those impressive machines and factories that had appeared sent a shiver through the community and represented a potential end to their independence, skills and autonomy.[50] The old legislation was regarded as the final safeguard to the new form of centralized production which was, they felt, fast breathing down their necks. The machine and factory were thus seen as the destruction of traditional relationships between the woollen masters and the workers in both the putting-out and domestic systems.[51] Not surprisingly, as Maxine Berg has shown, the 'machinery question became in fact the hinge which connected the new economic relations of production with the wider culture and consciousness of the new bourgeoisie and working class'. For many 'it became axiomatic that mechanical change was natural and evolutionary, the very motion of progress itself'. For others, by contrast, it was the exact opposite. The new discipline of political economy particularly emerged in tandem with the organizational and technical developments taking place in the new industries such as cotton and iron – along with certain older industries like woollens.[52]

Just as the common law and customary practices in the food market were being successfully challenged and eventually usurped in the late eighteenth and early nineteenth centuries by dismantling protective and regulating legislation, the same form of pressure was creating new ways to redefine and objectify the workplace and make it amenable to mechanization and mechanical organization.[53] However, such experimentation first required traditional roots to be eradicated. The west of England, and eventually the West Riding woollen workers, 'foresaw that the introduction of machinery would usher in the factory system and destroy the putting-out system'. In 1802 there were some seventy regulatory statutes in existence that controlled marketing, production and labour. During this period, writes Randall, the 'weavers of the West of England and the master clothiers and journeymen of the West Riding' instigated a 'campaign to uphold and strengthen the old acts in order to rest the rise of the weaving factory and loomshop'.[54]

The weavers and master clothiers told the parliamentary select committees of 1803 and 1806 that their main purpose in pressing for active enforcement of the old legislation was to stem the rise of the factory. This was a battle between the old regulated world of eighteenth-century manufactures, and the new desperate and pragmatic world of state deregulation. The latter, as we have seen, was primarily driven by the need to reduce the costs of a deeply unpopular state and promote the ever more important export-oriented industries. Changing work practices associated with the British Industrial Revolution cannot be severed from the urgent need to shrink the debt-ridden state.

Resistance was at its most intense in places with a history and a culture that was rich in pre-mechanical protest. Successful or at least sustained confrontation needed more than just widespread support; it also required organization through a trade combination or subsequently a trade union. This occurred in the west of England and, eventually, the West Riding woollen industries also succumbed once they found themselves faced with the loss of livelihood via the introduction of new technology. Meanwhile, after the repeal of the old woollen regulatory laws in 1809, there was a quick take-up of both gig mills and frames by woollen manufacturers. With the withdrawal of the state the woollen workers and skilled workers from numerous other industries found themselves isolated. One result, especially after the loss of the American market due to war in 1812, was Luddism.

Luddism was not just a loosely coordinated movement attacking machines but part of a much broader reaction to the loss of state regulation, the issue of skilled and unskilled labour and subsequent production of inferior products (Figure 9). Attacks also took place upon agricultural machinery and grain stacks. Luddism, as Katrina Navickas has shown, was not just an urban issue.[55] The most determined and successful of the Luddite attacks during 1812 were from the Yorkshire cloth dressers. The repeal of the woollen regulations was simply the tip of the iceberg, with the general repeal of various other

Figure 9 'The Leader of the Luddites', 1812.

trade regulatory and apprenticeship legislation about to take place.[56] One reason the woollen textile sector was slower to adopt new technology compared to cotton was the fact that it was under far less pressure to match foreign quality and, crucially, was a far older and more regulated industry.

The three main manufacturing areas associated with Luddism (Nottinghamshire, East Yorkshire and Lancashire) were united in the sense that the trades were fighting 'to extend or restore Parliamentary regulation of their particular industry'. They were, however, confronted by a government desperately seeking to shrink the sinews of the state and a new political economy was quickly filling the void. Thus, Malcolm Chase concludes, the repeal of the Statute of Artificers in 1814 had an even larger impact upon the shape trade unionism later took than the repeal of the Combination Acts in 1824. It was an assault upon the labourer's property of skill and 'one more brick in a wall being erected between employers and employed'.[57] All this, to repeat, was taking place in a political context urgently seeking ways to shrink an overblown and debt-ridden state.

The fear of political radicalism fusing with trade combinations had haunted government, particularly, during the 1790s; it once again expanded via the rise of the public platform and organized meetings in the post-Napoleonic War period.[58] The mass platform was unlike all previous political risings. It was characterized, as Nicholas Rogers writes, by 'large meetings and monster petitions' and 'a strategy of open, constitutional confrontation with the government that stood in marked contrast to the kinds of crowd interpretations that had characterised politics since the exclusion crisis'.[59] This became a rallying point for the now state-abandoned working classes. At Spa Fields in November 1816, a mass meeting heard one of the speakers, Mr Parkes, tell his audience that 'immorality' had never been as extensive as it was now. He claimed it had 'paved the way for corruption, and corruption had taken its permanent seat', and the only way to extricate it was for the people 'to dislodge them [those in political power]'. Next up was the star speaker, 'Orator' Henry Hunt, who focused his speech on the system of unjust taxation: 'Everything that concerned their subsistence or comforts was taxed. Was but their loaf taxed – was not their beer taxed – were not everything that they ate, drank, wore, and even said taxed? (*A laugh*). What impudence, what insolence was it then in the corrupt and profligate reasons of Government to say that the people suffered nothing by taxation.'[60]

William Cobbett more or less gave, word for word, the same argument in his *Political Register* of December 1819. These sentiments, in general, were widely diffused. Thomas Paine, for example, had given similar remarks in his *Rights of Man* in 1792 and in a letter to Secretary Dundas also that year. Likewise, John Thewall put this view forth in the *Tribune* during 1795.[61] The state had withdrawn its protective legislation within the food and labour markets, but still relied heavily upon the working classes for revenues. This was a volatile situation that would have to be sooner or later confronted and resolved. The explosive nature of the situation was demonstrated when several people were killed and hundreds of others injured at St Peter's Square, Manchester, where a crowd of seventy thousand had gathered to hear Hunt speak in 1819.

The Combination Acts

Two well-known pieces of labour legislation springing up during the Industrial Revolution were the 1799 and 1800 Combination Acts. Trade combination activity throughout the eighteenth century frequently hid behind a façade of being a friendly society that periodically met in an inn. The classification of a trade, and the increasing application of such a definition by journeymen, gained its sense from a clear clarification made by the Statute of Artificers. Thereafter, a concerted reform of such a specification only really commenced in the late seventeenth and eighteenth centuries, particularly with regard to England's leading industry, woollen textiles. By the mid-eighteenth century, a committee appointed by the House of Commons to investigate the laws concerning trade and manufacturers set the tone for the next generation. It stated in 1751: 'But your committee are of opinion, if the legal restraints were once removed, the particular by-laws would soon be reversed, as they cannot but observe that the most useful and beneficial manufactures are principally carried on, and trade most flourishing, in such towns and spaces as are under no such local disabilities.'[62]

The introduction of the general Combination Acts of 1799 and 1800 have been noted by some historians as the first overt example of class legislation born of the Industrial Revolution. J. L. and B. Hammond wrote in 1925: 'These two Acts, the second modifying the first, prohibiting all common action in defence of their common interests, remain the most unqualified surrender of the State to the discretion of a class in the history of England.' As we shall see, though, it is wrong to claim the second act reinforced the first. In addition, the legislation did not introduce any new principle or new offence, since there were numerous prior acts implemented to prevent combinations of workmen. However, it was the first time *all trades* were classified together as *one class*.[63]

The origin of the 1799 Act was due to a petition by the London millwrights for a bill making combination within their trade a summary offence. This would speed up cases by bypassing prosecutions on indictment at the Sessions or Assizes, which could lead to lengthy delays and high costs. As such many were put off prosecuting. By contrast, if the case went straight to magistrates, prosecutions would be much faster but with lighter punishments. It is also worth adding that the threat by excise officers to combine for higher wages in 1797 may also have added momentum to the 1799 Act. For if the most important source of revenue came to a halt the whole country would. In 1800 all excise officers were given a significant pay rise.[64]

The Millwright's Bill was passed but, after the intervention of the prominent slave abolitionist, William Wilberforce, it was extended to all trades. He told Parliament that all combinations should be 'regarded as a general disease in our society', although it took Prime Minister Pitt to actually get the broadened bill passed. Wilberforce's liberalism did not extend to all forms of labour. Pitt told Parliament that 'it was his intention to endeavour to provide a remedy to an evil of very considerable magnitude … of unlawful combinations of workmen in general – a practice that had become too general, and was likely, if left unchecked, to produce very serious mischief'.[65] Thus, to sum up, for the first time it was an act not concerned with just a single trade but all trades, with all prosecutions concerning combinations going to a single magistrate. The 1799 Act was subsequently amended the following year with the number of magistrates doubling. Significantly, too, all owners of production were defined as a class and also banned from combining.[66] Thence, at the legal level, there were now two clearly defined and opposing classes, namely, the bourgeoisie and the proletariat. This was, of course, at a time when punitive legislation had already been passed outlawing 'seditious assemblies' involving over fifty people, resulting, if the magistrate's orders were defied, in the perpetrators facing a punishment of possible death.[67]

Throughout this book we have looked at the rise of a highly regulated oeconomy that was central to the successful creation of a mighty fiscal–military state. However, in this chapter and the last we have seen the antithesis emerge, with the new emphasis upon a small inexpensive state and belief in freer trade, that is, a growing trust, forced via necessity, towards an unmanaged market. As with all credible alternatives it was accompanied by a carefully fashioned intellectual justification providing it with authority.

This could also be seen across the channel in France. Leonard N. Rosenband captures this fast-emerging transnational political economy: 'To ensure the operation of "natural", unencumbered labour markets, leading commentators on both sides of the Channel insisted that governments must clear the clutter of custom, combination and their own shopworn mandates.'[68] Again, as J. V. Orth emphasizes: 'Wages would no longer be state business; capital and labor would fight it out for themselves.' As such state regulation had to be abandoned, a key objective of the British government, and the only legal device would be the contract between employee and employer.[69]

As we have seen in the case of the woollen textile industry, social customs were a powerful force that could legitimate extremely powerful trade combinations to represent the interests of their workmen. There is no doubt that the more skilled a labour force was the more powerfully it could flex its muscle. In addition to Randall's example of the woollen cloth workers, Rosenband has shown the equally compact organization of the English paper workers. Such was their strength that it had led the paper manufacturers to successfully lobby Parliament for an anti-combination bill. The subsequent Papermakers Act erased all contracts that raised wages, that reduced hours or work, and that prevented the employment of other workers. This then became the model for the general Anti-Combination Act of 1799. Interestingly, concludes Rosenband, the British papermakers operated much more as a cartel. They were also located within a similar geographical area, predominantly in Kent and the southeast, compared to their far more widely dispersed French equivalents.[70]

It would be wrong to claim that the Combination Acts were a waste of time. As a leading historian of early trade unionism concludes: 'However infrequently the Acts may have been applied (another issue about which we simply cannot be clear), the Acts of 1799 and 1800 had immense psychological and practical import on the way trade unionism evolved.' There is no doubt that the relationship between the landed paternalists and labour during the eighteenth century was over.[71] Many in government recognized the urgent need to confront a perceived overblown and disliked British state. This, they now urgently thought, meant shrinking and reforming – especially from the regulatory spheres of food, trade, industry and anywhere else it could. Crucially, an alternative source of authority was thus needed. As far as possible the market, rather than the state, should now be the umpire of disputes and the arbiter between employees and employers. However, by severing manufacturing regulations, all legal protection of employees within the workplace disappeared; clearly, this served the interests of owners of production more than labour.[72] Thus, by 1800 there were two legally defined competing classes fighting it out in the labour market.

One could say the fiscal pressure on the state was bringing it closer to the demands of certain leading manufactures – something actually born out of the 1786 Anglo-French Trade Treaty. The two English Combination Acts were also a product of political pressure and the real fear of revolution that Parliament held during the 1790s. Growing political radicalism and social despair within a context of dire financial straits and war, particularly since 1763, were all panicking Parliament. Conditions continued to worsen between 1799 and 1801 as food became scarce and prices rocketed. These, as Wells has so clearly shown, were real famine conditions.[73] Not surprisingly, such an environment would intensify trades combining to preserve their standard of living.[74]

Debt, harvest failures, industrial change in the means of production, the severing of protectionary legislation in the food and labour markets, high indirect taxation, revolutionary activities across the Atlantic and later the Channel, and growing inflation were fuelling British political radicalism. This, in turn, informed landowners who took an increasingly hostile view of trade and society combinations.[75] The choice of the Papermakers Act of 1796 as the model for the 1799 Anti-Combination Act was deliberate.[76] The act was deeply significant in the sense of not introducing the usual counterbalance of official state wage-fixing. The employee would now have to rely on his employer and the market alone, unaided by the state, for the rate of pay. This was generalized in the 1799 Anti-Combination Act, which paved the way to removing all of the wage-setting clauses denoted in the Statute of Artificers when it was repealed in 1814. The implications of this were quickly recognized by workers across all trades. The chairman of the Manchester bench of magistrates, Thomas Butterworth Bayley, argued that labourers and mechanics deprived of the right to associate would be 'reduced to a state of slavery and subject to the capricious dispositions of those who employ them'; he also advocated for a state-enforced minimum wage and the regulation of child factory labour. The withdrawal of the state, the banning of worker combinations, and the aim of employers and employees settling claims independently amounted to, claimed Bayley, 'binding the hands of a dwarf upon his back'. This, along with an avalanche of appeals from workers' petitions, led to the Combination Amendment Act of 1800. Most notable here, as already noted, was the increase from one to two magistrates at the court of summary justice, and the attempt at appearing balanced by also banning employer combinations.[77]

In terms of papermaking such legislation failed to usurp the power of journeymen in both France and England. Thence the weary words addressed to the French Minister of the Interior in April 1816, 'This state of affairs … could only end with the installation of papermaking machines to replace the arms of the unruly workers.' Thus, despite all this anti-combination legislation, on both sides of the channel the workers and the employers continued to combine. The acts were certainly powerful symbols but, as Rosenband demonstrates, as long as manufacturers like the papermakers 'relied on the journeymen's know-how, turmoil persisted in the mills'. As with the woollen workers it was the introduction of the machine that ultimately thwarted the power of the paper journeymen. This solution to a 'trans-national problem' came at the close of the eighteenth century. A Frenchman called Nicolas-Louis Robert, disgusted by the conduct of French paper workers, sought to make a machine to replace a significant amount of their key skilled work. This was innovation out of desperation.[78]

The machine, however, was first introduced in Britain after being greatly improved by the engineer Bryan Donkin. By 1807 it was up and working, producing good quality reams of paper, and by 1837, it was estimated by one English papermaker that 240 of these machines was the equivalent of 1,200 hand-worked vats; this, in terms of labour costs, saved some £318,240 per year. The machine put an end to the journeymens' coalition. Not, however, without a fight. Like the Luddites' attack on woollen machinery earlier, paper workers started targeting new papermaking machinery in 1830 during the Captain Swing riots over farm machinery. The tactic temporarily worked, with some papermakers delaying the implementation of machinery.[79]

As well as being the path of least resistance, the machine also took on a particular symbolic meaning. For those of the new liberal and deregulating cast of mind, it was perceived as an emancipating tool exposing the jealously guarded property of elite artisan skills, which was the ultimate source of their power.[80] Unless this could be challenged, the manufacturer was always going to be dependent on good relations with his skilled workforce. A delegislative attack, unlike its success in the food market, was never going to be as successful in controlling the skilled workplace. What was needed was something else, and this came in the shape of the machine. Connected to all of this, at least as a form of intellectual legitimation, was the increasingly moral value of visibility. This became a central attack on the secretive, corrupt world of the politics that characterized 'Old Corruption'. It also became embedded in the values accumulating around an ideology invented to legitimate the shrinking of the state and lunge towards free trade. An open society also implied an open politics, workshop or manufactory; stripping labour of land rights and regulatory manufactory legislation was now joined by an attempt to remove skilled workers' property precisely via the usurpation of these skills.

As such this attachment to visibility was being used to reform both the body politic and workplace. Hiding skills, via an apprenticeship or simply shop-floor secrecy, made it difficult for employers to train unskilled, non-apprenticed workers, which thwarted the growth of a larger workforce and cheaper labour: free labour came at an expensive price. In this sense deregulating the workplace was also tied to demystifying it. For the so-called enlightened perspective, the social organization of work practices, no less than the method of making political decisions, should be visible like the divine regularity of the heavens, or, indeed, the more earthbound movement of a machine. The regularity of mechanization would discipline labour and act as a safeguard against dishonesty, mistakes and laziness. It would offer moral guidance, since consistency, efficiency and predictability in an age increasingly plagued by attacks on Old Corruption had come to be associated with high moral standing.[81]

However, a quest for visibility and efficiency does not mean a claim to objectivity or the moral high ground; rather, within this context, it can be read as a legitimation for exploitation and expropriation aided by desperate state deregulation. The acceleration towards free trade, mechanization and transparency was not hatched from some enlightened British culture but via urgent, volatile and changing socio-economic circumstances.

The struggle was not, however, one way. In many ways the repeal of the Combination Acts in 1824, and its less liberal reinterpretation the following year, was an acceptance that labour could not be prevented from coming together to protect their interests.[82] It also, of course, legalized what employers had long been doing, namely, also combining as a cartel to promote the interests of capital. The state, however, was now released from its former role of regulating industry, with capital and labour free in theory to discuss the basis of their contract although, tellingly, workers were still subject to criminal prosecution for breach of contract. This was underlined in the repressive 1823 Master and Servant Act, which reinforced legislation condemning an employee to be sentenced to three months hard labour or fined part of his wages if the contract between him and his employer was undermined.[83]

In addition, with the legal repeal of apprenticeships earlier in 1814, the eventual defence of skilled labour as property would fall to the trade societies or what would later get termed as trade unions. These organizations stepped in to occupy the area formerly negotiated by state regulation and riot. Although not a straightforward transition, these bodies became the mechanism to uphold what was once the moral economy.[84] The movement traced in this chapter represented a clear transition to nineteenth-century laissez-faire Britain. It can certainly be viewed, as John Rule concludes, 'as marking the end to the final crisis of paternalist protection'.[85] This, as we shall see in the final chapter, was part of an objective to sever the regulatory role of the state in general. The rise of an intellectual discipline defined by free trade was a necessary legitimation to such dismantling. The new political economy was a development that emerged during the Industrial Revolution.

CHAPTER 12
THE RISE OF POLITICAL ECONOMY DURING THE INDUSTRIAL REVOLUTION

The British Industrial Revolution is typically situated within an intellectual context characterized by the rise of a new political economy. This discipline has traditionally been seen as the trigger, prescription and rational legitimation of the economic and social structural reforms during this period. Indeed, as a reflection of a rational cultural transformation of the country, this was by no means unique in Britain and similar themes were also being discussed and applied elsewhere. Certainly, many of the key aspects of this creed were being defined and implemented across the channel in France. Like Britain, this was largely due to fraught economic imperatives rather than new enlightened rational prescription.

Deregulation: The market as arbiter of production

Over the course of the eighteenth century, French liberals increasingly condemned the role of the Bureau of Commerce, the inspectors of manufacturers and the guilds in the production of textiles. First, marking goods, they claimed, was simply an extravagant, hindering and extremely costly business. Secondly, uniform regulation was impossible since some regions varied so much in the quality of the woven thread that the mark became meaningless. Thirdly, regulations were geared to the top-of-the-range items and, increasingly, were not so relevant to the growing diversity of consumer demands. Fourthly, the regulating system was thwarting innovation and, lastly, an unregulated market would automatically ensure quality. In short, a number of commentators were advising that the traditional French regulated market should be completely dismantled and left to police itself.[1] In practice, however, it should be noted that these regulations were easily bypassed for a number of popular goods.[2]

By no means did everyone agree with the damning verdict of the French liberals. Many involved in the trade and production of goods wanted to retain the state and local system of regulation. For example, clearly a merchant could not personally check the dimensions and quality of all the cloth he or she bought, while the array of middlemen involved allowed numerous frauds to take place. Thus, to safeguard confidence required regulation, with the mark traditionally being a guarantee of quality. In this way the French inspectors carried out a function that merchants were unable to do, in much the same way the British Excise did. They were, therefore, much happier trading where the visible hand of the state was apparent.

Anne-Robert-Jacques Turgot and other liberals drew up an abstract notion of a perfect market where everyone had enough information to navigate his or her way efficiently around it. In reality, however, the chain between producer and consumer was far too long for such an idealized world, while those involved certainly did not conform to abstract notions of human behaviour. There were extensive price differences between regions while the level of transport was very poor, which made the flow of goods and commercial information fragmented and slow. Here, too, the much greater geographical size of France compared to Britain was a disadvantage. In short, the real lived experience was anything but a perfect situation. Consequently, the importance of regulatory marks was still considered by some as a crucial generator of trust in the product both domestically and internationally. The inspectors were the experienced front line in the process of guaranteeing product quality and were, therefore, the trust in the trade of such items. It was faith in regulatory labels and marks, rather than the market, which provided the crucial confidence for exchange. Turgot's 'theoretical scheme', concludes Philippe Minard, 'did not fit with the reality of the market as traders experienced it day in, day out. First-hand experience had enlightened them against liberal assumptions of invisible hands'.[3]

Nonetheless, the liberal critics were right to highlight the changing habits of consumers and the scale of demand. The old regulatory system was designed for traditional goods at the top end of the ladder. By contrast, the increasing role of fashion and surge in semi-luxury goods frequently meant the specifications for such items quickly changed. The market and consumer were no longer as static as they once were and the manufacturer had to keep up with such dynamism.[4] Within this context the market, argues Liliane Hilaire-Perez, 'was thought to be a wise judge of inventions and had to be allowed to play its part freely'. In other words, a regulated market could not keep up with the growth of such dynamism.[5]

As a result, those manufacturers involved in luxury top-of-the-line goods fought to retain regulation and fixed standards. By contrast, those producers plugging into the expanding and dynamic market of fashion goods, such as light textiles and semi-luxury manufactures, found the item and production process could quickly change; here clearly taste and price elasticity rather than quality was the key. For these producers, regulation and specified standards were a major source of contention and retardation.[6] A similar argument characterized the view of Britain's new export-oriented industries in the Midlands and northwest.

The French liberals claimed state regulation and the guilds were a monopoly that kept prices artificially high. They stifled innovation through technological change and flexibility when it came to consumer demand, and excluded numerous competent craftsmen with extremely high entry fees. They were, in short, the antithesis to liberty and long-term prosperity.[7] Despite this new increasing liberal impetus, France was still split over the pros and cons of manufacturing regulation. No new system was in place to substitute for the subsequent vacuum deregulation would leave. The role of laissez-faire in filling such a void may have been loudly applauded but it left many merchants, manufacturers and everyday folk bewildered at how to establish trust in a product.[8]

Predicted innovation might allow greater variety but also a great expansion in deception and reduction in quality.[9]

In conclusion, we can see that the French regulatory system turned upon the mark as a guarantee of quality. However, despite concerted attempts by Jean-Baptiste Colbert earlier in the seventeenth century to make this mark national, they varied across regions and frequently required more than one mark. By contrast, in Britain – with the exception of woollen textiles, metals and potteries – it was primarily just the Excise stamp on the wrapper, item or package that certified its legitimacy. Under this system, the production process had greater flexibility to legally evolve across the realm. In addition, with just a single national process of certification, the parliamentary system gave more unified trades greater power to lobby for effectual changes than those in absolutist France, which due to its political structure and institutional infrastructure would always remain piecemeal. In this sense, as Leonard N. Rosenband has argued, British manufacturing trades, compared with France, were far more of a cartel.[10]

Nonetheless, for the highly protected new British industries such as pottery, cotton and iron the excise was still too restrictive, particularly because of the fast-changing nature of their products. This accounts for these industries (potteries and iron were not excised but feared being so) being at the vanguard of anti-excise attacks during the 1780s. The nurturing and national regulation across the traditional domestic-oriented industries by the Excise was not appropriate for the newer, fast-changing, export-oriented industries. These manufacturers were frightened that their production techniques, flexible adaptability, recipes and technology would be exposed and restricted by the Excise.

Late-eighteenth-century Britain was a very different country from the earlier part of the century when it had been important to create and nurture manufactures to an internationally established level. Both the domestic and international market for different quality and priced products was now much wider and fast-changing. Although more adaptive compared to French stipulations, the excise regulations or simply the threat of their implementation on the new and dynamic industries was considered too restrictive by these manufacturers for the evolving environment.

Traditional manufacturers such as candle makers, glass makers, starch makers, soap makers, leather producers, paper makers and certain textile manufacturers that focused primarily upon the domestic market (all bred through tariff protection and the excise), may have squabbled over gauging techniques and levies, but accepted regulation as long as it was below the protective customs tariff. Not surprisingly, they were at the vanguard of opposing the 1786 Anglo-French Trade Treaty that we looked at in Chapter 10. By contrast, the new industries were at the forefront of supporting it.

These recent export-oriented industries in Britain were highly protected but only lightly taxed (cotton textiles) or untaxed altogether (potteries and iron), and therefore freer from the start to be adaptive to both domestic and foreign consumer demands – both in terms of price and quality – sheltered from foreign competition (at least in the home and to a certain extent colonial markets). One should also remember that cotton textiles, for example, were given a bounty for exports that lasted into the nineteenth century. In short, the new export-oriented industries were not directly vital to the fiscal demands of the country but were, crucially, in the sense that they were the most dynamic part of the broader economy. Consequently, they were critical in generating domestic capital from foreign trade and, increasingly, large employers with a labour force important to the consumption of taxed goods and servicing the national debt.

On both sides of the channel the state was seen as a parasite expanding at the expense of a growing disgruntled body of the highly taxed middling and, especially, labouring ranks. In France, state dismantling was dramatically executed with the advent of the revolution and the subsequent period. By contrast, despite its increasing withdrawal from the food and labour markets, Britain had to first intensify its reliance upon its economic institutions during the 1790s, before it could dismantle them in the nineteenth century.

The ballooning of the national debt in the war-ridden second half of the long eighteenth century (1757–1815) was pushing the British excise ever higher, to a point where for many industries it was spilling over the protective customs barriers, while the new industries simply despised the Excise's highly empirical and prescriptive accounting of the manufacturing process. A formal understanding of various industrial processes existed long before the French encyclopaedists attempted to depict it within beautifully illustrated and leather-bounded books. It should also be remembered that tax was a large component to total production costs during this period. Within this environment, the judgement of the Excise was increasingly questioned, which can be seen in the huge growth in revenue-related court trials. This, in turn, forced the Excise to turn to its most-experienced gaugers to defend and argue its methods in court.[11]

By the early nineteenth century, the issues had become ever more thorny and technical. Moreover, the desperate manufacturers turned to their own alternative sources of authority and, although using the same process of gauging pedalled by the state, they increasingly challenged the instrumentation and training used by the Excise. Out of this emerged experienced manufacturing authorities now typically trying to establish some formalized source of knowledge for legislation. This led to a growing emphasis upon precision measurement and increasing focus upon theory and instrumentation culminating in specialized manufacturing knowledge.[12]

Growing consumption of taxed products, in turn, further induced manufacturers to adulterate their products. From its initial role of helping to nurture quality in certain products, by the close of the century the efficiency of excise collection was, ironically, fuelling adulteration. Paradoxically, the revenue bodies were also the only possible source of protection for the consumer. Their first line of duty, however, was to safeguard the state's coffers and not the people's health. The consumer was seemingly digesting cheaper and frequently poisonous substances in ever-greater levels. The public concern over the adulteration of tea, for example, was fed by a number of well-publicized excise trials against manufacturers and sellers during the 1810s. This led to more sophisticated forms of testing tea, and to the emergence of a new set of tea dealers that played on the increasing public fear of adulteration; here, packaging and brand names started to come to the fore as a sign of quality.[13]

The world upside down

By 1800 a century had passed since most of the members of the Board of Trade and Plantations had legislated that free trade was a utopian fancy. As one of their leading commentators, John Pollexfen, wrote in 1697: 'Some are of opinion that Laws for regulating of Trade are unnecessary, if not inconvenient, and that it had better be left to take its own Course; but this opinion hath been contradicted by Experience; and if it should be allowed, as a General Rule, will upon inquiry be found lyable to many exceptions.'[14] By the close of the eighteenth century these sentiments were still, for many, at the heart of a correct oeconomic framework. As an anonymous woollen draper declared during the debate over the Anglo-French Trade Treaty in 1786: 'THE PRESERVATION OF THE HOME MARKET TO OUR OWN MANUFACTURES IS THE GREAT VITAL PRINCIPLE NEVER TO BE DEPARTED FROM.'[15] However, times were changing and Pitt confidently announced a year later, 'We have so avowedly superior a competition, that no danger can arise to any of our manufacturers.'[16]

The attack upon protectionism only truly and consistently commenced during the 1780s and, despite being put on hold in key areas during the wars with France, came to a head following the post-Napoleonic War slump. During the recovery of the 1820s, a creed of free trade started to take hold and inform economic policy in general. An anonymous and disgruntled commentator warned in 1826:

> Our cotton manufacture at one period gave no hope that we should excel in it as we do. … Under the new doctrines, no new manufacture must be established in this country, unless the manufacturers can, in the first moment, produce as good and cheap an article as foreign ones; and history shows this to be an impossibility. Of course, we must never have any additional manufactures; and, moreover, our old ones are all to be lost if ever foreigners can surpass us.[17]

The eighteenth-century fiscal–military–trading–industrial policy that had so successfully served the country and laid the foundations of the Industrial Revolution was being systematically dismantled. The impulse had, as we have seen, commenced after the Seven Years War and set in during the 1780s with attacks upon the overblown state and the rise of the new export-oriented industries, especially cotton, which now had little foreign, primarily Indian, competition to worry about.

Pitt proudly told the House of Commons in 1787 that Britain was now a fully clothed industrial country, and was totally different from France which depended 'upon the spontaneous offerings of her soil and her climate'. He confidently asserted: 'It is not surprising, that what arises from the industry of freemen should be superior to the rude produce of the earth.' France, or indeed any of Britain's industrial rivals, was now no longer an economic threat.[18] Pitt would never know how his particular notion of 'freemen' would be recast and generalized as a necessary axiom to industrialization during the next two centuries; indeed, for many, it would bizarrely become *the* central explanation to Britain's Industrial Revolution.

Growing wealth, global trade, industrialization and an emphasis upon free trade deflected regulation elsewhere. Consumption is most efficient in highly populated enclosed urban areas, making it potentially more volatile but easier to police. This was also a time when the protection of property was becoming ever more important. The rich wealth, born of war and a protected oeconomy, being sucked into Britain's ports needed better policing. *The Times*, for example, waded into the debate about establishing a new city police in 1788. The newspaper condemned 'The City Watch' as 'a muster of old decrepit and debilitated men, much better appropriated to keep *ward* in a hospital, than watch and *ward* in an opulent and populous city'. These inert guardians of property and social order were not 'citizens' but men recruited 'from the very dregs of mankind'. It was vital they be replaced by a uniformed 'city militia' composed of honest and sober men. In addition, they should wear a uniform, be given a unique number and be provided with a headquarters as impressive as the Guildhall or Bank of England.[19]

The increasing emphasis upon consumption, in general, and the voice of the consumer was increasingly acknowledged in new tracts. Earlier Adam Smith, for example, famously wrote: 'Consumption is the sole end and purpose of all production… . But in the mercantile system the interest of the consumer is almost constantly sacrificed to that of the producer and it seems to consider production and not consumption as the ultimate end and object of all industry and commerce.'[20] This criticism had been rapidly informing the dismantling of industrial regulation. One area that seemed to have greatly damaged the consumption of home-produced goods was the loss of much of British mainland America. However, this appeared less of a catastrophe by the mid-1780s when exports to the new United States of America started to grow by more than any other foreign market. The fruits of the old colonial system and the relative absence of manufacturing – especially concentrated production – particularly aided British commercial interests. By 1836 nearly a quarter of British exports went to the United States of America, with most of Lancashire's raw cotton coming from the American South's slave plantations. This forged an international economic union that would prove incredibly robust – particularly after transatlantic slavery was abolished in the old country. This, surely, was an example demonstrating that international economies left free, slavery and military superiority aside, could flourish without regulating policies. This view thus locked into prevalent political reforming and, indeed, radical sentiments; free trade would lead to a safer and more peaceful world. Debates over the empire were another intrinsic component in defining the new political economy.[21]

The Atlantic slave trade, as Eric Williams long ago argued, may have become unprofitable to Britain's interests, but had become absolutely vital to the new United States of America from which Britain greatly benefited.[22] Aspects of the work of Smith were selectively harnessed to aid, endorse and cast the new political economy. His subsequent association as the founder of the new creed has been greatly distorted and exaggerated.[23] He was, for example, an advocate of high wages and more tolerant of labourers' combinations than those of masters; he was not a major critic of the Poor Law and not in favour of primogeniture. Moreover, his political and theological views were surgically removed from his political oeconomy to extract it of any offence, particularly to the Church of England and social authority in general. By the time a posthumous edition of a memorandum by Edmund Burke was published in 1800 (probably written in 1795), declaring the need for total non-interference with the market, it was misleadingly interpreted as an exposition of Smith's teachings.[24] By contrast, all the pro-free-trade enunciations of the political radical, Thomas Paine, were expunged of the rising economics, with just the radicalism underlined. The centrality of commerce and British civilisation was thrust to the centre stage. The future was individualism, free trade, an ever broader movement of enclosure, technological determinism and a radical shrinking of the state's regulating activities.[25] The work of the twentieth-century economic historian and social philosopher, Karl Polanyi, is incisive on this development. He forcefully argued this was the first time in history a society was overtly subordinated to the invented logic of the market.[26]

Another key development in the rise of this political economy was the centrality of the gold standard. The year 1819 saw the return of the gold standard and the movement towards resumption; bullionists claimed too much paper money had been issued since its suspension in 1797. For a time, the government considered the possibility of retaining the temporary income tax (1799–1816) for social as well as fiscal reasons (it accounted for one-fifth or £16 million of all government revenue).[27] *The Times* editorial in February 1816, however, launched a furious attack on the tax. It was a war tax and should cease immediately: 'It is most obvious that no possible good can result from its continuance in any shape whatever, because there is no possible good, as a nation, we have not obtained.' The editorial concluded, 'The nation is ready to rise as one man against this break of faith which is now attempted to put in practice.'[28]

This view, reflected by Britain's leading broadsheet newspaper, won the day. Consequently, even higher indirect taxes would have to remain and the working ranks continue to try and make ends meet, but now without any protection in the food or workplace. To survive the government needed to ensure support from the propertied ranks for its subsequent repressive measures for containing widespread social discontent, namely the six notorious acts. The failure to retain the income tax would haunt successive governments for over two decades. This also, as Martin J. Daunton has shown, delayed Tory hopes of trying to achieve a new level of legitimacy and trust in the state.[29]

The years immediately following the war were some of the harshest to ever hit Britain and much of Europe. Initially, members of Lord Liverpool's government denied there was shrinking demand and paraded an array of excise statistics as proof that domestic consumption of certain commodities such as tea and malt had actually increased. Indeed, they argued, wartime prices and capitalization had caused overproduction. Speculation, cheap money and overtrading had to be expunged and the best policy for economic recovery was for the government, or so they thought, to leave things to find their natural state. As Boyd Hilton has argued, the government's inaction and reluctance to interfere with the economy was not evidence of a free-trade commitment but, literally, a policy for doing nothing; the premise being that left to itself the economy would naturally recover from the post-war slump and reach a natural, divinely ordained, equilibrium. The crucial input of confidence, namely, that convertibility had returned in the shape of cash payments and clear consistent government policy (i.e. inactivity) was now in place.[30] This, of course, was the ideal approach for a state desperately trying to shrink.

A pervasive form of Christian evangelical thought, what Hilton terms 'moderate' evangelicalism, had also penetrated the sinews of Lord Liverpool's liberal Tory administration. This clearly served to morally reinforce the economic and political pressure to reduce the state. He writes: 'They wished to make society operate as closely to "nature" as possible by repealing interventionist laws.' The only way people could reach salvation was through self-help and, consequently, it was vital the state should not interfere in people's lives. It was unnatural to intervene in God's socio-economic mechanism on earth; it should be left to function free of hindrance in the same manner as the heavens above.[31] Similarly, E. P. Thompson claimed: 'And already in the Twenties, Political Economy can be seen as a third partner alongside Morality and Useful Knowledge, in the shape of homilies upon the God-given and immutable laws of supply and demand. Capital, even nicer in its taste than the hog, would select only the industrious and obedient worker and reject all others.'[32] Capital was fast filling a void left by the rapid shrinking of the old regulatory state and the vital necessity of confronting the huge national debt. Not for the first or last time religion and/or claims to knowledge were conveniently harnessed during a period of economic and social urgency.

The free-trade wing of the Whigs found themselves on the side of the government as opposed to the protectionist demands of the agriculturists, skilled labour and traditional manufacturers. The only way to pluck the economy out of crisis was through the systematic destruction of all barriers. For different reasons, then, ministers were able to harness free-trade political economy as a compliment to its policy of crucial state shrinkage and perceived neutrality. Both saw the removal of, for example, trade obstacles, as necessary for getting the economy into its natural state. In this way the country would eventually emerge wealthier and much stronger since it would, it was argued, be based upon a real foundation.[33] Ironically, none of this pondering and formalizing of liberal policies would have been possible if the country's industrial base had not first been nurtured through protectionist policies.

This new mechanistic love of system, once seen as the predominant preserve of classical political economy and utilitarianism, was far more widespread during this period. The economic growth of the first half of the nineteenth century did not spell 'progress' for a large number of people. The very fabric of traditional society and authority seemed, as we have seen, under threat. Crucially, many were concerned that this growth had false foundations. In a world still predominantly observed as static or cyclical, the prevailing condition could, if constructed on false principles, quickly take a downward swing. The key, therefore, was to ensure trade and production was real and not a bubble.[34]

Hilton writes: 'Barriers to Free Trade, like monopolies, protective duties, and preferences, not only offended the unprivileged, but were elements of friction obscuring God's clockwork providence.' Of course, reference to 'unprivileged' would not have convinced many of the underprivileged poor who clearly still supported state regulation in certain areas of the food market and manufacturing. The terrestrial harbingers of the new political economy emphasized an industrial future and, although many still retained the belief of eventually reaching a static state, it clearly laid the seeds for a dynamic economic perspective. This was the moment when a concerted shift from a static to a dynamic view of expansion commenced.[35]

For the government, however, far more urgent than any theological or theoretical view was the fact the state had burst and was in no position to sustain its old balance. The only real alternative was the continued deregulation and the dismantling of the state. Pervasive Christian evangelicals seemed to think such actions would also lead to moral education and help build the path to salvation. Bankruptcy, for instance, like cholera or other epidemics, was simply God's way of intervening in the world to cure the mechanism. A clearly functioning laissez-faire economy would sniff out false businesses and rightly punish it; any intervention by the state was therefore artificial and wrong.[36] However, there were important exceptions to this movement such as the restriction of importing and exporting corn.

The 1815 Corn Law had been, in some sense, a bribe by the liberal Tory government to secure parliamentary support to extend the wartime income tax. The move, as we have seen, failed – culminating in the severing of the tax but the acceptance of the Corn Law. Landowners rejoiced, the labouring masses interpreted it as yet another blatant piece of oppressive legislation geared against their interests, most political economists were dismayed and the government was forced to introduce more draconian and coercive laws in an attempt to crush swelling social protest. The policy was also an attempt to protect imported Irish corn from European supplies. Importantly, it was designed to safeguard the marginal land that had been cultivated during the Napoleonic Wars, which was only viable when grain prices were high, as the stockbroker and political economist David Ricardo, especially, underlined. In this sense, landowners were not unified because only owners of rich land were capable of surviving foreign competition and even flourishing with the removal of cultivating marginal land; by contrast, tenant farmers feared such a move and greatly supported the new Corn Law. It was hoped the act would only be needed, however, for a brief period to allow farmers to adjust to lower prices, and for farmers of marginal lands to increase their efficiency.[37]

Many wanted the government to do a great deal more in putting down political agitation by force. Conversely, others in social authority wanted to reimpose the income tax and subdue popular clamour by reducing indirect tax on consumption in an attempt to woo the working ranks. Following this line of reasoning the assistant secretary to the Treasury and taxation authority, George Harrison, told Lord Liverpool that such a move would 'arrest the progress of those sentiments which if not arrested, must inevitably overturn the constitution and government'. Instead, he advised a property tax should be placed 'upon the Income of all *realised* Capital only to such an extent or percentage as might enable a Reduction of other Taxes to a corresponding amount, which may bear hardly or inconveniently upon the Income of labour. Such a measure would be the best of the calumnies of the Demagogues against the Rich'. Despite the appeals, the government rejected such a measure and opted to pass six acts of repression.[38] This was a bruising and, at times, contradictory battle.

The working masses began to relate much more closely; they combined and politicized through a diet of isolationism driven by the state's withdrawal from the food market, workplace, introduction of the Corn Laws and continued high indirect taxes. All this helped to fuel the rise of the radical political platform campaign. The social divide during the Industrial Revolution could not have been starker.

For the supporters of a gold standard it was clearly seen as providing a tangible, invariable and impartial standard of value and thence supplied the objective means of measuring the value of any economic enterprise. Crucial to this was the Bank of England, which functioned as a machine for self-regulating the money supply. Others simply saw the move as reducing the supply of money, thus shrinking consumption, damaging British industry and further fuelling the discontent of the working classes. Unimpressed by such claims, Huskisson rejoiced in 1818:

> The Bank would be the great steam engine of the State to keep the channel of the circulation always pressing full, and the power of converting its notes at any time into gold bullion at 78s the ounce the regulator and index of the engine, by which the extent of its operations and the sufficiency of the supply would be determined and ascertained.

Huskisson, from the 1820s until his untimely and ironic death by the dynamic icon of the times, a steam train, was at the vanguard of dismantling the old regulatory state.[39]

With monetary supply now seemingly flowing naturally, therefore neutral, and out of the political sphere, any economic disasters could not be seen as the fault of the government and its management of the rapidly shrinking state. This led to a clash between liberals and high Tories in 1825, when the latter wanted troubled firms to be bailed out using exchequer bills. The future prime minister Robert Peel quickly provided an answer, applauded by others of his ilk: 'Ultimate good, after some severe suffering, will result.'[40] There should not and would not be any easing in the supply of money. However, the need to substantially reduce taxation was, ultimately, the key to diluting the attacks on 'Old Corruption' and soothing the isolated but growing industrial working ranks. The shift to even higher duties to combat the fiscal burden resulting from the loss of the income tax in 1816 had resulted in additional taxes having an adverse impact upon, especially, the working classes.[41]

During this whole period the problem of smuggling was once again propelled to centre stage. Could the income of the state be significantly improved by decreasing the level of custom duties and therefore snatching a significant portion of the common economy? It was hoped the huge rise in legitimate goods would make up for the shortfall in lower taxes. Charles Long, a Treasury Commissioner, claimed in the 'Twelfth Report of the Commissioners of Inquiry into the Regulations of the Customs and Excise' in 1822, that 'the difficulty of protecting the Revenue while the present high duties continue' made it very difficult to prevent smuggling. Consequently, tariff reform was applied as the most effective way of fighting illicit trade. Equally, if not more, important in fuelling the free-trade movement was the agricultural debate, since it was now realized by most ministers that Britain could not feed its swelling population and would therefore need grain imports. The national food market may have been deregulated but now free trade in foreign corn was perceived as needed. The problem was the strength and resolve of the agricultural protectionists who aggressively opposed and challenged such a policy. They pointed to the protection that characterized manufactured goods as their main defence. Moreover, the wealth generated by domestic agriculture, they argued, fuelled the consumption of British manufactures – a key point underlined by the Duke of Wellington. Huskisson moaned: 'Unnecessary and excessive protection [on manufactured goods] is constantly thrown in our teeth by the Disciples of *Webb Hall*, and the advocates of extravagant duties on the productions of Foreign Agriculture.'[42]

With the state finances too depressed to allow effective cuts in the excise and assessed taxes, the government sought to expand foreign trade – as long as it was stable and not speculative trade. It was believed that freer global trade would generate genuine commerce, in which foreign countries would be able to sell more to Britain and, in turn, increase their income to purchase British manufactures. This would enlarge revenues from an expansion in customs and a wealthier taxpaying population. Such an optimistic view penetrated much of Britain's nineteenth-century economic policy.

It was now widely claimed that genuine trade and currency could ultimately never be established if there was an artificial wall of tariffs and a bloated interfering state. This had to be done cautiously. Huskisson first sought a uniform tariff and lower protectionary duties – as long as they were not prohibitory. All nations should be treated the same by being given equal facilities of commerce and navigation, and inducements to bring goods to British ports either in transit or consumption. It was the aim of Liverpool's government to consolidate Britain as the centre for all the world's goods. This process had already commenced in the seventeenth century, greatly expanded under Robert Walpole during the 1720s and later, especially with William Pitt's Great Warehouse Act in 1803. It would enable British merchants to fix world prices with capital further attracted into the country, while manufacturers would benefit even more since foreign merchants would make up gaps in their cargo with local products. This was underlined in 1823 with the first significant erosion of the Navigation Code by Huskisson's Reciprocity of Duties Act, which empowered the king in council to let the ships of any nation that responded in kind, transport goods to Britain on the same terms as British ships.[43] Ideally every nation participating in this projected world should operate to the gold standard. This weakening of the Navigation Acts was followed by the reduction of certain inland duties and, in 1825, the transference of import excise taxes on wine, foreign spirits, coffee, cocoa, pepper and tobacco to customs.

Tariff reform and the removal or reduction of excise duties obviously demanded careful thought and timing. Huskisson, for one, would only support the reduction of excise duties on malt and beer if it were part of a coherent system. There was, as yet, simply too little revenue to allow the government to sufficiently lower taxes to relieve the distress of the labouring ranks and stimulate consumption. Thus another source of revenue had to be found. As things stood something like three-quarters of the national revenue came from customs and excise as opposed to realized wealth. Future taxation therefore had to concentrate on fund holders, landlords, owners of production, mortgagees and annuitants and thus dilute the burden currently on the working ranks. The alternative would be for the Industrial Revolution to melt into a political revolution.

Trust in the fiscal future of the state needed something else. In 1828, Frederick John Robinson (Viscount Goderich), Huskisson and John Charles Herries were all agreed that a form of income tax should replace certain indirect taxes. However, another economic slump, the question of Catholic emancipation and the appointment of Wellington as prime minister put a temporary end to this view.[44] Equally important was the emergence of a powerful defence of the 'old system' of protection primarily propagated by conservative periodicals such as *Blackwood's Edinburgh Magazine* and the *Quarterly Review*.[45]

The political commentator, David Robinson, warned in 1825 that free-trade policies would be a disaster for British industry and dismissed the idea that foreign competition would improve domestic industry by forcing it to innovate. In a sharp and succinct historical analysis of Britain's industrial pathway he wrote:

> The greatest improvements have been made in our manufactures when they have been the most free from such [foreign] competition. Our cotton manufacturers have made the greatest varieties in their articles, and the greatest reductions in their prices, when it [free trade] has been perfectly unknown. Our iron and several other articles, which a few years since were greatly inferior to those provided in other countries, have been brought to equal, and in some cases to surpass those of all other parts, entirely without such competition. Under a system which studiously prevented such competition, which jealously excluded the foreigner from our home market, we have far outstripped all other nations in manufactures … we have rendered ourselves the first manufacturing nation in the universe.

This, Robertson rightly claimed, was the result of the 'Restrictive System', a system that 'leaves us at its death full of trade and prosperity'.[46] The British Industrial Revolution was not the result of an open system and culture of superior creativity as innovation, and the emergence of centralized production had taken place through a system of state protectionism and regulation.

Despite the block on the possibility of an income tax and the removal of all trade restrictions, such proposals were still bandied about and regularly put forward in Parliament. By January 1830 Huskisson privately admitted to the liberal Whig Evelyn J. Denison that the prevailing systems of indirect taxation 'press too hard on labour, and the capitals employed in productive industry'. In the budget that year some £3.4 million of tax cuts were made, of which a chunk was specifically aimed at reducing the expenditure of the agricultural and manufacturing classes upon mind-numbing goods such as spirits, beer and cider. Such a loss of revenue had to, sooner or later, be made up. Meanwhile, the simmering alliance between tax and constitutional reform was making headway. The government had, as yet, failed to rip the issue of tax from the clutches of political reformers or to soothe the angry protests of the labouring ranks.[47] The earlier marriage of finacialization and industrialization, forged by what Sven Beckert terms 'war capitalism', needed to be radically reconfigured.[48]

In his treatise *On Financial Reform*, first published in 1830, the Christian evangelical Whig Henry Parnell codified his views that he had cast during his work on the Finance Committee looking at the state of the nation's public income and expenditure. He confidently argued, with some justification for the short term: 'Our national productions of iron, coal, and other articles of raw materials will preserve our superiority in manufactures over other nations.' He posited that any duties still left on raw materials used for manufactures should be repealed, which included items such as hemp, barilla, bricks, tiles, raw silk, hides, skins and timber, while certain manufactured goods and fuel, which were beneficial to other manufactures, should also have their inland duties removed – including coal, tallow candles and soap. 'If all materials were free of duty,' he concluded, 'the consequences would be, that our woollens, cottons, silks, hardware, and other manufactures, might be sent to foreign markets two or three per cent cheaper than at present.' In other words, domestic industries that relied on protection could compensate for tariff reform through further reductions on raw material costs – even though they were already some of the lowest in Europe. By also decreasing the price of energy (coal) to produce popular items, the consumer would have more money to buy taxed items such as sugar, textiles, tea, beer, spirits and tobacco. This would also give a boost to employment for 'miners, sailors &c, in carrying on an increased trade'. In addition, excise regulations that now seemingly hampered innovation in trades like glass, paper and printed goods, should also be repealed.[49]

This latter attempt was gaining fast momentum. For example, a writer in *The Times* described excise laws as 'arbitrary, narrow, tormenting, and mind shackling'. In short, they were 'a very powerful instrument for checking the growth of British art, and giving to countries where they are unknown as sensitive advantages over Great Britain, in the career of manufacturing and commercial advantage'.[50] To tackle smuggling Parnell simply reiterated the old argument that tax on commodities like spirits and tobacco should be reduced. Crucially, to replace the lost revenue, he recommended that an income tax be reintroduced.

These themes became a central part of the Whig platform of reform during the 1830s. By contrast protectionists continued to claim – supported by history – that innovation could only flourish under a shielded but domestically competitive system. 'The old competition', moaned Robinson, 'was the only one to produce manufacturing improvements and discoveries.'[51] Another general fear propagated by the protectionists was a belief that the mechanization of manufactures, now seen as the potential impetus behind sustained economic success by free-traders, would 'produce beyond the means of consumption, whether domestic or foreign'. Instead, they wanted a stable balance between production and demand, with assurance that the income of manufacturers be safeguarded.[52]

In the short term the reform governments of the 1830s cut taxes too much in their attempt to meet the aim of cheap government and a much-reduced state. The Whigs gambled fiscal credibility and used surplus revenue, made possible by ending Pitt's once sacred Sinking Fund, to make tax cuts instead of servicing the national debt. The former golden rule that no tax should be totally repealed was severed. In the past, all-round reductions had been traditional policy, since it gave the option of increasing them again at a later date with much of the necessary staff and administrative infrastructure still in place. This option was now gone with twelve leading excises terminated between 1830 and 1840. The old world was being turned upside down too quickly. Peel and the Conservatives condemned the Whigs for running the government into debt. In an attempt to tackle the growing deficit, the new Whig Chancellor of the Exchequer, Francis Baring, reversed previous government policy and put a large duty on spirits, a general increase on all remaining excises by 5 per cent, all assessed taxes by 10 per cent, and took out a loan. This was followed by a powerful onslaught in the House of Commons by opposition MPs who continued to undermine an already weak Whig parliamentary standing.[53]

The Whigs were faced with two options: either they could introduce an income tax or make substantial reductions in the duties for sugar and timber. The latter was based on the hope that consumption of such products would increase by so much that the government would actually gain in tax revenues from such items. Russell also added a sliding scale proposal for the importation of foreign corn, with the final objective of replacing it with a fixed duty. By attacking the vested interest of the agricultural landed elite in this way, he hoped the Whigs would mobilize popular support by seeming to have the people's interest at heart. As a result, the policies over tariff reform and especially the Corn Laws had the impact of substantially reducing the attacks from the middling and lower ranks over elite greed and parasitism.[54] Conservatives typically hit back by condemning the Whigs for sacrificing sound fiscal policy to the clamours of the urban middling ranks and working-class protests.[55]

Cries from the Lancashire cotton industry for free trade had also been getting louder and more vociferous throughout the 1830s. Falling export prices were eroding the potential profits from the huge increase in cotton textile exports. Many manufacturers believed the root of the problem was a lack of capital in their foreign markets to pay for the cotton cloth. The solution, they claimed, was a rather neo-mercantilist measure, namely, to promote the import of primary goods into Britain from its cotton markets to allow them to purchase more cotton textiles. Such arguments were complimented in 1839 by the establishment of the Anti-Corn League; an organization, not surprisingly, widely supported by the cotton masters of Lancashire.[56] They also argued that if food was cheaper at home, then people would be able to purchase a greater amount of domestically produced taxed goods, while some manufacturers believed that the reduced price in food would lead to lower wages.

Protectionists, such as Alfred Mallalien of the Foreign Office, contested this last view, claiming it was the labour market and not the price of corn that influenced wages. It is also the case, too, that members of the Manchester Chamber of Commerce were not pro-free trade in all things. In particular, they fervently opposed the export of machinery, especially textile machinery. They had successfully fought this measure in 1824 and, again, prevented Parliament from allowing the free movement of skilled artisans in 1825. Indeed, the export of machinery was only legalized some two decades later in 1843.[57] By this date Britain had a global monopoly of cotton textiles including, ironically, the Indian market. Manchester cotton manufacturers were also now very active in lobbying the government to improve India's domestic transport infrastructure to aid the movement and accessibility to Indian raw cotton and distribution of British cotton textiles.[58]

The Whigs were subsequently defeated after a vote of no confidence in 1841, followed by a Peel-led Conservative victory with a respectable majority of 75. And it was Peel who emerged as the most powerful advocate of tax reform. He considered the policy of reducing duties to increase revenue as nonsense, but was facing deep social problems at large in the country. The urgency was made even worse in 1842 when a severe trade slump reduced wealth and revenues, a series of terrible harvests caused widespread hardship and Chartist agitation erupted in the Plug Riots that were ruthlessly squashed (Figure 10).

Peel's fiscal policy, regardless of ideology and other motivations, was at this point totally focused on trying to quell this social agitation and possible revolution. Central to his administration's economic and social policies was the pragmatic reintroduction of the income tax. The necessity for this was blamed squarely on the Whigs' alleged mismanagement of finances.[59] When this direct tax was reintroduced in 1842, all incomes below £150 were exempted but, unlike its predecessor of 1799, there was no graduated system above this level. Through this measure Peel was able to reduce duties on articles of popular consumption, and to shift the heart of 'Old Corruption' attacks and working-class agitation away from the landed political elite. It was within this arena that the duties on 1,200 articles were reduced and by 1842 some 750 duties had been abolished.[60] The customs now accounted for 43 per cent of all tax receipts and the excise at a much-reduced rate of 27 per cent. By 1844 there were also some twenty-seven reciprocating treatises with other countries.[61]

Figure 10 'Plug Plot Riot in Preston', *The Illustrated London News*, 20 August 1842.

In his budget speech of 11 March 1842, Peel told the House of Commons that the introduction of an income tax would enable him, 'with confidence and satisfaction to propose great commercial reforms, which will afford a hope of reviving commerce, and such an improvement in the manufacturing interests, as will react on every interest in the country'. Crucially, of course, it would hopefully dampen the threat of political uprising and possible revolution. As he continued, 'and by diminishing the prices of consumption and the cost of living, will, in a pecuniary point of view, compensate you for your present sacrifices, whilst you will be, at the same time, relieved from the contemplation of a great public evil'.[62]

This policy of tariff reform continued in the budget of 1844, when excise duties on flint glass and vinegar were reduced, coupled by a reduction in customs duties on coffee and currants. The duties on all glass were removed the following year. Implicit within Peel's manoeuvring, as Daunton usefully summarizes, was his hope that 'participation in the world of goods' would 'be an adequate substitute for exclusion from the world of politics'. This, as Frank Trentmann has shown, took root and the consumer became a vital component in the rise of free trade as a social movement and embedded, for a time, within the British national identity.[63]

It was also under the Peel government of the 1840s that attention was turned to reducing the protective duties upon non-British colonial sugar and therefore risking the wrath of the strong West Indies lobby. For some historians the imperial dimension was also critical to diluting social agitation and possible revolution. For example, Christopher Bayly and Miles Taylor both argue that by passing British costs onto the empire great savings were made domestically. As a result the home consumer benefited from free trade in commodities like sugar, but costs significantly increased for the colonial producer.[64]

After a heated and difficult battle, Peel's ministry were able to get their way after threatening to resign and, soon after, they reduced the sugar duties again. With a surplus of over £3 million the government went on to abolish half of the 813 duties on imports and all the export duties on British goods. Between 1841 and 1846 customs and excise revenue was reduced by 11 per cent of the total revenue. The key to these reforms was to directly tax the better off and therefore improve the life of the labouring ranks via lower indirect taxes. It was hoped, in retrospect correctly, that such a policy would dilute the overwhelming opposition to the political structure of the state and prevent possible revolutionary social turmoil.

Despite protectionist cries that free-trade induced fiscal reforms would, on the contrary, be a disaster and trigger revolutionary political sentiments further, Peel drew the opposite conclusion:

> It is not, in my mind, inconsistent with true conservative policy, that we have extinguished agitation and discouraged sedition, not by stringent coercive laws, but by encouraging the idea amongst the great body of people, that we, the rich and powerful, are willing to take a more than ordinary share of the public burdens, and to remove those burdens from the people as far as possible.

Many conservatives initially supported the reintroduction of the income tax, as it strengthened and underlined the interests of property with that of the state, and stemmed the tyranny of democracy.[65] As Cheryl Schonhardt-Bailey similarly suggests with regard to the repeal of the Corn Laws: 'In the end, Peel and his followers are deemed to have sacrificed protection to preserve their privileged status.' It was also the case that these laws had to be removed to enable the application of free trade to industry in general.[66]

The motor of all these reforms had commenced over half a century earlier with the gradual re-modelling of the state's administrative structure, the gradual removal of sinecures and placemen that characterized 'Old Corruption', and the withdrawal of the state from the food and labour market. However, ultimately, it was only the reintroduction of direct tax that made possible the final shrinking of the state and implementation of free trade.

The consolidation of the income tax, free trade and a small state

The groundwork for Peel to successfully introduce a sustainable income tax had taken several decades. For example, to levy the middling ranks had required a dilution of the prevailing status quo in the sense of an expansion of the franchise. This began in 1832 with the Great Reform Act and even more explicitly under William Gladstone's tax and income balancing act of the 1850s. As the latter wrote to the successful financial speculator and supporter of the income tax, J. L. Tabberner, in 1859: 'It is desirable in a high degree, when it can be effected, to connect the possession of the franchise with the payment in taxes.'[67]

The Reform Act of 1832 resulted in a small but significant proportion of the middling ranks being assimilated into the franchise.[68] This was crucial in selling the precedent for future electoral expansion and in providing the base for a future income tax; no taxation without representation was a critical factor. As Malcolm Chase puts it: 'Limited though the Act might appear with hindsight; it seemed to signal a sudden and massive potential for further political change.' Again, as Hilton reflects, subsequent historians may see the act as 'undaring' and limited, but for social authority at the time it was considered 'momentous'; the precedent for future Gladstonian reforms had been cast.[69]

The focus upon a stratum of the middling ranks was also a gamble since it spelt the defeat of 'artisan republicanism' and the complete isolation of working people's interests. With a small but symbolic proportion of the middling ranks now assimilated into the franchise, the working classes were becoming even more politically isolated. The result was the rise of Chartism and, for some historians with a credible degree of justification, a working-class consciousness.[70] Chartists sought to reform the unrepresentative political system by an attack on glaring injustices. Why, they asked, should the state protect certain forms of property but not the property of the worker (at least skilled labour)? Why should the state highly tax unrepresented workers but not its rivals (machines)? And why should the state protect landowners (Corn Laws) and fundholders (national debt) but not the source of this wealth (labour)?

The arguments utilized by Chartists were, as Gareth Stedman Jones has argued, drawn significantly from an older, pre-industrial, language devised to attack 'Old Corruption' and a perceived overstretched and inefficient state.[71] This, in turn, had evolved from libertarian urgings used to condemn the excise since its introduction by Parliament in 1643. In this sense the arguments had come full circle, and the Chartist attack upon taxation became embedded in the quest for parliamentary representation. Ultimately, as we have seen, it was Peel's reforms that took the venom out of this attack. His introduction of the income tax in 1842 may have been a risk, but it did, crucially, allow the severing of indirect tax (the source of many of the working-classes concerns). It was not a coincidence that 1842 was also the year of mass strikes often laced with Chartism.[72] In addition, the subsequent repeal of the Corn Laws (1846) and the introduction of legislation targeting the moneyed interests significantly deflected the focus from other constitutional issues. All this helped Britain avoid the wave of revolutions that swept Europe in 1848.

After the subsequent reform of the Corn Laws and further shrinking of the state, constitutional radicalism had been significantly diluted. By this stage the political economy of free trade had become dominant. The combative tone of Parnell's earlier 1830 free-trade manifesto, *On Financial Reform*, had become commonplace. The former policy of nurturing an infant industry via protectionism, had, it was claimed, now reached an adverse state. To change and improve, so the same argument now went, required industries, like glass manufacturers, to be let loose unregulated and, of course, unprotected. This, of course, was in contrast to the policies that led to the Industrial Revolution. Innovating against superior or cheaper competition was much harder in practice than theory. The excise on window glass was removed in 1845, followed by a reduction in import duties till they were completely abolished in 1857. The result was the sudden importation of cheaper Belgian window glass, with imports rising from zero during the 1840s to 28,000 cwt. in 1856 and 780,000 cwt. in 1870. Then came German glass, culminating in a serious depression for British domestic glass industries in general.[73]

Consider, too, the case of paper. When the customs duty on foreign paper was removed in 1860 the industry struggled to compete with foreign paper imports. The European continent and United States retained prohibitive tariffs, and an export duty on rags, which as the primary raw material needed at the time for making paper, constituted between 30 and 50 per cent of the cost of paper production. One papermaker reflected in 1860: 'The French are allowed to import paper into England but we're not allowed by the French tariff to import Rags, so as to give them plenty of cheap material for making paper & while with us it would be more expensive.' Another commentator could barely restrain his anger: 'To ask us to sustain a competition with foreign manufacturers under conditions such as these is to place before us a task more hopeless of accomplishment and more cruel in its exactions than that of which the Israelites complained during their bondage.'[74] Thomas Wrigley, writing on behalf of the papermakers concluded, like many others, that the evangelical pursuit of free trade was all about the producer at the vanguard of the Industrial Revolution, namely, cotton textiles: 'It is high time that the

Manchester Chamber of Commerce should be in reality what it professes to be by name. That it has watched with jealous care over the interests of cotton, no one will question.'[75]

By 1860 protective duties had also been removed from silk. The result was the decline of English-manufactured silk in Spitalfields, Macclesfield and Coventry. During the 1870s, there was a desperate attempt to adopt power looms and greater productive centralization as the only path for survival. However, such an approach for silk was challenged by some as in reality being more costly and less efficient than a cottage system. Henry Birchenough, a Macclesfield silk manufacturer, told a Royal Commission on trade depression some years later in 1886: 'They [France, Italy and Switzerland] have an advantage because they work lighter than we do. They are in a better position to produce more cheaply than we are, and they have not the same expensive establishments.' Moreover, unlike its European rivals the British domestic production of silk did not have an internal or cheap international supply of raw silk and now had no protective tariffs to shelter this disability.[76]

The leading advocate of British free trade, Richard Cobden, had spearheaded a commercial treaty with France in 1860 that removed the last 15 per cent *ad valorem* duty on foreign silk. In return, prohibitive duties on English textiles were replaced by a duty not exceeding 30 per cent *ad valumn*. Free-traders believed this would nurture a lean and competitive silk industry. The actual outcome was the opposite and foreign silk textiles flooded the British domestic market. Steven Ainscough writes: 'The result was the massive reduction in silk workers jobs, wages and working hours. This led to the closure of numerous silk mills and the migration of many silk workers from the trade and to new pastures in America.' Meanwhile, countries such as Italy, Russia and Austria all introduced tariff barriers. The impact on the British silk workforce is stark. In 1851, the year of London's Great Exhibition, 130,000 were employed in silk but by 1900 the number had dwindled by over three-quarters to 30,000.[77]

It had been hoped by free-traders that by glutting the market of other countries with British manufacturers it would prevent them from industrializing. As the Whig MP, Henry Brougham, had told the House of Commons as early as 1816: 'It is well worthwhile to incur a loss upon the first exportation, in order, by the glut, to stifle in the cradle those infant manufacturers in the United States which the (Napoleonic) war has forced into existence.' While Cobden, following John Stuart Mill, explained that by removing the Corn Laws, rival nations would concentrate on growing grain rather than trying to compete with British manufactures.[78] This was the promotion of liberal free trade for national self-interested reasons, defined by an arrogant belief that Britain was a natural industrial country, and the related view of international competitive specialization.

This is not to say, as we have seen, that there was not an articulate and clear defence of the traditional policies. Protectionists such as the MP and landowner Sir Richard Vyvyan, Robert Southey, John Barton and Albert Williams produced reams of statistical evidence demonstrating that there had been a decline in manufactured exports to corn-producing nations just as imports of corn had risen. Thus, the increased income in these countries through British agricultural purchases was not being spent on British manufactures as prophesized by free-traders. Moreover, increased reliance on these countries for corn put Britain in a dangerous position of being dependent upon a future enemy and having its food supplies cut off. Vyvyan and Williams pointed to the work of the fiercely protectionist American Henry Clay to support their claims. Protectionists also continued to argue the importance of dependent colonies as a market for high-end manufactures as opposed to independent foreign countries.[79]

However, the case for protection was fast disappearing. Peel's introduction of the income tax in 1842 and demonstration of the possibility of further tariff reforms aided the fervent belief in free trade, while the need for a more abundant and cheaper food supply, and thus a relaxation of agrarian import controls, was mounting. Any doubts about delaying this further were quickly brought into stark focus with the Irish famine and the negative role of the British government within this shocking and tragic event. As 21,000 Irish people died of starvation and a further 2 million emigrated, Britain continued to import corn from Ireland. Due to the Corn Laws the country had become an increasingly vital supplier of grain, butter, livestock and animal products to Britain (prohibitions on Irish livestock dating back to the late seventeenth century had been lifted during the mid-eighteenth century). Such supplies had been vital during Napoleon's blockade, with 35 per cent of all grains, meal and flour imported into Britain between 1800 and 1814 coming from Ireland. Brinley Thomas calculates that by the late 1830s something like '13 per cent of the entire output of English agriculture and over 85 per cent of England's imports of grains, meat, butter, and livestock' came from Ireland.[80]

The view of grain supplies was as complicated as it was contested. Within a European context, Britain was by no means alone in protecting its domestic production of corn. France, Holland, Switzerland and Spain all introduced, in varying forms, laws to stem grain imports. During the 1820s, the Corn Laws kept back a glut of cheap corn in Europe; however, by the period of concerted reform from 1838, corn had become much scarcer in Europe. Nonetheless, after the repeal of the Corn Laws, and despite the scarcity in Europe as a whole, unrestricted trade triggered a net fall in corn prices in Britain; there was also a decline in British production as marginal land was withdrawn.[81]

By 1846 free trade had become crucial to both Tories and Whigs alike. The reform of the Corn Laws that year was less a result of angry lobbying from the Anti-Corn League and more out of social urgency. The free-traders now occupied the moral high ground, claiming protection led to a bloated state, starvation, trade wars and high military expenditure.[82] The repeal of the Corn Laws represents a crucial departure from the earlier policies of Huskisson. The latter's emphasis on reciprocal free-trade agreements was abandoned and a unilateral policy was adopted. The Board of Trade, Peel and Gladstone had by this stage given up trying to negotiate such time-consuming commercial treaties.[83] It was also the case, as we have seen, that grain prices on the continent had risen closer to those in Britain making the repeal of the Corn Laws more palatable to the landed ranks. Indeed, it turned out to be a golden age for agriculture greatly aided by a shift to livestock farming.[84]

This year also saw the Colonial Possessions Act that repealed Britain's right to impose differential duties in the colonies. This was only fair, argued Lord Grey, since Britain had abandoned colonial preference. Finally, the Whigs set about repealing the Navigation

Acts; a natural progression after the repeal of preferential duties on sugar and timber. With revolution rife in Europe during 1848, this last act of deregulation was nearly defeated; however, it survived, and was passed, with shipping actually prospering in its wake.[85] The project of shrinking the state was near completion.

Free trade had evolved beyond an economic measure and become a notion of Britishness and crucial tool of state dismantling. For many, too, it was this country's mission as God's elect nation, demonstrated by commercial and industrial supremacy (ironically built upon illiberal and protectionist policies), to spread the doctrine of free trade. Within such a view, free-traders claimed that Britain was simply the best place in the world to produce cotton and woollen textiles, iron and steel, while protectionist nations would simply cultivate unnatural and unsuitable industries, which was something that went against the 'objective' laws of God and political economy.[86] The actual history of Britain's rise to industrial supremacy had seemingly evaporated into the ether.

Britain's staunch adherence to free trade during this period has baffled numerous commentators for generations. As a famous French historian of England, Elie Halevy, long ago observed, 'a barrier' was 'erected' by Britain's economic rivals, 'behind which the new-born industries were making in safety, for the day when they should be sufficiently strong to invade the British market'.[87] Certainly, there was strong opposition to unilateral free trade, such as the Fair-Trade League, but the Liberal Party would not budge. Free trade was what it always was: an ideological political movement, rather than what its prophets claimed, an objective creed based upon God's providence or a rational science. It was precisely the attempt to shrink and placate popular suspicion and dislike of the state that had fuelled a distinct British free-trade culture. The movement had subsequently become deeply embedded as the saviour of Britain from the old, hugely expensive, fiscal–military state. The fact it was precisely protectionist policies that had carved Britain's manufacturing pathway culminating in the Industrial Revolution was conveniently forgotten.

EPILOGUE

The recipe of free trade and democracy as a formula for sustained economic growth was invented after the rise and dominance of Western industrialization.[1] The shadow of this book is the way economic thought and ideology, since the nineteenth century to the present, has informed interpretations of the British Industrial Revolution. This reflexive dynamic has been most convincingly demonstrated in an essay by David Cannadine, who traced the varying interpretations of the Industrial Revolution between 1880 and 1980.[2] Since then, particularly after the fall of the Berlin Wall in 1989, a new reading has become dominant, reflecting the rise of neoliberalism and incorporating residues of Cold War rhetoric.[3]

To date the history of successful and sustainable finance, trade and industrialization has always predominantly involved some form of state regulation – despite an army of free-trade advocates arguing to the contrary. One problem is the sheer number of Western economists trained in a literal reading of free-trade ideology, who have subsequently become historians desperately seeking the origins of modern industrialization within such a context. This has been powerfully underlined in the recent work of a small but growing group of scholars, who have exposed how a dominant historiography has worked hard to misleadingly project back the origins of current economic values such as liberty, freedom of trade, an open and enlightened culture, science, the protection of property, individualism, expertise and materialism to a distinct Western past. By contrast, as they convincingly reveal, Britain and Western countries, in general, industrialized along illiberal nationalist lines, which raises the need for a concerted reinterpretation of the history of political economy.[4] As Sophus A. Reinert succinctly puts it: '"Enlightenment economics" cannot be equated with laissez-faire.'[5] The result has been the erasure of the British state from so much of the prevailing historiography of the Industrial Revolution.

This book has sought to put the state at the heart of understanding the history of British industrialization and, equally, to demonstrate that it cannot be grasped without placing it in a global framework. The dominance of a Western, if not Anglo-centric, perspective has meant much of the world has, until recently, been absent from the industrial historiography.[6] The most recent attempt at placing Britain's Industrial Revolution in a world context, despite the efforts of its editors, ends up as a serial of industrial revolutions.[7] The fact that the East, primarily China and India, were more industrialized well into the eighteenth century does not play much of a role in the histories of those seeking a distinct Western liberal interpretation. Reasons for this have a long trajectory. For example, the great neo-liberal economist Ludwig von Mises taught in his discussion of freedom in 1949 that the 'Orientals meekly acquiesced in this state of affairs'. In contrast, wherever

European Christians settled in the world they 'never tired in their struggle for liberty'. They worked relentlessly to eradicate 'all status and caste privileges and disabilities until they finally succeeded in establishing the system that the harbingers of totalitarianism try to smear by calling it the bourgeois system'. Likewise, another Austrian economist, Friedrich A. Hayek, concluded in 1988: The 'history of China provides many instances of government attempts to enforce so perfect an order that innovation became impossible'. Similarly, in 1998 the historian David Landes claimed the Chinese lacked curiosity and simply 'went to show themselves, not to see and learn. … They were what they were and did not have to take or make'. By contrast, the foundation of the West's free-market economy was liberty, entrepreneurial manufacturers left alone and the freeing of the individual consumer.[8]

Deirdre McCloskey has recently gone further and ferociously celebrates the rise of an apparent Western bourgeois dignity; this is an argument implicit in many of the recent volumes published on the birth of a consumer society in eighteenth-century Britain. And the recipient of the Hayek Prize for Lifetime Achievement (2012), Niall Ferguson, regularly celebrates Britain's gift to world civilization in an array of recent publications and work on television.[9] Ironically, the two nations that pride themselves as the home of liberty were built upon very illiberal foundations.[10]

It was a particularly powerful Western European, especially British, state that lay at the heart of this industrial ascendancy. Peer Vries has recently shown how the British state can ultimately be seen as the key to understanding the Great Divergence with China.[11] As Britain's industrial and commercial dominance during the eighteenth century grew, especially in the second half, so too did the translations of the country's oeconomic tracts. However, it was not the texts we are now told were important but those that confirmed illiberal British strategies at the time. This fact, of course, has got lost in the prescriptions now offered by economists and works highlighted in hindsight as being important.[12]

What really set eighteenth-century Britain apart was the peculiar strength and distinctive policies of its state born, primarily, of war. This body made possible a project of global trade, financialization, protectionism, coerced labour (slavery, women and children), colonization and an excruciatingly detail-obsessed, almost encyclopaedic, regulation of industry that culminated in the Industrial Revolution; all these components can't be separated. It was only once British industry had gained global supremacy over its continental European and Asian competitors that it embraced a more 'liberal' variant of economic policy and then proceeded to reinvent its own history along such a liberal vein.

In trying to dissolve clear and distinctive industrial trajectories we need to erase imagined or at least highly exaggerated cultural and even, recently, genetic interpretations.[13] However, for apologists of the rise of Western liberalism it is important to place an evolved culture or middle-class gene of creative rationality, characterized by what we now call 'science' at the heart of its historical ascendance. Within such grand narratives, fundamental factors such as the 'illiberal' policies pursued by the state, the role of the working population and cosmopolitanism become erased. The bourgeoisie, liberty and science can then be seen to have created an objective economic system that is natural and for the good of the many, that is, democratic, just and based on truth. In short, such an economic system is informed by the sentiments lying behind Karl Popper's 'open society' or Hayek's road to wealth rather than serfdom. An alliance between access to objective knowledge and a particular notion of freedom has become deeply entwined within Western politics, economics, morality and ideology.[14]

This perspective informs much of the latest historiography of the Industrial Revolution, however it is clothed. For example, Joyce Appleby has recently argued: 'Capitalist values could not be imposed by authority because the genius of the new entrepreneurial economy was individual initiative.' She then provides a traditional explanation of how this came together in eighteenth-century Britain. It was here that 'self-assertive individuals did the innovating' and proved to the rest of the world that 'unexpected social benefits' arose by 'allowing men and women to make their own self-interested choices'; individualism and intellectual openness were the keys. Similarly, Joel Mokyr has argued:

> In addition to the technology of access there was culture. The culture of 'open science' that evolved in the seventeenth century meant that observation and experience were placed in the public domain and that credit was assigned by priority. Its openness manifested itself in two dimensions, both in the full disclosure of findings and methods, and in the lack of barriers to entry for competent persons willing to learn the language.

The context for this was eighteenth-century Britain. It was here 'Scientific knowledge became a public good, communicated freely rather than confined to a secretive exclusive few as had been the case in medieval Europe' and, indeed, the rest of the world. Britain was, concludes Mokyr and more recently Margaret C. Jacob, the first-ever knowledge economy.[15]

This view has become a leading consensus in mainstream Western economics. For example, the director of the Earth Institute and former special advisor to the United Nations Secretary General (Kofi Annan), Jeffrey Sachs, writes in his recent book on prescriptions for economic development: 'The decisive breakthrough came with Isaac Newton's *Principia Mathematica* in 1687, one of the most important books ever written.' It was this book, he goes on to claim, which provided the perspective and tools that would ignite the Industrial Revolution: 'Newton set the stage for hundreds of years of scientists and technological discovery, and for the Industrial Revolution that would follow the scientific revolution.'[16] There is no room, as we have seen, for the state or the history of other countries in such claims purporting to trace the origins of modern economic growth. All this, to borrow Andre Wakefield's phrase in his recent demolition of the current trend in historical anachronisms, constitutes 'Disney history'.[17]

In opposition to the advocates of a distinct British-enlightened culture, there has been a gradual attempt by a growing group of scholars to reorient the Western-centric history of industrialization away from Europe, and especially Britain, to other parts of the world. Interest, particularly in the industrial and commercial history of China and increasingly India, has accompanied the economic rise of this region over the last twenty-five years. Here, it is argued, the British Industrial Revolution was merely a short moment within a much larger and longer global trajectory.[18] A central aspect to this moment, the subject of this book, was the creation of a strong and dynamic British state.

NOTES

Introduction

1. Stewart, *The Rise of Public Science*; Jacob, *Scientific Culture*; Jacob, *The First Knowledge Economy*; Jacob and Stewart, *Practical Matter*; Porter, *Enlightenment*; Mokyr, *Gifts of Athena* and *The Enlightened Economy*; Jones, *Industrial Enlightenment*; Greenfeld, *The Spirit of Capitalism*; Appleby, *The Relentless Revolution*; McCloskey, *Bourgeois Dignity*; and Ferguson, *Civilization*.

2. At the vanguard of the institutional emphasis has been Rosenberg and Birdzell, Jr., *How the West Grew Rich*; North and Weingast, 'The evolution of institutions'; North, *Institutions* and *Understanding the Process of Economic Change*; and Acemoglu and Robinson, *Why Nations Fail*.

3. For a historical critique of the institutional argument see, especially, Daunton, 'Rationality and institutions'; Hoppit, 'Compulsion, compensation and property rights'; Beckert, *Empire of Cotton*; and the various essays in Coffman, Leonard and Neal (eds), *Questioning Credible Commitment*.

4. Uglow, *The Lunar Men*, xiii.

5. Wrigley, *Continuity, Chance and Change* and *Energy and the English Industrial Revolution*; Pomeranz, *The Great Divergence*; Griffin, *A Short History of the British Industrial Revolution*; and Kander, Malanima and Warde, *Power to the People*.

6. Mathias, *The Transformation of England*.

7. Turnbull, 'Coal and regional growth'; Maw, Wyke and Kidd, 'Canals, rivers, and the industrial city'.

8. Allen, *The British Industrial Revolution*.

9. Parthasarathi, *Why Europe Grew Rich*; Riello, *Cotton*.

10. Berg, *Luxury and Pleasure* and 'The British product revolution'.

11. Williams, *Capitalism*; Inikori, *Africans and the Industrial Revolution*; and Blackburn, *The Making of New World Slavery*.

12. Esteban, 'The rising share of British industrial exports', 898; Eltis and Engerman, 'The importance of slavery', 141; and Engerman and O'Brien, 'Exports and the growth of the British economy'. For an overview of the debate involving slavery and capital to Britain's Industrial Revolution, see Morgan, *Slavery*, 44–8 and 53–4.

13. Esteban, 'The rising share of British industrial exports'; Inikori, *Africans and the Industrial Revolution*, 61–73; and Zahedieh, *The Capital*.

14. Beckert, *Empire of Cotton*; Baptist, *Half Has Never Been Told*.

15. Vries, *The Industrious Revolution*.

16. Humphries, 'Enclosures' and *Childhood and Child Labour*; Berg and Hudson, 'Rehabilitating'; Berg, 'What difference did women's work make'; and Sharpe, *Adapting to Capitalism*.

17. Rosenband, 'The industrious revolution'.

18. Crafts, 'British economic growth', 199, *British Economic Growth* and 'British industrialisation'. Similarly, Craig Muldrew has recently argued that any increased industry also meant an improvement in agricultural production and the supply of food; see his *Food*. Of course, such macro figures do not take into account dramatic regional differences; see, especially, Hudson (ed.), *Regions* and *The Industrial Revolution*, 101–32. It should also be noted that David S. Landes suggests that the early rate of growth (pre-1830s) was still faster by the tenor of the age – but he believed it went into capital formation rather than Albion's wage labour; see his 'The fable of the dead horse'.

19. Beckert, *Empire of Cotton*.

20. Vries, *State*.

21. Say, *England,* 5–6, 14–15, 21–6 and 29–31; Jones, *An End to Poverty*, 138–41.

22. Say, *England*, 35.

23. Compare, for example, this argument with Allen's emphasis upon high wages as the key to innovation in his *The British Industrial Revolution*.

24. Blanqui, *History of Political Economy* and quoted in Jones, *An End to Poverty*, 166.

25. Coleman, *British Paper Industry*, 141–2.

26. Fine, 'Production and excise', 185–6.

27. Parthasarathi, *Why Europe Grew Rich*, 132.

28. Fine, 'Production and excise', 224–5 and 204.

29. Dowell, *A History of Taxation*, vol. 4, 318–19.

30. Say, *England*, 37–9; Carnot, *Reflections*, 4.

31. Hartwell, 'Taxation in England', 131.

32. Beckert, *Empire of Cotton*; Baptist, *Half Has Never Been Told*. This complicated nexus is succinctly explained in Rockman, 'What makes the history of capitalism newsworthy?', 439–66.

33. See, especially, Brewer, *The Sinews of Power*, 221–49; Hoppit, 'Political arithmetic'; Innes, *Inferior Politics*, 109–75; Leng, 'Epistemology', 97–114; and Soll, *The Reckoning*, 107–8.

34. Turnbull, 'Coal and regional growth'; Maw, Wyke and Kidd, 'Canals, rivers, and the industrial city'.

35. Evans and Rydén, *Baltic Iron*.

36. Craven and Hay, 'The criminalization of "free" labour'.

37. Winch, *Riches and Poverty*, 8, 11 and 48; Rothschild, *Economic Sentiments*, 52–71, 82, 84, 93 and 109; and Jones, *An End to Poverty*, 234.

38. By far the best exception to this is Hudson, *The Industrial Revolution*; Daunton, *Progress and Poverty*; O'Brien, 'Imperialism and inseparable connections'; Beckert, *Empire of Cotton*; Vries, *State*; and Hardy, *Forgotten Voices*.

39. Chang, *Kicking Away the Ladder* and *Bad Samaritans*; E. Reinert, *How Rich Countries Got Rich*; S. Reinert, *Translating Empire*; Prasannan, *Why Europe Grew Rich*; Boldizzoni, *The Poverty of Clio*; and Mazzucato, *The Entrepreneurial State*.

Chapter 1

1. Samuel Pepys is quoted in Hill, *Some Intellectual Consequences*, 25.

2. Brewer, *The Sinews of Power*; Hont, *Jealousy of Trade*.

3. Scott, 'George Downing (1623-1684)', DNB; Brenner, *Merchants and Revolution*, 151; and Blackburn, *The Making of New World Slavery*, 238. For John Winthrop, see Bremer, *John Winthrop*. At a much more general level, the impact of colonial Americans upon the commerce of the Atlantic world was hugely important; see, especially, Hancock, *Citizens of the World*.

4. Scott, 'Downing'.

5. Lipson, *The Economic History of England*, vol. 3, 11; Pincus, 'Neither Machiavellian' and, especially, *1688*. Oeconomic emulation, of course, was not confined to England, but the country proved particularly good at it during this period; see Cipolla, *Before the Industrial Revolution*, 263 and, especially, Reinert, *Translating Empire*.

6. Coffman, 'Credibility'. This is expanded in her *Excise Taxation*.

7. Zook, *Radical Whigs*, xv.

8. Greaves, *Deliver Us From Evil* and *Enemies Under His Feet*; Leng, *Benjamin Worsley*; Pincus, *1688*; and Coffman, 'Credibility'.

9. Hill, *Some Intellectual Consequences*, 10–16; Greaves, *Deliver Us From Evil*, 227; and Coffman, 'Credibility'. For the post-Glorious Revolution period, focusing upon London, see the detailed study by Krey, *A Fractured Society*. This theme of continuity from the Cromwellian era is also demonstrated in colonial policy; see for example, Rich, 'The first earl of Shaftesbury's colonial policy'. By far the best examination of the reciprocal relationship between knowledge and social stability during this period is Shapin and Schaffer, *Leviathan and the Air-Pump*. For the emergence of 'facts' impregnating British society and their prominent role in, especially, oeconomic persuasion, see Poovey, *A History of the Modern Fact*, especially chs 2 and 3.

10. Scott, *England's Troubles*, 397 and 413–14. For a clear overview of the complicated relationship between the Crown and Parliament over (and the legality of) sources of revenue during the Elizabethan and early-Stewart period, see Braddick, *State Formation*, ch. 6. For a useful account of the traditional theory underpinning royal taxation, see Harris's 'Theory and practice in royal taxation' and 'Thomas Cromwell's "new principle" of taxation'.

11. Ship money was an ancient levy on London, maritime towns and counties to provide funds for the provisioning of ships in time of war. However, by 1636 it seemed Charles was trying to establish it as a permanent tax without parliamentary sanction. The best published history of the land tax is still Ward, *The English Land Tax*.

12. Nichols, 'English government borrowing', 83–4; Krey, *A Fractured Society*, 2.

13. Roseveare, *The Treasury 1660-1870*, 22–3; Chandaman, *The English Public Revenue*.

14. Soll, *The Reckoning*, 70–86.

15. For the importance of commercial knowledge and Amsterdam's predominant role as a centre of credible information exchange, see Smith, 'The function of commercial'; Poovey, *A History of the Modern Fact*, ch. 2. For London, see for example, Hancock, *Citizens of the World*, 32–6. Hancock provides some excellent detail and analysis concerning the mundane but vital role of the Counting-House, and its strategic geographical location near or within all the primary institutions in the City of London (85–114). For the precarious status of

financial information in the English financial markets during this period, see, especially, Murphy, *The Origins of English Financial Markets*, chs 4 and 5.

16. Rommelse, 'The role of mercantilism'; Scott, *When the Waves Ruled Britannia*, 5–9. For the impact of Dutch commerce and its stimulation of knowledge, see Cook, *Matters of Exchange*.

17. Gill, 'The Treasury', 601–2; D. L. Smith, 'Thomas Wriothesley, fourth earl of Southampton', DNB, 2004; and D. L. Smith, 'Warwick, Sir Philip (1609-1683)', DNB, 2004. The basis of the king's financial settlement was predominantly based upon John Pym's plan of 1641. Conrad Russell stated he was key in 'creating an administrative machine to run the Parliamentarian war effort. … He built up a system of standing committees at Westminster, and of county committees in the country, which worked. He and others succeeded, as he had not in 1641, in introducing the excise', see Conrad Russell, 'Pym, John (1584–1643)', DNB, 2004.

18. Coffman, 'Credibility', 78 and *Excise Taxation*, 13 and 163–70.

19. Tim Harris, 'Anthony Ashley Cooper, first earl of Shaftesbury', DNB, 2004; Rich, 'The first earl of Shaftesbury's colonial policy', 56–60.

20. Harris, 'Cooper'. The Exclusion Crisis describes a period between 1678 and 1681 when attempts were made to exclude the king's brother, the Duke of York, from being heir to the crown due to his Catholicism.

21. Roseveare, *The Evolution of a British Institution,* 414–15; Coffman, 'Credibility', 81.

22. Clarendon is quoted in Clapham, *The Bank of England*, vol. 1, 9.

23. Clarendon is quoted in Scott, *England's Troubles*, 415–16.

24. Bethel, *The Present Interest of England Stated* is quoted in Pincus, 'Neither Machiavellian moment', 721.

25. Roseveare, *The Evolution of a British Institution*, 62–4 and *The Treasury,* 31–4; Baxter, *The Development of the Treasury,* 4–5. For the Interrgenum, see, for example, *An Ordinance for Bringing the Publique Revenues* and Coffman, 'Credibility'. For a comparative history of the importance of financial accountability during this period and earlier, see Soll, *The Reckoning*.

26. Davenant, *An Essay upon the Natural Credit of England*, 9; Harley, *An Essay upon Publick Credit*, 3.

27. Gill, 'The relationship between the Treasury and the Excise'. Fiscal farms were composed of a group of financiers who paid an annual sum to the Crown to harvest the excise and customs in particular districts; see Braddick, *Parliamentary Taxation*.

28. O'Brien, 'Fiscal exceptionalism', 256.

29. Rommelse, 'The role of mercantilism', 598; Prak, *The Dutch Republic*, 75–84.

30. For a succinct account of Edward Hyde, first Earl of Clarendon, see Seaward, *The Cavalier Parliament*.

31. Edward Hyde, first Earl of Clarendon, 'News from Dunkirk'. This broadsheet was apparently sentenced by both Houses of Parliament to be burnt.

32. Gill, 'The Treasury', 601–2; Baxter, *Development of the Treasury*, 11 and 28.

33. Ibid., 602–3; ibid., 23–5.

34. Beckert, *Empire of Cotton*.

35. Scott, 'Good night Amsterdam', 347–52; Baxter, *Development of the Treasury*, 169; and Downing is quoted in Scott, 'Downing'. For an example of Downing's ruthless character, see Catterall, 'Sir George Downing and the regicides'.

36. Downing is quoted in Scott, 'Downing'; Hancock, *Citizens of the World*, 396; and Prak, *The Dutch Republic*, 75–134.

37. Scott, 'Good night Amsterdam', 339–41, *England's Troubles*, 309 and *When the Waves Ruled Britannia*, 62; Baxter, *Development of the Treasury*, 179.

38. Scott, *England's Troubles*, 67–8, 72–3 and 403. For the importance of revenue, new fiscal instruments and military success during the Interregnum, see Braddick, 'An English military revolution?' and *State Formation*, 177–290; Wheeler, 'Navy finance' and *The Making of a World Power*; and Coffman, 'Credibility' and *Excise Taxation*.

39. Downing is quoted in Scott, *England's Troubles*, 312.

40. George Downing, 'Negotiations and Letters to and from Sir George Downing at the Hague', vol. 1, August 1661, BLO: MS Clarendon 104, fols, 252–8.

41. Downing, 'Negotiations'.

42. Downing, 'Negotiations'. Downing was also one of the prime movers in attempting to introduce stamp duties during the mid-1660s; see Hughes, 'The English stamp duties', 235.

43. The Brewers of London, *Free-men Inslaved*, A2. Such concerns continued into the next century; see, for example, Ashworth, *Customs and Excise*, 63–84. The sustained importance of the Magna Carta has been underlined by Linebaugh, *The Magna Carta*.

44. Anon., *The General-Excise Considered*; Anon., *The Standard of Equality*, 11. The equitable nature of the excise was particularly emphasized during the mid-1690s in a doomed attempt to generate support for a significant expansion of the tax; see, for example, Anon., *The Excise Rectify'd*; W.C., *A Discourse Humbly Offer'd*. For a succinct overview of the array of arguments aimed at the possibility of a general excise, see Marquis of Hallifax, *An Essay upon Taxes*, 67–70. Although the excise was important to the Dutch, the system of excise collection was reliant on provinces and was not national like the English excise; see Prak, *The Dutch Republic*, 75–84.

45. Anon., *The Standard of Equality*, 18–23. For similar views, see also Anon., *Reasons and Grounds*, 1–3. Taxing luxuries and foreign-consumed imports was underlined by various subsequent commentators; see, for example, Petyt, *Britannia Languens*, 120.

46. *The Soapmakers Complaint*; Ibeson, *To the Supreme Authority*; and Prynne, *A Declaration*, 9 and 19. See also Ibeson, *To the Supreme Authority*; Anon., *The Excise-Mans Lamentation*. These arguments would continue to be repeated later and into the eighteenth century; see, for example, Anon., *The General-Excise Consider'd*; Anon., *The Congress of Excise-Asses* and Anon. (ed.), *Excise: Being a Collection of Letters*. A survey of seventeenth-century complaints are documented in Coffman, 'Credibility', 90 and *Excise Taxation*, 183–9.

47. Ramsey, *Bloudy Newes*, 1 and 8.

48. Seaward, 'The house of commons committee of trade', 437–40. The Duke of York was also governor of the Royal Fishing Adventurers.

49. Downing, *A Discourse*, 17–18; Seaward, 'The house of commons committee of trade', 450–2; Makepeace, 'English Traders', 246; and Rommelse, 'The role of mercantilism', 603.

50. Pincus, 'Popery', 194–201.

51. Gauci, *The Politics of Trade*. There is much in Christopher Hill's comment: 'Protestant ideology was ignored when the enemy was the Netherlands, remembered in Ireland and against France and Spain'; see his *Some Intellectual Consequences*, 23.

52. Downing, *A Discourse*, 8–10.

53. Pincus, 'Popery', 2–3.

54. Greaves, *Enemies Under His Feet*, 3–15, 16–32 and 47 and Pincus, 'Popery', 5–11.

55. Pincus, 'Popery', 19–27.

56. Downing, *A Discourse*, 14–15.

57. Harris, *Restoration*, 71.

58. Scott, *When the Waves Ruled Britannia*, 92–103.

59. The contemporary commentators are quoted in Pincus, 'From butterboxes', 337–9. For the English political motives, see Rommelse, 'The role of mercantilism', 606.

60. Pincus, 'From butterboxes', 342; Harris, *Restoration*, 71–5.

61. Ibid., 348–61.

62. Stein and Stein, *Silver, Trade, and War,* 110–11.

63. Pincus, 'From butterboxes', 361; Harris, *Restoration*, 74–6 and 80; and Greaves, *Deliver Us from Evil*; Krey, *A Fractured Society*, 12–13. Harris provides a very good overview of the Exclusion Crisis in his *Restoration*, 136–205. The best account of Shaftesbury's radical Whig circle is Zook, *Radical Whigs*.

64. Beckett, 'Land tax or excise', 288–301.

65. Anon., *The General-Excise Consider'd*, 2 and 6.

66. Roseveare, *The Evolution of a British Institution*, 75 and *The Treasury*, 51–2 and 56–8; Sainty, 'The tenure of offices'.

67. Hoppit, 'Checking leviathan', 274, 'Political arithmetic', 516–40 and *A Land of Liberty?*, 190–2; Brewer, *The Sinews of Power*, 221–49; Innes, *Inferior Politics*, 109–75; and Leng, 'Epistemology'.

68. See, for example, *Instructions to be Observed by the Officers of Excise*, 15.

69. Defoe, *The Complete English Tradesman*, vol. 1, 275 and 311.

70. Poovey, *A History of the Modern Fact,* 80–97 and 110–20; Leng, 'Epistemology', 100–1. See also Crosby, *The Measure of Reality,* 199–223. For Defoe and his adoption of factual narratives devised by the Royal Society and, no doubt, directly from his experiences as a merchant and one-time bookkeeper to the Excise, see Schaffer, 'Defoe's natural philosophy'. For the formal marrying of probity, prudence and precise bookkeeping in science and business during the early nineteenth century, see Ashworth, 'The calculating eye'.

71. Shapin and Schaffer, *Leviathan and the Air-Pump*.

72. For the Excise, from this perspective, see Brewer, *The Sinews of Power*; Ashworth, *Customs and Excise*.

73. R. Zaller, 'Robinson, Henry (*bap.* 1605, *d.* 1673)', DNB, 2004.

74. Cunningham, *The Growth of English Industry*, 411–12, and *Alien Immigrants*, 207; Dickson, *The Financial Revolution*, 54–6.

75. The Stop of the Exchequer happened when Charles II was no longer able to honour his debts, leading to a number of goldsmith bankers going bankrupt.

76. Quinn, 'Tallies or reserves?', 39–40.

77. Quinn, 'Tallies or reserves?', 40–1. For an in-depth study of the financial market during this period, see Murphy, *The Origins of English Financial Markets*.

78. Tomlinson, 'Financial and administrative developments', 96–104; Holmes, *Augustan England*, 252–3; and Brewer, *The Sinews of Power*, 3–24.

79. Brewer, 'The English state', 59–60.

80. For offices as property in late-eighteenth-century England, see Chester, *The English Administrative System*, 18–20.

81. Downie, 'The commission of public accounts'; Brewer, 'The English state', 59–60; and Hessenbruch, 'The spread of precision measurement', 195–8. For influence and patronage in the British system, see Ward, 'Some eighteenth century civil servants'; Sainty, 'Tenure of offices'; and Tomlinson, 'Place and profit'. For the wide differences between French and English practices, see Root, 'The redistributive role of government'.

Chapter 2

1. Robinson, *Briefe Considerations*, 1.

2. Petyt, *Britannia Languens,* 29–30.

3. Ash, 'A note and a caveat' and *Power*, 87–134; Epstein, 'Craft guilds', 171. For the crucial role of foreigners in fuelling London's production of philosophical instruments during this period, see Iliffe, 'Capitalizing expertise', 55–84; Harkness, *The Jewel House*.

4. Brenner, *Merchants and Revolution*, 23–8.

5. Stein and Stein, *The Colonial Heritage*, 26.

6. Thornton, *Africa and Africans,* 36; Bayly, *The Birth of the Modern World*, 62–4. For the sophistication of Chinese navigation, see Hobson, *The Eastern Origins*, 57–8, 121–6 and 140–4.

7. Beckert, *Empire of Cotton*; Vries, *State*, 295–323.

8. Ormrod, *The Rise of Commercial Empires* and 'English re-exports'; Inikori, *Africans and the Industrial Revolution*; and Zahedieh, *The Capital and the Colonies*.

9. Inikori, *Africans and the Industrial Revolution*, 363.

10. Brenner, *Merchants and Revolution*, 36–7; Allen*, The British Industrial Revolution*.

11. Berg, 'In pursuit of luxury', 87.

12. Parthasarathi, *Why Europe Grew Rich*; Riello, *Cotton*.

13. Rosenband, 'Becoming competitive' and 'The many transitions'; Berg, *Luxury and Pleasure*, 7 and 12.

14. R. Zaller, 'Robinson, Henry (*bap.* 1605, *d.* 1673)', DNB, 2004.

15. Robinson, *England's Safety*, 8–9 and 16–19.

16. Petyt, *Britannia Languens*, 30. Petyt emphasized Parliament's antiquity and its mandate derived 'from the popular will of England's ancient peoples'. In other words, Parliament was not subordinate to the will of the king; see Zook, *Radical Whigs*, 69–70.

17. Robinson, *England's Safety*, 24–5.

18. Robinson, *Briefe Considerations*, 3 and *England's Safety*, 44. The Dutch excise is described in Prak, *The Dutch Republic*, 75–84. For the implication of this view and its political manifestation, see Ashworth, *Customs and Excise*, 53–62.

19. This is in contrast to the market argument made by Jan De Vries in his *The Industrious Revolution*.

20. Robinson, *Briefe Considerations*, 4 and 7–10 and *England's Safety*, 26, 43 and 46.

21. Pincus, 'Neither Machiavellian moment', *1688* and 'Rethinking mercantilism'. The transition to a commercial culture has a long and impressive intellectual history; see, especially, Pocock, *The Machiavellian Moment*.

22. Hont, *Jealousy of Trade*, 28.

23. Davenant, *An Essay upon Ways and Means*, 16; Whiston, *A Discourse*, 2; Petyt, *Britannia Languens*, 16; and Cary, *An Essay on the State of England*, 170.

24. Pincus, *1688* and 'Rethinking mercantilism'.

25. Worsley, *The Advocate*, 1; Leng, *Benjamin Worsley*, xi and 22–3; Wennerlind, *Casualties of Credit*, 55–79; and Webster, 'Worsley, Benjamin (1617/18-1677)', rev. DNB, 2004.

26. Leng, *Benjamin Worsley*, 35 and 49–59.

27. Worsley, *The Advocate*, 3–7; Petyt, *Britannia Languens*, 51–4.

28. Webb, *1676*, 50, 152–3 and 203–4; Blackburn, *The Making of New World Slavery*, 256–8.

29. Webb, *1676*, 203; B. C. Murison, 'Povey, Thomas (*b.* 1613/14, *d.* in or before 1705)', DNB, 2004.

30. Bland, *Trade Revived*, 3–8 and 34–5.

31. Ibid., 8; Cunningham, *The Growth of English Industry*, vol. 2, 308.

32. Anon., *England's Interest*, 24.

33. Ibid., 25 and 34.

34. Bland, *Trade Revived*, 10.

35. Gauci, 'Fortrey, Samuel (1622-1682?)', DNB, 2004.

36. Gauci, 'Fortrey'.

37. Fortrey, *England's Interest*, 22–4.

38. Bland, *Trade Revived*, 16, 23, 25 and 29. The clamour over the adverse impact of customs officials and their illicit dealings regarding trade continued to grow in intensity; see for example, Anon., *For the Bill Against Clandestine Trade*; A Fair Merchant, *A Letter to a Member of Parliament*.

39. Farnell, 'The navigation act of 1651'; Wilson, *England's Apprenticeship*, 58–64; Hill, *God's Englishman*, 125–7; and Inikori, 'Slavery', 785. For a useful synthesis of the importance of the navy to the English/British state, see Rodger, 'From the "military revolution"'.

40. Morgan, 'Mercantilism', 168; Wilson, 'The economic decline', 111.

41. I. B., *The Merchants Remonstrance*, 3; Wilson, 'Cloth production', 210. For earlier migrations of Dutch and Flemish workers to Lancashire, see Attwood, 'Localization'.

42. Warren C. Scoville puts the figures slightly differently; between 4,000 and 6,000 'strangers' going to Norwich, 10,000 to London and significant pockets of Flemish, Walloon and Dutch Protestants in Sandwich, Canterbury, Southampton and several other places. See his 'Spread of techniques', 353.

43. Fisher, 'London's export trade', 154–5 and 158.

44. Bowden, 'The wool supply', 49; Allen, *The British Industrial Revolution*, 110.

45. Coleman, 'An innovation', 421.

46. Ibid.; Hudson, *The Genesis of Industrial Capital*, 63. For the limitations of kerseys see Brenner, *Merchants and Revolution*, 38.

47. Coleman, 'An innovation', 422–3.

48. Ibid., 425–9; Scoville, 'Spread of techniques', 353.

49. Cipolla, *Before the Industrial Revolution*, 239–42.

50. Wilson, 'Cloth production', 212.

51. Ibid., 213–14.

52. Brenner, *Merchants and Revolution*, 38–9.

53. Wilson, 'Cloth production', 219–20; Douglas, 'Cotton textiles', 30 and 33.

54. Sawyers, 'The navigation acts revisited'; Price, 'What did merchants do?', 270. For the Navigation Acts from the perspective of British America, see McCusker and Menard, *The Economy of British America*, 46–50.

55. Lipson, *The Economic History of England*, vol. 3, 198; Harris, *Restoration*, 95–6; and Pittar, *Customs Tariffs*, 27–30.

56. Priestley, 'Anglo-French trade', 37; Ormrod, *The Rise of Commercial Empires*, 141 and 173.

57. Anon., *At the Court at Whitehall*.

58. The Merchants trading to France, *To the Right Honourable the Lords Commissioners*, 1–3 and 6–8. This was an increasingly widespread view that was intensifying; see, for example, the long sermon on the danger of France by Petyt, *Britannia Languens*.

59. Reynel, *The True English Interest*, iv–v and 8–11. For the importance of Savary's *The Perfect Merchant or General Instructions Regarding the Mercantile Trade of France and Foreign Countries* (Paris, 1675), see Packard, 'International rivalry', 432. For an eighteenth-century review of the impact of Colbert's policies upon Britain's industrialisation, see, for example, Anon., *An Appeal to Facts*, 14–17.

60. Reynel, *The True English Interest*, 24–5 and 36–7; Trevers, *An Essay*. The clamour to start a serious linen industry was becoming more and more forceful; see, for example, Anon., *The Prevention of Poverty*, 4–5. For the extent of the illicit trade in raw wool, see Chatterton, *King's Cutters*, 24–5; Waugh, *Smuggling*, 12; and Platt, *Smuggling*, 84 and 107–12.

61. Thomas, *Mercantilism*, 115–17.

62. Scoville, 'Large-scale production'.

63. Cunningham, *The Growth of English Industry*, 458–9; Ormrod, 'English re-exports', 94–5. For commerce and status in France, see Grassby, 'Social status'.

64. Priestley, 'Anglo-French trade', 38–9; Cunningham, *The Growth of English Industry*, 458; Packard, 'International rivalry', 425; and Krey, *A Fractured Society*, 23.

65. Ashley, 'The Tory origins', 3–4.

66. N. E. Key, 'Birch, John (1615-1691)', DNB, 2004. Birch is now best remembered for introducing the Winchester Bushel Act in 1670 and attempting to standardize weights and measures; see Ashworth, *Customs and Excise*, 282.

67. Krey, 'Sir Patience Ward (1629-1696)', DNB, 2004; Zook, *Radical Whigs*, 19; Pincus, 'The making of a great power?', 539; and Harris, *Restoration*, 281–2. Although seemingly milder than the 1664 Conventicle Act, the new Act of 1670 legislated that only two JPs were needed to convict conventiclers (i.e. dissenters meeting in private to worship) and thus denying them the right of a trial – as was supposedly guaranteed by the Magna Carta.

68. Gauci, 'Thomas Papillon (1623-1702)', DNB, 2004; Papillon, *Memoirs*, 1–16; and Zook, *Radical Whigs*, 19.

69. Papillon [Robert Ferguson], *A Treatise Concerning The East India Trade*, 2. See also Petyt, *Britannia Languens*, 187–99. For Ferguson and Monmouth's *Declaration* see Pincus, *1688*, 105.

70. Roseveare, 'Sir John Houblon (1632-1712) and Sir James Houblon', DNB, 2004.

71. Stuart Handley, 'Michael Godfrey (1659-1695)', DNB, 2004.

72. Krey, 'John Dubois (1622-1684)', DNB, 2004.

73. Priestley, 'Anglo-French trade', 45–9.

74. Pitt, *Speech in the House of Commons*, 36–7.

75. Priestley, 'Anglo-French trade', 47–50; Hudson, *The Genesis of Industrial Capital*, 67.

76. Cunningham, *Growth of English Industry*, 459; Lipson, *The Economic History of England*, vol. 3, 104–5; Pincus, *England's Glorious Revolution*, 3 and 24–32; and *1688*, 160 and ch. 11.

77. Pincus, *1688*, 381 and 'Rethinking mercantilism'; Dudley, 'Party politics'. For an earlier account that also emphasizes a more dynamic mercantilism, see also Wiles, 'Mercantilism'.

78. 'House of Commons Committee Appointed to Examine into the Causes and Occasions of the Great Tumults of the Multitude', 29 January 1696, JHC, vol. 11, 682–4, on 683.

79. James, *England's Interest*, 3–4.

80. Thomas, 'The beginnings of calico-printing', 25–6.

81. The dominance of cotton textiles by India, China and other parts of the world for centuries prior to the relatively late emergence of European production is told in Beckert, *Empire of Cotton*, 3–28.

82. On the issue of wages and Indian agricultural advantage, see Parthasarathi, 'Rethinking wages', *The Transition*, 43–66 and *Why Europe Grew Rich*. On alleged high silver wages in England, see Broadberry and Gupta, 'The early modern great divergence'. Broadberry and Gupta place the emphasis upon technological innovation in cotton due to the wages in Britain being, they claim, four times higher than India – see their 'Lancashire'; Allen, *The British Industrial Revolution*; and Davis, *The Rise of the Atlantic Economies*.

83. Mun, *England's Treasure*; Thomas, *Mercantilism*, 13–15.

84. 'State of Trade: The Answer of the Commissioners to look after the Trade of England', 25 November 1696, JHC, vol. 11, 593–5.

85. 'Board of Trade and Plantations on the Woollen Manufacture', 18 January 1698, JHC, vol. 12, 425–7, on 427.

86. 'Petition of the Dyers, Setters, Callenders, Tillet-pressers, and packers of London, Norwich and Coventry', 18 May 1698, JHC, vol. 12, 274–6. An early attempt to manufacture and export dyed cloth (rather than the predominant export of unfinished white cloth) was attempted by James I in 1614 – the Cockayne Project – that banned the sale of unfinished cloth. However, the project failed and James had to revert back to the old trade; see Irwin, 'Strategic trade policy', 138.

87. Cunningham, 'The repression'.

88. The 1698 commentator is republished in Smith, *Chronicon Rusticum-Commerciale,* vol. 2, 18–22, 39–40, 157–8 and 262–5. The various woollen laws introduced by Britain between 1660 and 1800 are summarized in Sickinger, 'Regulation', 213–19.

89. Anon., *The Linnen and Woolen*, 10–11. William III and the anonymous commentator are quoted in Smith, *Chronicon Rusticum*, 29 and 312. For earlier and related sentiments, see Petyt, *Britannia Languens*, 166.

90. Ormrod, *The Rise of Commercial Empires*, 143–4, 152–4, 168–9 and 170–1; Inikori, *Africans and the Industrial Revolution*, 421–5; and Jubb, 'Economic policy', 128. For the deal with Austria, see Dickson, 'English commercial negotiations'. The various laws introduced to encourage linen in Britain between 1660 and 1800 are summarized in Sickinger, 'Regulation', 220–3.

91. Papillon [Ferguson], *A Treatise Concerning the East India Trade*, 10–11.

92. 'William and Mary, 1688: An Act for Prohibiting all Trade and Commerce with France', SOR, vol. 6: 1685–94 (1819), 98–103.

93. Ashworth, 'Manufacturing expertise'.

94. I. Robin, 'Second Memorial about Contraband Trade between France and England – Presented to the Ministry', n.d., probably 1719, CUL: Ch(H) 41/1 and 3.

95. 'William III, 1697-98: An Act for the Better Encouragement of the Royal Lustring Company and the More Effectual Preventing the Fraudulent Importation of Lustrings and Alamodes Manufacture', SOR, vol. 7: 1695–1701 (1820), 426–9.

96. 'William III, 1697-98: An Act for Increasing His Majesties Duties upon Lustrings and Alamodes', SOR, vol. 7: 1695–1701 (1820), 401; 'William III, 1697-98: An Act for the further Encouragement of the Manufacture of Lustrings and Alamodes within this Realme and for the better Preventing the Importation of the same', SOR, vol. 7: 1695–1701 (1820), 289–90. For the laws placed upon silk textiles between 1660 and 1800, see Sickinger, 'Regulation', 225–8.

97. Ormrod, *The Rise of Commercial Empires*, 91–2.

Chapter 3

1. Elliott, *Empires of the Atlantic World*, 27.

2. Swingen, 'Labor', 46–67.

3. Elliott, *Empires of the Atlantic World*, 27.

4. Beattie, *Crime and the Courts*, ch. 9; Linebaugh and Rediker, *The Many-Headed Hydra*.

5. Pincus, 'Rethinking mercantilism', 22–3.

6. Beer, *The Old Colonial System*; Hancock, *Citizens of the World* and '"A world of business to do"', 4; and Zahedieh, 'Overseas expansion'.

7. Zahedieh, *The Capital*, 4–33 and 184–5. For London's key place in Britain's industrialization, see Barnett, *London*.

8. Zahedieh, *The Capital*, 236–79.

9. Haffenden, 'The crown: part I', 299 and 305 and 'The crown: part II', 463.

10. Root, 'The lords of trade', 27–9.

11. Ibid., 30–2; B. C. Murison, 'Povey, Thomas (*b.* 1613/14, *d.* in or before 1705)', DNB, 2004. For an in-depth history of William Blathwayt, see Jacobsen, *William Blathwayt*; Murison, 'William Blathwayt's empire'.

12. Root, 'The lords of trade', 33–4; Steele, *Politics of Colonial Policy*, 9.

13. Webb, 'William Blathwayt, imperial fixer: from popish plot', 3–5; Cappon, 'The Blathwayt papers', 317–18.

14. Ibid., 5–8; Elliott, *Empires of the Atlantic World*, 155 and 164.

15. Ibid., 12–14; Pincus, *1676*.

16. Webb, 'William Blathwayt, imperial fixer: muddling through to empire', 373–8.

17. Ibid., 379–80 and 394.

18. Ibid., 398–411.

19. Lees, 'Parliament', 45 and 57–61; Steele, *Politics of Colonial Policy*, 10–14; and N. Glaisyer, 'Whiston, James (*bap* 1641?, *D.* 1706)', DNB, 2004. Davenant's proposal is reprinted in Lees's essay. Whiston was instrumental in convincing the government to change the way brandy

was taxed and rewarded with a payment of £100. For his proposal, see his *A Discourse*, 2, 5 and 9, and *The Causes*. Steele, unlike Lees, places most emphasis upon Davenant for the scheme of a new Board of Trade and Plantations, see *Politics of Colonial Policy*, 12.

20. Bland, *Trade Revived*, 45–6; Reynel, *The True English Interest*, 16; Child, *A Treatise*, 3; Cary, *An Essay*, 139–40; and Gauci, 'Thomas, Sir Dolby (c.1650-1711)', DNB, 2004.

21. Reinert, *Translating Empire*.

22. 'Answer of the Commissioners of Trade & Plantations to the Honourable the House of Commons', 22 March 1700, in A Collection of Papers Respecting Trade, Imports and Exports, Taxes etc, by Abraham Hill Esq., BL: SP 2902; Steele, *Politics of Colonial Policy*, 3 and 18. For the eventual fate of the Board of Trade and Plantations and the creation of a replacement body in the 1780s, see Lingelbach, 'The inception'. The French also created a Board of Commerce slightly later in 1700 with a number of similarities to the English board; see Smith, 'Structuring politics'.

23. L. A. Knafla, 'John Ederton, third Earl of Bridgewater (1646-1701)', DNB, 2004; Steele, *Politics of Colonial Policy*, xiv, 15 and 17.

24. T. Venning, 'Sir Philip Meadows (*bap.* 1626, *d.* 1718)', DNB, 2004; Steele, *Politics of Colonial Policy*, 20–1; and Meadows, *Observations*. For an in-depth study of the 1654 Anglo-Portuguese Trade Treaty, see Shaw, *The Anglo-Portuguese Alliance*.

25. Maddison, 'Abraham Hill', 173–6; L. Mulligan, 'Abraham Hill (*bap.* 1635, *d.* 1722)', DNB, 2004.

26. Colbin, *The Unseen Hand*, 142.

27. G. F. R. Barker revised by T. Doyle, 'John Methuen (1650-1706)', DNB, 2004.

28. Barker with Doyle, 'John Methuen'; Cunningham, *The Growth of English Industry*, 459–61; Hewins, *English Trade*, 129–33; Shaw, *The Anglo-Portuguese Alliance*, 98; and Nye, *War, Wine, and Taxes*, 46–55.

29. R. Grassby, 'Pollexfen, John (1636-1715)', DNB, 2004.

30. Ibid.; Steele, *Politics of Colonial Policy*, 22.

31. Robbins, 'Absolute liberty'; Laslett, 'John Locke', 390–1; and Zook, *Radical Whigs*, 100.

32. Arneil, 'Trade, plantations, and property', 591–3. For the profound impact of the first Earl of Shaftesbury and his circle – such as Benjamin Worsley and Henry Slingsby – on Locke, see Laslett, 'Introduction', in Locke, *Two Treatises of Government*, 25–37.

33. Arneil, 'Trade, plantations, and property', 595–601.

34. Arneil, 'Trade, plantations, and property', 602–9. The fate of English labour during this period, as well as local ethnic populations and African slaves, in the Americas is told in Linebaugh and Rediker, *The Many-Headed Hydra*.

35. Ferguson, 'The measurement', 96–7.

36. L. Frey and M. Frey, 'Stepney, George (1663-1707)', DNB, 2004.

37. Stepney, *Essay*.

38. Greaves, 'Grey, Ford, earl of Tankerville (*bap.* 1655, *d.* 1701)', DNB, 2004; Laslett, 'Introduction', in Locke, *Two Treatises of Government*, 24; and Zook, *Radical Whigs*, 37. For the argument that Locke was involved in the Rye House Plot, see Ashcraft, *Revolutionary Parties*, and for the view he was not, see Milton, 'John Locke'. For Grey's accused involvement in the plot, see Zook, *Radical Whigs*, 103–5.

39. See, for example, Anon., *News*, 1–2.

40. Greaves, 'Grey'; Zook, *Radical Whigs*, 141. Many of those involved in the planned revolts of late 1682 and early 1683, especially those associated with in the Rye House Plot, subsequently ended up joining the doomed Monmouth and Argyll rebellions of 1685; see Harris, *Restoration*, 200 and 309–23 and his *Revolution*, 73–100.

41. Scott, *England's Troubles*, 192, 371 and 399.

42. Scott, *Algernon Sidney*, 214–16.

43. Krey, 'Political radicalism', 594, 602–3 and 606 and *A Fractured Society*, 61 and 70–3. For an older but very useful account of the early to mid-1690s, see Kenyon, 'The earl of Sunderland'.

44. Richard L. Greaves, 'Grey, Thomas, second earl of Stamford (1653/4-1720)', DNB, 2004; Pincus, *1688*, 234.

45. Greaves, 'Grey'.

46. P. Woodfine, 'Sutton, Robert, second Baron Lexington (1661-1723)', DNB, 2004.

47. 'Board of Trade and Plantation's to the King's most Excellent Majesty', 23 December 1697, in A Collection of Papers Respecting Trade, Imports and Exports, Taxes etc., by Abraham Hill Esq., BL: SP 2902.

48. Landes, *The Unbound Prometheus*, 32; Leng, 'Epistemology'. For the migration of slave plantation bookkeeping to British cotton factory labour bookkeeping, see Beckert, *Empire of Cotton*, 61. For the historical importance, in general, of accounting to a nation's success, see Soll, *The Reckoning*.

49. For examples and debates concerning the history of quantification, see, especially, Frangsmyr, Heilbron and Rider (eds), *The Quantifying Spirit* and Porter, *Trust*.

50. 'Board of Trade and Plantation's to the King's most Excellent Majesty'. A similar survey, without the figures, was earlier provided by Cary in his *An Essay* and almost in conjunction with the board's report, one of its members, John Pollexfen, published *A Discourse of Trade*, 84–110. For Baltic iron, see the excellent account given by Evans and Rydén, *Baltic Iron*.

51. Ibid. See also Pollexfen, *Discourse of Trade*, 84–90.

52. Ibid.; Pollexfen, *Discourse of Trade*, 92–6.

53. Ibid.

54. Morgan, 'Cary, John (b. 1649 and d. 1719 or 22)', DNB, 2004 and, especially, Reinert, *Translating Empire*, 73–128.

55. Reinert, *Translating Empire*, 6, and 81–3.

56. Cary, *An Essay*, 129 and 131.

57. 'Board of Trade and Plantation's to the King's most Excellent Majesty'.

58. Stein and Stein, *The Colonial Heritage*, 7–9.

59. Beckert, *Empire of Cotton*, 36.

60. 'Board of Trade and Plantation's to the King's most Excellent Majesty'; Pollexfen, *Discourse of Trade*, 86–7.

61. Cary, *An Essay*, 74–7 and 84. Here Cary and the board were joined by a number of petitions; see, for example, Anon., *Some Considerations*.

62. For the origins of Atlantic slavery in Spanish and Portuguese South America, see Blackburn, 'The old world'.

63. Nettels, 'England', 1–2; Stein and Stein, *Silver, Trade, and War*, 107–8; and Elliott, *Empires*, 100. Extensive details of the Treaty of Peace can be found in McLachlan, 'Documents', 304–8. The actual term 'Assiento' is one of 'Spanish public law that designates every contract

made for the purpose of public utility, for the administration of a public service, between the Spanish Government and private individuals. The administration of a tax, an enterprise of colonization, of public works, of recruiting the militia, of providing manual labour or materials was done by the *Assiento*'; see Scelle, 'The slave-trade', 614–15. A useful account of the Assiento is also given in Beltran, 'The slave trade'.

64. Nettels, 'England', 4–5.

65. The impact of pirates in the Caribbean is discussed in Fryman, 'Pirates and smugglers'.

66. Nettels, 'England', 6–8 and 13–15; Zook, 'The royal adventurers', 209; Stein and Stein, *Silver, Trade, and War*, vii and for the massive illicit transfer of silver to Western Europe, 23–6; Martin, 'Power, cloth and currency'; and Makepeace, 'English traders', 237–40 and 250. Makepeace shows the global and diverse array of goods traded by the English along the Guinea coast and the continued need for African bullion in the Asian trade. In 1675 African stock was owned by 194 mainly London based investors. A great blow came to the company when Clifford, Shaftesbury, Arlington and Buckingham withdrew their investment due to the exclusion crisis; see Davies, 'Joint-stock investment', 298.

67. Manning, 'Asia and Europe', 420; Wong, 'The search for European differences', 463. For a detailed examination of silver and Asia in the global economy, see Frank, *ReOrient*, ch. 3 and 277–83.

68. Inikori, *Africans and the Industrial Revolution*, 203–4 and 266.

69. Nettels, 'England', 16–17; Inikori, 'Slave trade', 787. For the Company of Royal Adventurers and background to the supply of slaves, planters and the Spanish colonies, see Zook, 'The royal adventurers'. For an examination of the company's constitution, problems and system of management, see Carlos, 'Principal-agent problems'; Carlos and Nicholas, 'Theory and history'; and Carlos, Key and Dupree, 'Learning'.

70. Pettigrew, 'Free to enslave'.

71. Sir John Trenchard is quoted in Nettels, 'England', 17; Stein and Stein, *Silver, Trade, and War*, 36–9; and Inikori, *Africans and the Industrial Revolution*, 204.

72. Ames, 'Colbert's Indian ocean strategy', 539–42.

73. Ibid., 550–7.

74. Pollexfen, *Discourse of Trade*, 163; The Board of Trade and Plantations, 'Report on the Trade of the Kingdom as well as the defence of the Plantations', 29 November 1707, HL: HM 821.

75. Scelle, 'The slave-trade', 618 and 626–8; Beltran, 'The slave trade', 423; and Stein and Stein, *Silver, Trade, and War*, 7. The importance of the Spanish empire in Britain's economic ambitions during the eighteenth century has recently been underlined by John J. McCusker in his 'Special section'.

76. Nettels, 'England', 18–19 and 32; Scelle, 'The slave-trade', 644–5; and Stein and Stein, *The Colonial Heritage*, 10–11 and *Silver, Trade, and War*, 121.

77. Blackburn, *The Making of New World Slavery*, 97 and 102.

78. See, for example, Mintz, *Sweetness and Power*; Beckert, *Empire of Cotton*, 61.

79. Stein and Stein, *The Colonial Heritage*, 21–3.

80. Stein and Stein, *The Colonial Heritage*, 24 and 40–2 and *Silver, Trade, and War*, 131. For the importance of trade with Portugal see, for example, Davis, 'English foreign trade'; Fisher, 'Anglo-Portuguese trade'.

81. Scelle, 'The slave-trade', 644 and 653; Stein and Stein, *The Colonial Heritage*, 86–7 and 92–3 and *Silver, Trade, and War*, 137–44; and Beltran, 'The slave trade', 429.

82. Scelle, 'The Slave-Trade', 656.

83. Blackburn, *The Making of New World Slavery*, 219 and 229; Inikori, *Africans and the Industrial Revolution*, 208. For an in-depth look at England's involvement in sugar and the Caribbean during this period, see, especially, Dunn, *Sugar and Slaves*.

84. Mintz, *Sweetness and Power*, 47.

85. Blackburn, *The Making of New World Slavery*, 260 and 268.

86. See especially Blackburn, *The Making of New World Slavery*; Inikori, *Africans and the Industrial Revolution*; and Solow, 'Introduction'. For the array of goods absent from most consumer histories that were exported specifically to plantations, see Evans, 'The plantation hoe'.

87. Esteban, 'The rising share', 898; Eltis and Engerman, 'The importance of slavery', 141; and Engerman and O'Brien, 'Exports'. For a synthesis of competing views, see Morgan, *Slavery*, 44–8 and 53–4.

88. 'Board of Trade and Plantation's to the King's most Excellent Majesty'. The attempt to nurture naval substitutes had long occupied England; see, for example, Robinson, *England's Safety*, 20.

89. Ibid. The idea and attmpts to use the plantations for such items came up regularly throughout the eighteenth century. For a later example, see Board of Trade and Plantations, *Representation from the Commissioners for Trade and Plantations*.

90. Ibid.

91. Ibid. For the establishment of the Riding Officers, see Ashworth, *Customs and Excise*, 169–70. The contemporary literature on raw wool smuggling and its adverse impact upon England's economy is vast, but for a useful summary, see Carter, *An Abstract of the Proceedings*. Further details can be found in Chatterton, *King's Cutters*, 20–5; Waugh, *Smuggling*, 12–13; and Platt, *Smuggling*, 107–25.

92. Ibid.; Pollexfen, *Discourse of Trade*, 89; and Tryon, *England's Grandeur*, 4–5.

93. Cary, *An Essay*, 92–109.

94. 'Board of Trade and Plantation's to the King's most Excellent Majesty'; Cunningham, 'The repression'; and O'Brien, *The Economic History of Ireland*, 185.

95. Ibid.

96. Page (ed.), *A History of the County of Middlesex*, vol. 2, 132–7.

97. 'Board of Trade and Plantation's to the King's most Excellent Majesty'.

98. Ibid.

99. 'Answer of the Commissioners of Trade & Plantations to the Honourable the House of Commons', 22 March 1700, in A Collection of Papers Respecting Trade, Imports and Exports, Taxes etc., by Abraham Hill Esq., BL: SP 2902. An act had already been introduced in 1695 to encourage linen production in Ireland; see 'William III, 1695-96: An Act for Encouraging the Linen Manufacture of Ireland and bringing Flax and Hemp into and the Making of Sail Cloth in this Kingdome', SOR, vol. 1: 1695–1701, 156.

100. A. Gordon, 'Crommelin, (Samuel-) Louis (1652-1727)', rev. L. A. Clarkson, DNB, 2004.

101. Gordon, 'Crommelin'; 'Answer of the Commissioners of Trade'; and Scoville, 'The Huguenots I', 308–9. Another Huguenot was also important in introducing a successful silk industry to Dublin; see Scoville, 'The Huguenots II', 310; Longfield, 'History of the Irish linen'.

102. 'Answer of the Commissioners of Trade'.

103. Ibid.

104. Ibid.

Notes

Chapter 4

1. Blanch, *The Interest*, 53.

2. Goose, 'Immigrants', 4–6 and 16–21; Cipolla, *Before the Industrial Revolution*, 262.

3. Fortrey, *England's Interest*, 11; 'Charles II, 1663: An Act for Encouraging the Manufactures of Making Linen Cloath and Tapistry', SOR, vol. 5: 1628–80, 498. The controversial contemporary issue of immigration is explored in Luu, 'Natural-born'.

4. Wilson, 'The Anglo-Dutch establishment', 11–32; Ormrod, *The Rise of Commercial Empires*, 96–7; and Scoville, 'The Huguenots II', 404.

5. Schomberg, *Historical and Political Remarks*; Bosher, 'Huguenot merchants', 77–8, 88–9, 93 and 98–100; and Wilson, 'New introduction', xv.

6. The Spanish attempts were, perhaps, overly ambitious in the construction of large mills vertically integrated while, in contrast, the emphasis for much of the century in Britain was on the putting-out process. Skills were one thing, but getting an appropriate production system and export markets were another. See Force, 'Royal textile', 346–56 and 361. For institutional differences – from transport and lack of market integration to contractual law and taxation – see Grafe, *Distant Tyranny*.

7. Statt, 'The city of London', 45–9 and 'Daniel Defoe'.

8. Anon., *A Discourse of the Necessity*, 27.

9. Statt, 'The city of London', 50–3 and 'Daniel Defoe', 299–313; Luu, 'Natural-born', 72; Cunningham, *Alien Immigrants*, 249–53; Dickinson, 'The Poor Palatines'; and Steele, *Politics of Colonial Policy*, 116–17. For a useful list of the fleeing Palatines to England in 1709, including their occupations, see Tribbeko and Ruperti, *Lists of Germans*.

10. Gauci, *The Politics of Trade*, 38–42 and 67; Krey, *A Fractured Society*, 19–22. This is also underlined in the earlier work of William Cunningham; see especially his *Alien Immigrants*.

11. Wilson, 'The Anglo-Dutch establishment', 11–12 and 20. See also S. D. Chapman, *Merchant Enterprise*, for the continued importance of foreigners in the City of London in a later period.

12. Scoville, 'The Huguenots I'; Cunningham, *Alien Immigrants*, 235. For subsequent developments, see Rothstein, 'Huguenots in the English silk industry'.

13. Ibid., 300–1.

14. 'Foreigne Lustrings and Clandestine Trade: Petition of the Royal Lustring Company', 20 April 1698, JHC, 239–41.

15. Williams, *Contraband Cargoes*, 87–8.

16. Scoville, 'The Huguenots I', 301.

17. Dupin, *Proposals of Nicholas Dupin*, 3.

18. Scoville, 'The Huguenots I', 302.

19. Ibid., 302–3; Cunningham, *Alien Immigrantsin*, 242; Shorter, *Studies on the History of Papermaking*, 203; and Pollard, 'White paper-making'; Hazen, 'Eustace Barnaby's manufacture'.

20. Barker, *The Glassmakers*, 3–4.

21. Goose, 'Immigrants', 143–4.

22. Grew, *Meanes of a Most Ample Encrease*, 56–60, HL: HM 1264. Since I viewed the original manuscript, this has been published in an edited volume by Julian Hoppit, *Nehemiah Grew*. For Grew's biography, see Michael Hunter, 'Grew, Nehemiah (bap. 1641, d. 1712)', DNB, 2004.

23. Cunningham, *Alien Immigrants*, 243. The two French officials are quoted in Scoville, 'The Huguenots I', 306.

24. Grew, *Meanes of a Most Ample Encrease*, 74–88.

25. Walpole, *King's Speech*.

26. *The Case of the British and Irish Manufacture of Linens, Threads and Tapes*, 297.

27. Pollexfen, *A Discourse of Trade*, 99.

28. Petyt, *Britannia Languens*, 126–38.

29. Cary, *An Essay*, 52. For later attacks upon the detrimental impact of the East India trade, see, for example, Anon., *An English Winding Sheet*; Anon., *A Short Abstract of a Case*.

30. Blanch, *The Naked Truth*, 53–60.

31. John Pollexfen and Daniel Sheldon are quoted in Cherry, *Early English Liberalism*, 284–5.

32. Coleman, 'Introduction', 4–5; Wilson, 'The other face', 120–1 and 128–9; Morgan, 'Mercantilism', 176; and Inikori, *Africans and the Industrial Revolution*, 206. It is also the case 'that Europe offered nothing to Africa that Africa did not already produce' during this period; see Thornton, *Africa and Africans*, 44.

33. Harley, 'Trade', 179. For an estimate of the size of world bullion flows during this period, see Barrett, 'World bullion flows'.

34. Brenner, *Merchants and Revolution*, 43–9. For the arrival and impact of such new exotics, see, for example, Mintz, *Sweetness and Power* and, more generally, Walvin, *Fruits of Empire*.

35. Krey, *A Fractured Society*, 24–9; Lawson, *The East India Company*, 55–6; and Pincus, *1688*, 188. In 1691 Child owned £51,150 of stock, Sir Thomas Cooke £40,850, Sir James Edwards, deceased, £15,500, Sir Joseph Hearne £12,938 6s. 8d., Richard Hutchinson senior £13,950, Sir John Moore £25,009 10s. and Sir Jeremy Sambrooke £17,750; see Davies, 'Joint-stock investment', 297.

36. Davenant, *An Essay*, 6 and 10.

37. Anon., *The Petition and Case of the Embroiderers*. For perceived female weakness, cotton textiles and fashion during this period, see Smith, ' "Calico Madams" '.

38. Brisco, *Economic Policy*, 129–31.

39. Davenant, *An Essay*, 12, 15, 20–1 and 28.

40. There is not much on Ferguson since his switch from radical Whig to Jacobite consigned him to the footnotes of subsequent Whig historiography. For a recent attempt to resurrect his significance and work, see Zook, *Radical Whigs*, 87–113 and 'Turncoats', 365.

41. Ferguson, *The East-India-Trade*, 2 and 6–8. It should also be noted that Ferguson was implicated in a possible assassination plot of the king led by the first Earl of Shaftesbury; see Milton, 'John Locke', 654–5. Indeed, Ferguson was implicated with just about every plot from the Exclusion Crisis to the Jacobite Rising of 1715; see Zook, 'Turncoats', 363–64. Playing the naval card was a popular argument during this period; see, for example, Anon., *The Mischief of the Five Shillings Tax*, 4 and 19.

42. Ferguson, *The East-India-Trade*, 9–10 and 12.

43. Richard Grassby, 'Child, Sir Josiah, first baronet (*bap.* 1631, *d.* 1699)', DNB, 2004; Lawson, *The East India Company*, 51; and Keay, *The Honourable Company*, 174–5.

44. Child, *A Treatise on the East-India Trade*, 4–7 and 25–7. Child went on to focus even more intensely on the role of the East India Company to England's naval power; see *A Supplement to a former Treatise, concerning the East-India Trade*. The view of bullion as simply a

commodity like any other was fairly widespread. For example, James Houblon had made this explicit in the examination of a committee of the commons set up to consider ways to prevent the draining of England's bullion; see Cherry, *Early English Liberalism*, 286.

45. Martyn, *Considerations upon the East-India Trade*, 36–40, 55–8 and 69–73.

46. T. S., *England's Danger*, 1–5. Tammet's were a worsted in which the yarn had been 'shrunk and smoothed by scouring' and then woven; see Kerridge, *Textile Manufactures*, 53.

47. Pollexfen, *Discourse of Trade*, 6–8.

48. Ormrod, 'English re-exports', 104.

49. Thomas, *Mercantilism*, 52 and 59–60.

50. Pollexfen, *Discourse of Trade*, 43, 105 and 125. The Board of Trade were more successful in their critique of the Royal African Company; see Pettigrew, 'Free to enslave'.

51. Thomas, *Mercantilism*, 79–80 and Martyn is quoted in Thomas, *Mercantilism*, 90. For Martyn's 'volte-face' to protectionism in his writings for *The British Merchant* in 1713, see MacLeod, 'Henry Martin'.

52. Pollexfen, *England and East-India*, 6, 8, 14 and 18–19. See also Anon., *An Answer to the Most Material Objections*, 1.

53. Pollexfen, *England and East-India*, 25; Anon., *An Answer to the Most Material Objections*, 3.

54. N. C., *The Great Necessity*, 5–8.

55. T. S., *Reasons Humbly Offered*, 34–5. For an English translation of the 1686 edict and the subsequent immigration of French printers to England, see W. C., *An Alarum to England*, 35–7.

56. Douglas, 'Cotton textiles', 35; Lipson, *The Economic History of England*, vol. 3, 41–2; Wilson, 'Treasure and trade balances', 152; Inikori, *Africans and the Industrial Revolution*, 431–3; Jubb, 'Economic policy', 124; Berg, 'From imitation to invention' and *Luxury and Pleasure*; and Parthasarathi, *Why Europe Grew Rich*, chs 4–6.

57. Griffiths, 'Sherwin, William (b. 1645, d. in or after 1709)', DNB, 2004; Thomas, *Mercantilism*, 209–10; and Wadsworth and Mann, *The Cotton Trade*, 130. Mezzotinting was a process of engraving that allowed producers to print tones either light or shaded upon textiles and derived from a technique of engraving copper by Ludwig von Sieger of Utrecht.

58. Thomas, *Mercantilism*, 210.

59. Parthasarathi, *Why Europe Grew Rich* and Riello, *Cotton*.

60. *Stuff Weaver's Case*; The Board of Trade and Plantations, 'Report on the Trade of the Kingdom'.

61. The Board of Trade and Plantations is quoted in Thomas, *Mercantilism*, 122.

62. Haynes, *A View of the Present State*, 10–11, 19, 25–7, 62, 68 and 81–93 and Blanch, *The Interest of Great Britain*, 13 and 20–1.

63. The Board of Trade and Plantations, 'Report on the Trade of the Kingdom'. This reinforces John Styles's recent emphasis upon the far more pervasive reach of the new textiles among the lower ranks; see his *The Dress of the People*.

64. Frendenberger, 'Fashion', 41–3.

65. Parthasarathi, *Why Europe Grew Rich*, 133; Riello, *Cotton*, 124–5. See also Longfield, 'History of the Irish linen', 27.

66. A Merchant, *The Weavers Pretences*, 419–20.

67. Anon., *A Brief State of the Question*, 23.

68. Asgill, *A Brief Answer*, 7–9; The Silk Manufactures, *The Produce of India*. As we have seen, the attempt to make the colonies staple suppliers of raw materials for British manufactures was a central colonial policy. For an articulate exponent of this objective, see the work of the former writer for the *British Merchant*, Joshua Gee, and his widely-read *The Trade and Navigation*.

69. Asgill, *A Brief Answer*, 12–13 and 20–1.

70. Rey, *Observations on Mr Asgill's Brief Answer*, 9; *The Weavers True Case*, 14. Interestingly, a few years later Rey wrote another pamphlet blaming the woes of the domestic silk industry upon smuggling and the adulteration of silks; see his *A Scheme to Settle*.

71. Wadsworth and Mann, *The Cotton Trade*, 125.

72. Dowell, *A History of Taxation*, vol. 4, 332; Wadsworth and Mann, *The Cotton Trade*, 134–41 and 154.

73. Lipson, *The Economic History of England*, vol. 3, 44.

74. Thomas, 'The beginnings of calico-printing', 215–16.

75. Wadsworth and Mann, *The Cotton Trade*, 144; Rostow, *How it All Began*, 64.

Chapter 5

1. Dowell, *A History of Taxation*, vol. 4, 282.

2. Dickson, *The Financial Revolution*.

3. Ashworth, *Customs and Excise*, part 5 and 'The intersection of industry'. For smuggling during this period, see, for example, Smith, *Something to Declare*; Platt, *Smuggling*; Chatterton, *King's Cutters and Smugglers*.

4. Dickinson, *Walpole*, 94–5.

5. O'Brien, 'The political economy', 9; Beckett, 'Land tax or excise', 306.

6. Stasavage, *Public Debt*, 77; Fine, 'Production and Excise', 162. Walpole's attempts to win over landowners and his dislike of the land tax is succinctly described in Brisco, *The Economic Policy*, 84–9, while the attempt to introduce the excise on tobacco and wine is extensively discussed in Langford, *The Excise Crisis* and Ashworth, *Customs and Excise*, ch. 4. For an overview of debates that informed the rate of interest during this period, see, for example, Keirn and Melton, 'Thomas Manley' and McNally, *Political Economy*, 18, 30–3, and 55–60.

7. North and Weingast, 'The evolution of institutions'; North, *Institutions*.

8. Child, *A Discourse*, 18; 'Board of Trade and Plantation's to the King's most Excellent Majesty', 1697, in A Collection of Papers Respecting Trade, Imports and Exports, Taxes etc., by Abraham Hill Esq., BL: SP 2902; Davenant, 'A memorial concerning credit', 73.

9. Fine, 'Production and the Excise', 129–32. The great fear of a 'general excise' may not have been realized, but the reality was not far off. For an early articulation of this fear, see, for example, Anon., *The General-Excise Consider'd*.

10. Brewer, *The Sinews of Power*, 67.

11. Davenant, *A Second Report*.

12. Anon., *Torism and Trade*, 12.

13. Anon., *An Account of the Woolen Manufactures*.

14. Lipson, *The Economic History of England*, vol. 3, 106.

15. Carswell, *The South Sea Bubble*, 39.

16. Pincus, 'Rethinking mercantilism', 25–6.

17. Gibbs, 'Boyer, Abel (1667?-1729?)', DNB, 2004.

18. Boyer, *An Account of the State*, 31–2.

19. Extracts from these forty-six petitions can be found in Anon., *The Two Treaties between Great Britain and France*, 10–13.

20. Gauci, *The Politics of Trade*, 240–7; Dudley, 'Party politics', 1091–6.

21. Hewins, *English Trade*, 137–8.

22. Miquelon, 'Envisioning the French empire'.

23. Gauci, *The Politics of Trade*, 247–9, 256, 262 and 268; Hewins, *English Trade and Finance*, xxx, xxxiv and 139–41. For the political reasons underpinning Martyn's changed stance in *The British Merchant* compared to his free-trade analysis in *Considerations upon the East India Trade* of 1701, see MacLeod, 'Henry Martin', 225–6.

24. Thompson, 'Moore, Arthur (d. 1730)', DNB, 2004.

25. King (ed.), *The British Merchant*, vol. 1, 4 and vol. 2, 229–30; Anon., *The State of the Silk and Woolen Manufactures*; and Defoe (ed.), *Extracts from Several Mercators*, 12.

26. King (ed.), *The British Merchant*, vol. 1, 6 and vol. 2, 231–4. See also Anon., *The Consequences of a Law*, 6 and 14.

27. Ibid., 15 and 141–9.

28. Ibid., 143–9 and 176–7.

29. The original document was reproduced in King (ed.), *The British Merchant*, vol. 1, 181.

30. King (ed.), *The British Merchant*, vol. 1, 155–62 and 183 and vol. 2, 29–34 and 61–5.

31. Defoe (ed.), *Extracts from Several Mercators,* 16.

32. King (ed.), *The British Merchant*, vol. 1, 185–99, 215–30, 253, and 280, and vol. 2, 76–87, 99–102, 122–4 and 155–6; Defoe (ed.), *Extracts from Several Mercators*, 14–19. For the importance of Portugal, see King (ed.), *The British Merchant*, vol. 3, 1–78.

33. King (ed.), *The British Merchant*, vol. 1, 300 and 342–3, and vol. 2, 129 and 194–5.

34. Coleman, 'Politics and economics', 190–1 and 205–6; Krey, *A Fractured Society*, 245; and Price, *Overseas Trade*. For the French objectives of the treaty, see Miquelon, 'Envisioning the French empire'.

35. Davis, 'The rise of protection', 312; Hayton, 'Hanmer, Sir Thomas, fourth baronet (1677-1746)', DNB, 2004.

36. Groenewegan, 'Gee, Joshua (1667-1730)', DNB.

37. Langford, *The Excise Crisis*; Ashworth, *Customs and Excise*, ch. 4.

38. O'Brien, 'The political economy', 14 and 27; Davis, 'The rise of protection', 307; and Brisco, *The Economic Policy of Robert Walpole*, 166–87.

39. Ashworth, *Customs and Excise*, 207–315; Bosher, *The Single Duty Project*, 95.

40. Defoe, *Taxes No Charge*, 9, 12 and 25.

41. Turnbull, 'Coal and regional growth'; Maw, Wyke, and Kidd, 'Canals, rivers, and the industrial city'.

42. Calvert, *Salt in Cheshire*; Newbury, 'The history of the common salt industry'; and Gittins, 'Innovations in textile bleaching' and 'Salt, salt making, and the rise of Cheshire'.

43. Hudson (ed.), *Regions and Industries*; Hudson, *The Industrial Revolution*, 101–32.

44. Price, 'The imperial economy', 88 and 99; Inikori, *Africans and the Industrial Revolution*, 39 and 54–88; and Zahedieh, *The Capital,* 279–85.

45. Inikori, *Africans and the Industrial Revolution*, 192–93 and 208.

46. Humphries, 'Enclosures, common rights, and women' and *Childhood and Child Labour*; Berg and Hudson, 'Rehabilitating the industrial revolution'; Berg, 'What difference did women's work make'; and Sharpe, *Adapting to Capitalism*.

47. Inikori, *Africans and the Industrial Revolution*, 211–12; Berg, *Luxury and Pleasure*, 144.

48. Ibid., 407–16; Hudson, *The Industrial Revolution*, 32–3.

49. Ibid., 368–74.

50. Beckett and Turner, 'Taxation and economic growth', 397 and 401–2; Crafts, *British Economic Growth*.

51. Paine, *The Rights of Man, Part II*, 182.

Chapter 6

1. Minard, 'Facing uncertainty', 284; Horn, *The Path Not Taken*; Parker, 'Two administrative bureaus'; and Potofsky, 'The construction of Paris'.

2. See, for example, Sonenscher on the Hatters in *The Hatters of Eighteenth-Century*.

3. Root, *The Fountain of Privilege*, xiii and 9–18; Potofsky, 'The construction of Paris'.

4. Smith, 'Learning politics' and 'Structuring politics'; Parker, *An Administrative Bureau*; and Gillispie, *Science and Polity*.

5. Jones, *The Great Nation*; Horn, *The Path Not Taken*; and Minard, 'Facing uncertainty'.

6. Minard, 'Facing uncertainty'.

7. Ashworth, 'The intersection of industry' and 'Manufacturing expertise'.

8. Brewer, *The Sinews of Power*; Ashworth, *Customs and Excise*, 117–20.

9. For an array of other comparative histories documenting the rise of quantification during the eighteenth century, see, for example, Frangsmyr, Heilbron and Rider (eds), *The Quantifying Spirit*.

10. I. Robin, 'Second Memorial about Contraband Trade between France and England – Presented to the Ministry', 1719, Cholmondley Houghton Papers 41/1 and 3, Cambridge University Library. The battle between manufacturing fraud and the excise is told in Ashworth, *Customs and Excise*, 209–57.

11. This is not to generalize across all trades since there were regional differences and diverse product-types with different needs preventing an industry to lobby as one.

12. Parker, *An Administrative Bureau*, 13; Bosher, 'Current writing'; and Jones, *The Great Nation*.

13. Bosher, *French Finances*.

14. Behrens, *Society*, 68–78.

15. Minard, 'Colbertism continued?', 478–9.

16. Smith, 'Structuring politics', 501–2 and 511–17.

17. Minard, 'Colbertism continued?', 479–80; Minard, 'Trade without institution?', 84.

18. Ibid., 480.

19. Ibid., 481 and 483–4. See also Parker, *An Administrative Bureau*, 18–19.

20. Porter, *Trust in Numbers*, xi.

21. Leadbetter, *The Royal Gauger*, 179.

22. Ibid., 180–1. For the hydrometer and the excise, see Ashworth, "'Between the trader and the public'".

23. Anon., *Instructions to be Observed by the Officers of Excise*, 13.

24. Huie, *An Abridgement*, 21.

25. Anon., *Instructions for Officers Who Survey Printers of Callicoe*, 5–7.

26. Locke, *A New Abstract of the Excise Statutes*, 42–3.

27. Mackay, *An Abridgement of the Excise-Laws*, 42–3. See also Highmore, *A Practical Arrangement*, 45–50.

28. Highmore, *A Practical Arrangement*, 146–9.

29. 'Petition of George Blackman', 1801, NA: CUST: 48/33. For paper production and the Excise see Jarvis, 'The papermakers'; Rosenband, 'Making the fair trader'.

30. Highmore, *A Practical Arrangement*, 146–9 and 246–9; Locke, *A New Abstract*, 181–7. The best overview of soap and the excise is Gittins, 'Soapmaking'.

31. Fine, 'Production and Excise', 234, 241 and 248.

Chapter 7

1. It is precisely from the 1760s that Alexander Hamilton detected a rapid increase in British manufacturers committing tax evasion and the level of penalties greatly increasing; see his *An Enquiry into the Principles of Taxation*.

2. Coleman, *British Paper Industry*, 141–2.

3. Fine, 'Production and Excise', 185–6.

4. Ibid., 224–5 and 204.

5. Dowell, *A History of Taxation*, vol. 4, 318–19.

6. Barker, *The Glassmakers*, 1–2.

7. Ibid., 4–5; A. Thrash, 'Mansell, Sir Robert (1570/71-1652)', DNB, 2004.

8. Turnbull, 'Canals, coal and regional growth', and Maw, Wyke, and Kidd, 'Canals, rivers, and the industrial city'.

9. 'Committee Appointed to Consider the Act for Duties on Glassware, Stone and Earthen Bottles, Coal, and Culm', 24 January 1695 and 'Committee to Whom the Several Petitions of the Glass-makers were Referred', 17 February 1696, JHC.

10. John Cary is quoted in Dowell, *A History of Taxation*, vol. 4, 297.

11. Anon., *The Case of the Poor Work-men Glass-makers*; Anon., *An Account of the Produce of the Glass Duty*; and Anon, *The Miserable Case of the Poor Glass-Makers*.

12. Anon., *The Allegations of the Glass-Makers*.

13. 'William III, 1697-98: An Act for Taking away Half the Duties imposed on Glass, Wares and Tobacco Pipes and for Granting (in lieu thereof) new Duties upon Whole, Fine and Scotch linen. [Chapter XLV. Rot. Parl. 9 Gul. III. p. 7. n. 5]', SOR: Volume 7: 1695–1701, 447–8.

14. 'Committee to Whom the Several Petitions of the Glass-makers were Referred', 1 April 1698, JHC; 'William III, 1698: An Act for Taking off the remaining Duties upon Glass and Wares. [Chapter XXIV. Rot. Parl. 10 Gul. III. p. 4. n. 9.]', SOR: Volume 7: 1695–1701, 533–4.

15. *The Case of the Glass-Makers*; Jarvis, 'The papermakers', 114.

16. *Instructions to be Observed by the Officers concerned in Ascertaining the Duties on Glass*, 5–10.

17. Ibid., 16–17.

18. Ibid., 27–9.

19. 'Glass Makers Memorial', April 1760, NA: CUST 48/16.

20. 'Memorial of the Flint Glass Makers within the City of London and Bills of Mortality, and of Stourbridge in the County of Worcester, on behalf of themselves and several other makers of Flint glass in England', 3 June 1766, NA: CUST 42/17.

21. 'Memorial of the Flint Glass Makers'.

22. Barker, *The Glassmakers*, 8–15 and 123.

23. 'Committee to Whom the Petition of Charles Fitzroy and twelve others was Referred', 24 February 1773 and 'House of Commons Committee of the Whole House to Consider of the Report which was made from the Committee to Whom the Petition of the Honourable Charles Fitzroy … Was referred', 2 March 1773, JHC.

24. Barker, *The Glassmakers*, 15–16.

25. Powell, *Glass-Making in England*, 123.

26. Dowell, *A History of Taxation*, vol. 4, 298.

27. 'Memorial of the Governor and Company of British Cast Plate Glass Manufacturers', November/December 1778, NA: CUST 48/19.

28. Excise to Treasury, 12 February 1779, NA: CUST 48/19. Protest also arose from glass bottle manufacturers; see 'Memorial of the Proprietors of the Glass Bottle Manufacturers in and near the City of Bristol', June 1778, NA: CUST 48/19.

29. 'Memorial of the Governor and Company of the British Cast Plate Glass Manufacturers', August 1782, NA: CUST 48/20.

30. Excise to Treasury, 1 April 1783, NA: CUST 48/21.

31. 'House of Commons Committee to whom the Petition of the Governor and Company of British Cast Plate Glass Manufacturers was Referred', 18 June 1784 and 'House of Commons Committee of the Whole House to Whom it Was Referred to Consider of … the Petition of the Governor and Company of British Plate Glass Manufacturers', 28 April 1785, JHC.

32. Treasury to Excise, 27 May 1785; Excise to Treasury 2 June 1785, NA: CUST 48/22.

33. Ibid., 9 June 1785, NA: CUST 48/22.

34. Excise to Treasury, 9 June 1785; Treasury to Excise, 17 June 1785; Excise to Treasury, 21 June 1785; Excise to Treasury, 23 June 1785; and Excise to Treasury, 26 June 1785, NA: CUST 48/22.

35. Treasury to Excise, 26 October 1785, NA: CUST 48/22; Excise to Treasury, 3 March 1786, CUST 48/22. Bartholemew Sikes was the same experienced excise officer who represented the Excise in an important trial over the credibility of the hydrometer used to measure spirit density. He subsequently developed a new hydrometer that was used by the Excise into the late twentieth century; see Ashworth, '"Between the trader and the public"'.

36. Excise to Treasury, 4 January 1787, NA: CUST 48/22.

37. 'House of Commons Committee to Consider the Duties and Drawbacks on Glass', 14 May 1787, JHC.

38. Treasury to Excise, 19 November 1787; Excise to Treasury, 29 November 1787; and Treasury to Excise, 13 December 1787, NA: CUST 48/23.

39. 'Memorial of British Plate Manufactory', 25 April 1793; Excise to Treasury, n.d.; and Treasury to Excise, 17 February 1794, NA: CUST 48/26.

40. See, for example, 'Memorial of the Proprietors of Glass Manufactories in the Counties of Northumberland and Durham, and in the Town and County of Newcastle-upon-Tyne', 2 July 1794, NA: CUST 48/27 and Excise to Treasury, 18 July 1794, NA: CUST 48/27.

41. Excise to Treasury, 6 February 1795, NA: CUST 48/27; Treasury to Excise, 2 June 1795 and 8 June 1795, NA: CUST 48/27.

42. Barker, *The Glassmakers*, 21.

43. Dowell, *A History of Taxation*, vol. 4, 299–300.

44. *The Case of the Company of White Paper Makers Humbly Presented to the Consideration of the Present Parliament* (London, 1689), 1–2. For a useful map of English paper mills in England during the 1690s, see Shorter, *Studies on the History of Papermaking*, 5–9.

45. Anon., *The Case and Circumstances of Paper-making*.

46. An excellent overview of the quality of English paper in comparison to Europe is given in Rosenband, 'Becoming competitive'.

47. Anon., *The Case and Circumstances of Paper-making*.

48. Cherry, *Early English Liberalism*, 287–8; Pettigrew, 'Free to enslave'.

49. Pollexfion, *Discourse of Trade*, 96.

50. 'William and Mary, 1694: An Act for Granting to their Majesties Severall Dutyes upon Velum Parchment and Paper for four Years towards Carrying on the War Against France: [Chapter XXI. Rot. Parl. pt. 5. nu. 1]', SOR: Volume 6: 1685–94, 495–502.

51. Details of the Act are provided in Jarvis, 'The Papermakers'.

52. Dowell, *A History of Taxation*, vol. 4, 325–6; Fine, 'Production and Excise', 175. For Whatman, see, especially, Rosenband, 'Becoming competitive'.

53. 'Committee appointed by a General Meeting of the Paper makers of Great Britain', 7 June 1765, NA: CUST 42/17.

54. See, for example, 'Memorial of the Manufacturers of Marbled Paper', 18 August 1784, NA: CUST 48/21; 'Memorial of the Manufacturers of Marbled Paper'. It is worth also adding that producers and retailers of wallpaper wanted painted walls and ceilings to be also equally taxed; see 'Petition of the Paper Stainers, Retailers of Paper Hangings and Several Journeymen', NA: CUST 48/19, 28 April 1778; James Woodmason to the Treasury, 10 November 1786, and Excise to the Treasury, 22 March 1787, NA: CUST 48/23.

55. 'An Account of the Gross amount of duties on paper in England from the introduction of the duty in 1713 to 1785', and Excise to Treasury, 28 November 1786, NA: CUST 48/22.

56. Rosenband, 'Becoming competitive'.

57. Say, *England*, 5–6, 14–15, 21–6 and 29–31; Jones, *An End to Poverty*, 138–41.

58. *The Case and Humble Petition of the Hard Cake and White Soap Makers*.

59. Musson, *Enterprise in Soap*, 26–7 and 30–1.

60. Dowell, *A History of Taxation*, vol. 4, 318–19; Gittins, 'Soapmaking'. For fears by soap makers over fraud and smuggling, see, for example, NA:CUST 42/17, April 1765; CUST 48/19, 30

April 1774; CUST 48/19, 28 February 1775; CUST 48/19, February 1776; CUST 48/21, 30 April 1783; CUST 48/21, 30 April 1783; and CUST 48/21, 21 June 1784.

61. 'House of Commons Committee to whom the Petition of the Manufacturers of Fustian was Referred', 16 February 1735, JHC; Dowell, *A History of Taxation*, vol. 4, 331–2.

62. 'House of Commons Committee to Whom the Manufacture of Striped and Chequered Linens and the Traders and Dealers in the Linen Manufactory in the Town and Parish of Manchester were Referred', 6 May 1751, JHC.

63. Turnbull, 'Canals, coal and regional growth'; Clemens, 'The rise of Liverpool'.

64. Dowell, *A History of Taxation*, vol. 4, 333; 'House of Commons Committee of the Whole House to Whom It Was Referred to Consider of the … Petition of Richard Arkwright and Company, Spinner of Cotton', 10 May 1774, JHC.

65. 'Memorial of the Linen Dealers in Scotland', 15 December 1779, NA: CUST 48/20. For the continuation of these concerns, see 'Memorial of Linen makers in Perth, Dundee, Forfar, Cupar and St. Andrews', 19 April 1782, NA: CUST 48/20.

66. 'Committee of the Whole House to Whom it was Referred to Consider of the State of the Linen Manufacture of Great Britain', 30 April 1781 and 'Committee Who Were Appointed to Consider the Several Petitions … Respecting the Fund Established for the Growth of Hemp and Flax in Great Britain', 12 June 1781, JHC; 'Memorial of the Manufacturers of Linen and Cotton in the town of Nottingham', 22 April 1783, 'Memorial of the General Convention of the Royal Borough of Scotland', April 1783 and 'Memorial of the Manufacturers of Calico Printers, Bleachers and others residing in the City and Neighbourhood of Carlisle', April 1783, NA: CUST 48/21.

67. 'Committee of the Whole House to Whom It was Referred to Consider of the Bounties Now Payable on … Linens and on Calicoes or Cottons Mixed with Linen', 13 March 1783, JHC.

68. 'Memorial of the Calico Printers at Manchester', 26 May 1783, NA: CUST 48/21.

69. Ibid., 26 May 1783.

70. Dowell, *A History of Taxation*, vol. 4, 335–6. For Eli Whitney and the cotton gin, see, especially, Angela Lakwete's account, *Inventing the Cotton Gin*.

71. Tomlinson, *The Useful Arts*, 14; Riello, *Cotton*, 254.

72. Beckert, *Empire of Cotton*; Baptist, *Half Has Never Been Told*.

73. Mokyr, *The Gifts of Athena*; Jacob, *The First Knowledge Economy*; and Black, *The Power of Knowledge*.

Chapter 8

1. For institutions and political context, see Rosenberg and Birdzell, *How the West Grew Rich*; North and Weingast, 'The evolution of institutions'; North, *Understanding*; and Robinson and Acemoglu, *Why Nations Fail*. For an overview of the current historiography, see Ashworth, 'The ghost of Rostow' and 'The industrial revolution'.

2. Hobson, *The Eastern Origins of Western Civilisation*, 57. Hobson has developed his critique of Eurocentrism in *The Eurocentric Conception of World Politics*.

3. Dear, 'Historiography', 201–2.

4. Webster, *The Great Instauration*; Wennerlind, *Casualties of Credit*, 54–61.

Notes

5. For Francis Bacon, see, for example, Porter, *Enlightenment*, 14, 56–7 and 131–2; Ash, *Power*, 186–212; and Mokyr, 'The intellectual origins', 41. For the diffusion of Newtonian experimental natural philosophy through the marketplace, see Ashton, *The Industrial Revolution*, 16–21; Musson and Robinson, *Science and Technology*, 10–59; Stewart, *The Rise of Public Science*; Jacob, *Scientific Culture* and *The First Knowledge Economy*; and Jacob and Stewart, *Practical Matter*.

6. Goody, *The East in the West*; Hobson, *The Eastern Origins*, chs 6–9. Aspects of knowledge and technology, deemed important to the West, have been mapped in India between 1600 and 1800 by Prasannan Parthasarathi in his *Why Europe Grew Rich*, 185–222.

7. Gee, *The Trade and Navigation*, 2 and 98–9; Goody, *The Theft of History*, 292–4; MacLeod, *Inventing the Industrial Revolution*, 10–13; Cunningham, *The Growth of English Industry*, 56.

8. Colbin, *The Unseen Hand*, 26–31; Cunningham, *The Growth of English Industry*, 57–8; and Brenner, *Merchants and Revolution*, 20. The growing transnational nature of Elizabethan London can clearly be seen in Iliffe, 'Capitalizing expertise' and Harkness, *The Jewel House*.

9. Dowell, *A History of Taxation*, vol. 4, 291–4; Barker, *The Glassmakers*, 4.

10. W. T. MacCaffrey, 'Cecil, William, first Baron Burghley (1520/21-1598)', DNB, 2004.

11. Dowell, *A History of Taxation*, vol. 4, 317; Thirsk, *Economic Policy*, 53–9; and Gittins, 'Soapmaking', 265–6.

12. Cunningham, *Alien Immigrants*, 122–3. For the importance of German experience and the problems they faced in England, see Ash, *Power,* 19–54.

13. Ash, *Power*, 24; Cunningham, *The Growth of English Industry*, 59–60 and 72 and *Alien Immigrants*, xiv and 150–7; and Colbin, *The Unseen Hand*, 19.

14. Thirsk, *Economic Policy*, 56–7; Cunningham, *The Growth of English Industry*, 75.

15. Ibid., 67.

16. Reynel, *The True English Interest*, 197–8; Thirsk, *Economic Policy*, 68–9 and *Alternative Agriculture*, 73–6; and Warner, *Bloody Marsh*.

17. Thirsk, *Alternative Agriculture*, 79–83.

18. B. Morgan, 'Bradley, Humphrey (1584-1625)', DNB, 2004.

19. Ash, 'Amending nature', 122–3.

20. McGurk, 'Russell, William, first Baron Russell of Thornhaugh (c. 1553-1613)', DNB, 2004.

21. Russell, 'Russell, Francis, fourth earl of Bedford (bap. 1587, d. 1641)', DNB, 2004. Land and money details are given in Anon., *The History or Narrative of the Great Level of the Fens*, 12.

22. Anon., *The Anti-Projector* and quoted in Ash, 'Amending Nature', 125.

23. This fundamental and ongoing clash is best described in Linebaugh, *Stop, Thief!*

24. Ash, 'Amending nature'.

25. Vries and Wonde, *The First Modern Economy*; Prak, *The Dutch Republic*.

26. Ash, 'Amending nature', 129–30.

27. Skempton, 'Vermuyden', 739.

28. Ibid., 743.

29. Vermuyden, *A Discourse touching the Drayning the Great Fennes*; Burrell, *Exceptions Against Sir Cornelius Virmudens*, A2 and 19 and *A Briefe Relation*.

30. The anonymous writer of *The Anti-Projector* is quoted in Ash, 'Amending nature'. There are a great number of pamphlets printed during this period condemning the forced appropriation of common land for drainage.

31. Vermuyden, *A Discourse*, 349; Ash, 'Amending nature', 131–2.

32. Ash, 'Amending nature', 140.

33. The issue of capital and space is best approached through the work of David Harvey; for example, *The Urban Experience* and *The Condition of Postmodernity*.

34. Ash, *Knowledge*, 87–134; Iliffe, 'Capitalizing expertise', 62. For the Elizabethan Principal Secretary Sir Francis Walsingham and his sponsoring of voyages into the arctic, see Adams, Bryson and Leimon, 'Walsingham, Sir Francis (c. 1532-1590)', DNB, 2004.

35. Ash, *Knowledge*, 186–216 and 'Introduction', 22–3.

36. Mokyr, 'Intellectual origins', 336–7.

37. Jacob, *Scientific Culture*, 29.

38. Bacon is quoted in Gee, *The Trade and Navigation*, 3.

39. Musson and Robinson, *Science and Technology*, 16–17; Jacob, *Scientific Culture*, 53–5. For a succinct overview of this trajectory, see Porter, *Enlightenment*, 142–5.

40. Turnbull, 'Peter Stahl'; Meynell, 'Locke, Boyle and Peter Stahl'; Clericuzio, 'Vigani, John Francis (c. 1650-1713)', DNB, 2004; Musson and Robinson, *Science and Technology*, 32–5.

41. For Pierre Blondeau, see MacLeod, *Inventing the Industrial Revolution*, 34. Iliffe documents a number of foreign engineers during the seventeenth century; see his 'Capitalizing expertise', 65–6. Between 1680 and 1720 sixteen Huguenots were elected Fellows of The Royal Society – including the leading mathematician, Abraham de Moivre, and John (Jean) Theophilus Desaguliers. See Gibbs, 'Huguenot contributions'.

42. Reinert, *Translating Empire*, 171.

43. Shapin, 'The house of experiment'.

44. Stewart, 'Other centres of calculation', 134–5.

45. For the explicit, but ultimately failed, attempt to tie the new philosophy to practical trades, see Ochs, 'The Royal Society'.

46. Henry, *The Scientific Revolution*, 100.

47. Stewart, 'Other centres of calculation', 138–9. See also Musson and Robinson, *Science and Technology*, 37–43.

48. Stewart, *The Rise of Public Science*, xv, xxxii–xxxiii and 116. For the problematic term 'Newtonianism', see Schaffer, 'Newtonianism', and for a more diluted interpretation of the impact of Newton's work, see his 'Newton on the beach'.

49. Stewart, 'Other centres of calculation', 141; Jacob and Stewart, *Practical Matter*, 75–8.

50. Ibid., 143–4.

51. Morton, 'Lectures on natural philosophy', 411–34. An attempt at mapping the diffusion of public lectures can be found in Musson and Robinson, *Science and Technology*, ch. 3.

52. Stewart, *The Rise of Public Science*, 113–17, 170–1, 187 and 269–78.

53. Ashworth, *Customs and Excise*, 210 and 'The intersection of industry', 348–77.

54. Stewart, 'Other centres of calculation', 152.

55. Stewart, *The Rise of Public Science*, 111–17 and 'A meaning for machines', 266; Jacob and Stewart, *Practical Matter*, 75–8; and Dickson, *The Sun Insurance Office*, 268.

56. Stewart, 'Other centres of calculation', 139.

57. Morton, 'Men and machines', 49.

58. Morton, 'Men and machines', 49 and 54; Schaffer, '"The charter'd Thames"'; and Fox, *The Arts of Industry*, 138–40. The volumes of Excise trials held in the National Archives under CUST103 frequently refer to models taken to trial to demonstrate a fraud.

59. Brewer, *The Sinews of Power*, 34–7; Rodger, 'From the "military revolution"'; and Rosier, 'The construction costs'.

60. For a useful summary of this argument, see, for example, Arrighi, *Adam Smith in Beijing*, 265–74.

61. Beckert, *Empire of Cotton*, 295–323; Vries, *State*.

62. Gee, *The Trade*, 51.

63. Douglas, 'Cotton textiles in England', 38; Thomas, 'The beginnings of calico-printing', 209; and Clayton and Oakes, 'Early calico printers', 136.

64. Ibid., 38–9; Styles, 'Design for large-scale production', 12; and Riello, *Cotton*, 159.

65. Berg, *Luxury and Pleasure*, 23.

66. Ibid., 24–5, 55, 69–72 and 81; Styles, 'Design for large-scale production' and 'Product innovation'.

67. Styles, *The Dress of the People*.

68. Berg, *Luxury and Pleasure*, 95–8. *Marchands-merciers* were originally entrepreneurial craftsmen independent of the guild system and, as such, were the only craftsmen allowed to work with foreign items such as Chinese porcelain and Japanese lacquer.

69. Puetz, 'Design instruction', 217–18; Berg, *Luxury and Pleasure*, 98, 102 and 132–3; Styles, 'Manufacturing', 543–8; Clifford, 'The ornament of nations'; Uglow, *The Lunar Men*, 322–38; and Dolan, *Josiah Wedgwood*, 321–2 and 327.

70. Puetz, 'The society', 18.

71. Bowrey, 'Art, craft, good taste', 6.

72. Craske, 'Plan and control', 188–92.

73. Ibid., 201 and 206–9.

74. 'House of Commons Committee to Whom the Petition of the Callicoe Printers, Artists, designers of Drawings, Engravers, and others, Proprietors of original Patterns for printing Linens, Cottons, Callicoes, and Muslins', 8 March 1785, JHC.

75. 'House of Commons Committee to Whom the Petition of the Callicoe Printers, Artists, designers of Drawings, Engravers, and others, Proprietors of original Patterns for printing Linens, Cottons, Callicoes, and Muslins'.

76. Bowrey, 'Art, craft, good taste', 8–10.

77. Ibid., 11. A petition in 1788 advocated the creation of a 'General Hall' in the City of London to display the variety of cotton textiles and designs to potential buyers, see *Observations on the Means of Extending the Consumption of British Callicoes*.

78. *The Penny Magazine* is quoted in Kriegel, 'Culture and the copy', 239.

79. Chapman, 'Quantity versus quality', 178–80.

80. Kriegel, 'Culture and the copy', 259.

81. Fairlie, 'Dyestuffs', 489; Wolff, 'Textile bleaching', 150; Musson and Robinson, *Science and Technology*, ch. 9; and Wadsworth and Mann, *The Cotton Trade*, 48.

82. Fairlie, 'Dyestuffs', 491–2. The difficulty in importing various dyes and the superiority of Indian dyeing see Turnbull, *A History of the Calico Printing*, 1–30.

83. Ibid., 494.

84. Ibid., 501–2.

85. Fairlie, 'Dyestuffs', 505; Beer, 'Eighteenth-century theories'.

86. Nash, 'South Carolina indigo'. Attempts to cultivate Virginia for textile dyes had commenced from the moment English colonists had arrived; see, for example, Colvin, *The Unseen Hand*, xix and 22.

87. Fairlie, 'Dyestuffs', 507; Gillispie, 'The discovery', 152 and 159 and *Science and Polity in France*, 137–8 and 411–12; Musson and Robinson, *Science and Technology*, 252–5.

88. Turnbull, *A History of the Calico Printing*, 32.

89. Wolff, 'Bleaching', 146–8; Durie, 'Textile bleaching', 339–41.

90. Gittins, 'Innovations', 195–6; Landes, *The Unbound Prometheus*, 109; Clow and Clow, 'Vitriol', 149–50.

91. Gillespie, *Science and Polity in France*, 411–12; Clow and Clow, 'Vitriol', 156–7; Wolff, 'Bleaching', 155; Hardie, 'The Macintosh's', 181–5; Musson and Robinson, *Science and Techology*, 273–6 and 326–7; and Turnbull, *A History of the Calico Printing*, 32.

92. Gittins, 'Innovations', 199 and 201–2 and 'Salt', 87; Turnbull, *A History of the Calico Printing*, 32–4.

93. Barker, Dickinson and Hardie, 'The origins', 163; Gittins, 'Innovations', 199.

94. Ibid., 164–6; Musson and Robinson, *Science and Technology*, ch. 10. For a critical look at Leblanc's role in the process given his name, see Gillispie, 'The discovery'.

95. Rees, 'Evolution'; Calvert, *Salt in Cheshire*; and Newbury, 'The history of the common salt industry'.

96. Clow and Clow, 'Vitriol', 160–3; Barker, Dickinson and Hardie, 'The origins', 169–70; and T. I. Williams, 'Muspratt, James (1793-1886)', DNB, 2004.

97. Barker, Dickinson and Hardie, 'The origins', 171. The Leblanc process, unfortunately, also produced highly noxious hydrochloric acid – a problem not overcome till the work associated with Ernest Solvay in Belgium; see Williams, 'Muspratt'.

Chapter 9

1. Wadsworth and Mann, *The Cotton Trade*, 143; Turnbull, *A History of the Calico Printing*, 18.

2. O'Brien, Griffiths and Hunt, 'Political components'; Daunton, *Progress and Poverty*, 543; Riello, *Cotton*, 125; and Colvin, *The Unseen Hand*, 103.

3. Chapman, *The Cotton Industry*, 12–15.

4. Parthasarathi, *Why Europe Grew Rich*, 222; Riello, *Cotton*, 149.

5. Griffiths, Hunt and O'Brien, 'Scottish, Irish, and imperial connections', 630–6.

6. For Kay and the shuttle see, especially, Wadsworth and Mann, *The Cotton Trade*, 449–71.

7. Griffiths, Hunt and Brien, 'Scottish, Irish, and imperial connections', 636–42; Mokyr, *The Lever of Riches,* 96. For an account of Lewis Paul and John Wyatt, see Wadsworth and Mann, *The Cotton Trade*, 419–71.

8. Wadsworth and Mann, *The Cotton Trade*, 484–8; Berg, *The Age of Manufactures*, 236–43. A very useful overview of technological developments in cotton production is also given in Tomlinson, *The Useful Arts*, 3–39; Mann, *The Cotton Trade*, 1–24.

9. Wadsworth and Mann, *The Cotton Trade*, 412–13 and 471; MacLeod, 'The European Origins', 115. See also Landes, *The Unbound Prometheus*, 83 and Rosenberg, 'Science', 102.

10. *The Case of the British Cotton Spinners*, 1.

11. Tunzelmann, *Steam Power*, 180–1; Mokyr, *Lever of Riches*, 98–100; and Berg, *The Age of Manufactures*, 245.

12. Ibid., 195–6 and 216–17.

13. Beckert, *Empire of Cotton*, 85–97; Riello, *Cotton*, 242.

14. Wadsworth and Mann, *The Cotton Trade*, 183–5 and 208; Inikori, *Africans and the Industrial Revolution*, 143; Chapman, *The Cotton Industry*, 16; Parthasarathi, *Why Europe Grew Rich*; and Riello, *Cotton*, 150. The African context is hugely complex and in terms of its industrial history poorly researched. However, for the immensely important status of cloth within various African ethnic groups and rise in imported cloth from the mid-seventeenth century, see Martin, 'Power'. The best overview of African industry during this period is Thornton, 'Precolonial African industry' and *Africa and Africans*. Thornton should be read with the critical remarks made by Austen, 'On company pre-industrial African'.

15. Beckert, *Empire of Cotton*, 67.

16. Allen, *The British Industrial Revolution*, 197–206; Beckert, *Empire of Cotton*, 73. For an in-depth look at Lancashire and horology, see Treherne, 'The contribution'.

17. Turnbull, 'Canals, coal and regional growth'; Maw, Wyke and Kidd, 'Canals, rivers, and the industrial city'.

18. Wrigley, *Continuity* and *Energy*; Sieferle, *The Subterranean Forest*, ch. 3; Brinkley, 'Escaping'; and Allen, *The British Industrial Revolution*, 163. For Allen it was the demand from growing urban areas, especially London, that provided the impetus to the growth of Britain's coal industry. The most recent statement to emphasize Britain's ecology to its Industrial Revolution is Kander, Malanima and Warde, *Power to the People*.

19. Harris, *The British Iron Industry*, 30–1.

20. Hayman, 'The Shropshire Wrought-Iron Industry', 146.

21. Harris, *The British Iron Industry*, 32–3; Usher, *A History*, 373–4.

22. Ibid., 38–9.

23. Ibid., 39–40; Hayman, 'The Shropshire Wrought-Iron Industry', 12–13.

24. Evans and Rydén, *Baltic Iron in the Atlantic World*; Evans, 'The plantation hoe'.

25. Evans and Rydén, *Baltic Iron in the Atlantic World*, 51.

26. Ibid., 298; Harris, *The British Iron Industry*, 41.

27. Mathias, *The Transformation of England*, 33–5.

28. Harris, *The British Iron Industry*, 45–6; Treherne, 'The contribution', 466.

29. Evans and Rydén, *Baltic Iron in the Atlantic World*, 250.

30. Ibid., ch. 4; Hyde, 'Technological change', 200–5.

31. Wakefield, *The Disordered Police State*, 81–110.

32. Mokyr, 'Editors Introduction', 22 and 'Secrets of Success'; Harris, 'Reviewed work', 180.

33. Wrigley, *Energy*, 41–2; Allen, *The British Industrial Revolution*, 81–2; and Brinkley, 'Escaping', 737–9.

34. MacLeod, 'The European origins', 117–18; Rolt, *Thomas Newcomen,* 42 and 94. Desaguliers is quoted in J. S. Allen, 'Newcomen, Thomas (bap. 1664, d. 1729)', DNB, 2004.

35. Marsden, *Watt's Perfect Engine*, 36–40.

36. Clavering, 'The coal mills'; Hollister-Short, 'Before and after'.

37. Tunzelmann, *Steam Power*; Daunton, *Progress and Poverty*, 191–3.

38. Lindquist, *Technology on Trial*, 34–6 and 296.

39. Hills, *James Watt*, vol. 1, 312–80; Usher, *A History*, 353–4; and Marsden, *Watt's Perfect Engine*, 50–60.

40. Marsden, *Watt's Perfect Engine*, 70–7.

41. Hills, *Power from Steam*, 62–9.

42. Harris, *Essays in Industry*; MacLeod, 'European origins', 119; Berg, 'The genesis'; Hilaire-Perez, 'Technology'; and Marsden, *Watt's Perfect Engine*, 99–104.

43. Wrigley, *Energy*, 45; Allen, *The British Industrial Revolution,* 83; Harris, *Essays in Industry*; and Brinkley, 'Escaping from constraints'.

44. Pomeranz, *The Great Divergence* and 'Political economy', 427 and 437.

45. Mathias, *Transformation*, 57–60.

Chapter 10

1. Eden, *Four Letters*, 123.

2. Hume, 'Of credit', 213. Hont has masterfully traced Hume's view towards public credit and the Scottish thinker's fear of the inevitable dire conclusion of war and debt to Britain; see his *Jealousy of Trade*, 84–8 and 325–53.

3. For a useful overview of the quest for economic reform during this period, see Reitan, *Politics,* 16–113. For the modernization of the Royal Navy, see Knight, *Britain Against Napoleon*, part one.

4. Thompson, 'Eighteenth-century English society', 161.

5. Kwass, *Privilege*.

6. Mathias and O'Brien, 'Taxation', 626–9; Engerman and O'Brien, 'The industrial revolution', 452.

7. Behrens, *Society,* 68–78.

8. White, 'The French revolution'; Sonenscher, *Before the Deluge*.

9. Bosher, *The Single Duty*, 75; Nye, *War, Wine, and Taxes*, 57; Ormrod, *The Rise of Commercial Empires*, 45; and White, 'The French revolution', 229. For an overview of French taxes and accompanying administration, see Matthews, *The Royal General Farms*, part two.

10. Steuart, *An Inquiry*, vol. 2, 697.

11. Ashworth, *Customs and* Excise, 117–30; Smith, *An Inquiry*, vol. 2, 883.

12. Eden, *Letter to the Earl of Carlisle*, 26.

13. Brewer, *Party Ideology*, 215; Binney, *British Public Finance*, 11; Hilton, *A Mad, Bad & Dangerous People?*, 41 and 46; and Ashworth, *Customs and Excise*, ch. 19.

14. Hoppit, 'Checking the leviathan', 287 and 'Political arithmetic'; Brewer, *The Sinews of Power*, 221–49; and Innes, *Inferior Politics*, 109–75.

15. Root, 'The redistributive role of government', 339.

16. Excise to Treasury, 26 February 1783, NRO: CUST 48/21.

17. Ibid., 9 April 1783, NRO: CUST 48/21. For a useful overview of the abuse of permits, see Hamilton, *An Enquiry*, 29–32 and 40–4.

18. Waugh, *Smuggling*, 7.

19. Ashworth, *Customs and Excise*, 196.

20. 'Petition of the Lancashire and Glasgow Calico Printers', 31 May 1785, NRO: CUST 48/22; Colquhoun, *A Treatise*.

21. Hardy, *Forgotten Voices*, 123.

22. Ehrman, *The Younger Pitt*, 240–2; Henderson, 'The Anglo-French commercial treaty', 105.

23. Eden, *Four Letters to the Earl of Carlisle*, 130–1 and 203–9.

24. Mui and Mui, 'William Pitt' and *Shops and Shopkeeping*, 162; Ehrman, *The Younger Pitt*, 5 and 243–5; and Rose, *William Pitt*, 184–5.

25. Charles Fox is quoted in Kennedy, *English Taxation*, 161.

26. Henderson, 'Anglo-French commercial treaty', 111; Ehrman, *The Younger Pitt*, 245–6.

27. For Walpole's 1733 scheme, see Langford, *The Excise Crisis*; Ashworth, *Customs and Excise*, 67–81.

28. Ehrman, *The Younger Pitt*, 250; Fine, 'Production and the Excise', 142; Ward, 'The administration', 534–42; and Dowell, *A History of Taxation*, vol. 2, 189.

29. Ehrman, *The Younger Pitt*, 246.

30. Ibid., 252–3; Norris, 'Samuel Garbett', 453 and 458–9; Kelly, 'British Parliamentary politics', 741–2; and Rose, *William Pitt*, 186–7. For Boulton and Watt see Jacob, *The First Knowledge Economy*, 39–40. For the ill-fated shop tax, see Mui and Mui, *Shops and Shopkeeping*, 34–6 and 73–85. The context, interests and reasons fuelling early industrial lobbying and the formation of manufacturing associations is usefully examined in Dietz, 'Before the Age of Capital'.

31. Dowell, *History of Taxation*, vol. 4, 333; Bowden, 'The influence of the manufacturers', 656.

32. 'House of Commons Committee of the Whole House to Whom it was Referred to Consider of the Petition of the Gentlemen, Clergy, Land Owners, Merchants, Manufacturers, Dyers, Bleachers, and Others Interested in Printed Linens, Dyed Stuffs of Cotton and Cotton and Linen Mixed, and Licenses for Bleaching or Dying', 21 April 1785, JHC.

33. Wright, *An Address*, 9–10, 12, 19 and 56.

34. Josiah Wedgwood is quoted in Dietz, 'Before the Age of Capital', 106–7; Wright, *An Address*, 45.

35. Bowden, 'The Influence of the Manufacturers', 656 and *Industrial Society*, 170; Polanyi, *The Great Transformation*, 142. For pottery and patents, see MacLeod, *Inventing the Industrial Revolution*, 111.

36. Bowden, 'The influence of the manufacturers', 656–8 and 665.

37. O'Brien, 'The triumph', 29–30.

38. O'Brien, *The Economic History of Ireland*, 230–3 and 'The Irish Free Trade Agitation (Part 1)'; Henry, *Dublin Hanged*. For the American consumer protest movement, see Breen, *The Marketplace*.

39. O'Brien, 'The Irish free trade agitation of 1779 (Part 1)', 569–70.

40. Ibid., 573–6.

41. Ibid., 576–80.

42. O'Brien, 'The Irish free trade agitation of 1779 (Part 2)', 96; Sickinger, 'Regulation', 218–19. Foster is quoted in A. P. W. Malcomson, 'Foster, John, first Baron Oriel (1740-1828)', DNB, 2004.

43. Breen, *The Marketplace of Revolution*.

44. O'Brien, 'The Irish free trade agitation of 1779 (Part 2)', 98–106.

45. *Premiums Offered by the Dublin Society*, 7–14 and 16; Longfield, 'History of the Irish Linen', 25–56.

46. Ehrman, *The Younger Pitt*, 196–7.

47. Bolton, 'Some British reactions', 367; Evans, *William Pitt the Younger*, 62–4.

48. Kelly, 'British and Irish politics', 534–41; Ehrman, *Pitt the Younger*, 206–7; and Bowden, 'The influence of the manufacturers', 663. Lord Sheffield was educated in Dublin; see J. Cannon, 'Holroyd, John Baker, first earl of Sheffield (1741-1821)', DNB, 2004.

49. Mann, *The Cotton Trade*, 23.

50. Bowden, 'The influence of the manufacturers', 666–72 and *Industrial Society in England*, 172–5.

51. Kelly, 'British and Irish politics', 542–4; O'Brien, *The Economic History*, 250–5.

52. A succinct and detailed contemporary overview of these concerns are given in Anon., *An Address to the Members of both Houses of Parliament on the Late Tax on Fustian*, 19. It is sometimes forgotten that cotton textiles were also Scotland's leading industry during the Industrial Revolution; see Cooke, *The Rise and Fall*.

53. Kelly, 'British and Irish politics', 544–9; Hilton, *A Mad, Bad & Dangerous People?*, 52. For succinct details of the proposed Irish propositions, see Ehrman, *The Younger Pitt*, 209–13.

54. O'Hearn, 'Innovation and the world-system hierarchy', 598–601. The Irish were able to wield significant weight in protecting its linen industry in the negotiations of the 1786 trade treaty with France; see Kelly, 'The Anglo-French commercial treaty'.

55. Ibid., 601–2.

56. Ibid., 602–7. Once the cotton gin was established in the United States, it made it economic to process upland cotton in the South, resulting in its revolutionary expansion that propelled it by 1803 to being Britain's primary supplier. For the ideal environment of Lancashire for cotton, see the early, but still useful, Atwood, 'Localization'.

57. Pitt the younger, *Speech in the House of Commons*, 4.

58. Ehrman, *The British Government*.

59. *The British Merchant, from 1787*, 8, 12 and 28 and quoted in Bowden, 'The English manufacturers', 23–4.

60. Rose, 'The Franco-British commercial treaty', 710.

61. Bowden, 'The English manufacturers', 24–8 and, especially, Beckert, *Empire of Cotton*.

62. Stephen E. Lee, 'William Eden, first Baron Auckland (1744-1814)', DNB, 2004. For Eden's earlier, more liberal and sympathetic views towards Ireland, see his *Four Letters to the Earl of Carlise*, 137–67.

63. Kelly, 'The Anglo-French commercial treaty'. For the French perspective on the treaty, see Donaghay, 'Calonne' and, especially, 'The exchange of products'.

64. Mokyr, *The Enlightened Economy*, 153 and 418.

65. Lipson, *The Economic History*, vol. 3, 114–16; Murphy, 'DuPont de Nemours', 575; and Browning, 'The treaty of commerce', 359.

66. Henderson, *The Genesis*, 45–6.

67. Rose, 'The Franco-British commercial treaty', 716; Browning, 'The treaty of commerce', 350–3; Bolton and Kennedy, 'William Eden'; and Donaghay, 'The Marechal de Castries'.

68. For a succinct overview of the treaty's contents, see Hewins, *English Trade*, 147–9; Rose, 'The Franco-British commercial treaty', 717–23.

69. Pitt, *Speech*, 18.

70. Murphy, 'DuPont De Nemours', 577.

71. Horn, *The Path Not Taken*, 52–60 and 67; Bosher, *The Single Duty*.

72. Pitt, *Speech*, 20–32; Horn, *The Path Not Taken*, 65.

73. Ibid., 43.

74. Horn, *The Path Not Taken*, 65.

75. See, for example, Anon., *Historical and Political Remarks*, 56–69.

76. Browning, 'The treaty of commerce', 358; Brace, 'The Anglo-French treaty', 154; and Henderson, *The Genesis*, 50. Fox is quoted in Hilton, *A Mad, Bad & Dangerous People?*, 189. For the physiocrats in relation to the treaty, see Horn, *The Path Not Taken*, 52–3.

77. Pitt is quoted in Ehrman, *The British Government*, 45. For further context, see Crowley, 'Neo-Mercantilism'.

78. A Woollen Draper's Letter, *On the French Treaty*, 5.

79. Ibid., 8–14.

80. See 'The Normandy chamber', 308–9; Hirsch, 'Revolutionary France', 1283; and Henderson, *The Genesis*, 51–2.

81. See 'The Normandy chamber', 310; Hewins, *English Trade*, 156.

82. Parthasarathi, *Why Europe Grew Rich*. This point is reiterated by Giorgio Riello in his *Cotton*.

83. See 'The Normandy chamber', 312. For French cotton and its mechanization, see the old, but still informative, article by Dunham, 'Development of the cotton industry', 281–91.

84. See, for example, Harris, *Industrial Espionage*.

85. Cone, 'Richard Price', 251; Ehrman, *The Younger Pitt*, 260–3; Hilton, *A Mad, Bad & Dangerous People?*, 114–15; O'Brien, 'The political economy', 13; and Harling, *Waning of 'Old Corruption'*, 53–6.

86. Dowell, *A History of Taxation*, vol. 2, 209. For an in-depth overview of British taxation during this period of war against the French, see O'Brien, 'The triumph'.

87. 'EXCISE', *The Times*, 30 April 1790, 2.

88. Ibid., 26 May 1790, 3.

89. William Pitt is quoted in Kennedy, *English Taxation*, 165–71.

90. Cooper, 'William Pitt', 99.

91. Seligman, *Progressive Taxation*, 31–3 and 114–15; Daunton, *Progress and Poverty*, 518; and Cooper, 'William Pitt', 101.

92. O'Brien, 'Political economy', 21–2 and 'The triumph', 22–8; Dowell, *History of Taxation*, vol. 2, 221–2; and Cooper, 'William Pitt', 100–3.

93. Daunton, *Trusting Leviathan*, 44–5.

94. Knight, *Britain Against Napoleon*, 214–16; Breihan, 'The Addington party'; and Ashworth, '"System of terror"'.

95. Crouzet, 'Wars'; Knight, *Britain Against Napoleon*, 400–5.

96. Harling, *The Waning of 'Old Corruption'*, 80–95; Hilton, *A Mad, Bad & Dangerous People?*, 65–74.

97. 'Frauds on the Revenue', *The Times*, 8 November 1811, 1.

98. 'Bow-STREET: Government has been Induced by the Recent Outrages of Smugglers to make the most Active Exertions', *The Times*, 15 November 1815, 3.

99. Harling and Mandler, 'From fiscal-state', 46 and 52–3. The adverse spectre of the eighteenth-century 'fiscal-military state' loomed large in the forging of taxation policy in nineteenth-century Britain; see Daunton, *Trusting Leviathan* and his various essays in *State and Market*. For the discontent of the middling ranks, see Brown, '"A just and profitable commerce"', 326–8.

Chapter 11

1. Thelwall, *The Tribune*, 23 May 1795 and quoted in Thompson, *The Making of the English Working Class*, 174.

2. Thompson, *The Making of the English Working Class*, 842.

3. Jones, *Languages of Class*, 90–178.

4. Thompson, *The Making of the English Working Class*, 68–72; Thompson, 'The moral economy', 258.

5. Randall, *Riotous Assemblies*, 151.

6. Linebaugh, *Stop, Thief!*, 37 and 80.

7. Thompson, 'The patricians and the plebs', 89. But see Williams, 'Morals'. For the growing voice of the middling ranks see, especially, Harling, *The Waning of 'Old Corruption'* and Daunton, *Trusting Leviathan*. Thompson does not, as Nicholas Rogers points out, allow enough agency to the growing middling ranks; see his *Crowds*.

8. Thompson, 'The patricians and the plebs', 95–6 and 'Eighteenth-century English society', 164.

9. Thompson, 'The patricians and the plebs', 74 and 'Eighteenth-century English society', 158; Hay and Rogers, *Eighteenth-Century English Society*, 85; and Randall, *Riotous Assemblies*, 45. Although notions of new rights were also being generated within the Atlantic and, particularly, towards slavery; see Linebaugh and Rediker, *The Many-Headed Hydra*; Blackburn, *The American Crucible*.

10. Randall, *Riotous Assemblies*, 78–81. For turnpike roads and canals, see, especially, Bagwell, *The Transport Revolution*; Szostak, *The Role of Transportation*. For the linked nexus of urbanization, enclosure and consuming, see Linebaugh, *Stop, Thief!*, 26.

11. Randall and Charlesworth, 'Comment'; Hay and Rogers, *Eighteenth-Century English Society*, 137–44.

12. Thompson, 'The moral economy', 193–4 and 224–6; Rogers, *Crowds*, 64–74.

13. Ibid., 197. The issue of metrology is examined in detail by Sheldon, Randall, Charlesworth and Walsh in their 'Popular Protest', 25–45; Ashworth, 'Metrology and the state'.

14. Ibid., 199–200; Randall, *Riotous Assemblies*, 88–90; Hay and Rogers, *Eighteenth-Century English Society*, 110; and Rogers, *Crowds*, 68–9, 74 and 82.

15. Randall, *Riotous Assemblies*, 91–5.

16. Thompson, *Customs in Common*; Linebaugh, *Stop, Thief!*

17. Thompson, 'The moral economy', 200–3.

18. Ibid., 205–7.

19. Ibid., 208–9; Randall, *Riotous Assemblies*, 115.

20. Thompson, 'custom and culture', 14 and 'The moral economy', 249–50; Hay and Rogers, *Eighteenth-Century English Society*, 108.

21. The classic account of the growth of architectural enclosure and its association with a new micro-physics of power is Foucault, *Discipline and Punish*. The relationship between land enclosure, growing urbanization and capitalism is powerfully explored in Linebaugh, *Stop, Thief!*, 80–1 and 101. For the impact of capitalism upon space in general, see Harvey, *The Condition of Postmodernity*.

22. Randall, *Riotous Assemblies*, 228–31. This transition is convincingly told in Hay, 'The state and the market'.

23. Ibid., 238–9.

24. Randall, *Before the Luddites*, 7; Rule, *The Experience of Labour*, 96–7.

25. Hammond and Hammond, *The Rise of Modern Industry*, 101; Cunningham, *The Growth of English Industry*, vol. 2, 26–30; and Lipson, *The Economic History*, vol. 1, 252–3.

26. Chase, *Early Trade Unionism*, 48.

27. Cunningham, *The Growth of English Industry*, vol. 2, 31–5.

28. Rule, *The Experience of Labour*, 99.

29. Cunningham, *The Growth of English Industry*, vol. 2, 37–9; Lipson, *The Economic History*, vol. 1, 254.

30. Epstein, 'Craft guilds', 688.

31. 'House of Commons Committee to Whom the Petition of the Serge or Worsted Weavers was referred', 4 December 1702, JHC.

32. Randall, *Riotous Assemblies*, 122–3. For a succinct overview of early trade combinations, see Lipson, *The Economic History*, vol. 1, 386–409; Orth, 'English combination acts'; and Chase, *Early Trade Unionism*, 15–69.

33. Randall, *Riotous Assemblies*, 124–6, 129 and 136–7.

34. Lipson, *The Economic History*, vol. 3, 267.

35. Biggs, 'A tale untangled'.

36. Rogers, *Crowds*, 66.

37. 'Bill for more effectual preventing the abuses and frauds of persons employed in working up the woollen, linen and cotton manufactures of this Kingdom', 1756, JHC.

38. Orth, 'English combination acts', 187–9.

39. Randall, *Riotous Assemblies*, 150–1. See also Lipson, *The Economic History*, vol. 1, 264.

40. Clapham, 'The Spitalfields acts', 460; Randall, *Riotous Assemblies*, 144–5. For the hanging of Valline and Doyle, see Spraggs, 'The Spitalfield riots'.

41. Clapham, 'The Spitalfield acts', 461; Orth, 'English combination acts', 190–1.

42. 'House of Commons Committee to Whom the Petition of Several Master Dyers and Calico Printers within the Counties of Middlesex, Essex, Surrey and Kent was Referred', 12 March 1790, JHC.

43. Chase, *Early Trade Unionism*, 9–15 and 26–8.

44. Clapham, 'The Spitalfield acts', 462–4. The request to have the act extended to Coventry had long been made; see, for example, 'House of Commons Committee to whom the Petition of Several Journeymen Silk Weavers for Coventry was Referred', 12 March 1790, JHC. The desire for standardized piece rates was also fought for by cotton mule spinners; see Lazonick, 'Industrial relations', 234.

45. Clapham, 'The Spitalfield acts', 464, 466 and 470.

46. Ibid., 469.

47. Innes, 'Regulating wages', 215.

48. Montoux, *The Industrial Revolution*, 411–13.

49. Randall, *Before the Luddites*, 2–3, 7–8, 26–7 and 44.

50. The continued dominance of hand technology is best told in Samuel, 'Workshop of the world'.

51. Montoux, *The Industrial Revolution*, 419 and 462.

52. Berg, *The Machinery Question*, 2. The machinery question was not just confined to physical production but intellectual production; see Ashworth, 'Memory, efficiency and symbolic analysis'.

53. Randall, *Before the Luddites*, 47–8 and 'The philosophy of luddism'; Berg, *The Machinery Question*; Behagg, *Politics and Production*; Charlesworth, 'From the moral economy'; and Ashworth '"System of terror"'.

54. Randall, *Before the Luddites*, 9.

55. Hammond and Hammond, *The Rise of Modern Industry*, 104; Thompson, *The Making of the English Working Class*, 537–45; Rule, *The Experience of Labour*, 116; and Navickas, 'Luddism'.

56. Attacks upon machines stem from at least the seventeenth century and were originally not directed specifically at new technology but at employers of the putting-out system; see Hobsbawm, 'The machine breakers', especially 58–62. For a broader analysis of Luddism, see Chase, *Early Trade Unionism*, 91–5; Binfield (ed.), *Writings of the Luddites*; Bailey, *The Luddite Rebellion*; and Navickas, 'The search for "General Ludd"'.

57. Chase, *Early Trade Unionism*, 92 and 100. Although apprenticeships were greatly weakened by the 1814 Act many continued; see Humphries, 'Rent seeking'.

58. Belchem, *Orator Hunt* and *Industrialisation*, 73–83.

59. Rogers, *Crowds*, 279.

60. 'Meeting at Spa Fields', *The Times*, 16 November 1816, 2.

61. Cobbett, *Political Register*, December 1819; Paine, *The Rights of Man*, Part II, 158 and 'To Mr Secretary Dundas', 6 June 1792, 22; and Thelwall, 'On the exhausted state of our natural resources', 14.

62. The committee is quoted in Lipson, *The Economic History*, vol. 1, 290.

63. J. L. and B. Hammond are quoted in George, 'Revisions in economic history', 172.

64. The excise as a factor is suggested in Hughes, *Studies in Administration and Finance*, 348.

65. Wilberforce is quoted in Orth, 'English combination acts', 195; Pitt in Chase, *Early Trade Unionism*, 86.

66. George, 'Revisions in economic history', 173; Chase, *Early Trade Unionism*, 84.

67. Thompson, *The Making of the English Working Class*, 158–9 and 183–5.

68. Rosenband, 'Comparing combination acts', 166–7.

69. Orth, 'English combination acts', 207. A test run outlawing both combinations of manufacturers and journeymen had been first tried in Ireland in 1780; see Henry, *Dublin Hanged*, chs 3 and 7. Compare, too, the different way Scotland dealt with combinations during this period; see Gray, 'The law of combination'.

70. Rosenband, 'Comparing combination acts', 170; Orth, 'English combination acts', 193–4.

71. Chase, *Early Trade Unionism*, 84–5.

72. Rosenband, 'Comparing combination acts', 172.

73. Wells, *Wretched Faces*.

74. Dicey, 'The combination laws', 519.

75. Chase, *Early Trade Unionism*, 72–3.

76. Rosenband, 'Comparing combination acts', 172–3.

77. Ibid., 173–4. Bayley is best known as a Unitarian reformer, founder of the Manchester Board of Health in 1796, and follower of Wilkite radicalism; see P. Carter, 'Bayley, Thomas Butterworth (1744-1802)', DNB, 2004.

78. Ibid., 170 and 177 and 'The industrious revolution'.

79. Ibid., 178–80 and 'Becoming competitive'.

80. Behagg, *Politics and Production*.

81. For one major example of visibility tied to workplace reform during this period, see Ashworth, '"System of terror"'. For the parallel rise of efficiency, see Alexander, *The Mantra of Efficiency*, and for the emphasis upon precision measurement, see the collection of essays in Wise (ed.), *The Values of Precision*.

82. For the 1825 repeal, see the old, but useful, Dicey, *Lectures*, 190–8.

83. This legislation dated back to the Statute of Labourers in 1349 and was reinforced during the sixteenth century; see Steinfeld, *Coercion*, 40–7.

84. Chase, *Early Trade Unionism*, 28 and 54.

85. Rule, *The Experience of Labour*, 212.

Chapter 12

1. Minard, 'Colbertism continued?', 485–7 and 'Facing uncertainty'; Rosenband, 'The competitive cosmopolitanism'; Reynard, 'Manufacturing quality', 510; and Potofsky, 'The construction of Paris', 31–48.

2. Fairchilds, 'The production and marketing'.

3. Minard, 'Colbertism continued?', 487–8 and 'Facing uncertainty', 274–6; Minard and Terrier, 'Review of Jean-Pierre Hirsch'; Kaplan, 'Social classification'; and Hirsch, 'Revolutionary France'.

4. Minard, 'Colbertism continued?', 491 and 'Facing uncertainty', 285.

5. Hilaire-Perez, 'Invention and the state', 924.

6. Minard, 'Colbertism continued?', 492–3.

7. Horn, 'Marx was right!', 227 and *The Path Not Taken*, 89–125; Vardi, 'The abolition of the guilds'.

8. Minard, 'Trade without institution?', 87; Maitte, 'Labels'.

9. Minard, 'Colbertism Continued?', 478 and 'Trade without institution?', 87; Bossenga, 'Protecting merchants', 694–5. For Jacques Necker's reforms see, for example, Boscher, *French Finances*, 142–65; Jones, *The Great Nation*, 310–17.

10. I am indebted to discussions with Leonard N. Rosenband on this point.

11. The growth of these hugely informative trials can be found at the National Archives under CUST103 and I engage with some of them in *Customs and Excise*, 209–57.

12. Ashworth, 'Practical objectivity' and 'Manufacturing expertise'. This culminated in the establishment of the country's first state laboratory to scrutinize certain excsed items; see Hammond and Egan, *Weighed in the Balance*. For the emergence of specialization in theoretical matters, as opposed to observational matters of fact, within the court room during this period, see Golan, *Laws of Men*.

13. Ashworth, *Customs and Excise*, 307–15.

14. Pollexfen, *Discourse of Trade*, 148.

15. Woollen Draper, *Letter on the French Treaty*, 21.

16. Pitt, *The Speech of William Pitt*, 40.

17. Anon., 'Mr Huskisson's speech in defence of free trade', 479.

18. Pitt, *The Speech of William Pitt*, 65. For the centrality of agriculture to the French economy and the physiocrats' model of free trade in grain see, for example, Miller, 'European ideology'.

19. 'A Plan of Police for the City of London', *The Times*, 26 March 1788, 3.

20. Adam Smith is quoted in Wilson, *Mercantilism*, 5. Smith and consumption from this perspective is discussed in Hont, *Jealousy of Trade*, 55.

21. For debates over empire and the forging of political economy, see DuRivage, *Revolution against Empire*.

22. Williams, *Capitalism and Slavery*. This is especially shown in Beckert, *Empire of Cotton*; Baptist, *The Half Has Never Been Told*.

23. For the conservative reinterpretation of Smith, see Berg, *The Machinery Question*, 17, 35–6 and 90–4; Winch, *Riches and Poverty*, 8, 11 and 48; Rothschild, *Economic Sentiments*, 52–71, 82, 84, 93 and 109; and Jones, *An End to Poverty*, 234.

24. Jones, *An End to Poverty*, 70–89.

25. Ibid., ch. 2; Linebaugh, *Stop Thief!*, 142–58; and Winch, *Riches and Poverty*, 48.

26. Polanyi, *The Great Transformation*, 60–80.

27. Hilton, *A Mad, Bad & Dangerous People?*, 251 and 257–60.

28. 'INCOME TAX', *The Times*, 24 February 1816, 2.

29. Daunton, *Trusting Leviathan*, 51–5.

30. Hilton, *Corn, Cash, Commerce*, 71–4 and *A Mad, Bad & Dangerous People?*, 253.

31. Hilton, *The Age of Atonement*, 16–23; Daunton, *Trusting Leviathan* and *State and Market*, 4–5.

32. Thompson, *The Making of the English Working Class*, 813.

33. Hilton, *The Age of Atonement*, 76, 79 and 117; Jones, 'Rethinking Chartism', 115; and Daunton, *Trusting Leviathan* and *State and Market*, chs 2–4.

34. Ibid., 33, 65–6 and 80 and *A Mad, Bad, & Dynamic People?*, 309–14 and 599–611.

35. For an interesting example of the parallel change in economic doctrine and science, see M. Norton Wise with the collaboration of Smith, 'Work and waste (II)' and Alexander, *The Mantra of Efficiency*.

36. Hilton, *The Age of Atonement*, 69, 85–122 and 220–1.

37. Daunton, *Progress and Poverty*, 549–50; Hilton, *A Mad, Bad, & Dynamic People?*, 264–8; and Hardy, *Forgotten Voices*, 127–8.

38. Ibid., 519.

39. Hilton, *Age of Atonement*, 127–8 and 223. For an old, but succinct, summary of Huskisson's measures, see Lingelbach, 'William Huskisson', 766–74.

40. Hilton, *Age of Atonement*, 224.

41. Hilton, *Corn, Cash, Commerce*, 143–7, 164 and 176; Hilton, *A Mad, Bad, & Dynamic People?*, 295–6.

42. Hilton, *Corn, Cash, Commerce*, 177–8; Hardy, *Forgotten Voices*, 139–41. For Webb Hall, see Spring and Crosby, 'George Webb Hall'.

43. Hilton, *Corn, Cash, Commerce*, 183–6 and 198; Ashworth, *Customs and Excise*, 358–78; Harling, *The Waning of 'Old Corruption'*, 182–3; and Howe, *Free Trade*, 3.

44. Hilton, *Corn, Cash, Commerce*, 259–61.

45. Gambles, 'Rethinking the politics of protection' and *Protection and Politics*.

46. Robinson, 'The Silk trade', 743.

47. Harling, *Waning of 'Old Corruption'*, 152–3 and 180–93; Dowell, *History of Taxation*, vol. 2, ii and 288–92.

48. Beckert, *Empire of Cotton*.

49. Parnell, *On Financial Reform*, 205; Harling, *Waning of 'Old Corruption'*, 214–15; and Dowell, *History of Taxation*, vol. 2, 288–9. An emphasis on access to cheaper and more abundant raw materials is evident throughout the various reports made by the Commissioners of Inquiry into the Excise Establishment (1835).

50. *The Times*, 21 May 1827, 6.

51. Robinson, 'Silk trade', 746.

52. Gambles, 'Rethinking the politics of protection', 936. For a succinct overview of the protectionist argument, see Hardy, *Forgotten Voices*, 143–50.

53. Brown, 'The Board of Trade', 395; Harling, *Waning of 'Old Corruption'*, 220; Dowell, *History of Taxation*, vol. 2, 311–12; Hughes, *Studies in Administration and Finance*, 504–5; and Fine, 'Production and Excise', 144.

54. Harling, *Waning of 'Old Corruption'*, 222–3; Dowell, *History of Taxation*, vol. 2, 313–14.

55. Gambles, *Protection and Politics*, 60.

56. Schonhardt-Bailey, *From the Corn Laws*, 11.

57. Mathias, *First Industrial Nation*, 297–8; Turner, '"The Bonaparte of free trade"'; Gambles, 'Rethinking the politics of protection', 937; and Daunton, *Progress and Poverty*, 554.

58. Moore, 'Imperialism' and, especially, Beckert, *Empire of Cotton*, 74–5 and 125–8.

59. Halevy, *The Age of Peel*, 14–16.

60. Harling, *Waning of 'Old Corruption'*, 225–9 and 241–2; Daunton, *Progress and Poverty*, 520 and *Leviathan*, ch. 4; Hilton, *Corn, Cash and Commerce*, 261; Dowell, *History of Taxation*, vol. 2, 326–7; Mathias, *First Industrial Nation*, 300; Matthew, *Gladstone*, 121–2; Howe, *Free Trade*, 4; and Fine, 'Production and Excise', 144.

61. For details on the origins and earlier examples of this shift, see Musgrave, 'Notes and Extracts', 7 October 1823, 26 January and 22 February 1825, NA: CUST 29/7; Dowell,

History of Taxation, vol. 2, 276–80; Fine, 'Production and Excise', 143; and Hughes, *Studies in Administration*, 481–2.

62. Peel is quoted in Blunden, 'The position and function of the income tax', 638.

63. Daunton, *Leviathan*, 78–80; Trentmann, *Free Trade Nation*.

64. Bayly, 'The British military-fiscal state'; Taylor, 'The 1848 revolutions'.

65. Harling, *Waning of 'Old Corruption'*, 246 and 252–3; Dowell, *History of Taxation*, vol. 2, 330; and Hilton, *Corn, Cash, Commerce*, 267. Peel is quoted in Harling and Mandler, 'From fiscal-state', 70; Gambles, *Protection and Politics*, 61.

66. Schonhardt-Bailey, *From the Corn Laws*, 19; Halevy, *The Age of Peel*, 104–5.

67. Gladstone is quoted in Matthew, *Gladstone*, 127.

68. LoPatin, *Political Unions*.

69. Chase, *Early Trade Unionism*, 135; Hilton, *A Mad, Bad & Dangerous People?*, 424.

70. Chase, *Chartism*.

71. Jones, 'Rethinking chartism', 90–178.

72. Chase, *Early Trade Unionism*, 190–200. For an attempt to reconcile class-based interpretations of Chartism with Jones's argument, see Taylor, 'Rethinking the chartists'. The introduction of the income tax was welcomed by Daniel O'Connell in 1842, although the association, in general, of any tax remained connected with anti-government attacks; see Chase, *Chartism*, 271–2 and 296–7.

73. Barker, *An Age of Glass*, 25–6; Pilbin, 'External relations', 314. The view that excise duties had a completely crippling impact upon technology has typically been generalized by one small section of industry, namely, glass. Even this impact was limited to one particular type of glass, namely, that used in highly specialized precison instruments such as telescopes. The origins of this seem to lie with Robert E. Schofield's rather narrowly-focused essay titled 'Josiah Wedgwood and the technology of glass manufacturing'.

74. Crocker and Kane, *The Diaries of James Simmons*, 141.

75. Wrigley, *Mr Milner Gibson*, 5–7 and *The Manchester Chamber of Commerce and the Paper Trade*, 3–4. It is also the case that rival leather manufacturers in Germany and the United States continued to be protected by formidable tariffs to the detriment of British producers. See Church, 'The British leather industry', 563–4. A useful comparison of British economic policy to its main industrial competitors can be found in Gourevitch, 'International trade'.

76. Ainscough, 'Macclesfield Elites', 109–24. Distress among silk weavers in Spitalfields and Nottingham had been growing for some time. See, for example, 'Report on the Spitalfield and Nottingham Weavers', June 1837, JHC.

77. Ibid., 143 and 158–61.

78. Reinert, 'The role of the state', 290.

79. Gambles, 'Rethinking the politics of protection', 938.

80. Thomas, 'Escaping from constraints', 742–5.

81. Farlie, 'The nineteenth-century corn law reconsidered', 562–6 and 'The corn laws'.

82. Hilton, *A Mad, Bad & Dangerous People?*, 503.

83. Howe, 'Restoring free trade', 204–5 and *Free Trade*, 7.

84. Thomas, 'Escaping from constraints', 747.

85. Howe, *Free Trade*, 58–61.

Notes

86. Daunton, *Leviathan*, 29 and *State and Market*, part 3; Trentmann, 'National identity', 223–4.

87. Colbin, *The Unseen Hand*, 221–38; Elbaum and Lazonick, 'The decline of the British economy', 573. Elie Halevy is quoted in Zebel, 'Fair trade', 164.

Epilogue

1. For the contradictions between present economic prescriptions and the history of economic development, see, especially, Chang, *Kicking Away the Ladder, Bad Samaritans, 23 Things* and *Economics*; Reinert, *How Rich Countries Got Rich*; Parthasarathi, *Why Europe Grew Rich*; Boldizzoni, *The Poverty of Clio*; and Reinert, *Translating Empire*.

2. Cannadine, 'The present and the past'. For the later historiography, see, especially, Sewell, 'A strange career'; Jonsson, 'The industrial revolution'.

3. Ashworth, 'The ghost of Rostow' and 'The industrial revolution'. There are a number of excellent books tracing the rise of neoliberalism. See, especially, Cockett, *Thinking the Unthinkable*; Harvey, *A Brief History*; Mirowski and Plehwe (eds), *The Road from Mont Pelerin*; Peck, *Constructions of Neoliberal Reason*; Crouch, *The Strange Non-Death of Neoliberalism*; and Jones, *Masters of the Universe*.

4. Chang, *Kicking Away the Ladder, Bad Samaritans, 23 Things* and *Economics*; Reinert, *How Rich Countries Got Rich*; Parthasarathi, *Why Europe Grew Rich*; Boldizzoni, *The Poverty of Clio*; Reinert, *Translating Empire*; and Wakefield, 'Butterfield's nightmare'.

5. Reinert, *Translating Empire*, 276.

6. This can clearly be seen in the history of texts written on the subject of industrialization. See Ashworth, 'Industrialisation'. The neglect and distortion of the East in Western histories has been underlined by a steadily expanding group of historians and commentators; see, especially, Amin, *Eurocentrism*; Balut, *1492, Eight Eurocentric Historians* and *The Colonizers Model of the World*; Said, *Orientalism*; Goody, *The East in the West, Capitalism and Modernity* and the *Theft of History*; Washbrook, 'From Comparative Sociology'; Hobson, *The Eastern Origins* and *The Eurocentric Conception*; and Santos, 'A non-occidentalist West?'.

7. Horn, Rosenband and Smith (eds), *Reconceptualizing*.

8. Mises, *Economic Freedom*, 4 and *Human Action*, vol. 1, 10; Hayek, *The Fatal Conceit*, 33 and 44–5; and Landes, *The Wealth and Poverty of* Nations, 78, 96, 108 and 112.

9. McCloskey, *Bourgeois Dignity*; Ferguson, *Civilization*.

10. Losurdo, *Liberalism*; Beckert, *Empire of Cotton*; Baptist, *Half Has Never Been Told*; and Rockman, 'What makes the history of capitalism newsworthy?'.

11. Vries, *State*.

12. Reinert, *Translating Empire*, 52 and 71. A recent economist, Mazzucato, has put the state back to the centre of recent technological innovations. See her *The Entrepreneurial State*. Short-term venture capitalists do not invest in risky long-term projects – typically only the state does this. The reward is national wealth and thus greater employment and revenues. For an excellent critique of liberal economic dogmas and its adverse impact upon democracy, see Self, *Rolling Back the Market*.

13. For the recent emphasis upon a genetic interpretation, see Clark, *A Farewell to Alms*.

14. This has a long intellectual trajectory but for a good start compare Hayek, *The Road to Serfdom* and Popper, *The Open Society* to Mokyr, *The Enlightened Economy* and McCloskey,

Bourgeois Dignity. For a recent critical historical interpretation of American notions of freedom, see Rana, *The Two Faces of American Freedom*.

15. Mokyr, 'Eurocentricity triumphant', *Gifts of Athena*, 'The intellectual origins', 302 and 336–7, 'Intellectual property rights', 350, *The Enlightened Economy* and co-authored with Nye, 'Distributional coalitions', 59–60, 62–3 and 65–6; Jacob, *The First Knowledge Economy*; and Black, *The Power of Knowledge*.

16. Sachs, *The End of Poverty*, 34 and 41.

17. Wakefield, 'Butterfield's nightmare'.

18. Washbrook, 'From Comparative sociology'; Wong, *China Transformed* and with Rosenthal, *Before and Beyond Divergence*; Frank, *ReOrient*; Hanley, *Everyday Things*; Pomeranz, *The Great Divergence*; Bray, *Technology and Society*; and Parthasarathi, *The Transition to a Colonial Economy* and *Why Europe Grew Rich*.

BIBLIOGRAPHY

Abbreviations

BL SP	Sloane Papers, British Library
BLO	Bodleian Library, Oxford University
CUL Ch(H)	Cholmondley Houghton Papers, Cambridge University Library
CUST 48	Excise Board and Secretariat: Entry Books of Correspondence with Treasury (144 vols, 1668–1839), NA
DNB	*Dictionary of National Biography* (Oxford, 2004)
JHC	Journals of the House of Commons, House of Commons Parliamentary Papers online, University of Southampton
HCSP	House of Commons Sessional Papers, ed. S. Lambert (147 vols, Delaware, 1975)
HL	Huntington Library, California
HPHC	History and Proceedings of the House of Commons, British History Online
NA	National Archives, Kew, London
SOR	Statutes of the Realm, British History Online

Primary sources

An Act of the Commons of England in Parliament for the speedy raising and levying of Monies by way of New Impost or Excise (London 1649).

Anon., *The Anti-Projector. Or The History of the Fen Project* (London 1646).

Anon., *The Standard of Equality in Subsidiary Taxes and Payments, or a Just and Strong Preserver of Publique Liberty* (London 1647).

Anon., *Reasons and Grounds for the Necessitie, Equalitie, and Expedience of an Excise, to be Granted upon the Particulars Contained Herein* (London 1649).

Anon., *The Excise-Mans Lamentation* (London 1652).

Anon., *England's Interest Asserted in the Government of Its Native Commodities. And more Especially the Manufacture of Wool* (London 1669).

Anon., *At the Court at Whitehall* (London, 6 June 1673).

Anon., *The Prevention of Poverty. Or, New Proposals Humbly Offered for Enriching the Nation* (London 1677).

Anon., *News From Sir. William Waller, The Lord Grey and Sir. Thomas Armstrong, And of Several other Fled from Justice* (London 1684).

Anon., *The History or Narrative of the Great Level of the Fens, Called Bedford Level* (London 1685).

Anon., *The Case and Circumstances of Paper-making in England Truly Stated* (London 1689).

Anon., *A Discourse of the Necessity of Encouraging Mechanick Industry* (London 1689).

Anon., *The Linnen and Woolen Manufactory Discoursed: with the Nature of Companies and Trade in General* (London 1691).

Anon., *The General-Excise Considered* (London 1692).

Anon., *The Allegations of the Glass-Makers Examin'd and Answer'd* (London 1694).

Anon., *The Excise Rectify'd* (London 1695).

Anon., *Some Considerations Humbly Offered to Demonstrate How Prejudicial It Would Be to the English Plantations, Revenues of the Crown, the Navigation and General Good of This Kingdom, That the Sole Trade for Negroes Should Be Granted to a Company with a Joynt-Stock Exclusive to All Others* (London 1695).

Anon., *The Case of the Poor Work-men Glass-makers* (London 1695).

Anon., *The Petition and Case of the Embroiderers, Flourishers, Raisers and Stichers of East-India Silks, and other Goods, and Stainers thereof* (London 1696).

Anon., *An Account of the Produce of the Glass Duty* (London 1696).

Anon, *The Miserable Case of the Poor Glass-Makers, Artificers, and Several Hundred Families that were Imployed in the said Manufacture. Humbly offered in reference to the Duty on Glass* (London 1696).

Anon., *The Mischief of the Five Shillings Tax upon Coal* (London 1698).

Anon., *An Answer to the Most Material Objections Against the Bill for Restraining the East-India Wrought Silks &c* (London 1699).

Anon., *An English Winding Sheet for the East-India Manufactures* (London 1700).

Anon., *A Short Abstract of a Case which was last sessions presented to Parliament: Being a true relation of the Rise and Progress of the East India Company shewing how their Manufactures have been, are, and will be prejudicial to the Manufactures of England* (London 1700).

Anon., *For the Bill Against Clandestine Trade* (London 1700).

Anon., *Instructions to be Observed by the Officers of Excise* (Edinburgh 1707).

Anon., *Torism and Trade can never Agree: To which is added, An Account and Character of the Mercator and his Writing* (London 1713).

Anon., *An Account of the Woolen Manufactures made in the Province of Languedoc, and at Abbeville, in Picardy* (London 1713).

Anon., *The State of the Silk and Woolen Manufactures. Considered in Relation to a French Trade* (London 1713).

Anon., *The Consequences of a Law for Reducing the Dutys upon French Wines, Brandy, Silk and Linen, to those of other Nations, with Remarks on the Mercator* (London 1713).

Anon., *A Brief State of the Question, Between the Printed and Painted Callicoes and the Woolen and Silk Manufacture* (London 1719).

Anon., *The Congress of Excise-Asses* (London 1733).

Anon. (ed.), *Excise: Being a Collection of Letters, &c* (London 1733).

Anon., *A Collection of Scarce and Valuable Tracts* (London 1748, 4 vols).

Anon., *An Appeal to Facts. Regulating the Home Trade and Inland Manufactures of Great Britain and Ireland* (London 1751).

Anon., *Instructions for Officers Who Survey Printers of Callicoe, &c* (London 1777).

Anon., *An Address to the Members of both Houses of Parliament on the Late Tax on Fustian, and Other Cotton Goods* (London 1785).

Anon., *The Two Treaties between Great Britain and France, the Former Ratified in the Reign of Queen Anne, 1713, and the Latter Signed by Mr. Eden in the Year 1786* (London 1786).

Anon., *Historical and Political Remarks of the Commercial Treaty* (London 1787).

Anon., 'Mr Huskisson's speech in defence of free trade'. *Blackwood's Edinburgh Magazine* 19 (1826): 474–88.

Bibliography

An Ordinance for Bringing the Publique Revenues of This Commonwealth into one Treasurie (London 1654).

Ashley, William, 'The tory origins of free trade policy'. *Journal of Economics* 11 (1897): 1–19.

Asgill, John, *A Brief Answer to A Brief State of the Question Between the Printed and Painted Callicoes, And the Woolen and Silk Manufactures* (London 1719).

Bethel, Slingsby, *The Present Interest of England Stated* (London 1671).

Blanch, John, *The Naked Truth, in an Essay upon Trade* (London 1696).

Blanch, John, *The Interest of Great Britain Consider'd in an Essay upon Wool, Tin and Leather* (London 1707).

Bland, John, *Trade Revived, or, A Way Proposed to Restore, Increase, Inrich, Strengthen and Preserve the Decayed and even Dying Trade of this our English Nation, in its Manufactories, Coin, Shiping and Revenue whereby Taxes may be lessened if not totally taken away, to the great content of the people* (London 1659).

Blanqui, Jérôme-Adolphe, *History of Political Economy in Europe* (1837, English translation, New York 1880).

Blunden, G. H., 'The position and function of the income tax in the British fiscal system'. *Economic Journal* 2 (1892): 637–52.

Board of Trade and Plantations, *Representation from the Commissioners for Trade and Plantations, To the Right Honourable the Lords Spiritual and Temporal, In Parliament Assembled* (London 1734).

Boyer, Abel, *An Account of the State and Progress of the Present Negotiation of Peace with the Reasons For and Against a Partition of Spain, &c* (London 1711).

Brewers of London, *Free-men Inslaved: Or, Reasons humbly offered to the right Honorable, the Commons of England in Parliament assembled, for the taking off the Excise upon BEER and ALE* (London 1642).

British Merchant, from 1787: Addressed to the Chamber of Manufacturers (London 1787).

Browning, Oscar, 'The treaty of commerce between England and France in 1786'. *Transactions of the Royal Historical Society* 2 (1885): 349–64.

Burrell, Andrewes, *Exceptions Against Sir Cornelius Virmudens Discourse for the Draining of the Great Fennes, &c* (London 1642).

Burrell, Andrewes, *A Briefe Relation Discovering Plainely the true Causes why the Great Levell of Fens … have been Drowned, and made Unfruitful for Many Years Past* (London 1642).

Carnot, Sadi, *Reflections on the Motive Power of Fire and on Machines Fitted to Develop that Power* (1824, New York 1988).

Carter, W., *An Abstract of the Proceedings of W. Carter. Being a Plan to some Objectives urged against them* (London 1694).

Cary, John, *An Essay on the State of England in Relation to Its Trade, Its Poor, and Its Taxes* (Bristol 1695).

Case of the British and Irish Manufacture of Linens, Threads and Tapes fairly stated, and all the Objections against the Encouragement proposed to be given to that Manufacture, fully answered (London 1738) in Smith (ed.), *Chronicon Rusticum – Commerciale*, 296–300.

Case of the Glass-Makers in and About the City of London (London 1699).

Case of the Company of White Paper Makers Humbly Presented to the Consideration of the Present Parliament (London 1689).

Case and Humble Petition of the Hard Cake and White Soap Makers (London 1711).

Case of the British Cotton Spinners and Manufacturers of Piece Goods (London 1790).

Child, Josiah, *A Treatise on the East-India Trade* (London 1681).

Child, Josiah, *A Supplement to a Former Treatise, concerning the East-India Trade* (London 1689).

Child, Josiah, *A Discourse of the Nature, Use and Advantages of Trade* (London 1694).

Cobbett, William, *Political Register* (London, December 1819).

Colquhoun, Patrick, *A Treatise on the Police of the Metropolis* (London 1797).

Conway, M. D. (ed.), *The Writings of Thomas Paine* (London 1996, 4 vols).

Cunningham, William, 'The repression of the woolen manufactures in Ireland'. *English Historical Review* 1 (1886): 277–94.

Cunningham, William, *Alien Immigrants in England* (1897, 2nd edn, London 1969).

Davenant, Charles, *An Essay upon Ways and Means* (London 1695) and reprinted in Whitworth (ed.), *The Political and Commercial Works of Charles Davenant*, vol. 1, 1–81.

Davenant, Charles, *An Essay on the East-India-Trade. By the Author of the Essay upon Wayes and Means* (London 1696).

Davenant, Charles, 'A memorial concerning credit and the means and methods by which it may be restored', 15 July 1696, and reprinted in Davenant, *Two Manuscripts by Charles Davenant*.

Davenant, Charles, *An Essay upon the Natural Credit of England* (London 1710).

Davenant, Charles, *A Second Report to the Honourable the Commissioners for Putting in Execution the Act, intitled, An Act, for the Taking, Examining, and Stating the Publick Accounts of the Kingdom. From Part I* (London 1712).

Davenant, Charles, *Two Manuscripts by Charles Davenant*, with an Introduction by Abbott Payson Usher (Baltimore 1942).

Defoe, Daniel, *Taxes no Charge: In A Letter from a Gentleman, To A Person of Quality* (London 1689).

Defoe, Daniel (ed.), *Extracts from Several Mercators. Being Considerations on the State of the British Trade* (Dublin 1713).

Defoe, Daniel, *The Complete English Tradesman* (1725, repr., Oxford 1841, 2 vols).

Dowell, Stephen, *A History of Taxation and Taxes in England: From the Earliest Times to the Present Day* (1884, 3rd edn, New York 1965, 4 vols).

Downing, George, *A Discourse written by Sir George Downing, The King of Great Britain's Envoy Extraordinary to the States of the United Provinces* (London, 1664).

Dupin, Nicholas, *Proposals of Nicholas Dupin … To All the Parishes in and about the City of London, and within the Weekly Bills of Mortality, to set the Poor to Work* (London 1698).

Eden, William, *Four Letters to the Earl of Carlisle from William Eden to which is added a Fifth Letter* (1779, 3rd edn, London 1780).

Eden, William, *Letter to the Earl of Carlisle from the Right Honourable William Eden* (Dublin 1786).

Fair Merchant, *A Letter to a Member of Parliament Concerning Clandestine Trade* (London 1700).

Ferguson, Robert, *The East-India-Trade: A Most Profitable Trade to the Kingdom* (London 1677).

Fortrey, Samuel, *England's Interest and Improvement, consisting in the Increase of the Store and Trade of this Kingdom* (London 1663).

Gee, Joshua, *The Trade and Navigation of Great Britain* (1729, 4th edn, London 1738).

Harley, Robert, *An Essay upon Publick Credit*, 1710 and reprinted in Anon., *A Collection of Scarce and Valuable Tracts* (London 1748, 4 vols).

Halifax, Marquis of, *An Essay upon Taxes, Calculated for the Present Juncture of Affairs in England*, 1693, in Scott (ed.), *A Collection of Scarce and Valuable Tracts*, vol. 11, 75–81.

Hamilton, Alexander, *An Enquiry into the Principles of Taxation, Chiefly Applicable to Articles of Internal Consumption* (London 1790).

Haynes, John, *A View of the Present State of the Clothing Trade in England* (London 1706).

Hewins, W. A. S., *English Trade and Finance Chiefly in the Seventeenth Century* (London 1892).

Highmore, A., *A Practical Arrangement of the Laws Relative to the Excise* (London 1796, 2 vols).

Huie, J., *An Abridgement of All the Statutes Now in Force, Relative to the Revenue of Excise* (Edinburgh 1797).

Hume, David, 'Of Credit', in his *Essays*, 207–17.

Hume, David, *Essays, Literary, Moral and Political* (1777, repr., London, n.d.).

Hyde, Edward, first earl of Clarendon, 'News from Dunkirk: or, Clarendon's farewell to England', London, 12 December 1667.

Bibliography

I. B., *The Merchants Remonstrance: Wherein is set Forth the Inevitable Miseries which may suddenly befall this kingdome by want of Trade, and decay of Manufactures* (London 1644).

Ibeson, James, *To the Supreme Authority the Parliament of the Common-wealth of England* (London 1650).

Instructions to be Observed by the Officers of Excise (Edinburgh 1707).

Instructions to be Observed by the Officers concerned in Ascertaining the Duties on Glass (London 1758).

James, William, *England's Interest: Or, Means to Promote the Consumption of English Wool* (London 1689).

Jones, Richard, *An Essay on the Distribution of Wealth and on the Sources of Taxation* (London 1844).

King, Charles (ed.), *The British Merchant: A Collection of Papers Relating to the Trade and Commerce of Great Britain and Ireland* (1724, 2nd edn, London 1743, 3 vols).

Kuklick, B. (ed.), *Thomas Paine: Political Writings* (1792, Cambridge 1994).

Leadbetter, Charles, *The Royal Gauger. Or, Gauging made Easy, As it is actually Practised by the Officers of His Majesty's Revenue of Excise* (1739, 2nd edn, London 1743).

Locke, S., *A New Abstract of the Excise Statutes* (London 1788).

Mackay, H., *An Abridgement of the Excise-Laws, and of the Custom-Laws therewith Connected, now in Force in Great Britain* (Edinburgh 1779).

Manchester Chamber of Commerce and the Paper Trade – Free trade: What is it? (Bury 1865).

Mann, J. A., *The Cotton Trade of Great Britain* (Manchester 1860).

Martyn, Henry, *Considerations upon the East-India Trade* (London 1701).

Meadows, Philip, *Observations Concerning the Dominion and Sovereignty of the Seas: Being an Abstract of the Marine Affairs of England* (London, 1689).

Merchants trading to France, *To the Right Honourable the Lords Commissioners Appointed for the Treaty of Commerce with France* (London, 29 November 1674).

Merchant, A., *The Weavers Pretences Examined* (London 1719).

Mun, Thomas, *England's Treasure by Foreign Trade* (London 1664).

N. C. a Weaver of London, *The Great Necessity and Advantage of Preserving our own Manufactories. Being An Answer To a Pamphlet Intitl'd The Honour and Advantage of the East-India Trade, &c* (London 1697).

Observations on the Means of Extending the Consumption of British Callicoes, Muslins and Other Cotton Goods (London 1788).

Paine, Thomas, *The Rights of Man* (London 1792, Part II), in Kuklick (ed.), *Thomas* Paine, 145–203.

Paine, Thomas, 'To Mr Secretary Dundas', 6 June 1792, in Conway (ed.), *The Writings of Thomas Paine*, vol. 3, 15–29.

Papillon, A. F. W., *Memoirs of Thomas Papillon, of London, Merchant* (Reading 1887).

Papillon, Thomas [Robert Ferguson], *A Treatise Concerning The East India Trade To The Kingdom, And Best Secured and Improved by A Company and A Joint-Stock* (London 1680).

Parnell, Henry, *On Financial Reform* (London 1830).

Petyt, William, *Britannia Languens. Or, A Discourse of Trade: Shewing the Grounds and Reasons of the Increase and Decay of Land-rents, National Wealth and Strength* (1680, London 1689).

Pitt the Younger, William, *The Speech of William Pitt in the House of Commons, 12 February 1787* (London 1787).

Pittar, T. J., *Customs Tariffs of the United Kingdom from 1800 to 1897. With Some Notes Upon the History of the More Important Branches of Receipt from the Year 1660* (London 1897).

Pollexfen, John, *A Discourse of Trade, Coyn and Paper Credit* (London 1697).

Pollexfen, John, *England and East-India Inconsistent in Their Manufactures. Being an Answer to a Treatise, Intitled, An Essay on the East-India Trade* (London 1697).

Premiums Offered by the Dublin Society (Dublin 1782).

Prynne, William, *A Declaration and Protestation Against the Illegal, Detestable, Oft-condemned, New Tax and Extortion of Excise* (London 1654).

Ramsey, James, *Bloudy Newes from the East-Indies* (London 1651).

Reasons Humbly Offered to the Honourable House of Commons by the Callicoe-Printers against the Duty Intended to be Laid on Printed Callicoes (London 1711).

Rey, Claudius, *Observations on Mr Asgill's Brief Answer to a brief State of the Question between the Printed and Painted Callicoes, &c* (London 1719).

Rey, Claudius, *The Weavers True Case. Or, the Wearing of Printed Callicoes and Linnen Destructive to the Woolen and Silk Manufactures* (London 1719).

Rey, Claudius, *A Scheme to Settle and Establish the Silk Weaving Trade on a Solid Foundation* (London 1728).

Reynel, Carew, *The True English Interest: Or An Account of the Chief National Improvements* (London 1674).

Robinson, David, 'The silk trade', *Blackwood's Edinburgh Magazine* 18 (1825): 736–50.

Robinson, Henry, *England's Safety in Trades Encrease* (London 1641).

Robinson, Henry, *Briefe Considerations concerning the Advancement of Trade and Navigation* (London 1649).

Savary, Jacques, *The Perfect Merchant or General Instructions Regarding the Mercantile Trade of France and Foreign Countries* (Paris 1675).

Say, Jean-Baptiste, *England, and The English People*, translated by John Richter (London 1816).

Schomberg, J. Alexander Crowcher, *Historical and Political Remarks upon the Tariff of the Commercial Treaty* (London 1787).

Scott, Walter, *A Collection of Scarce and Valuable Tracts* (1809, 2nd edn, London 1814, 16 vols).

Seligman, Edwin R. A., *Progressive Taxation in Theory and Practice* (Baltimore 1894).

Silk Manufactures, *The Produce of India, Italy, and France, raised in England* (London 1720).

Smith, Adam, *An Inquiry into the Nature and Causes of the Wealth of Nations* (1776, Indianapolis 1981, 2 vols).

Smith, John (ed.), *Chronicon Rusticum – Commerciale. Or Memoirs of Wool* (London 1747, 2 vols).

Soapmakers Complaint for the Losse of their Trade (London 1650).

Stepney, G., *Essay upon the Present Interest of England* (London 1701).

Steuart, James, *An Inquiry into the Principles of Political Oeconomy*, edited with an Introduction by A. S. Skinner (1767, Edinburgh 1966, 2 vols).

Stuff Weaver's Case against Printing Callicoes Examined (London 1704).

Thelwall, John, 'On the exhausted state of our natural resources and the consequent condition of our labourers and manufacturers'. *The Tribune*, 1795, in Claeys (ed.), *The Politics of English Jacobinism*, 14.

Tomlinson, Charles, *The Useful Arts and Manufacturers of Great Britain: First Series, Textile Fabrics, &c* (London 1852).

T. S. a Weaver in London, *Reasons Humbly Offered for the Passing a Bill for the Hindering the Home Consumption of East-India Silks, Bengals &c* (London 1697).

Trevers, J., *An Essay to the Restoring of Our Decayed Trade* (London 1677).

Tryon, T., *England's Grandeur, and Way to Get Wealth: Or, Promotion of Trade* (London 1699).

T. S., *England's Danger by Indian Manufactures* (London 1701).

Vermuyden, Cornelius, *A Discourse touching the Drayning the Great Fennes … as it was presented to his Majestie* (London 1642) and reprinted in Wells, *The History of the Draining of the Great Level of the Fens*, 339–66.

Walpole, Robert, *King's Speech to both Houses of Parliament, 19 October 1721* (London 1721).

W. C., *An Alarum to England, To Prevent its Destruction by the Loss of Trade and Navigation* (London 1700).

Bibliography

W. C., *A Discourse Humbly Offer'd to the Consideration of the Honourable House of Commons, Towards the Raising Moneys by an Excise* (London 1695).

Whiston, James, *A Discourse of the Decay of Trade* (London, 1693).

Whiston, James, *The Causes of Our Present Calamities In reference to the Trade of the Nation* (London 1695).

Whitworth, C. (ed.), *The Political and Commercial Works of Charles Davenant* (London 1771, 5 vols).

Woollen Draper, A., *Letter on the French Treaty* (London 1786).

Worsley, Benjamin, *The Advocate: Or A Narrative of the State and Condition of Things between the English and Dutch Nation in Relation to Trade* (London 1651).

Wright, John, *An Address to the Members of Both Houses of Parliament on the late Tax Laid on Fustian, and Other Cotton Goods* (London 1785).

Wrigley, T., *Mr Milner Gibson and the Papermakers* (Manchester 1864).

Secondary sources

Acemoglu, Daron, and James A. Robinson, *Why Nations Fail: The Origins of Power, Prosperity and Poverty* (London 2012).

Ainscough, Steven, 'Macclesfield elites, 1832-1918' (unpublished PhD, University of Liverpool 2004).

Alexander, J. K., *The Mantra of Efficiency: From Waterwheel to Social Control* (Baltimore 2008).

Allen, Robert C., *The British Industrial Revolution in Global Perspective* (Cambridge 2009).

Ames, G. J., 'Colbert's Indian ocean strategy of 1664-1674: A reappraisal'. *French Historical Studies* 16 (1990): 536–59.

Amin, Samir, *Eurocentrism* (1988, 2nd edn, New York 2009).

Appleby, Joyce, *The Relentless Revolution: A History of Capitalism* (New York 2010).

Arneil, Barbara, 'Trade, plantations, and property: John Locke and the economic defence of colonialism'. *Journal of the History of Ideas* 55 (1994): 591–609.

Arrighi, Giovanni, *Adam Smith in Beijing: Lineages of the Twenty-First Century* (London 2007).

Ash, Eric, '"A note and a caveat for the merchant": Mercantile advisors in Elizabethan England'. *Sixteenth Century Journal* 33 (2002): 1–31.

Ash, Eric, *Power, Knowledge and Expertise in Elizabethan England* (Baltimore 2004).

Ash, Eric, 'Amending nature: draining the English Fens', in L. S. Roberts, S. Schaffer and P. Dear (eds), *The Mindful Hand: Inquiry and Invention from the Late Renaissance to Early Industrialization* (Amsterdam 2007), 117–43.

Ash, Eric, 'Introduction: expertise and the early modern state'. *Osiris* 25 (2010): 1–24.

Ashcraft, Richard, *Revolutionary Parties and Locke's Treatises of Government* (Princeton 1986).

Ashton, T. S., *The Industrial Revolution, 1760-1830* (London 1948).

Ashworth, William J., 'The calculating eye: Baily, Herschel, Babbage and the business of astronomy'. *British Journal for the History of Science* 27 (1994): 409–41.

Ashworth, William J., 'Memory, efficiency and symbolic analysis: Charles Babbage, John Herschel and the industrial mind'. *Isis* 87 (1996): 629–53.

Ashworth, William J., '"System of terror": Samuel Bentham, accountability and dockyard reform during the Napoleonic Wars'. *Social History* 23, 1 (January 1998): 63–79.

Ashworth, William J., '"Between the trader and the public": British alcohol standards and the proof of good governance'. *Technology and Culture* 42 (2001): 27–50.

Ashworth, William J., *Customs and Excise: Trade, Production and Consumption, 1660-1842* (Oxford 2003).

Ashworth, William J., 'Practical objectivity: the excise, state, and production in eighteenth century England'. *Social Epistemology* 18 (2004): 181–97.

Ashworth, William J., 'Metrology and the state: science, revenue, and commerce'. *Science* 306 (2004): 1314–17.

Ashworth, William J., 'The ghost of Rostow: Science, culture, and the British industrial revolution'. *History of Science* 46 (2008): 249–74.

Ashworth, William J., 'Manufacturing expertise: the excise and production in eighteenth-century Britain'. *Osiris* 25 (2010): 231–54.

Ashworth, William J., 'The intersection of industry and the state in eighteenth-century Britain', in Roberts, Schaffer and Dear (eds), *The Mindful Hand*, 348–77.

Ashworth, William J., 'Industrialisation', Oxford Bibliography Online, 2013.

Ashworth, William J., 'The industrial revolution and the ideological revolution: Science, neoliberalism and history'. *History of Science* 52 (2014): 178–99.

Attwood, Rollin S., 'Localization of the cotton industry in Lancashire, England'. *Economic Geography* 4 (1928): 187–95.

Austen, R. A., 'On company pre-industrial African and European economies'. *African Economic History* 19 (1990–1): 21–4.

Bagwell, Philip S., *The Transport Revolution from 1770* (London 1974).

Bailey, Brian, *The Luddite Rebellion* (Stroud 1998).

Balut, J. M., *1492: The Debate on Colonialism, Eurocentrism and History* (New Jersey 1992).

Balut, J. M., *The Colonizers Model of the World: Geographical Diffusionism* (New York 1993).

Balut, J. M., *Eight Eurocentric Historians* (New York 2000).

Baptist, Edward E., *Half Has Never Been Told: Slavery and the Making of Modern American Capitalism* (New York 2014).

Barker, T. C., R. Dickinson and D. W. F. Hardie, 'The origins of the synthetic alkali industry in Britain'. *Economica* 23 (1956): 158–71.

Barker, T. C., R. Dickinson and D. W. F. Hardie, *The Glassmakers Pilkington: The Rise of an International Company 1826-1976* (London 1977).

Barker, T. C., R. Dickinson and D. W. F. Hardie, *An Age of Glass: The Illustrated History* (London 1994).

Barnett, David, *London, Hub of the Industrial Revolution: A Revisionary History 1775-1825* (London 1998).

Barrett, Ward, 'World bullion flows, 1450-1800', in Tracy (ed.), *The Rise of Merchant Empires*, 224–54.

Baxter, S. B., *The Development of the Treasury 1660-1702* (London 1957).

Bayly, C. A., 'The British military-fiscal state and indigenous resistance in India, 1750-1820', in Lawrence Stone (ed.), *An Imperial State at War: Britain from 1689 to 1815* (London 1994), 322–54.

Bayly, C. A., *The Birth of the Modern World 1780-1914* (Oxford 2004).

Beattie, J. M., *Crime and the Courts in England 1660-1800* (Princeton 1986).

Beckert, Sven, *Empire of Cotton: A New History of Global Capitalism* (London 2014).

Beckett, J. V., 'Land tax or excise: the levying of taxation in seventeenth and eighteenth-century England'. *English Historical Review* 100 (1985): 285–308.

Beckett, J. V., and M. Turner, 'Taxation and economic growth in eighteenth-century Britain'. *Economic History Review* 43 (1990): 377–403.

Beer, G. L., *The Old Colonial System 1660-1754* (2 vols, New York 1912).

Behagg, Clive, *Politics and Production in the Early Nineteenth Century* (London 1990).

Behrens, C. B. A., *Society, Government and the Enlightenment: The Experiences of Eighteenth-Century France and Prussia* (London 1985).

Belchem, John, *Orator Hunt: Henry Hunt and the English Working Class* (Oxford 1985).

Belchem, John, *Industrialisation and the Working Classes: The English Experience, 1750-1900* (Aldershot 1990).

Bibliography

Beltran, G. A., 'The slave trade in Mexico'. *Hispanic American Historical Review* 24 (1944): 412–31.

Berg, Maxine, *The Machinery Question and the Making of Political Economy 1815-1848* (Cambridge 1980).

Berg, Maxine, 'What difference did women's work make to the industrial revolution'. *History Workshop Journal* 35 (1993): 22–40.

Berg, Maxine, *The Age of Manufactures 1700-1820: Industry, Innovation and Work in Britain* (1985, 2nd edn, London 1994).

Berg, Maxine, 'From imitation to invention: Creating commodities in eighteenth-century Britain'. *Economic History Review* 55 (2002): 1–30.

Berg, Maxine, 'In pursuit of luxury: Global history and British consumer goods in the eighteenth century'. *Past and Present* 82 (2004): 85–142.

Berg, Maxine, 'The genesis of "useful Knowledge"'. *History of Science* 45 (2007): 123–33.

Berg, Maxine, *Luxury and Pleasure in Eighteenth-Century Britain* (Oxford 2007).

Berg, Maxine, 'The British product revolution of the eighteenth century', in Horn, Rosenband and Smith (eds), *Reconceptualizing the Industrial Revolution*, 47–64.

Berg, Maxine, and Pat Hudson, 'Rehabilitating the industrial revolution'. *Economic History Review* 45 (1992): 24–50.

Biggs, N., 'A tale untangled: measuring the fineness of yarn'. *Textile History* 35 (2004): 120–9.

Binfield, Kevin (ed.), *Writings of the Luddites* (Baltimore 2004).

Binney, J. E. D., *British Public Finance and Administration 1774-92* (Oxford 1958).

Black, Jeremy (ed.), *Britain in the Age of Walpole* (London 1984).

Black, Jeremy (ed.), *The Power of Knowledge: How Information and Technology Made the Modern World* (New Haven 2014).

Blackburn, Robin, 'The old world background to European colonial slavery'. *William and Mary Quarterly* 54 (1997): 65–102.

Blackburn, Robin, *The Making of New World Slavery: From the Baroque to the Modern, 1492-1800* (1997, 2nd edn, London 2010).

Blackburn, Robin, *The American Crucible: Slavery, Emancipation and Human Rights* (London 2011).

Boldizzoni, Francesco, *The Poverty of Clio: Resurrecting Economic History* (Princeton 2012).

Bolton, G. C., 'Some British reactions to the Irish act of union'. *Economic History Review* 18 (1965): 367–75.

Bolton, G. C., and B. E. Kennedy, 'William Eden and the treaty of Mauritius, 1786-7'. *Historical Journal* 16 (1973): 681–96.

Bosher, J. F., *The Single Duty Project: A Study of the Movement for a French Customs Union in the Eighteenth Century* (London 1969).

Bosher, J. F., *French Finances 1770-1795: From Business to Bureaucracy* (Cambridge 1970).

Bosher, J. F., 'Current writing on administration and finance in eighteenth-century France'. *Journal of Modern History* 53 (1981): 73–83.

Bosher, J. F., 'Huguenot merchants and the protestant international in the seventeenth century'. *William and Mary Quarterly* 52 (1995): 77–102.

Bossenga, Gail, 'Protecting merchants: guilds and commercial capitalism in eighteenth-century France'. *French Historical Studies* 15 (1988): 693–703.

Bowden, P. J., 'The wool supply and the woollen industry'. *Economic History Review* 9 (1956): 44–58.

Bowden, Witt, 'The English manufacturers and the commercial treaty of 1786 with France'. *American Historical Review* 25 (1919): 18–35.

Bowden, Witt, 'The influence of the manufacturers on some of the early policies of William Pitt'. *American Historical Review* 29 (1924): 655–74.

Bowden, Witt, *Industrial Society in England Towards the End of the Eighteenth Century* (New York 1925).

Bowrey, Kathy, 'Art, craft, good taste and manufacturing: the development of intellectual property laws'. http://www.chickenfish.cc/copy/. This is an electronic version of an essay that first appeared in *Law in Context* 15 (1997): 78–104.

Brace, Richard Munthe, 'The Anglo-French treaty of commerce of 1786: a reappraisal'. *The Historian* 9 (1947): 151–62.

Braddick, Michael J., 'An English military revolution?'. *Historical Journal* 36 (1993): 965–75.

Braddick, Michael J., *Parliamentary Taxation in Seventeenth-Century England: Local Administration and Response* (Woodbridge 1994).

Braddick, Michael J., *State Formation in Early Modern England 1550-1700* (Cambridge 2000).

Bray, Francesca, *Technology and Society in Ming China 1368-1644* (Washington 2000).

Breen, T. H., *The Marketplace of Revolution: How Consumer Politics Shaped American Independence* (Oxford 2005).

Breihan, J. R., 'The Addington party and the navy in British politics 1801-1806', in Symonds (ed.), *New Aspects of Naval History*, 163–88.

Bremer, Francis J., *John Winthrop: America's Forgotten Founding Father* (Oxford 2003).

Brenner, Robert, *Merchants and Revolution: Commercial Change, Political Conflict, and London's Overseas Traders, 1550-1653* (1993, London 2003).

Brewer, John, *Party Ideology and Popular Politics at the Accession of George III* (Cambridge 1976).

Brewer, John, 'The English state and fiscal appropriation, 1688-1789'. *Parliament and Society* 16 (1988): 288–385.

Brewer, John, *The Sinews of Power: War, Money and the English State, 1688-1783* (London 1989).

Brewer, John, and Roy Porter (eds), *Consumption and the World of Goods* (London 1993).

Brinkley, T., 'Escaping from constraints: the industrial revolution in a Malthusian context'. *Journal of Interdisciplinary History* 15 (1985): 729–53.

Brisco, N. A., *The Economic Policy of Robert Walpole* (New York 1907).

Broadberry, S., and B. Gupta, 'The early modern great divergence: Wages, prices and economic development in Europe and Asia, 1500-1800'. *Economic History Review* 59 (2006): 2–31.

Broadberry, S., and B. Gupta, 'Lancashire, India, and shifting competitive advantage in cotton textiles, 1700-1850: the neglected role of factor prices'. *Economic History Review* 62 (2009): 279–305.

Brown, Lucy, 'The board of trade and the tariff problem, 1840-1842'. *English Historical Review* 68 (1953): 394–421.

Brown, S. E., '"A just and profitable commerce": moral economy and the middle classes in eighteenth-century London'. *Journal of British Studies* 32 (1993): 305–32.

Calvert, Albert Frederick, *Salt in Cheshire* (1915, London 2010).

Cannadine, David, 'The present and the past in the English industrial revolution'. *Past and Present* 103 (1984): 131–72.

Canny, Nicholas (ed.), *The Origins of Empire: British Overseas Enterprise to the Close of the Seventeenth Century* (Oxford 1998).

Cappon, Lester J., 'The Blathwayt papers of colonial Williamsburg, Inc.'. *William and Mary Quarterly* 4 (1947): 317–31.

Carlos, A. M., 'Principal-agent problems in early trading companies: a tale of two firms'. *American Economic Review* 82 (1992): 140–5.

Carlos, A. M., and S. Nicholas, 'Theory and history: Seventeenth-century joint-stock chartered trading companies'. *Journal of Economic History* 56 (1996): 916–24.

Carlos, A. M., J. Key and J. L. Dupree, 'Learning and the creation of stock-market institutions: evidence from the Royal African and Hudson Bay Companies, 1670-1700'. *Journal of Economic History* 58 (1998): 318–44.

Carswell, John, *The South Sea Bubble* (1960, Stroud 2001).

Bibliography

Catterall, R. C. H., 'Sir George Downing and the regicides'. *American Historical Review* 17 (1912): 268–89.

Chandaman, C. D., *The English Public Revenue 1660-1688* (Oxford 1975).

Chang, Ha-Joon, *Kicking Away the Ladder: Development Strategy in Historical Perspective* (London 2003).

Chang, Ha-Joon, *Bad Samaritans: Rich Nations, Poor Policies and the Threat to the Developing World* (London 2007).

Chang, Ha-Joon, *23 Things They Don't Tell You About Capitalism* (London 2010).

Chang, Ha-Joon, *Economics: The User's Guide* (St. Ives 2014).

Chapman, S. D., *The Cotton Industry in the Industrial Revolution* (London 1972).

Chapman, S. D., 'Quantity versus quality in the British industrial revolution: the case of printed textiles'. *Northern History* 21 (1985): 175–92.

Chapman, S. D., *Merchant Enterprise in Britain: From the Industrial Revolution to World War 1* (1992, Cambridge 2004).

Charlesworth, Andrew, 'From the moral economy of Devon to the political economy of Manchester, 1790-1812'. *Social History* 18 (1993): 205–17.

Chase, Malcolm, *Early Trade Unionism: Fraternity, Skill and the Politics of Labour* (Aldershot 2000).

Chase, Malcolm, *Chartism: A New History* (Manchester 2007).

Chatterton, E. K., *King's Cutters and Smugglers 1700-1855* (1912, London 2010).

Cherry, G. L., 'The development of the English free-trade movement in Parliament, 1689-1702'. *Journal of Modern History* 25 (1953): 103–19.

Cherry, G. L., *Early English Liberalism: Its Emergence Through Parliamentary Action, 1660-1702* (New York 1962).

Chester, N., *The English Administrative System 1780-1870* (Oxford 1981).

Christie, John, and Sally Shuttleworth (eds), *Nature Transformed: Science and Literature 1700-1900* (Manchester 1984).

Church, R. A., 'The British leather industry and foreign competition, 1870-1914'. *Economic History Review* 24 (1971): 543–70.

Cipolla, Carlo M., *Before the Industrial Revolution: European Society and Economy, 1000-1700* (New York 1976).

Claeys, Gregory (ed.), *The Politics of English Jacobinism: Writings of John Thelwall* (Pennsylvania 1995).

Clapham, J. H., 'The Spitalfields acts, 1773-1824'. *The Economic Journal* 26 (1916): 459–71.

Clapham, J. H., *The Bank of England: A History* (2 vols, Cambridge 1944).

Clark, Gregory, *A Farewell to Alms: A Brief Economic History of the World* (Princeton 2007).

Clarke, M. P., 'The board of trade at work'. *American Historical Review* 17 (1911): 17–43.

Clavering, Eric, 'The coal mills of northeast England: the use of waterwheels for draining coal mines, 1600-1750'. *Technology and Culture* 36 (1995): 211–41.

Clayton, M., and A. Oakes, 'Early calico printers around London'. *The Burlington Magazine* 96 (1954): 135–9.

Clemens, Paul G. E., 'The rise of Liverpool, 1665-1750'. *Economic History Review* 29 (1976): 211–25.

Clifford, Helen, 'The ornament of nations: the society of arts and the "arts of design" 1754-1806', in S. Bennett (ed.), *Cultivating the Human Faculties: James Barry Commemorated*, online (RSA/William Shipley Group 2005), 6–11.

Clow, Archibald, and Nan L. Clow, 'Vitriol in the industrial revolution', in A. E. Musson (ed.), *Science, Technology and Economic Growth in the Eighteenth Century* (London 1972), 148–67.

Cockett, Richard, *Thinking the Unthinkable: Think-Tanks and the Economic Counter-Revolution, 1931-1983* (London 1994).

Coffman, D'Maris, Adrian Leonard and Larry Neal (eds), *Questioning Credible Commitment: Perspectives on the Rise of Financial Capitalism* (Cambridge 2013).

Coffman, D'Maris, 'Credibility, transparency, accountability, and the public credit under the long Parliament and commonwealth, 1643-1653', in D'Maris Coffman, Adrian Leonard and Larry Neal (eds), *Excise Taxation and the Origins of Public Debt* (Basingstoke 2013), 76–103.

Coffman, D'Maris, *Excise Taxation and the Origins of Public Debt* (Basingstoke 2013).

Colbin, Ian D., *The Unseen Hand in English History* (1917, London 2012).

Coleman, Donald C., *British Paper Industry 1495-1860* (Oxford 1958).

Coleman, Donald C. (ed.), *Revisions in Mercantilism* (London 1969).

Coleman, Donald C., 'Introduction', in Coleman (ed.), *Revisions in Mercantilism*, 1–18.

Coleman, Donald C., 'An innovation and its diffusion: the "new draperies"'. *Economic History Review* 22 (1969): 417–29.

Coleman, Donald C., and A. H. John (eds), *Trade, Government and Economy in Pre-Industrial England: Essays Presented to F. J. Fisher* (London 1976).

Coleman, Donald C., and Peter Mathias (eds), *Enterprise and History: Essays in Honour of Charles Wilson* (Cambridge 1984).

Coleman, Donald C., 'Politics and economics in the age of Anne: the case of the Anglo-French trade treaty of 1713', in Coleman and John (eds), *Trade, Government and Economy in Pre-Industrial England*, 187–211.

Cone, C. B., 'Richard Price and Pitt's sinking fund of 1786'. *Economic History Review* 4 (1951): 243–51.

Cook, Harald J., *Matters of Exchange: Commerce, Medicine, and Science in the Dutch Golden Age* (New Haven 2008).

Cooke, Anthony, *The Rise and Fall of the Scottish Cotton Industry, 1778-1914* (Manchester 2010).

Cooper, Richard, 'William Pitt, taxation, and the needs of war'. *Journal of British Studies* 22 (1982): 94–103.

Crafts, N. F. R., 'British economic growth, 1700-1831: a review of the evidence'. *Economic History Review* 36 (1983): 177–99.

Crafts, N. F. R., *British Economic Growth during the Industrial Revolution* (Oxford 1985).

Crafts, N. F. R., 'British industrialisation in an international context'. *Journal of Interdisciplinary History* 19 (1989): 415–28.

Craske, Matthew, 'Plan and control: Design and the competitive spirit in early and mid-eighteenth-century England'. *Journal of Design History* 12 (1999): 187–216.

Craven, Paul, and Douglas Hay, 'The criminalization of "free" labour: Master and servant in comparative perspective'. *Slavery and Abolition* 15 (1994): 71–101.

Crocker, A., and M. Kane, *The Diaries of James Simmons: Papermaker of Haslemere 1831-1868* (Oxshot 1990).

Crosby, A. W., *The Measure of Reality: Quantification and Western Society 1250-1600* (Cambridge 1997).

Crouch, Colin, *The Strange Non-Death of Neoliberalism* (Cambridge 2011).

Crouzet, Francois, 'Wars, blockade, and economic change in Europe, 1792-1815'. *Journal of Economic History* 24 (1964): 567–88.

Crowley, J. E., 'Neo-Mercantilism and the wealth of nations: British commercial policy after the American revolution'. *Historical Journal* 33 (1990): 339–60.

Cunningham, William, *The Growth of English Industry and Commerce in Modern Times* (2 vols, 1903, 4th edn, 1907, New York 1968).

Daunton, Martin J., *Progress and Poverty: An Economic and Social History of Britain 1700-1850* (Oxford 1995).

Bibliography

Daunton, Martin J., *Trusting Leviathan: The Politics of Taxation in Britain 1799-1914* (Cambridge 2001).

Daunton, Martin J., *State and Market in Victorian Britain: War, Welfare and Capitalism* (Woodbridge 2008).

Daunton, Martin J., 'Rationality and institutions: reflections on Douglass North'. *Structural Change and Economic Dynamics* 21 (2010): 147–56.

Davies, K. G., 'Joint-stock investment in the late seventeenth century'. *Economic History Review* 4 (1952): 283–301.

Davis, Ralph, 'English foreign trade, 1700-1770'. *Economic History Review* 6 (1954): 150–66 and reprinted in Minchinton (ed.), *The Growth of English Overseas Trade*, 99–120.

Davis, Ralph, 'The rise of protection in England, 1689-1786'. *Economic History Review* 19 (1966): 306–17.

Davis, Ralph, *The Rise of the Atlantic Economies* (London 1973).

Dear, Peter, 'Historiography of not-so-recent science'. *History of Science* I (2012): 197–210.

Dicey, A. V., 'The combination laws as illustrating the relation between law and opinion in England during the nineteenth century'. *Harvard Law Review* 17 (1904): 511–32.

Dicey, A. V., *Lectures on the Relations between Law and Public Opinion in England* (1905, 2nd edn, London 1940).

Dickinson, H. T., 'The poor Palatines and the parties'. *English Historical Review* 83 (1967): 464–85.

Dickinson, H. T., *Walpole and the Whig Supremacy* (London 1973).

Dickson, P. G. M., *The Sun Insurance Office 1710-1960: The History of Two and a Half Centuries of British Insurance* (Oxford 1960).

Dickson, P. G. M., *The Financial Revolution in England: A Study in the Development of Public Credit 1688-1756* (London 1967).

Dickson, P. G. M., 'English commercial negotiations with Austria, 1737-1752', in Whiteman, Bromley and Dickinson (eds), *Statesmen, Scholars and Merchants*, 81–112.

Dietz, V. E., 'Before the age of capital: manufacturing interests and the British state, 1780-1800' (unpublished PhD thesis, Princeton University 1991).

Dolan, Brian, *Josiah Wedgwood: Entrepreneur to the Enlightenment* (St Ives 2004).

Donaghay, Marie M., 'Calonne and the Anglo-French Treaty of 1786'. *Journal of Modern History* 50, 3 – supplement (1978): D1157–84.

Donaghay, Marie M., 'The Marechal de Castries and the Anglo-French commercial negotiations of 1786-1787'. *Historical Journal* 22 (1979): 295–312.

Donaghay, Marie M., 'The exchange of products of the soil and industrial goods in the Anglo-French commercial treaty of 1786'. *Journal of European Economic History* 19 (1990): 377–401.

Douglas, A. W., 'Cotton textiles in England: the East India Company's attempt to exploit developments in fashion 1660-1721'. *Journal of British Studies* 8 (1969): 28–43.

Downie, J. A., 'The commission of public accounts and the formation of the country party'. *English Historical Review* 91 (1976): 33–51.

Dudley, Christopher, 'Party politics, political economy, and economic development in early eighteenth-century Britain'. *Economic History Review* 66 (2013): 1084–1100.

Dunham, Arthur L., 'Development of the cotton Industry in France and the Anglo-French treaty of commerce 1860'. *Economic History Review* 1 (1927): 281–307.

Dunn, R. S., *Sugar and Slaves: The Rise of the Planter Class in the English West Indies, 1624-1713* (Chapel Hill 1973).

DuRivage, Justin, *Revolution against Empire: Taxes, Politics and the Origins of American Independence* (New Haven, forthcoming).

Durie, A. J., 'Textile bleaching: a note on the Scottish experience'. *Business History Review* 49 (1975): 337–45.

Ehrman, John, *The British Government and Commercial Negotiations with Europe 1783-1793* (Cambridge 1962).

Ehrman, John, *The Younger Pitt: The Years of Acclaim* (London 1969).

Elbaum, B., and W. Lazonick, 'The decline of the British economy: an institutional perspective'. *Journal of Economic History* 44 (1984): 567–83.

Elliott, John H., *Empires of the Atlantic World: Britain and Spain in America 1492-1830* (New Haven 2006).

Eltis, David, and Stanley L. Engerman, 'The importance of slavery and the slave trade to industrializing Britain'. *Journal of Economic History* 60 (2000): 123–44.

Engerman, Stanley L., and Patrick K. O'Brien, 'Exports and the growth of the British economy from the glorious revolution to the peace of Amiens', in Solow (ed.), *Slavery and the Rise of the Atlantic System*, 177–209.

Engerman, Stanley L., and Patrick K. O'Brien, 'The industrial revolution in global perspective', in Floud and Johnson (eds), *The Cambridge Economic History of Modern Britain*, 451–64.

Epstein, Stephan R., 'Craft guilds, apprenticeship and technological change in preindustrial Europe'. *Journal of Economic History* 53 (1998): 684–713.

Epstein, Stephan R., 'Craft guilds in the pre-modern economy: a discussion'. *Economic History Review* 61 (2008): 155–74.

Escosura, Leandro Prados de la (ed.), *Exceptionalism and Industrialisation: Britain and its European Rivals* (Cambridge 2004).

Esteban, Javier Cuenca, 'The rising share of British industrial exports in industrial output, 1700-1851'. *Journal of Economic History* 57 (1997): 879–906.

Evans, Chris, 'The plantation hoe: the rise and fall of an Atlantic commodity, 1650-1850'. *The William and Mary Quarterly* 69 (2012): 71–100.

Evans, Chris, and Goran Rydén, *Baltic Iron in the Atlantic World in the Eighteenth Century* (Leiden 2007).

Evans, E. J., *William Pitt the Younger* (London 1999).

Fairchilds, Cissie, 'The production and marketing of populuxe goods in eighteenth-century Paris', in Brewer and Porter (eds), *Consumption and the World of Goods*, 228–48.

Fairlie, Susan, 'Dyestuffs in the eighteenth century'. *Economic History Review* 17 (1965): 488–510.

Fairlie, Susan, 'The nineteenth-century corn law reconsidered'. *Economic History Review* 18 (1965): 562–75.

Fairlie, Susan, 'The corn laws and British wheat production, 1829-76'. *Economic History Review* 22 (1969): 88–116.

Farnell, J. E., 'The navigation act of 1651, the first Dutch war, and the London merchant community'. *Economic History Review* 16 (1964): 439–54.

Ferguson, Eugine S., 'The measurement of the "man-day"'. *Scientific American*, October (1971): 96–103.

Ferguson, Niall, *Civilization: The West and the Rest* (London 2011).

Fine, S. E., 'Production and excise in England, 1643-1825' (unpublished PhD thesis, Radcliffe College, Harvard University, 1937).

Fisher, F. J., 'London's export trade in the early Seventeenth Century'. *Economic History Review* 3 (1950): 151–61.

Fisher, H. E. S.,'Anglo-Portuguese trade 1700-1770'. *Economic History Review* 16 (1963): 219–33 and reprinted in Minchinton (ed.), *The Growth of English Overseas Trade*, 144–64.

Flood, R., and P. Johnson (eds), *The Cambridge Economic History of Modern Britain* (3 vols, Cambridge 2003).

Force, J. C. L., 'Royal textile factories in Spain, 1700-1800'. *Journal of Economic History* 24 (1964): 337–63.

Foucault, Michel, *Discipline and Punish: The Birth of the Prison* (1975, St. Ives 1991).

Fox, Celina, *The Arts of Industry in the Age of Enlightenemnt* (New Haven 2009).

Frangsmyr, Tore, J. L. Heilbron and Robin E. Rider (eds), *The Quantifying Spirit in the Eighteenth Century* (Berkeley 1990).

Bibliography

Frank, Andre G., *ReOrient: Global Economy in the Asian Age* (Berkeley 1998).

Frendenberger, H., 'Fashion, sumptuary laws, and business'. *Business History Review* 37 (1963): 37–48.

Fryman, Niklas, 'Pirates and smugglers: political economy in the red Atlantic', in Stern and Wennedlind (eds), *Mercantilism Reimagined*, 218–36.

Gadd, I. A., and P. Wallis (eds), *Guilds and Association in Europe, 900-1900* (London 2006).

Gambles, Anna, 'Rethinking the politics of protection: Conservatives and the corn laws 1830-52'. *English Historical Review* 113 (1998): 928–52.

Gambles, Anna, *Protection and Politics: Conservative Economic Discourse, 1815-1852* (Woodbridge 1999).

Gauci, Perry, *The Politics of Trade: The Overseas Merchant in State and Society, 1660-1720* (Oxford 2003).

Gauci, Perry (ed.), *Regulating the British Economy 1660-1850* (Aldershot 2011).

Gavroglu, K. (ed.), *The Sciences in the European Periphery During the Enlightenment* (Dordrecht 1999).

George, M. D., 'Revisions in economic history: IV. the combination laws'. *Economic History Review* 6 (1936): 172–8.

Gibbs, G. C., 'Huguenot contributions to England's intellectual life, and England's intellectual commerce with Europe, c. 1680-1720', in Scouloudi (ed.), *Huguenots in Britain*, 20–46.

Gill, D. M., 'The treasury, 1660-1714'. *English Historical Review* 46 (1931): 600–22.

Gill, D. M., 'The relationship between the treasury and the excise and customs commissioners (1660-1714)'. *Cambridge Historical Journal* 4 (1932): 94–9.

Gillispie, Charles C., 'The discovery of the Leblanc process'. *Isis* 48 (1957): 152–70.

Gillispie, Charles C., *Science and Polity in France: The End of the Old Regime* (Princeton 1980).

Gittins, L., 'Soapmaking and the excise laws, 1711-1853'. *Industrial Archaeological Review* 1 (1977): 265–75.

Gittins, L., 'Innovations in textile bleaching in Britain in the eighteenth century'. *Business History Review* 53 (1979): 194–204.

Gittins, L., 'Salt, salt making, and the rise of Cheshire'. *Transactions of the Newcomen Society* 75 (2005): 139–59.

Golan, Tal, *Laws of Men and Laws of Nature: The History of Scientific Expert Testimony in England and America* (Cambridge, MA 2003).

Goody, Jack, *The East in the West* (Cambridge 1996).

Goody, Jack, *Capitalism and Modernity: The Great Debate* (Cambridge 2004).

Goody, Jack, *Theft of History* (Cambridge 2006).

Goose, Nigel, 'Immigrants in Tudor and early Stuart England', in Goose and Luu (eds), *Immigrants in Tudor and Early Stuart England*, 1–38.

Goose, Nigel, and L. Luu (eds), *Immigrants in Tudor and Early Stuart England* (Brighton 2005).

Gourevitch, P. A., 'International trade, domestic coalitions and liberty: Comparative responses to the crisis of 1873-1896'. *Journal of Interdisciplinary History* 8 (1977): 281–313.

Grafe, Regina, *Distant Tyranny: Markets, Power, and Backwardness in Spain, 1650-1800* (Princeton 2012).

Grassby, R. B., 'Social status and commercial enterprise under Louis XIV'. *Economic History Review* 13 (1960): 19–38.

Gray, J. L., 'The law of combination in Scotland'. *Economica* 24 (1928): 332–50.

Greaves, Richard L., *Deliver us from Evil: The Radical Underground in Britain, 1660-1663* (Oxford 1986).

Greaves, Richard L., *Enemies under his Feet: Radicals and Nonconformists in Britain, 1664-1677* (Stanford 1990).

Greenfeld, Liah, *The Spirit of Capitalism: Nationalism and Economic Growth* (Cambridge, MA 2001).

Griffin, Emma, *A Short History of the British Industrial Revolution* (London 2010).

Griffiths, T., P. Hunt and P. K. O'Brien, 'Scottish, Irish, and imperial connections: Parliament, the three kingdoms, and the mechanization of cotton spinning in eighteenth-century Britain'. *Economic History Review* 61 (2008): 625–50.

Habermas, Jürgen, *The Structural Transformation of the Public Sphere: Inquiry into a Category of Bourgeois Society* (1962, Cambridge 1992).

Haffenden, P. S., 'The crown and the colonial charters, 1675-1688: part I'. *William and Mary Quarterly* 15 (1958a): 297–311.

Haffenden, P. S., 'The crown and the colonial charters, 1675-1688: part II'. *William and Mary Quarterly* 15 (1958b): 452–66.

Halevy, Elie, *The Age of Peel and Cobden* (London 1947).

Hall, A. R., 'Engineering and the scientific revolution'. *Technology and Culture* 4 (1961): 333–41.

Hammond, J. L., and Barbara Hammond, *The Rise of Modern Industry* (London 1925).

Hammond, P. W., and H. Egan, *Weighed in the Balance: A History of the Laboratory of the Government Chemist* (London 1992).

Hancock, David, *Citizens of the World: London Merchants and the Integration of the British Atlantic Community, 1735-1785* (Cambridge 1995).

Hancock, David, '"A world of business to do": William Freeman and the foundations of England's commercial empire, 1695-1707'. *William and Mary Quarterly* 57 (2000): 3–34.

Hanley, Susan B., *Everyday Things in Premodern Japan: The Hidden Legacy of Material Culture* (Berkeley 1999).

Hardie, D. W. F., 'The Macintosh's and the origins of the chemical industry', in Musson (ed.), *Science, Technology and Economic Growth*, 168–94.

Hardy, William, *Forgotten Voices of the Industrial Age* (Shepperton 2014).

Harkness, Deborah, *The Jewel House: Elizabethan London and the Scientific Revolution* (New Haven 2007).

Harley, C. Knick, 'Trade: discovery, mercantilism and technology', in Flood and Johnson (eds), *The Cambridge Economic History of Modern Britain*, vol. 1, 175–203.

Harling, Philip, *The Waning of 'Old Corruption': The Politics of Economic Reform in Britain, 1779-1846* (Oxford 1996).

Harling, Philip, and Peter Mandler, 'From fiscal-state to laissez-faire state, 1760-1850'. *Journal of British Studies* 32 (1993): 44–70.

Harris, John R., *The British Iron Industry 1700-1850* (London 1988).

Harris, John R., *Essays in Industry and Technology in the Eighteenth Century: England and France* (Aldershot 1992).

Harris, John R., 'Reviewed work: the British industrial revolution: an economic perspective (ed.) Joel Mokyr'. *Technology and Culture* 37 (1996): 180–1.

Harris, John R., *Industrial Espionage and Technology Transfer: Britain and France in the Eighteenth Century* (Aldershot 1998).

Harris, Tim, *Restoration: Charles II and His Kingdoms 1660-1685* (London 2005).

Harris, Tim, *Revolution: The Great Crisis of the British Monarchy, 1685-1720* (London 2006).

Harriss, G. L. 'Thomas Cromwell's "new principle" of taxation'. *English Historical Review* 93 (1978): 721–38.

Harriss, G. L., 'Theory and practice in royal taxation: Some observations'. *English Historical Review* 97 (1982): 811–19.

Hartwell, Ronald Max, 'Taxation in England during the industrial revolution'. *Cato Journal* 1 (1981): 129–53.

Harvey, David, *The Urban Experience* (Baltimore 1989).

Harvey, David, *The Condition of Postmodernity: An Enquiry into the Origins of Cultural Change* (Oxford 1991).

Harvey, David, *A Brief History of Neoliberalism* (Oxford 2005).

Bibliography

Hay, Douglas, 'The state and the market in 1800: Lord Kenyon and Mr Waddington'. *Past and Present* 162 (1999): 101–62.

Hay, Douglas, and Nicholas Rogers, *Eighteenth-Century English Society* (Oxford 1997).

Hayek, Frederick A., *The Road to Serfdom* (1944, London 2001).

Hayek, Frederick A., *The Fatal Conceit: The Errors of Socialism*, ed. W. W. Bartley III (London 1988).

Hayman, Richard, 'The Shropshire wrought-iron industry c. 1600-1900: a study of technological change' (Unpublished PhD thesis, University of Birmingham, 2003).

Hazen, A. T., 'Eustace Barnaby's manufacture of white paper in England'. *Papers of the Biographical Society of America* 48 (1954): 326–8.

Henderson, W. O., 'The Anglo-French commercial treaty of 1786'. *Economic History Review* 10 (1957): 104–12.

Henderson, W. O., *The Genesis of the Common Market* (London 1962).

Henry, Brian, *Dublin Hanged: Crime, Law Enforcement and Punishment in Late Eighteenth-Century Dublin* (Dublin 1993).

Henry, John, *The Scientific Revolution and the Origins of Modern Science* (1997, Basingstoke 2002).

Hessenbruch, A., 'The spread of precision measurement in Scandinavia 1660-1800', in Gavroglu (ed.), *The Sciences in the European Periphery*, 179–224.

Hilaire-Perez, Liliane, 'Invention and the state in eighteenth-century France'. *Technology and Culture* 32 (1991): 911–31.

Hilaire-Perez, Liliane, 'Technology as a public culture in the eighteenth century: the artisans' legacy'. *History of Science* 45 (2007): 135–53.

Hill, Christopher, *God's Englishman: Oliver Cromwell and the English Revolution* (Harmondsworth 1970).

Hill, Christopher, *Some Intellectual Consequences of the English Revolution* (1980, London 1997).

Hills, Richard L., *Power from Steam: A History of the Stationary Steam Engine* (Cambridge 1989).

Hills, Richard L., *James Watt* (3 vols, Ashburne 2002).

Hilton, Boyd, *Corn, Cash, Commerce: The Economic Policies of the Tory Governments 1815-1830* (1977, Oxford 1980).

Hilton, Boyd, *The Age of Atonement: The Influence of Evangelicalism on Social and Economic Thought, 1795-1865* (Oxford 1988).

Hilton, Boyd, *A Mad, Bad & Dangerous People? England 1783-1846* (Oxford 2006).

Hirsch, Jean-Pierre, 'Revolutionary France, cradle of free enterprise'. *American Historical Review* 94 (1989): 1281–9.

Hobsbawm, Eric J., 'The machine breakers'. *Past and Present* 1 (1952): 57–70.

Hobson, John M., *The Eastern Origins of Western Civilisation* (Cambridge 2004).

Hobson, John M., *The Eurocentric Conception of World Politics: Western International Theory, 1760-2010* (Cambridge 2012).

Hollister-Short, Graham, 'Before and after the Newcomen engine of 1712: Ideas, gestalts, practice'. *Le Journal de la Renaissance* 5 (2007): 57–76.

Holmes, G., *Augustan England: Professions, State and Society, 1680-1730* (London 1982).

Hont, Istvan, *Jealousy of Trade: International Competition and the Nation-State in Historical Perspective* (Cambridge, MA 2010).

Hoppit, Julian, 'Political arithmetic in eighteenth-century England'. *Economic History Review* 49 (1996): 516–40.

Hoppit, Julian, 'Checking leviathan', in Winch and O'Brien (eds), *The Political Economy of British Historical Experience*, 267–94.

Hoppit, Julian, *A Land of Liberty? England 1689-1727* (Oxford 2000).

Hoppit, Julian, 'Compulsion, compensation and property rights in Britain, 1688-1833'. *Past and Present* 210 (2011): 93–128.

Hoppit, Julian, 'The nation, the state, and the first industrial revolution'. *Journal of British Studies* 50 (2011): 307–31.

Hoppit, Julian, *Nehemiah Grew and England's Economic Development: The Means of a Most Ample Increase of the Wealth and Strength of England (1706-7)* (Oxford 2012).

Horn, Jeff, 'Marx was right! the guilds and technological change'. *Proceedings of the Western Society for French History* 33 (2005): 224–39.

Horn, Jeff, *The Path Not Taken: French Industrialisation in the Age of Revolution 1750-1830* (Cambridge, MA 2006).

Horn, Jeff, L. N. Rosenband and M. R. Smith (eds), *Reconceptualising the Industrial Revolution* (Cambridge, MA 2010).

Howe, Anthony, *Free Trade and Liberal England 1846-1946* (Oxford 1997).

Hudson, Pat, *The Genesis of Industrial Capital: A Study of the West Riding Woollen Textiles Industry c. 1750-1850* (Cambridge 1986).

Hudson, Pat (ed.), *Regions and Industries: A Perspective on the Industrial Revolution in Britain* (Cambridge 1989).

Hudson, Pat, *The Industrial Revolution* (London 1992).

Hughes, Edward, *Studies in Administration and Finance, 1558-1825* (Manchester 1934).

Hughes, Edward, 'The English stamp duties, 1664-1764'. *English Historical Review* 56 (1941): 234–64.

Humphries, Jane, 'Enclosures, common rights, and women: the proletarianization of families in the late eighteenth and early nineteenth centuries'. *Journal of Economic History* 50 (1990): 17–142.

Humphries, Jane, *Childhood and Child Labour in the British Industrial Revolution* (Cambridge 2010).

Humphries, Jane, 'Rent seeking or skill creating? Apprenticeship in early industrial Britain', in Gauci (ed.), *Regulating the British Economy*, 235–58.

Hyde, C. K., 'Technological change in the British iron industry, 1750-1815: a reinterpretation'. *Economic History Review* 27 (1974): 190–206.

Iliffe, Robert, 'Capitalizing expertise: Philosophical and artisanal expertise in early modern London', in Rabier (ed.), *Fields of Expertise*, 55–84.

Inikori, Joseph E., 'Slavery and the development of industrial capitalism in England'. *Journal of Interdisciplinary History* 17 (1987): 771–93.

Inikori, Joseph E., *Africans and the Industrial Revolution in England: A Study in International Trade and Economic Development* (Cambridge 2002).

Innes, Joanna, *Inferior Politics: Social Problems and Social Policies in Eighteenth-Century Britain* (Oxford 2009).

Innes, Joanna, 'Regulating wages in eighteenth and early nineteenth-century England: Arguments in context', in Gauci (ed.), *Regulating the British Economy*, 195–215.

Irwin, Douglas A., 'Strategic trade policy and mercantilist trade rivalries'. *American Economic Review* 82 (1992): 134–9.

Jacob, Margaret C., *Scientific Culture and the Making of the Industrial West* (Oxford 1996).

Jacob, Margaret C., and Larry Stewart, *Practical Matter: Newton's Science in the Service of Industry and Empire, 1687-1851* (Cambridge, MA 2005).

Jacob, Margaret C., *The First Knowledge Economy: Human Capital and the European Economy, 1750-1850* (Cambridge 2014).

Jacobsen, G. A., *William Blathwayt: A Late Seventeenth Century English Administrator* (New Haven 1932).

Bibliography

Jarvis, Rupert, 'The paper-makers and the excise in the eighteenth century'. *The Library* 19 (1959): 100–16.

Jones, Colin, *The Great Nation: France from Louis XV to Napoleon* (St Ives 2002).

Jones, Daniel Stedman, *Masters of the Universe: Hayek, Friedman, and the Birth of Neoliberal Politics* (Princeton 2012).

Jones, Gareth Stedman, 'Rethinking Chartism', in Jones (ed.), *Languages of Class*, 90–178.

Jones, Gareth Stedman, *Languages of Class: Studies in the English Working Class History 1832-1982* (Cambridge 1983).

Jones, Gareth Stedman, *An End to Poverty: A Historical Debate* (London 2004).

Jones, J. R. (ed.), *The Restored Monarchy 1660-1688* (London 1979).

Jones, Peter M., *Industrial Enlightenment: Science, Technology and Culture in Birmingham and the West Midlands 1760-1820* (Manchester 2008).

Jonsson, Fredrik Albrittonb, 'The industrial revolution in the Anthropocene'. *Journal of Modern History* 84 (2012): 679–96.

Jubb, M., 'Economic policy and economic development', in Black (ed.), *Britain in the Age of Walpole*, 121–44.

Kander, Astrid, Paolo Malanima and Paul Warde, *Power to the People: Energy in Europe Over the Last Five Centuries* (Princeton 2013).

Kaplan, Steven Laurence, 'Social classification and representation in the corporate world of eighteenth-century France: Turgot's "carnival"', in Kaplan and Koepp (eds), *Work in France*, 176–228.

Kaplan, Steven Laurence, and Cynthia J. Koepp (eds), *Work in France* (Ithaca 1986).

Kearney, H. F., 'The political background to English mercantilism, 1695-1700'. *Economic History Review* 11 (1959): 484–96.

Keay, John, *The Honourable Company: A History of the East Indian Company* (London 1991).

Keirn, T., and F. T. Melton, 'Thomas Manley and the rate of interest debate, 1688-1673'. *Journal of British Studies* 29 (1990): 147–73.

Kelly, James, 'The Anglo-French commercial treaty of 1786: the Irish dimension'. *Eighteenth-Century Ireland/Iris an da Chultur* 4 (1989): 93–111.

Kelly, Paul, 'British Parliamentary politics, 1784-1786'. *Historical Journal* 17 (1974): 733–53.

Kelly, Paul, 'British and Irish politics in 1785'. *English Historical Review* 90 (1975): 536–63.

Kennedy, W., *English Taxation 1640-1799: An Essay on Policy and Opinion* (London 1913).

Kenyon, J. P., 'The earl of Sunderland and the king's administration, 1693-1695'. *The English Historical Review* 71 (1956): 576–602.

Kerridge, Eric, *Textile Manufactures in Early Modern England* (Manchester 1988).

Knight, Roger, *Britain Against Napoleon: The Organisation of Victory 1793-1815* (St. Ives 2013).

Koot, G. M., *English Historical Economics, 1870-1926: The Rise of Economic History and Neomercantilism* (Cambridge 1987).

Krey, Gary S. D., 'Political radicalism in London after the Glorious Revolution'. *Journal of Modern History* 55 (1983): 585–617.

Krey, Gary S. D., *A Fractured Society: The Politics of London in the First Age of Party, 1688-1715* (Oxford 1985).

Kriegel, Lara, 'Culture and the copy: Calico, capitalism, and design copyright in early Victorian Britain'. *Journal of British Studies* 43 (2004): 233–65.

Kwass, Michael, *Privilege and the Politics of Taxation in Eighteenth-Century France* (Cambridge 2000).

Lakwete, Angela, *Inventing the Cotton Gin: Machine and Myth in Antebellum America* (Baltimore 2003).

Landes, David S., *The Unbound Prometheus: Technological Change and Industrial Development in Western Europe from 1750 to the Present* (1969, Cambridge 1987).

Landes, David S., *The Wealth and Poverty of Nations: Why Some Are Rich and Some Poor* (1998, London 1999).

Landes, David S., 'The fable of the dead horse; or, the industrial revolution revisited', in Mokyr (ed.), *The British Industrial Revolution*, 128–59.

Langford, Paul, *The Excise Crisis: Society and Politics in the Age of Walpole* (Oxford 1975).

Laslett, Peter, 'Introduction', in Laslett (ed.), Locke, *Two Treatises of Government*, 3–120.

Laslett, Peter (ed.), John Locke, *Two Treatises of Government* (1960, Cambridge 1990).

Lawson, Philip, *The East India Company: A History* (Harlow 1993).

Lazonick, William, 'Industrial relations and technical change: the case of the self- acting mule'. *Cambridge Journal of Economics* 3 (1979): 231–62.

Lees, R. M., 'Parliament and the proposal for a council of trade, 1695-6'. *English Historical Review* 54 (1939): 38–66.

Leng, Thomas, *Benjamin Worsley (1618-1677): Trade, Interest and the Spirit in Revolutionary England* (Basingstoke 2008).

Leng, Thomas, 'Epistemology: Expertise and knowledge in the world of commerce', in Stern and Wennedlind (eds), *Mercantilism Reimagined*, 97–114.

Lindquist, Svante, *Technology on Trial: The Introduction of Steam Power Technology into Sweden, 1715-1736* (Uppsala 1984).

Linebaugh, Peter, *The Magna Carter Manifesto: Liberties and Commons for All* (Berkley 2008).

Linebaugh, Peter, *Stop, Thief! The Commons, Enclosures, and Resistance* (Oakland 2014).

Linebaugh, Peter, and Marcus Rediker, *The Many-Headed Hydra: Sailors, Commoners, and the Hidden History of the Revolutionary Atlantic* (Boston 2000).

Lingelbach, A. L., 'The inception of the British board of trade'. *American Historical Review* 30 (1925): 701–27.

Lingelbach, A. L., 'William Huskisson as president of the board of trade'. *American Historical Review* 43 (1938): 759–74.

Lipson, Ephraim, *The Economic History of England* (3 vols, 1931, 4th edn, London 1947).

Longfield, Ada K., 'History of the Irish linen and cotton printing industry in the eighteenth century'. *Journal of the Royal Society of Antiquaries of Ireland* 7 (1937): 25–56.

LoPatin, Nancy D., *Political Unions, Popular Politics and the Great Reform Act of 1832* (London 1999).

Losurdo, Domenico, *Liberalism: A Counter-History* (2006, London 2011).

Luu, L., 'Natural-born versus stranger-born subjects: Aliens an their status in Elizabethan London', in Goose and Luu (eds), *Immigrants*, 57–75.

MacLeod, Christine, 'Henry Martin and the authorship of "considerations upon the East India trade"'. *Bulletin of the Institute of Historical Research* 56 (1983): 222–9.

MacLeod, Christine, *Inventing the Industrial Revolution: The English Patent System 1660-1800* (1988, Cambridge 2002).

MacLeod, Christine, 'The European origins of British technological predominance', in Escosura (ed.), *Exceptionalism and Industrialisation*, 111–26.

Maddison, R. E. W., 'Abraham Hill, F.R.S. (1635-1722)'. *Notes and Records of the Royal Society of London* 15 (1960): 173–82.

Maitte, Corine, 'Labels, brands, and market integration in the modern era'. *Business and Economic History Online* 7 (2009): 1–16.

Makepeace, M., 'English traders on the Guinea coast, 1657-1668: an analysis of the East India Company archive'. *History in Africa* 16 (1989): 237–84.

Manning, Patrick, 'Asia and Europe in the world economy: Introduction'. *American Historical Review* 107 (2002): 419–24.

Marsden, Ben, *Watt's Perfect Engine: Steam and the Age of Invention* (Cambridge 2002).

Marshall, P. J. (ed.), *The Oxford History of the British Empire: The Eighteenth Century* (6 vols, Oxford 1998) vol. 2.

Bibliography

Martin, P. M., 'Power, cloth and currency on the Loango coast'. *African Economic History* 15 (1986): 1–12.

Mathias, Peter, *The Transformation of England: Essays in the Economic and Social History of England in the Eighteenth Century* (London 1979).

Mathias, Peter, and Patrick K. O'Brien, 'Taxation in Britain and France, 1715-1810'. *Journal of Economic History* 5 (1976): 601–40.

Matthews, G. T., *The Royal General Farms in Eighteenth Century France* (New York 1958).

Matthew, H. C. G., *Gladstone 1809-1874* (1986, Oxford 1991).

Matthew, H. C. G., *Gladstone, 1809-1898* (Oxford 1997).

Maw, Peter, Terry Wyke, and Alan Kidd, 'Canals, rivers, and the industrial city: Manchester's industrial waterfront, 1790-1850'. *Economic History Review* 65 (2012): 1495–1523.

Mazzucato, Mariana, *The Entrepreneurial State: Debunking Public Versus Private Sector Myths* (London 2013).

McCloskey, Deirdre, *Bourgeois Dignity: Why Economics Can't Explain the Modern World* (Chicago 2010).

McCraw, Thomas, *Prophet of Innovation: Joseph Schumpeter and Creative Destruction* (Cambridge, MA 2007).

McCusker, John J., 'Special section: Trade in the Atlantic world'. *Business History Review* 79 (2005): 697–713.

McCusker, John J., and R. R. Menard, *The Economy of British America, 1607-1789* (Chapel Hill 1985).

McLachlan, J., 'Documents illustrating Anglo-Spanish trade between the commercial treaty of 1667 and the commercial treaty and the Assiento contract of 1713'. *Cambridge Historical Journal* 4 (1934): 299–311.

McNally, David, *Political Economy and the Rise of Capitalism: A Reinterpretation* (Berkeley 1994).

McNeil, Maureen, *Under the Banner of Science: Erasmus Darwin and His Age* (Manchester 1987).

Meynell, G., 'Locke, Boyle and Peter Stahl'. *Notes and Records of the Royal Society of London* 49 (1995): 185–92.

Miller, Judith A., 'European ideology, 1750-1800: the creation of the modern political economy'. *French Historical Studies* 23 (2000): 497–511.

Milton, P., 'John Locke and the rye house plot'. *Historical Journal* 43 (2000): 647–68.

Minard, Philippe, 'Colbertism continued? the inspectorate of manufactures and strategies of exchange in eighteenth-century France'. *French Historical Studies* 23 (2000): 477–96.

Minard, Philippe, 'Trade without institution? French debates about restoring guilds at the start of the nineteenth century', in Gadd and Wallis (eds), *Guilds and Association in Europe*, 83–100.

Minard, Philippe, 'Facing uncertainty: Markets, norms and conventions in the eighteenth century', in Gauci (ed.), *Regulating the British Economy*, 177–94.

Minard, Philippe, and D. Terrier, 'Review of Jean-Pierre Hirsch, *Les Deux Reves du Commerce: Entreprise et Institution dans la Region Lilloise (1780-1860)* (Paris, 1992)'. *European Journal of the History of Economic Thought* 1–3 (1994): 625–30.

Minchinton, W. E. (ed.), *The Growth of English Overseas Trade in the Seventeenth and Eighteenth Centuries* (London 1969).

Mintz, S. W., *Sweetness and Power: The Place of Sugar in Modern History* (Harmondsworth 1986).

Mirowski, Philip, and Dieter Plehwe (eds), *The Road from Mont Pelerin: The Making of the Neoliberal Thought Collective* (Cambridge, MA 2009).

Mises, Ludwig Von, *Human Action: A Treatise on Economics* (1949, 3rd edn, 4 vols, 1966, Indianapolis 2007).

Mises, Ludwig Von, *Economic Freedom and Interventionism: An Anthology of Articles and Essays*, selected and edited by Bettina Bien Greaves (Indianapolis 2007).

Miquelon, Dale, 'Envisioning the French empire: Utrecht, 1711-1713'. *French Historical Studies* 24 (2001): 653–77.

Mokyr, Joel, *The Lever of Riches: Technological Creativity and Economic Progress* (Oxford 1990).

Mokyr, Joel, 'Editors introduction', in Mokyr (ed.), *The British Industrial Revolution*, 1–127.

Mokyr, Joel (ed.), *The British Industrial Revolution: An Economic Perspective* (1993, 2nd edn, Boulder 1999).

Mokyr, Joel, 'Secrets of success'. *Reasononline: Free Minds and Free Markets*, December 1998, http://www.reason.com/news/show/30804.html.

Mokyr, Joel, 'Eurocentricity triumphant'. *American Historical Review* 104 (1999): 1241–6.

Mokyr, Joel, *Gifts of Athena: Historical Origins of the Knowledge Economy* (Princeton 2004).

Mokyr, Joel, 'The intellectual origins of modern economic growth'. *Journal of Economic History* 65 (2005): 285–351.

Mokyr, Joel, *The Enlightened Economy: An Economic History of Britain 1700-1850* (New Haven 2009).

Mokyr, Joel, 'Intellectual property rights, the industrial revolution, and the beginnings of modern economic growth'. *American Economic Review* 99 (2009): 349–55.

Mokyr, Joel, 'Cultural entrepreneurs and the origins of modern economic growth'. *Scandinavian Economic History Review* 61 (2013): 1–33.

Mokyr, Joel, and John V. C. Nye, 'Distributional coalitions, the industrial revolution, and the origins of economic growth in Britain'. *Southern Economic Journal* 74 (2007): 50–70.

Montoux, Paul, *The Industrial Revolution in the Eighteenth Century* (London 1928).

Moore, R. J., 'Imperialism and "free trade" policy in India, 1853-4'. *Economic History Review* 17 (1964): 135–45.

Morgan, Kenneth, 'Mercantilism and the British empire, 1688-1815', in Winch and O'Brien (eds), *The Political Economy of British Historical Experience*, 165–91.

Morgan, Kenneth, *Slavery, Atlantic Trade and the British Economy, 1660-1800* (Cambridge 2000).

Morton, Alan Q., 'Lectures on natural philosophy in London, 1750-1765: S. C. T. Demainbray (1710-1782) and the "inattention" of his countrymen'. *British Journal for the History of Science* 23 (1990): 411–34.

Morton, Alan Q., 'Men and machines in mid-eighteenth century London'. *Transactions of the Newcomen Society* 64 (1993–4): 47–56.

Mui, H., and L. H. Mui, 'William Pitt and the enforcement of the commutation act, 1784-1788'. *English Historical Review* 76 (1961): 447–65.

Mui, H., and L. H. Mui, *Shops and Shopkeeping in Eighteenth-Century England* (London: Routledge, 1989).

Muldrew, Craig, *Food, Energy and the Creation of Industriousness: Work and Material Culture in Agrarian England, 1550-1780* (Cambridge 2012).

Murison, Barbara Cresswell, 'William Blathwayt's empire: Politics and administration in England and the Atlantic colonies, 1668-1710' (Unpublished PhD thesis, University of Ontario, 1981).

Murphy, Anne L., *The Origins of English Financial Markets: Investment and Speculation Before the South Sea Bubble* (Cambridge 2009).

Murphy, Orville T., 'DuPont de Nemours and the Anglo-French commercial treaty of 1786'. *Economic History Review* 19 (1966): 569–80.

Musson, A. E., *Enterprise in Soap and Chemicals: Joseph Crosfield and Sons Limited, 1815-1965* (1965, New York 1967).

Musson, A. E., (ed.), *Science, Technology and Economic Growth in the Eighteenth Century* (London 1972).

Musson, A. E., 'Introduction', in Musson (ed.), *Science, Technology and Economic Growth*, 57–61.

Musson, A. E., and E. Robinson, 'Science and industry in the late eighteenth century'. *Economic History Review* 13 (1960): 222–44.

Musson, A. E., *Science and Technology in the Industrial Revolution* (Manchester 1969).

Bibliography

Nash, R. C., 'South Carolina indigo, European textiles, and the British Atlantic economy in the eighteenth century'. *Economic History Review* 63 (2010): 362–92.

Navickas, Katrina, 'The search for "General Ludd": the mythology of Luddism'. *Social History* 30 (2005): 281–95.

Navickas, Katrina, 'Luddism, incendiarism and the defence of rural "task-scapes" in 1812'. *Northern History* 48 (2011): 59–73.

Nettels, Curtis, 'England and the Spanish-American trade, 1680-1715'. *Journal of Modern History* 3 (1931): 1–32.

Newbury, N. F., 'The history of the common salt industry on Merseyside'. *Annals of Science* 3 (1938): 138–48.

Nichols, G. O., 'English government borrowing, 1660-1688'. *Journal of British Studies* 10 (1971): 83–104.

Norris, J. M., 'Samuel Garbett and the early development of industrial lobbying in Great Britain'. *Economic History Review* 10 (1958): 450–60.

North, Douglas C., *Institutions, Institutional Change and Economic Performance* (Cambridge 1990).

North, Douglas C., *Understanding the Process of Economic Change* (Princeton 2010).

North, Douglas C., and Barry W. Weingast, 'The evolution of institutions governing public choice in seventeenth century England'. *Journal of Economic History* 49 (1989): 803–32.

Nye, J. V. C., *War, Wine, and Taxes: The Political Economy of Anglo-French Trade, 1689-1900* (Princeton 2007).

O'Brien, George, *The Economic History of Ireland in the Eighteenth Century* (1918, Philadelphia 1977).

O'Brien, George, 'The Irish free trade agitation of 1779 (part 1)'. *English Historical Review* 38 (1923): 564–81.

O'Brien, George, 'The Irish free trade agitation of 1779 (part 2)'. *English Historical Review* 39 (1924): 95–109.

O'Brien, Patrick K., 'The political economy of British taxation, 1660-1815'. *Economic History Review* 41 (1988): 1–32.

O'Brien, Patrick K., 'Inseparable connections: Trade, economy, fiscal state, and the expansion of empire, 1688-1815', in Marshall (ed.), *The Oxford History of the British Empire*, 53–77.

O'Brien, Patrick K., 'Imperialism and the rise and decline of the British economy'. *New Left Review* 238 (1999): 48–80.

O'Brien, Patrick K., 'Fiscal exceptionalism: Great Britain and its European rivals from civil war to triumph at Trafalgar and Waterloo', in Winch and O'Brien (eds), *The Political Economy of British Historical Experience*, 245–65.

O'Brien, Patrick K., 'The triumph and denouement of the British fiscal state: Taxation for the wars against revolutionary and Napoeonic France, 1793-1815'. *Working Papers in Economic History*, LSE, No. 99/07 (2007): 1–56.

O'Brien, Patrick K., T. Griffiths and P. Hunt, 'Political components of the industrial revolution: Parliament and the English textile industry, 1660-1774'. *Economic History Review* 44 (1991): 395–423.

Ochs, K. H., 'The Royal Society of London's history of trades programme: an early episode in applied science'. *Notes and Records of the Royal Society* 39 (1985): 129–58.

O'Hearn, D., 'Innovation and the world-system hierarchy: British subjugation of the Irish cotton industry, 1780-1830'. *American Journal of Sociology* 100 (1994): 587–621.

Olby, R. C., G. N. Cantor, J. R. R. Christie and M. J. S. Hodge (eds), *Companion to the History of Modern Science* (London 1990).

Ormrod, David, 'English re-exports and the Dutch staplemarket in the eighteenth century', in Coleman and Mathias (eds), *Enterprise and History*, 89–115.

Ormrod, David, *The Rise of Commercial Empires: England and the Netherlands in the Age of Mercantilism, 1650-1770* (Cambridge 2003).

Orth, J. V., 'English combination acts of the eighteenth century'. *Law and History Review* 5 (1987): 175–211.

Packard, L. B., 'International rivalry and free trade origins, 1660-78'. *Quarterly Journal of Economics* 37 (1923): 412–35.

Page, William, 'Industries: Silk weaving', in Page (ed.), *A History of the County of Middlesex: Volume 2*, 132–37.

Page, William (ed.), *A History of the County of Middlesex: Volume 2* (London 1911).

Parker, H. T., 'Two administrative bureaus under the directory and Napoleon'. *French Historical Studies* 4 (1965): 150–69.

Parker, H. T., *An Administrative Bureau during the Old Regime: The Bureau of Commerce and its Relations to French Industry from May 1781 to November 1783* (Newark 1993).

Parthasarathi, Prasannan, 'Rethinking wages and competitiveness in the eighteenth century: Britain and South India'. *Past and Present* 158 (1998): 79–109.

Parthasarathi, Prasannan, *The Transition to a Colonial Economy: Weavers, Merchants and Kings in South India, 1720-1800* (Cambridge 2001).

Parthasarathi, Prasannan, *Why Europe Grew Rich and Asia Did Not: Global Economic Divergence, 1600-1850* (Cambridge 2011).

Peck, Jamie, *Constructions of Neoliberal Reason* (Oxford 2010).

Pettigrew, William A., '"Free to enslave": Politics and the escalation of Britain's transatlantic slave trade, 1688-1714'. *William and Mary Quarterly* 64 (2007): 3–38.

Pilbin, P., 'External relations of the Tyneside glass industry'. *Economic Geography* 13 (1937): 301–14.

Pincus, Steve, 'Popery, trade and universal monarchy: the ideological context of the outbreak of the second Anglo-Dutch war'. *English Historical Review* 107 (1992): 1–29.

Pincus, Steve, 'From butterboxes to wooden shoes: the shift in English popular sentiment from anti-Dutch to anti-French in the 1670s'. *Historical Journal* 38 (1995): 333–61.

Pincus, Steve, 'Neither Machiavellian moment nor possessive individualism: Commercial society and the defenders of the new commonwealth'. *American Historical Review* 103 (1998): 705–36.

Pincus, Steve, 'The making of a great power? Universal monarchy, political economy, and the transformation of English political culture'. *The European Legacy* 5 (2000): 531–545.

Pincus, Steve, *England's Glorious Revolution: A Brief History with Documents* (London 2006).

Pincus, Steve, *1688: The First Modern Revolution* (New Haven 2009).

Pincus, Steve, 'Rethinking mercantilism: Political economy, the British empire, and the Atlantic world in the seventeenth and eighteenth centuries'. *William and Mary Quarterly* 69 (2012): 3–34.

Platt, R., *Smuggling in the British Isles: A History* (Stroud 2007).

Pocock, J. G. A., *The Machiavellian Moment: Florentine Political Thought and the Atlantic Tradition* (Princeton 1975).

Polanyi, Karl, *The Great Transformation: The Political and Economic Origins of Our Time* (1944, Boston 2001).

Pollard, M., 'White paper-making in Ireland in the 1690s'. *Proceedings of the Royal Irish Academy* 77 (1977): 223–34.

Pomeranz, Kenneth, *The Great Divergence: China, Europe, and the Making of the Modern World Economy* (Princeton 2000).

Pomeranz, Kenneth, 'Political economy and ecology on the eve of industrialisation: Europe, China and the global conjuncture'. *American Historical Review* 107 (2002): 425–46.

Poovey, Mary, *A History of the Modern Fact: Problems of Knowledge in the Sciences of Wealth and Society* (Chicago 1998).

Bibliography

Popper, Karl, *The Open Society and Its Enemies* (2 vols, London 1945).

Porter, Roy, *Enlightenment: Britain and the Creation of the Modern World* (London 2000).

Porter, Theodore M., *Trust in Numbers: The Pursuit of Objectivity in Science and Public Life* (Princeton 1995).

Potofsky, A., 'The construction of Paris and the crises of the ancien regime: the police and the people of the Parisian building sites, 1750-1789'. *French Historical Studies* 27 (2004): 9–48.

Powell, H. J., *Glass-Making in England* (Cambridge 1923).

Prak, Maarten, *The Dutch Republic in the Seventeenth Century* (Cambridge, 2005).

Price, Jacob M., *Overseas Trade and Traders: Essays on some Commercial, Financial and Political Challenges Facing British Atlantic Merchants, 1660-1775* (Aldershot 1996).

Price, Jacob M., 'What did merchants do? Reflections on British overseas trade, 1660-1790'. *Journal of Economic History* 49 (1989): 267–84.

Price, Jacob M., 'The Imperial Economy, 1700-1776', in Marshall (ed.), *The Oxford History of the British Empire*, vol. 2, 78–104.

Priestley, M., 'Anglo-French trade and the "unfavourable balance" controversy, 1660-1685'. *Economic History Review* 4 (1951): 37–52.

Puetz, Anne, 'Design instruction for artisans in eighteenth-century Britain'. *Journal of Design History* 12 (1999): 217–39.

Quinn, Stephen, 'Tallies or reserves? Sir Francis Child's balance between capital reserves and extending credit to the crown, 1685-1695'. *Business and Economic History* 23 (1994): 39–51.

Rabier, C. (ed.), *Fields of Expertise: A Comparative History of Expert Procedures in Paris and London, 1600 to Present* (Newcastle 2007).

Rana, Aziz, *The Two Faces of American Freedom* (Cambridge, MA 2010).

Randall, Adrian, 'The philosophy of luddism: the case of the West of England woolen workers, ca. 1790-1809'. *Technology and Culture* 27 (1986): 1–17.

Randall, Adrian, *Before the Luddites: Custom, Community and Machinery in the English Woollen Industry, 1776-1809* (Cambridge 1991).

Randall, Adrian, *Riotous Assemblies: Popular Protest in Hanoverian England* (Oxford 2006).

Randall, Adrian, and Andrew Charlesworth, 'Comment: morals, markets and the English crowd in 1766'. *Past and Present* 114 (1987): 200–13.

Randall, Adrian, and Andrew Charlesworth (eds), *Markets, Market Culture and Popular Protest in Eighteenth-Century Britain and Ireland* (Liverpool 1996).

Rees, Henry, 'Evolution of Mersey estuarine settlements'. *Economic Geography* 21 (1945): 97–103.

Reinert, Erik S., 'The role of the state in economic growth'. *Journal of Economic Studies* 26 (1999): 268–326.

Reinert, Erik S., *How Rich Countries Got Rich … and Why Poor Countries Stay Poor* (London 2007).

Reinert, Sophus A., *Translating Empire: Emulation and the Origins of Political Economy* (Cambridge, MA 2011).

Reinert, Sophus A., 'Rivalry: greatness in early modern political economy', in Stern and Wennerlind (eds), *Mercantilism Reimagined*, 348–65.

Reitan, Earl A., *Politics, Finance, and the People: Economical Reform in England in the Age of the American Revolution, 1770-92* (Basingstoke 2007).

Reynard, Pierre Claude, 'Manufacturing quality in the pre-industrial age: Finding value in diversity'. *Economic History Review* 53 (2000): 493–516.

Rich, E. E., 'The first earl of Shaftesbury's colonial policy'. *Transactions of the Royal Historical Society*, 5th ser., 7 (1957): 47–70.

Riello, Giorgio, *Cotton: The Fabric That Made the Modern World* (Cambridge 2013).

Robbins, Caroline, 'Absolute liberty: the life and thought of William Popple, 1638-1708'. *William and Mary Quarterly* 24 (1967): 190–223.

Roberts, L., S. Schaffer and P. Dear (eds), *The Mindful Hand: Inquiry and Invention from the Late Renaissance to Early Industrialisation* (Amsterdam 2007).

Rockman, Seth, 'What makes the history of capitalism newsworthy?'. *Journal of the Early Republic* 34 (2014): 439–66.

Rodger, N. A. M., 'From the "military revolution" to the "fiscal-naval state"'. *Journal for Maritime Research* 13 (2011): 119–28.

Rogers, Nicholas, *Crowds, Culture and Politics in Georgian Britain* (Oxford 1998).

Rolt, L. T. C., *Thomas Newcomen: The Prehistory of the Steam Engine* (London: David and Charles, 1963).

Rommelse, Gijs, 'The role of mercantilism in Anglo-Dutch political relations, 1650-74'. *Economic History Review* 63 (2010): 591–611.

Root, Hilton L., 'The redistributive role of government: Economic regulation in old regime France and England'. *Comparative Studies in Society and History* 33 (1991): 338–69.

Root, Hilton L., *The Fountain of Privilege: Political Foundations of Markets in Old Regime France and England* (Berkeley 1994).

Root, Winfred T., 'The lords of trade and plantations, 1675-1696'. *American Historical Review* 23 (1917): 20–41.

Rose, J. H., 'The Franco-British commercial treaty of 1786'. *English Historical Review* 23 (1908): 709–24.

Rose, J. H., *William Pitt and National Revival* (London 1911).

Rosenband, Leonard N., *Papermaking in Eighteenth-Century France: Management, Labor, and Revolution at the Montgolfier Mill* (Baltimore 2000).

Rosenband, Leonard N., 'The competitive cosmopolitanism of an old regime craft'. *French Historical Studies* 23 (2000): 454–76.

Rosenband, Leonard N., 'Comparing combination acts: French and English papermaking in the age of revolution'. *Social History* 29 (2004): 165–85.

Rosenband, Leonard N., 'Becoming competitive: England's papermaking apprenticeship, 1700-1800', in Roberts, Schaffer and Dear (eds), *The Mindful Hand*, 379–401.

Rosenband, Leonard N., 'The many transitions of Ebenezer Stedman: a biographical and cross-national approach to the industrial revolution', in Horn, Rosenband and Smith (eds), *Reconceptualizing the Industrial Revolution*, 201–28.

Rosenband, Leonard N., 'Making the fair trader: Papermaking, the excise, and the English state, 1700-1815', in Walton (ed.), *Into Print*, 71–81.

Rosenband, Leonard N., 'The industrious revolution: a concept too many?'. *International Labor and Working Class-History* (forthcoming).

Rosenberg, Nathan, 'Science, invention and economic growth'. *Journal of Economic History* 84 (1974): 90–108.

Rosenberg, Nathan, and L. E. Birdzell Jr., *How the West Grew Rich: The Economic Transformation of the Industrial World* (New York 1986).

Roseveare, Henry, *The Evolution of a British Institution: The Treasury* (New York 1969).

Roseveare, Henry, *The Treasury 1660-1870: The Foundations of Control* (London 1973).

Roseveare, Henry, 'Prejudice and policy: Sir George Downing as Parliamentary entrepreneur', in Coleman and Mathias (eds), *Enterprise and History*, 135–50.

Rosier, Barrington, 'The construction costs of eighteenth-century warships'. *Mariner's Mirror* 96 (2010): 162–72.

Rostow, Walt W., *How it All Began: Origins of the Modern Economy* (New York 1975).

Rothschild, Emma, *Economic Sentiments: Adam Smith, Condorcet, and the Enlightenment* (Cambridge, MA 2001).

Rothstein, Natalie, 'Huguenots in the English silk industry in the eighteenth century', in Scouloudi (ed.), *Huguenots in Britain*, 125–40.

Bibliography

Rule, John, *The Experience of Labour in Eighteenth-Century Industry* (London 1981).

Sachs, Jeffrey, *The End of Poverty: How We Can Make It Happen in Our Lifetime* (St. Ives 2005).

Said, Edward W., *Orientalism* (1995, Harmondsworth 2003).

Sainty, J. C., 'The tenure of offices in the Exchequer'. *English Historical Review* 80 (1965): 449–75.

Samuel, Raphael, 'Workshop of the world: Steam power and hand technology in mid-Victorian Britain'. *History Workshop* 3 (1977): 6–72.

Santos, Boaventura de Sousa, 'A non-occidentalist west?: Leaned ignorance and ecology of knowledge'. *Theory, Culture and Society* 103 (2009): 103–125.

Sawyers, Larry, 'The navigation acts revisited'. *Economic History Review* 45 (1992): 262–84.

Scelle, G., 'The slave-trade in the Spanish colonies of America: the Assiento'. *American Journal of International Law* 4 (1910): 612–61.

Schaffer, Simon, 'Newtonianism', in Olby, Cantor, Christie and Hodge (eds), *Companion to the History of Modern Science*, 610–26.

Schaffer, Simon, 'Defoe's natural philosophy and the worlds of credit', in Christie and Shuttleworth (eds), *Nature Transformed*, 13–44.

Schaffer, Simon, '"The charter'd Thames": Naval architecture and experimental spaces in Georgian Britain', in Roberts, Schaffer and Dear (eds), *The Mindful Hand*, 278–305.

Schaffer, Simon, 'Newton on the beach: the information order of *Principia Mathematica*'. *History of Science* 47 (2009): 243–76.

Schofield, Robert E., 'Josiah Wedgwood and the technology of glass manufacturing'. *Technology and Culture* 3 (1962): 285–97.

Schofield, Robert E., *Lunar Society of Birmingham* (Oxford 1963).

Schonhardt-Bailey, Cheryl, *From the Corn Laws to Free Trade: Interests, Ideas, and Institutions in Historical Perspective* (Cambridge, MA 2006).

Scott, David B., *A School History of the United States, from the dawning of America to the Year 1870* (Washington 1870).

Scott, Jonathan, *England's Troubles: Seventeenth-Century English Political Instability in European Context* (Cambridge 2000).

Scott, Jonathan, '"Good night Amsterdam": Sir George Downing and Anglo-Dutch statebuilding'. *English Historical Review* 476 (2003): 334–56.

Scott, Jonathan, *Algernon Sidney and the English Republic 1623-1677* (Cambridge 2004).

Scott, Jonathan, *When the Waves Ruled Britannia: Geography and Political Identities, 1500-1800* (Cambridge 2011).

Scouloudi, Irene (ed.), *Huguenots in Britain and their French Background, 1550-1800* (Basingstoke 1987).

Scoville, Warren C., 'Large-scale production in the French plate-glass industry, 1665-1789'. *Journal of Political Economy* 50 (1942): 669–98.

Scoville, Warren C., 'Spread of techniques: minority migrations and the diffusion of technology'. *Journal of Economic History* 11 (1951): 347–60.

Scoville, Warren C., 'The Huguenots and the diffusion of technology I'. *Journal of Political Economy* 60 (1952): 294–311.

Scoville, Warren C., 'The Huguenots and the diffusion of technology II'. *Journal of Political Economy* 60 (1952): 392–411.

Seaward, Paul, 'The house of commons committee of trade and the origins of the second Anglo-Dutch War, 1664'. *Historical Journal* 30 (1987): 437–52.

Seaward, Paul, *The Cavalier Parliament and the Reconstruction of the Old Regime* (Cambridge 1988).

See, H., 'The Normandy chamber of commerce and the commercial treaty of 1786'. *Economic History Review* 2 (1930): 308–13.

Sewell, William H. Jr, 'A strange career: the historical study of economic life'. *History and Theory* 49, 4 (2010): 146–66.

Shapin, Steven, 'The house of experiment in seventeenth-century England'. *Isis* 79 (1988): 373–404.

Shapin, Steven, and Simon Schaffer, *Leviathan and the Air-Pump: Hobbes, Boyle, and the Experimental Life* (Princeton 1985).

Sharpe, Pamela, *Adapting to Capitalism: Working Women in the English Economy, 1700-1850* (Basingstoke 1996).

Shaw, L. M. E., *The Anglo-Portuguese Alliance and the English Merchants in Portugal, 1654-1810* (Aldershot 1998).

Sheldon, R., A. Randall, A. Charlesworth and D. Walsh, 'Popular protest and the persistence of customary measures: Resistance to the Winchester bushel in the English West', in Randall and Charlesworth (eds), *Markets, Market Culture and Popular Protest*, 25–45.

Shorter, A. H., *Studies on the History of Papermaking in Britain* (Aldershot 1993).

Sickinger, Raymond L., 'Regulation or ruination: Parliament's consistent pattern of mercantilist regulation of the English textile trade, 1660-1800'. *Parliamentary History* 19 (2000): 211–32.

Sieferle, Rolf P., *The Subterranean Forest: Energy Systems and the Industrial Revolution* (1982, Cambridge 2001).

Skempton, Alec W., 'Vermuyden, Sir Cornelius (1590-1677)', in Skempton (ed.), *A Biographical Dictionary of Civil Engineers*, 739–47.

Skempton, Alec W. (ed.), *A Biographical Dictionary of Civil Engineers in Great Britain and Ireland* (London 2002).

Smith, C. W., '"Calico madams": servants, consumption, and the calico crisis'. *Eighteenth-Century Life* 31 (2007): 29–55.

Smith, D. K., 'Learning politics: the nimes hosiery guild and the statutes controversy of 1706-1712'. *French Historical Studies* 22 (1999): 493–533.

Smith, D. K., 'Structuring politics in early eighteenth-century France: the political innovations of the French council of commerce'. *Journal of Modern History* 74 (2002): 490–537.

Smith, Graham, *Something to Declare: One Thousand Years of Customs and Excise* (London 1980).

Smith, W. D., 'The function of commercial centers in the modernization of European capitalism: Amsterdam as an information exchange in the seventeenth century'. *Journal of Economic History* 44 (1984): 985–1005.

Soll, Jacob, *The Reckoning: Financial Accountability and the Rise and Fall of Nations* (St. Ives 2014).

Solow, B. L., 'Introduction', in Solow (ed.), *Slavery and the Rise of the Atlantic System*, 1–20.

Solow, B. L. (ed.), *Slavery and the Rise of the Atlantic System* (Cambridge 1993).

Sonenscher, Michael, *The Hatters of Eighteenth-Century France* (Berkley 1992).

Sonenscher, Michael, *Before the Deluge: Public Debt, Inequality, and the Intellectual Origins of the French Revolution* (Princeton 2007).

Spraggs, G., 'The Spitalfield riots, 1769'. London Metropolitan Archives, http://www. CityofLondon.gov.uk/Corporation/Ima_learning/schoolmate/Irish/sm_irish_stories_detail

Spring, D., and T. L. Crosby, 'George Webb Hall and the agricultural association'. *Journal of British Studies* 2 (1962): 115–31.

Stasavage, David, *Public Debt and the Birth of the Democratic State: France and Great Britain, 1688-1789* (Cambridge 2002).

Statt, Daniel, 'The city of London and the controversy over immigration, 1660-1722'. *Historical Journal* 33 (1990): 45–61.

Statt, Daniel, 'Daniel Defoe and immigration'. *Eighteenth-Century Studies* 24 (1991): 293–313.

Steele, Ian K., *Politics of Colonial Policy: The Board of Trade in Colonial Administration 1696-1720* (Oxford 1968).

Bibliography

Stein, S. J., and B. H. Stein, *The Colonial Heritage of Latin America: Essays on Economic Dependence in Perspective* (1970, Oxford 1978).

Stein, S. J., and B. H. Stein, *Silver, Trade, and War: Spain and America in the Making of Early Modern Europe* (Baltimore 2000).

Steinfeld, Robert J., *Coercion, Contract, and Free Labor in the Nineteenth Century* (Cambridge 2001).

Stern, Philip J., and Carl Wennedlind (eds), *Mercantilism Reimagined: Political Economy in Early Modern Britain and Its Empire* (Oxford 2014).

Stewart, Larry, *The Rise of Public Science: Rhetoric, Technology, and Natural Philosophy in Newtonian Britain, 1660-1750* (Cambridge 1992).

Stewart, Larry, 'A meaning for machines: Modernity, utility, and the eighteenth-century British public'. *Journal of Modern History* 70 (1998): 259–94.

Stewart, Larry, 'Other centres of calculation, or, where the Royal Society didn't count: Commerce, coffee-houses and natural philosophy in early modern London'. *British Journal for the History of Science* 32 (1999): 133–53.

Stone, Lawrence (ed.), *An Imperial State at War: Britain from 1689 to 1815* (London 1994).

Styles, John, 'Design for large-scale production in eighteenth-century Britain'. *Oxford Art Journal* 11 (1988): 10–16.

Styles, John, 'Manufacturing, consumption and design in eighteenth-century England', in Brewer and Porter (eds), *Consumption and the World of Goods* (London 1993), 527–54.

Styles, John, 'Large-scale production and Product Innovation in Early Modern London'. *Past and Present* 168 (2000): 124–69.

Styles, John, *The Dress of the People: Everyday Fashion in Eighteenth-Century England* (New Haven 2007).

Swingen, Abigail, 'Labor: Employment, colonial servitude, and slavery in the seventeenth-century Atlantic', in Stern and Wennerlind (eds), *Mercantilism Reimagined*, 46–67.

Symonds, C. L. (ed.), *New Aspects of Naval History* (Maryland 1981).

Szostak, Rick, *The Role of Transportation in the Industrial Revolution: A Comparison of England and France* (Montreal 1991).

Taylor, Miles, 'Rethinking the chartists: Searching for synthesis in the historiography of chartism'. *Historical Journal* 39 (1996): 479–95.

Taylor, Miles, 'The 1848 revolutions and the British empire'. *Past and Present* 166 (2000): 146–80.

Thirsk, Joan, *Economic Policy and Projects: The Development of a Consumer Society in Early Modern England* (1978, Oxford 1988).

Thirsk, Joan, *Alternative Agriculture: A History from the Black Death to the Present Day* (Oxford 1997).

Thomas, P. J., 'The beginnings of calico-printing in England'. *English Historical Review* 39 (1924): 206–16.

Thomas, P. J., *Mercantilism and East India Trade* (1923, London 1963).

Thompson, E. P., *The Making of the English Working Class* (1963, Harmondsworth 1988).

Thompson, E. P., 'Eighteenth-century English society: Class struggle without class?'. *Social History* 3 (1978): 133–65.

Thompson, E. P., 'The moral economy of the English crowd in the eighteenth century', in Thompson, *Customs in Common*, 185–258.

Thompson, E. P., 'The patricians and the plebs', in Thompson, *Customs in Common*, 16–96.

Thompson, E. P., *Customs in Common* (Harmondsworth 1993).

Thornton, John, 'Precolonial African industry and the Atlantic trade, 1500-1800'. *African Economic History* 19 (1990–1): 1–19.

Thornton, John, *Africa and Africans in the Making of the Atlantic World, 1400-1800* (1992, 2nd edn, Cambridge 1998).

Tomlinson, H., 'Financial and administrative developments in England, 1660-88', in Jones (ed.), *The Restored Monarchy*, 94–117.

Tomlinson, H., 'Place and profit: an examination of the ordnance office, 1660-1714'. *Transactions of the Royal Historical Society* 25 (1975): 55–75.

Tracy, James D. (ed.), *The Rise of Merchant Empires: Long-Distance Trade in the Early Modern World, 1350-1750* (Cambridge 1993).

Treherne, A. A., 'The contribution of South-West Lancashire to horology'. *Antiquarian Horology* June (2009): 457–76.

Trentmann, Frank, 'National identity and consumer politics – free trade and tariff reform', in Winch and O'Brien (eds), *The Political Economy of British Historical Experience*, 215–42.

Trentmann, Frank, *Free Trade Nation: Commerce, Consumption, and Civil Society in Modern Britain* (Oxford 2008).

Tribbeko, John, and George Ruperti, *Lists of Germans from the Palatinate who came to England in 1709* (London 1990).

Tunzelmann, G. N. von, *Steam Power and British Industrialisation to 1860* (Oxford 1978).

Turnbull, Geoffrey, *A History of the Calico Printing Industry of Great Britain* (Altringham 1951).

Turnbull, G. H., 'Peter Stahl, the first public teacher of chemistry at Oxford'. *Annals of Science* 9 (1953): 265–70.

Turnbull, Gerard, 'Canals, coal and regional growth during the industrial revolution'. *Economic History Review* 40 (1987): 537–60.

Turner, Michael J., '"The Bonaparte of free trade" and the anti-corn law league'. *Historical Journal* 41 (1998): 1011–34.

Uglow, Jenny, *The Lunar Men: The Friends who made the Future* (Bath 2002).

Usher, Abbott Payson, *A History of Mechanical Inventions* (1929, New York 1988).

Vardi, L., 'The abolition of the guilds during the French revolution'. *French Historical, Studies* 15 (1988): 704–17.

Vries, Jan de, *The Industrious Revolution: Consumer Behaviour and the Household Economy, 1650 to the Present* (Cambridge 2008).

Vries, Jan de, and A. V. D. Wonde, *The First Modern Economy: Success, Failure and Perseverance of the Dutch Economy, 1500-1815* (Cambridge 1997).

Vries, Peer, *State, Economy and the Great Divergence* (London 2015).

Wadsworth, Alfred P., and Julia De Lacy Mann, *The Cotton Trade and Industrial Lancashire 1600-1780* (1931, New York 1968).

Wakefield, Andre, *The Disordered Police State: German Cameralism as Science and Practice* (Chicago 2009).

Wakefield, Andre, 'Butterfield's nightmare: the history of science as Disney history'. *History and Technology* 30 (2014): 232–51.

Walton, Charles (ed.), *Into Print: Limits and Legacies of the Enlightenment: Essays in Honor of Robert Darnton* (Philadelphia 2011).

Walvin, James, *Fruits of Empire: Exotic Produce and British Taste, 1660-1800* (London 1997).

Ward, W. R., 'The administration of the window and assessed taxes, 1696-1798'. *English Historical Review* 67 (1952): 523–42.

Ward, W. R., *The English Land Tax in the Eighteenth Century* (Oxford 1953).

Ward, W. R., 'Some eighteenth century civil servants: the English revenue commissioners, 1754-1798'. *English Historical Review* 70 (1955): 25–54.

Warner, Peter, *Bloody Marsh: A Seventeenth-Century Village in Crisis* (Macclesfield 2000).

Washbrook, David, 'From comparative sociology to global history: Britain and India in the pre-history of modernity'. *Journal of Economic and Social History of the Orient* 40 (1997): 410–43.

Waugh, M., *Smuggling in Kent and Sussex 1700-1840* (Newbury 1985).

Webb, Stephen Saunders, 'William Blathwayt, imperial fixer: From popish plot to Glorious Revolution'. *William and Mary Quarterly* 25 (1968): 3–21.

Webb, Stephen Saunders, 'William Blathwayt, imperial fixer: Muddling through to empire 1689-1717'. *William and Mary Quarterly* 26 (1969): 373–415.

Webb, Stephen Saunders, *1676: The End of American Independence* (1984, New York 1995).

Webster, Charles, *The Great Instauration: Science, Medicine, and Reform, 1626-1660* (London 1976).

Weightman, Gavin, *The Industrial Revolutionaries: The Creation of the Modern World 1776-1914* (London 2007).

Wennerlind, Carl, *Casualties of Credit: The English Financial Revolution, 1620-1720* (Cambridge, MA 2011).

Wheeler, James Scott, 'Navy finance, 1649-1660'. *Historical Journal* 39 (1996): 457–66.

Wheeler, James Scott, *The Making of a World Power: War and the Military Revolution in Seventeenth-Century England* (Stroud 1999).

Whiteman, A., J. S. Bromley and P. G. M. Dickinson (eds), *Statesmen, Scholars and Merchants: Essays in Eighteenth-Century History Presented to Dame Lucy Sutherland* (Oxford 1973).

White, Eugene Nelson, 'The French revolution and the politics of government finance, 1770-1815'. *Journal of Economic History* 55 (1995): 227–55.

Wiles, Richard C., 'Mercantilism and the idea of progress'. *Eighteenth-Century Studies* 8 (1974): 56–74.

Williams, D. E., 'Morals, markets and the English crowd in 1766'. *Past and Present* 104 (1984): 56–73.

Williams, Eric, *Capitalism and Slavery* (Chapel Hill 1944).

Williams, Neville, *Contraband Cargoes: Seven Centuries of Smuggling* (London 1959).

Wilson, Charles, 'The economic decline of the Netherlands'. *Economic History Review* 9 (1939): 111–27.

Wilson, Charles, *Mercantilism* (London 1958).

Wilson, Charles, 'Cloth production and international competition in the seventeenth century'. *Economic History Review* 13 (1960): 209–21.

Wilson, Charles, 'New introduction', in Cunningham (ed.), *Alien Immigrants to England* (1897, 2nd edn, London 1969).

Wilson, Charles, 'The other face of mercantilism', in Coleman (ed.), *Revisions in Mercantilism*, 118–39.

Wilson, Charles, 'The Anglo-Dutch establishment in eighteenth century England', in Wilson, Hooykaas, Hall and Waszink (eds), *The Anglo-Dutch Contribution*, 11–32.

Wilson, Charles, R. Hooykaas, A. R. Hall, and J. H. Waszink (eds), *The Anglo-Dutch Contribution to the Civilization of Early Modern Society* (Oxford: Oxford University Press, 1976).

Wilson, Charles, *England's Apprenticeship 1603-1763* (London 1979).

Winch, Donald, *Riches and Poverty: An Intellectual History of Political Economy in Britain, 1750-1834* (Cambridge 1996).

Winch, Donald, and P. K. O'Brien (eds), *The Political Economy of British Historical Experience, 1688-1914* (Oxford 2002).

Wise, M. Norton, with the collaboration of Crosbie Smith, 'Work and waste: Political economy and natural philosophy in nineteenth century Britain (II)'. *History of Science* 27 (1989): 391–449.

Wise, M. Norton (ed.), *The Values of Precision* (Princeton 1994).

Wolff, Klaus H., 'Textile bleaching and the birth of the chemical industry'. *Business History Review* 48 (1974): 143–63.

Wong, R. Bin, *China Transformed: Historical Change and the Limits of European Experience* (Ithaca 1997).

Wong, R. Bin, 'The search for European differences and domination in the early modern world: a view from Asia'. *American Historical Review* 107 (2002): 447–69.

Wong, R. Bin, and Jean-Laurent Rosenthal, *Before and Beyond Divergence: The Politics of Economic Change in China and Europe* (Cambridge, MA 2011).

Wrigley, E. A., *Continuity, Chance and Change: the Character of the Industrial Revolution in England* (Cambridge 1990).

Wrigley, E. A., *Energy and the English Industrial Revolution* (Cambridge 2010).

Zahedieh, Nuala, 'Overseas expansion and trade in the seventeenth century', in Canny (ed.), *The Origins of Empire*, 398–422.

Zahedieh, Nuala, *The Capital and the Colonies: London and the Atlantic Economy 1660-1700* (Cambridge 2012).

Zebel, S. H., 'Fair trade: an English reaction to the breakdown of the Cobden treaty system'. *Journal of Modern History* 12 (1940): 161–85.

Zook, G. F., 'The royal adventurers and the plantations'. *Journal of Negro History* 4 (1919): 206–31.

Zook, Melinda S., *Radical Whigs and Conspiratorial Politics in Late Stuart England* (Pennsylvania 1999).

Zook, Melinda S., 'Turncoats and double agents in restoration and revolutionary England: the case of Robert Ferguson, the plotter'. *Eighteenth-Century Studies* 42 (2009): 363–78.

INDEX

Index

Index

Index

Index

Index